PENGUIN BOOKS
TELLING TALES: NEW ONE-ACT PLAYS

Eric Lane is co-editor with Nina Shengold of *Moving Parts: Monologues from Contemporary Plays* and *The Actor's Book of Scenes from New Plays*. He is Artistic Director of Orange Thoughts, a not-for-profit theater company in New York City. His writing has been performed at LaMama, St. Mark's Church, Nikolais/Louis ChoreoSpace, the Ethnic Folk Arts Center, and the Nat Horne Theatre. Mr. Lane has acted in several off-off Broadway productions and is author of *Crunchy Apples*, a children's musical performed at Symphony Space. His plays include "Dancing on Checkers' Grave," "The Heart of a Child," "Glass Stirring," "So Slow It Whirls," "Blue Christmas," and "Jersey Bounce." For his television work on *Ryan's Hope*, he received a Writer's Guild Award. Mr. Lane is an honors graduate of Brown University.

TELLING TALES

NEW
ONE-ACT
PLAYS

EDITED BY
ERIC LANE

PENGUIN BOOKS

PENGUIN BOOKS
Published by the Penguin Group
Penguin Books USA Inc., 375 Hudson Street, New York, New York 10014, U.S.A.
Penguin Books Ltd, 27 Wrights Lane, London W8 5TZ, England
Penguin Books Australia Ltd, Ringwood, Victoria, Australia
Penguin Books Canada Ltd, 10 Alcorn Avenue, Toronto, Ontario, Canada M4V 3B2
Penguin Books (N.Z.) Ltd, 182–190 Wairau Road, Auckland 10, New Zealand

Penguin Books Ltd, Registered Offices:
Harmondsworth, Middlesex, England

First published in Penguin Books 1993

10 9 8 7 6 5 4 3 2 1

LIBRARY OF CONGRESS CATALOGING IN PUBLICATION DATA
Telling tales : new one-act plays / edited by Eric Lane.
    p.   cm.
    Includes index.
    ISBN 0 14 048.237 7
    1. One-act plays, American.   2. One-act plays, English.   I. Lane,
  Eric.
  PS627.O53T45   1993
  812'.04108—dc20   92 – 23876

Printed in the United States of America
Set in Garamond No. 3
Designed by Ann Gold

EDITOR'S PREFACE

Telling Tales collects twenty-eight new one-act plays, offering a wide range of original voices. From the comic to the tragic, political to personal, each play presents memorable characters and strong challenges for the actors. The plays can be easily produced with simple sets and costumes. The challenge is not so much in the technical requirements of the production, but rather in the development of the characters and the telling of their stories in a compressed amount of time—spanning anywhere from a little over an hour to ten minutes in length.

Many of the plays were selected from the numerous one-act festivals springing up across the country. You'll find works developed at the Ensemble Studio Theatre, Actor's Theatre of Louisville, Love Creek Productions, the Dramatists Guild's Young Playwrights Festival (for writers under the age of nineteen), and Manhattan Punch Line's Festival of One-Act Comedies. The one-act play has become a staple of these theaters, as well as colleges, universities, and emerging theater companies. Commercial producers generally avoid the pairings of one-acts, with their multiple casts, rehearsal schedules, sets, and costumes, and the sometimes erratic quality within a single evening. Yet it is precisely these "problems" which make the form so appealing to actors, writers, directors, designers, and audiences. Within a single evening, an audience is led into several completely different worlds and offered an array of stories, characters, and emotions with which to connect. Each story is complete, yet it feels as though the characters have a life beyond the one depicted in the play. They existed before it began and continue after its conclusion; yet somehow they've been changed by this experience. The playwright has granted us a window into their world at this particular moment. They tell their stories with amazing efficiency. In the race to tell our stories in record time, my favorite entry is the Lamia Ink! International One-Page Play Festival.

The plays in this collection comprise a variety of cast sizes, from the large, predominately male casts of "Fun" and "Throwing Smoke," to the smaller, all-male casts of "Vivien," "Slaughter in the Lake,"

"Vito on the Beach," and "Flyer." From the large, predominately female cast of "Women and Wallace," to the smaller, all-female casts of "Telling Tales," "Dancing on Checkers' Grave," "The Coal Diamond," "Haiku," and "Final Placement." Others offer diverse roles for both sexes. The authors include internationally recognized playwrights Athol Fugard, Arthur Miller, and Harold Pinter; as well as writers whose works have been widely produced, including Christopher Durang, Maria Irene Fornes, David Henry Hwang, Craig Lucas, John Patrick Shanley, George C. Wolfe, and Zora Neale Hurston. Others, David E. Rodriguez, Samuel Schwartz, and Barbara Wiechmann, are being published here for the first time.

Reading so many plays, naturally I've wondered why, out of a huge stack, one suddenly reaches up and grabs me. The play may be funny, sad, poignant, beautiful, ugly. But the situation and characters are always ones which on some level we know. They offer a strong emotional connection for performer and audience. In David Ives's comedy "Sure Thing," I recognize myself and laugh; I know what it's like to be single and meet someone for the first time. Unlike the title character in Percy Granger's "Vivien," my father has never been in a mental institution or on Thorazine. But like Paul, I and most of us have felt the desire to connect with our father and the inability to. I've never lived under South African apartheid like the characters in Athol Fugard's "Statements after an Arrest under the Immorality Act." But as a gay man, I have felt threatened and restricted in fully expressing my love in public.

You'll find plays with gay and lesbian characters, and many roles specifically written for minority actors. I strongly encourage actors to find roles which speak to them, regardless of category. And I hope current advances in nontraditional casting continue to grow.

After choosing a play to perform, please contact the author's agent or publisher listed in the back of the book and secure the rights. The financial incentive for writing plays, particularly one-acts, is little enough as is. Please pay the authors the royalties to which they are entitled and rightfully deserve.

The playwrights in this anthology continue to write against terrifying odds. Theaters are closing all over. Every day gifted men and women in the theater community are dying of AIDS. Governmental and corporate sponsorship of the arts is dwindling. The National Endowment for the Arts has become increasingly conservative as innovative works on a wide range of subjects including religion, sexism, racism, homophobia, sex, and sexuality are attacked as "obscene" by the New Right. The fact that these works are being attacked so vehemently also proves their power. For those who say the theater is dead, pick up a play and start to read. Go to the Young Playwrights Festival or any school show. Put on a play. There is great power and joy in these works. I hope they give you the same pleasure I have had compiling them.

—Eric Lane,
March 1992

ACKNOWLEDGMENTS

I wish to thank the many people who contributed to this anthology, especially Sam Ambler of Berkeley Rep, Michael Biello, Debby Brown, Tisa Chang of Pan Asian Rep, Todd Cooper, Migdalia Cruz, Kate Cummings, Douglas Daven, Michael Bigelow Dixon of Actor's Theatre of Louisville, Florence Eichen of NAL, Ensemble Studio Theatre, Eileen Falcone, Mary Flower of Grove Press, Michael Goodwin, Cynthia Granville of Love Creek Productions, Gary Jennings, Dr. Shari Kogan, Jeffrey Lane, James Luse of Long Wharf, Sophie Maletsky of New Dramatists, Susan Marcus, Dan Martin, John McCormack, Ken Mueller, Bob Najjar, Terry Nemeth of TCG, Sarah Noll, Orange Thoughts, Mark Owen of 3 Dollar Bill Theatre, Christine Owens, Nancy Quinn of Young Playwrights Festival, Ed Rubin, Lawry Smith of La MamaLa Galleria, Eleanore Speert of Dramatists Play Service, Michael Swanberg, Glenn Young of Applause, Bruce E. Whitacre of Manhattan Theatre Club. Special thanks to my family and friends.

Once again, Michael Millman, my editor at Penguin, was a constant support. I've had the pleasure of co-editing two previous books with Nina Shengold; her contribution to this book was invaluable.

Thanks to all the agents for their submissions and help in obtaining permission to include the plays in the collection; also for their willingness to represent new and exciting writers in a time when opportunities are unfortunately diminishing. Much appreciation to the theaters that continue to present these works. And most of all, to the writers themselves, for the wonderful and varied worlds they have lived, dreamed, and shared.

CONTENTS

TELLING
TALES

TELLING TALES

MIGDALIA CRUZ

TELLING TALES was developed at INTAR's Hispanic Playwrights-in-Residence laboratory under the direction of Maria Irene Fornes. The production at HOME for Contemporary Theatre and Art, 44 Walker Street, in May 1990, featured Monique Cintron, Sonia Medina, and Cristina San Juan, and was co-directed by Jonathan Rosenberg and Joumana Rizk, with slides by James M. Kent. This play is dedicated to Gloria, Pedro, Nancy and Virginia Cruz.

▪ ▪

Sand

She wasn't supposed to go on the roof. I tole her not to. But she wouldn't listen to me. She never listens to me. She's always the brave one.

I cried for a long time after that. I cried for her and I cried for me, because I din't go with her. I din't know what was gonna happen. And now I'll always wonder what woulda happened if I'da gone.

I was on the fire escape when they caught him. A whole army of men from the neighborhood were carrying him up above their heads. And he squirmed like a rat, like a fucking rat in a corner surrounded by hungry cats.

They took him into the playground and threw him down into the sandbox. Everybody stood around him and screamed at him. You couldn't even understand what they were saying.

I closed my eyes for a minute and when I opened them again, he was buried in the sand. Two men held him down while everybody else threw sand in his face. His eyes were filled with it and he was screaming. Then they filled up his mouth and the screaming stopped. He threw up and choked and he kept choking on his own blood and spit and sand.

And I smiled. . . .

That's when I thought there must be a God, because there was justice.

They picked him up and my daddy tied his legs to the back of his '58 Plymouth Valiant. He got that car the day I was born—two months before Anita was born. That car was us. It was as old as us. Eight years old. So wise for eight. So strong. Stronger than we could ever be. Stronger than my father. They dragged him through the streets he knew so well. The streets we played in. Where he watched us and made his plan. I hoped that car would climb to the roof and jump over—like Anita. Rip him up, like he ripped Anita. Take his hands and make him pull his own guts out. And then the balls. Slash. Cut. Tear.

He tore her clothes off with his teeth. He ripped her open with his teeth. His teeth were yellow and sharp—like gold. Golden teeth. Now he had vomit and blood caked onto his teeth. They weren't so pretty like they used to be. They looked good now. Like they were supposed to look.

We keep away from the sandbox now. It's strange when people from an island are scared of sand.

Jesus

I don't understand anything. I just keep seeing a pincushion shaped like a heart. It's pink with yellow fringe and where the pins are stuck, there's blood dripping. I remember where that comes from. . . .

When I was very little, about one, my sister Tati, who was two, got very sick. I didn't see my parents much for the next five years because they were always at the hospital. Turns out she had lead poisoning. My mom gave me a picture of Jesus when I was two and told me to pray to it—that Tati would get better if only I did this.

Jesus had light brown hair and blue eyes and his heart showed and it was bluish red with swords going through it and blood dripping from the wounds. But he was smiling.

For Mother's Day, when I was in first grade, we had to sew pincushions for our moms. I made mine heart-shaped. The teacher liked it very much. So did my mother. Everytime she stuck a pin in it, I snuck a look. Would it bleed? I wondered.

Tati was pale when she came back. I missed her. We played rocking horse together. That's where you cradle each other and rock back and forth in the middle of the sofa where the springs are loosest. After awhile only I could do the cradling. That was okay. But nobody ever explained it to me.

Yellow Eyes

I'm sitting in front of my great-grandfather. He is telling me a story about how he fell in love with my great-grandmother, but I can't hear him. He has beautiful yellow eyes and I'm hypnotized by them.

I just sit staring at him. I can see every line of his skull. Every vein. His skin is like coffee with milk, like my father's coffee with milk. He doesn't get out of bed anymore. He sits up though and we dress him. He's wearing a brownish-green sweater, a cardigan. His dirty undershirt shows beneath it. It is stained with cherry chewing tobacco. His words smell like mucus and tobacco. People think mucus doesn't smell. But I think it smells. It smells yellow. His pants are brown; they are too short and cuffed. One cuff is torn and hanging off his thin, long legs. He has the longest legs I've ever seen. He's the tallest man I've ever known. He has scars on his arms and his legs from chains. He is strong.

He used to hold me over his head with his feet. Like a circus act. Like a balancing act. We could be famous I always thought. He's so strong and I'm so graceful.

He has on the socks I bought him for Christmas. My ma said to buy him socks because old people's feet get very cold.

He was one hundred six when he died and she was ninety-nine. She was also nuts. She'd wake up a different person every day. We always had to guess three or four times before we hit on the right name to call her. She thought she lived in a great manor in the country and my great-grandfather was her valet instead of her husband. My mother was the poor woman who came in once a week to do laundry. She pitied all of us and gave us chocolates because "Poor people like chocolates. It takes their minds off their little problems. . . ." They weren't really chocolates though—she used to cut out cubes from bars of soap and pretend they were chocolates. She'd watch you too. She'd watch you put 'em in your mouth and wait till your mouth foamed up before she'd turn away. "Good chocolates, huh? You people always enjoy my chocolates. You're like dogs for them. Hungry for them. I never liked sweets myself. They weaken your heart. People fall in love when they eat too much candy. Always with the wrong person. That's why so many children have children. They don't know. Their minds are in the sweets, covered with sugar. No sense."

Papo Chibirico

Papo Chibirico was fifteen when I was seven. He was my first love. He bought me coloring books and candy and took me to the zoo. Anthony Vargas tried to give me coloring books too, but I punched him in the nose and made him bleed. Papo thought it was a good idea. "Don't let the boys bully you," he always said.

Every summer we formed softball teams. Once we were playing and I walked backwards to make a catch. I didn't know I was on a hill and fell off into a pile of beer bottles. Papo carried me the fifteen blocks home with one hand holding my left knee together. He pulled the glass out of the wound and went with my Mom and me to the hospital. He was mature for a kid. That's what I thought.

When I turned eleven, I went to P.R. for the summer. I returned a foot and a half taller and five shades darker. Papo was six inches shorter than me then. How could he be six inches shorter, if he was eight years older? Papo changed that summer too, he got more muscles and was training to become a wrestler. My dad and I watched his first televised fight on Channel Forty-seven. That's when I found out he was a midget—because he was a midget wrestler.

Papo fought the Jamaican Kid. The strength was in their arms really. Their little legs just kicked the air. With their arms they pinned each other to the floor. My Dad laughed and I wondered what was so funny. He explained to me that it was supposed to be funny—that's why you watch midget wrestling, to laugh. The Jamaican Kid won.

The next day I saw Papo. He was still friendly to me even though he was a TV star. All the kids on the block wanted to talk to him. But he talked just to me. The big kids were always challenging him to a fight. He would say "No," but they would push him and hit him until there was nothing left to say. Sometimes three or four would gang up on him and hold him up in the air. His useless legs would swing wildly at his attackers always missing their mark. "Some tough guy!" Then they'd throw him into a dumpster. I used to watch and cry because I didn't know what else to do. All I could do was wait for them to leave and help Papo out of the garbage. He always got mad at me then. "Don't you know you could get hurt?! Stay away from me, will you! I don't need your help!" But he always needed my help.

He got to be a really good wrestler. The kind the crowd stands up for. He got tougher too. Carried a knife and stabbed somebody, so I couldn't see him anymore. He'd look at me from across the street when I was sitting on the fire escape doing my homework. He waved and I waved back, but he always turned away before he saw me wave. I guess he was afraid I wouldn't.

When he got a little money saved, he got a special bicycle on which he could reach the pedals. He spent hours on that bike, circling the neighborhood. I watched him go by and go by and go by again. He looked normal on that bike—happy. He walked with a limp now. The Jamaican Kid went crazy one night and bit a chunk out of his calf. He got an infection from it. The Jamaican Kid never even apologized. I know because I asked. That's the last thing we ever talked about.

It was one of those real hot August nights, when everybody's on the street because nobody can sleep. Some guys are playing the congas in the playground, small children are playing tag, mothers are gossiping and the men are playing dominoes. Papo comes by on his bike. It's a pretty one—black with a red seat and Papo's in red and black too. He looks sharp. His face is pretty. He's the only one on the block with green eyes. Everybody wanted those eyes. Everybody says hello. He starts showing off, making the bike jump and taking turns real fast and low. People applaud. He does this over and over, people finally stop watching but he keeps saying "Look at me, look at me!" Now people are embarrassed to look. Papo goes by one more time. . . .

I don't know where the car came from. It was a new car, I think. Shiny. Maybe just freshly waxed. People always wax their cars in the summer. He wouldn't have lived long anyway—that's what people said. "God bless him. Midgets don't live very long."

But he wasn't a midget, he was a dwarf.

Parcheesi

The stage of a school auditorium. The walls are mint green. The stage is just a platform. No walls. The floor of the stage is brown. It's two thirty in the afternoon. Assembly time. All the children are saying the pledge of allegiance, except the Jehovah's Witnesses. The principal is seated in the front row. She's seven and a half feet tall with long, blonde hair and long, white teeth. Her bangs touch her eyebrows. Her ears touch her chin. Whenever there's an announcement made, she yells at the child to speak up. "How can you say something on a stage that no one can hear?!" I hated that stage.

I was My Fair Lady on that stage. Eliza Doolittle. I had a voice then. My friend Sharon Gray always forgot her lines and the principal would yell at her. "How can we enjoy the show if we can't hear you? Only stupid people forget their lines."

Sharon was very pretty . . . she's a cop now. I used to hate cops but I could never hate Sharon. She was my dumbest best friend. She didn't know how to read in the fifth grade and I taught her.

On my eleventh birthday, she came to my house with a Parcheesi game. I already had a Parcheesi game. I said "Oh, I have one just like that." I felt bad because as soon as I said it I knew she was embarrassed, so then I knew she had brought it for me. She was going to take it back, but I told her I lost all the pieces out of my other game and so it was a good thing she had bought this new set. It was prettier than the one I had. She bought it at John's Bargain Store. That was our favorite store because everything was either fifty-nine cents or eighty-eight cents. I couldn't believe she had bought me anything . . . it was a lot of money to spend on a friend.

We sat right in front of the television and watched Captain Jack's Popeye cartoons first—"Ahoy, ye maties!"—"Ahoy, Captain Jack." And then we played Parcheesi. She ate me first and went twenty spaces. I hate when someone eats me first because then I'm bound to lose. The first eater always wins in Parcheesi. She ate me second and third too. But then she stopped eating me even though she could. I guess because it was my birthday. I ended up winning.

Sharon had the blackest skin I've ever seen except in *National Geographic*. It was polished wood. My mother used to say she must use lemon Pledge on her face because it was so shiny. And she smelled like lemons too, because of our business. We sold coconut ices and lemonade. My dad showed us how to make the ices so we gave him part of our profits—that was Sharon's idea. Sharon made the lemonade because she was an expert. Her mother made lemonade for her to take to school on Pot Luck Lunch Day and all the kids loved it. It had rosehips in it. But we didn't know what they were then—we thought it was a drug because it tasted so good.

In sixth grade, we got separated by Mrs. Newman because she said Sharon wasn't smart enough to be in the same class with me. I was in six-one and they put her in six-twelve. That wasn't too bad though because we had up to six-twenty-six. The kids in six-twenty-six were called the F-Troop. They weren't bad but they were stupid. The kids in six-twelve weren't real stupid, they just smoked too much. The kids in six-fifteen were the school terrors. They started a war against all the other classes. Sharon got stabbed in the stomach after she stood up for me when some girls from six-fifteen tried to steal my bus pass. The next day they were waiting for her in the yard and worked her over. Sharon said if there'd only been three she could have handled it, but there were five.

I used to wonder what happened to Sharon until I met her on the bus. She saw me first and came over and hugged me. She remembered me. I was so glad to see her because I almost never stop thinking about her. She's always there in the back of my head—like a soft spot that babies have that if struck kills them instantly. Dogs have a spot like that too. It's on their sides.

Sharon had a dog. His name was Don. Junie, her little brother named him—he just couldn't say dog, it came out like don. It was a big poodle with all its hair—not a clipped, ugly, French one. We took Don everywhere with us. He would come into the bathroom and watched everything you did in there. He was curious and I don't blame him. I always liked watching dogs pee in the street. So shameless. I wanted a life like that. Sharon wanted order. She wanted money. She wanted to have a history and I wanted to have a past.

So now she can blow your head off with a three fifty-seven magnum and I can tell you about it.

Fire

When our apartment building caught on fire, my mother braved the flames to save our four-foot-tall statue of Jesus Christ. It was a very nice statue, when my father found it in the street, but someone had painted the eyes white. It was also missing a hand. The right one, of course. At the age of five, nine years before the fire, I attached a hand from a doll to Christ's arm. My mother didn't speak to me for months after that. Everytime I tried to appeal my case, my father would nod his head sadly and pat me on the back. He couldn't do anything about the punishment, but he was certainly sympathetic.

As she re-entered the smoky building to recover her treasures, I tried to soothe the fears of my two sisters. One was seven and the other a year older than myself. She was the most scared. She really couldn't understand what was happening. That's when I first realized that she would never get any better. I held her in my arms and she rocked furiously, searching the eyes of the rude crowd—the kind that always gathers lasciviously at tragedies. I don't know what she was looking for—maybe she was looking for Mother too.

Anyway, there we were in the January cold, huddled in our pajamas in the middle of the street, when this angel appeared. No ordinary angel. She was too old to be wearing a mini-dress and too ugly to be wearing so much make-up. She gathered us together and led us to her apartment under the cover of a bright orange blanket. That's when I thought, Maybe I'm dead already. Maybe we didn't get out on time. The blanket became the fire to me and I tried to break free, but she was very strong. She sat us down in her living room and made us hot chocolate with the kind of chocolate you grate. She kept the chocolate in a beautiful tin box. I thought she must be very rich to grate her lovely chocolate for us.

I told her I was afraid that Mother was dead. The people in the street told me she was dead. Because she went to save Jesus. She smiled at me and said, "Of course, she's not dead. You think the firemens would let her back in if it wasn't safe? They don't do that. Firemen's are good people."

I drank five cups of that chocolate. My dad kidded her when he came to get us. He told her he owed her a gallon of milk for the life of his daughters. Where was she? "Why din't Mommy come with you?" "She's guarding the statues. She thinks the firemen will break them with axes." We went back to our apartment. My mother was sitting in the middle of the bed holding a baseball bat.

"Okay. Everybody's okay. What are you crying for?" I couldn't stop crying. "Make her stop crying, Pe." "If she wants to cry, let her cry." "What are you crying about?" I couldn't tell her—then I told her. "You're alive, Ma. They tole me you were dead." "Who told you that?" "The people in the street." "And you believe them? What a crazy daughter I have. What can we do about those windows?" She paced furiously in front of the shattered windows. It was then that I realized that the statues still stood in front of the windows, unbroken, untouched by the fire that was hot enough to shatter every window in the apartment. They guarded our apartment and Mom guarded them.

My mother and father hung blankets over the window frames to keep out the wind and I sat on the bed and cried. "What's she crying about?" "Let her cry." My sisters were already fast asleep.

A month later, we were packed into a van covered with Bronx art, as my little sister calls graffiti, and moved to a better place. Better for me anyway. Only three blocks from the Bronx Zoo. I was in heaven. There was only one person left to say good-bye to—the garish lady with chocolate suitable for shaving. I was in love with her because she took me so seriously. I appreciated her and wanted to tell her so. My parents said it wasn't necessary, they'd already thanked her. "You don't want to embarrass her, do you?" No, I didn't want to do that. . . . "I want to go anyway." They forbade me to see her. It only took a few hours for me to figure out why. No wonder she had that kind of chocolate . . . but I still loved her.

I heard three years later that she had been brutalized by the Black Spades, the South Bronx equivalent to the Nazi Brown Shirts. When she got out of the hospital, she went to the commuter rails and put her head on the track. As the story goes, she was such a stupid whore that she put her head on the local track instead of the express and lay there for hours, awaiting her fate. Of course, you hear so many stories, you hardly ever know what's true. I know she doesn't live where she used to live. Her building's gone.

Loose Lips

I would have killed her if I had the courage. At first, I hated only her personality. Brutal, cunning, selfish, self-serving, inhuman, alien. Foreign matter. Mindless body proteins. Wasted flesh. But then it was everything about her that I despised. Lipstick color. The length of her fingernails. The dried skin that flaked away from behind her left ear. She really doesn't know how to put on make-up. It looks like a series of mistakes. Big ones. For example . . . lipstick. She makes her mouth look like a wound. A bright red gash too close to her neck to be lips. Not human lips. Goat lips. *Levres à chevres*. Is that how you say goat in French? *Chevre?* It sounds like goat. In French.

Have you ever eaten a goat? She has. She eats it every day and on Saturdays—twice. When she can get it. When she can get some "kid" to come home with her. It's not easy. Goats are like bulls—they're stubborn animals. And they have horns and they eat grass. That's why they go home with her—she has the best grass around. "Hey, that's a nice grass you got there lady!" Yeah.

And the clothes. The clothes. *(Long silence.)* The clothes.

The walk is worse. On her toes. On her tippy-toes. She could be four years old the way she walks. She's closer to fifty. She walks like she's afraid she might step in something awful. Something that's somewhere someone else has been. She could be one of those beautiful Japanese ladies who have their feet bound—but she's not. She doesn't have that flowing grace. She does seem to float though. Spooky. Creepy. The willies. She scares the shit out of me. Because she floats right up to you and bites off your tits. That's the type she is. The tit-tearing type. The terrible type. The type I hate the most in the world. A fake. A false friend. A fiend.

She destroys children. She tears the sweetness out of their hearts by making them believe they're wrong. They're always wrong. She's always right. She made only one mistake . . . she had children. "They suck you down. They want your blood." They can't have her blood. She'll have theirs first. She'll have yours too. She'll take it all from a slit in your finger. She gulps it down. Slurps it up. That's why her lips are so close to her chin. So she can open wide . . . I saw the Grand Canyon once. Her mouth was bigger. Deeper. Denser. More dangerous. No one will take care of you, if you fall in. It's your own fault if she takes you. Got to be ready. Got to carry a stake. Big one. Silver, if possible.

Silver's my favorite color. It was hers too when I told her I liked it. I don't like it as much as I used to, but it's still my favorite.

She never knew what she wanted, but she always wanted what you had. Everything—from dresses to diseases. She wanted to be sick all the time. It gave her power. She collected used tissues and tore them into her salads like lettuce. Or grated them into casseroles like Swiss cheese. Those were tasty.

I went to visit my mother in the hospital once. Big hospital. Ninth floor. She was there by mistake. That's what she told me anyway. The woman next to her was black. Charcoal-colored. Small. She raised her legs all the time and ate her own snots. She was tied. They had to tie her up. She would pull on the ropes until her wrists would bleed. Pulling up. Pulling her hands up to her nose. An African ritual. "Look at that!" I said to Ma. And she said, "African ritual." She knew because she was part African. That makes me part of a part. My friend Lorenzo says he always knew it. "Your purple gums give it away," he says. I know. I'm easy to read.

I got the history of the world on my face. See? This line under my left eye, looks like somebody knifed me, but somebody didn't. It's the Euphrates River. It's a piece of the cradle of civilization. My face is a cradle for the baby of the world.

You think I'm not afraid, but I am. Don't go. You don't have to be afraid of me. Give me your hand. You don't have to stop. You think I want to stop? I do. But I've got something else to say.

You don't think I killed her, do you? It's not murder. You can't murder somebody without lips. They're not worth killing. Without lips, there's no place to put the knife. If I was going to kill somebody, I would use a knife. Knives are user friendly. I could go in deep. Up to my elbow. Up, in, around. Twist, twist, rip. Carve hard. Hard to carve. Carving is a man's job. Daddy carves the turkey. He's the man. I knew that. I'm not stupid. I know the difference between men and women. I've known for a long time—since my first Thanksgiving.

Life's so tasty isn't it? I like it. I like it a lot. It's my favorite thing. I want to have a silver life. I always wanted to paint myself silver. There's silver nail polish and silver eyeshadow, but no silver foundation. Not in this country anyway. Not yet. I bet the Asian countries have it. They're much more mystical. They listen to their dead. Americans don't do that. Go to any cemetery in anyplace, U.S.A. and you'll see people talking to their loved ones, but they're just reporting. Watch. Listen. They say "Roger got a new minibike" and "Sally's on solids again," but they don't ask any questions. That's the thing. They never ask for advice.

They just don't understand yet. They'll find out. Just not yet. Don't go.

Sky

(She lies on the ground looking at the sky.)

This is the only way to watch the world. This is how you tell what's important. From here you know that what's important isn't you. You are so small in the universe. In its vastness, you are lost. In its beauty, you are dirt.

(She stands.)

That's how white people think we talk. If I were lying on a beach, looking up at the sky, and I was white, they'd expect me to say "God, it's hot!" or "Gee, I hope there are some cute guys on the beach!" It's funny what people expect. I don't expect anything. I mean, just basic things, maybe, like I expect people won't walk into me when they're walking towards me. But people do that. They do it all the time, in all the big cities. And the only reason they don't do it in small towns is there's room to walk and fewer people.

I grew up in a small town. No. Not a reservation. With my mother and my father and my sister. Just the four of us. Four little Indians. I hated it. I loved them though. My father had a hard time there. He never learned to speak English very well. Although he could say "Another beer, please." That he could say.

One of the most exciting things about being an Indian in the nineteen-sixties was the access to natural drugs. That's when heritage comes in handy. It offers classic methods of disposal. The first time we did mushrooms—my sister Vee and I—we bought a pound of butter cookies at the local bakery and ate a head with each cookie. We finished the box. That's when the lights began to flicker. She accused me of turning them on and off—when I knew it was she. She was closer to the light switch. I remember it clearly. I had my back to the window, and she was by the door. The very door which is near the very light switch of which I spoke. You see, it was she. It was.

That's when she got out of hand. Irrational. You see, I had an old conch shell, my grandfather brought back from Iwo Jima, on my dresser. She thought it was her right ear. She thought her ear had fallen off and landed on my dresser. I picked it up and talked into it. "Hello! Hello in there!" She turned green. She said she could feel it—my breath entering the side of her head through the seashell and she was about six feet away. I tried to reason with her—"No," I said. "It's not your ear, it's my voice." It was. I could never have talked to her without the shell. Like Rudy Vallee and his megaphone—we were nothing without each other. The loudest people are the ones you hear first. "Give me my ear," she said. "It's not your ear, can't you see that? Can't you hear me? You couldn't hear me if I had your ear." "What?" she said. "Speak into it. I can't hear you otherwise." We went back and forth like this for quite some time. You can imagine. Finally, I decided on a daring move. To swallow the shell and take back my voice. We struggled over it. It never made contact with the floor. She jumped on me and stomped on me. When I pushed her off, she went sailing through the window.

It was only the second floor though . . . most people would've survived it. But she fell into the back of Dad's pick-up that was loaded up with chicken manure. I didn't look until later. It was later, I saw she was dead.

And then I looked at the shell, but it wasn't a shell . . . it was an ear. I can't say anything that she won't hear ever again. She's on every beach now. I look at the sky because I just might see her. I might see her and I can wave and she'll come down to me. She has to see me. Because she can't hear me. I've got both her ears now.

(She picks up two conch shells and places them over her ears.)

And I can't speak.

Coconuts

The first thing I saw was a tongue. I love tongues. That's why I like lichee nuts . . . it's like eating tongue. I could live on lichees . . . or talcum powder. I adore talcum. That's why I spend so much time in the toilet. People think it's for other reasons, but it's not. I crave that taste . . . the same way I crave coconuts.

That sweet, moist pulp and that delicious milk . . . I never tire of it. In fact, I never have to eat anything else if I don't want to. I'm not like the rest of you. *(Pause.)* Is it a fruit of a nut? *(Pause.)* I know it's not a vegetable, although I think it looks like a hairy potato— sort of. *(Pause.)* I don't know why I kid myself. I'm no tropical beauty, no placid vegetarian . . . I am a carnivore. *(Running her fingers through her pubic hair.)* I like untangling the knots . . . Can you use hot oil on pubic hair?—How about henna?—I bet the ancient Egyptians used it on everything. *(Pulls on a pubic hair, unrolling it so it's flush against her thigh.)* Look at that! It almost reaches my knee . . . the human body is incredible. It holds all these little secrets. *(Rubs her arms as if she is cold.)* I have my mother's knees. *(Squats down, holding her knees and rocking back and forth.)* She always told me not to go running with the boys. She feared for my knees. "You must protect the skin. You only get one set." She never tired of giving advice. It was genetic.

Anyway . . . I won't eat meat. I can't stand the smell. *(Pause.)* But fish is different. It doesn't smell when you cook it—except like fish. *(Pause.)* Is there such a thing as smelling through your skin? *(Long pause.)* So this is how it feels . . . to be brain dead I mean. I must be because I talk and nobody listens because nobody answers back —that's how I know. Well . . . it's not bad. Not bad at all. Peaceful. Calm. Straightforward. A straight line. My life has structure now. I'm a new person. Not a thought in my pretty little head. So now I'll have it made.

Pretty little heads with pretty little bodies—they're the leaders.

What's between your ears never counts as much as what's between your legs. Isn't that right? The sexually attractive are the living gods. We worship them. Give them anything they desire because we desire them. . . . More than anything, we want to touch their hands and kiss their smooth cheeks and place a tongue between their pearly whites.

And they are the happiest of people. They can stay home and watch *Wheel of Fortune* and pump a pillow and they'd be content. Not a bad life.

I want to be that object of desire. Everyone's. . . . Young, old, ugly, pretty, pathetic, athletic . . . I want them all. Not that I really want them, I just want them to want me. I want everyone in my pocket. I want big pockets. From my breasts to my knees. I wanna bury my arms, shoulders and head in that cave. I wanna feel thousands of little teeth pulling at my body hairs. I wanna make a home for them with my breath and my spit. My fingers would reach into the center of their passion and tear at it, picking off little pieces to put into my mouth. I have a hunger for everyone. I can't stop eating, drinking, sucking in their senses. That's why I'm brain dead. . . . A good fuck strokes you out. You go numb. You'd throw yourself into a fire if it would keep you coming.

I have an "A," "B" and "C" spot—not just a "G." I have two of those. One below . . . and one up here, in my head. That's why I wear a hat. Especially on windy days. Especially when there's a sun out and there's a wind. When something touches my head, I go crazy. I collapse against buildings. And always . . . I always try to keep my thighs from touching. I have to be careful I don't kill myself as I start to come from my eyes down. They turn into my head and see the past. But it's an old story. I mean, I know how it ends.

Rats

He says violence isn't the answer. They're just looking for a warm place to live out the winter, and in the spring they'll be gone. But I hear them. In the walls. In the drawers. Every day I check the flour for them. They get everywhere. He says we shouldn't kill them. That won't keep them from coming back. He's a scientist, so he knows. He also says how can you kill anything that's so cute.

"But they ate all my sweet corn and my marigolds and my squash seeds," I say. "We can buy more," he says. I say, "Why should we have to?" I say, "They're aliens, invaders. Get the hell out of my seeds and grains." I'm not a monster. I'm willing to give them my thyme. It's all dried up now anyway, but there's plenty of it. And it's right there in the front yard. Right where they can get their grimy little teeth on it. But no. They gotta come inside my house.

I never liked mice. The ones in my parents' apartment were gray—baby rats, really. Nobody cared about the souls of those guys. They were dirty, ugly and smelled like urine, other animals' urine —not even their own urine, you know what I mean? City mice are nobody's friends. You kill city mice. You don't gently catch them in Hav-A-Heart traps and release them into some pretty country field. There are no fields so if you let 'em go they will (a) Come back or (b) bite you and give you rabies. So you have no choice. You use those lovely, backbreaking snap traps. By doing this, you prevent disease, death, desolation. You keep little rats from becoming big rats that will eat small children.

My father caught rats at work. They had contests to see who could catch the biggest one. The danger, of course, was that the rat might break out of the plastic bag it was caught in and rush the crowd of laughing men, throwing down their dollar bills in drunken bets. The rats usually lost.

There was this one guy—Paco Loco—my dad says Dominicans will do anything for money—who was offered twenty dollars to catch a rat with his bare hands and strangle it. Paco went after a big one, but he slipped when he got right up to it and had cornered it. As he grabbed for it, the rat jumped smack into his face, bit him and kept running past the other men who all ran screaming out the door. My dad was the only one who stayed. He says the rat stopped and looked at him. He said it looked scared. Imagine that. Even with blood hanging off his teeth, he was still scared of people. Then he kept right on going, under the steel machinery, disappearing into the wall. My dad went over to Paco and helped him up. Paco was crying. The rat got his left eye. I mean, it was completely gone. It was just a hole.

They stopped playing with the rats after that.

I thought I left those things behind me. In the Bronx. But they followed me here. To white suburbia. I'm the only Puerto Rican in New Canaan, Connecticut. I figure as long as I don't open my mouth I'm safe. I was at a party once and some WASPy lady in tennis whites asked if I was from England. England?! Can you imagine?! She said she thought I was from England because I had an accent. She looked real surprised when I told her I was from the South Bronx. "South what?" But once she got used to the idea, it seemed quite wonderful and she grabbed my elbow and brought me around to all of her friends. "Have you met this wonderful creature, yet? She's from the Bronx—the South Bronx!" "Amazing! Is anybody still living there?"

No—nobody important . . . just people. My mother, my father, my sisters. The priest who gave me first communion. My friend Sharon whose little brother Junie died of sickle cell anemia when we were twelve and he was ten. She's a cop now. I bet she's a good cop. Forty-fourth precinct. Otherwise known as Fort Apache. It's funny . . . when I lived there it seemed more like Fort Navajo or Fort Chippewa. My people are a peaceful people. It's when they herd us into *barrios* that we turn—like a rat in a plastic bag. When you're fighting for your life, you get ugly. You get bitter. Or if you're like my mother, you spend a lot of time in church lighting candles. And you bring your children with you so they forget for a time that they've been forsaken.

The church is beautiful. It smells wonderful. It smells purple, like a purple, powerful drug. I loved the church. When I was sixteen I decided to become a part of the church. You know, settle down, get married to the Son of God. But it didn't work out too well. I liked to read too much. And I liked to write. Mother Superiors don't like that kind of stuff. After three weeks, four days, nine hours, I left. I think my mom was disappointed. Back to the Bronx. Wasn't any one of us going to get out? The Bronx—where people talk with such intriguing accents.

He doesn't understand why they upset me so much. With their cute little noses and big, brown eyes. They look just like his eyes. Just like mine. But they squeak. I don't squeak, do I? Maybe I do. Maybe I shouldn't be afraid of them, but I am. The scuttling sounds behind the wall remind me. I wonder if what they say is true—that you have the memories of all your ancestors inside your head. I wonder if my children will jump when they hear mice in the walls. I wonder if they'll remember too and get up in the middle of the night to check on people who aren't there anymore. . . .

Maybe he's right. Maybe it's time to put away the knife.

She Was Something . . .

There was a wonderful wall on the southside of China.
It was mean and lowdown and just about everybody there
standing by that lowdown wall—laughed at me.
And Shit! I was just trying to balance . . . The wall. This new
    wall.
Walking it. Trying to see if all the bricks were in place.
    And I saw a girl and she was something. She had eyes like
flames

with nostrils to match and ooh, she made fire appear on most
everything . . . Like . . . shower caps . . . and parking meters
    and beautiful
red-haired girls—She liked them red-haired girls.
    She was a saint too. To some. To some she was a queen.

I found her once inside me like a Chinese dinner—including
    soup.
Egg drop soup. To be exact. She had rubies on her lips and
    when she spoke
they came running down her chin like the tears we all shed in
    the war.
    But that's something else. We're talking about jewels. And
    gems.

And if you want gems go to South Africa. Because man, Africa,
    Shit,
South Africa. It don't got a soul. It's divided—like a mirror
    thrown
against a wall. And now—we're back at the wall. And the wall
    is moaning.
It's crying. But I don't know. I don't know what she's crying
    for.
    Maybe she's crying 'cause she's on the southside of the
    eastside.

And walls, they don't like it when you change direction. No-
    body likes it. . . .
They all whisper. And . . . Shit, as she walks down the road—
    everybody, crows
turn, yes—even crows, turn their heads around and stare at
    her eyes
and their wings are singed by her fiery pupils. And I know
    why. . . .
    She was a coffee-colored gal on the southside of China,

And I know her feet were hurting 'cause her toenails were
    popping.
She caught each nail in her mouth. Like in the circus.
She loves the circus. She wants a seal to play her horns
    and I'd like to see that too. So would you. But it's so hot
    in the south.
People burn there. Flames shoot out of their mouths. The soles
    of her feet
are burning too. Now ain't that something. . . .

THE ACTOR'S NIGHTMARE

CHRISTOPHER DURANG

THE ACTOR'S NIGHTMARE was first presented by Playwrights Horizons, in New York City, on a double bill with "Sister Mary Ignatius Explains It All For You" on October 14, 1981. The production was directed by Jerry Zaks; set design by Karen Schulz; costume design by William Ivey Long; lighting design by Paul Gallo; sound design by Aural Fixation; production stage manager was Esther Cohen. The original cast was as follows:

GEORGE SPELVIN	Jeff Brooks
MEG	Polly Draper
SARAH SIDDONS	Elizabeth Franz
ELLEN TERRY	Mary Catherine Wright
HENRY IRVING	Timothy Landfield

The final performance off-Broadway was January 29, 1984.

■ ■

Scene—Basically an empty stage, maybe with a few set pieces on it or around it. George Spelvin, a young man (20 to 30), wanders in. He looks baffled and uncertain where he is. Enter Meg, the stage manager. In jeans and sweatshirt, perhaps, pleasant, efficient, age 25 to 30 probably.

GEORGE: Oh, I'm sorry. I don't know how I got in here.

MEG: Oh, thank goodness you're here. I've been calling you.

GEORGE: Pardon?

MEG: An awful thing has happened. Eddie's been in a car accident, and you'll have to go on for him.

GEORGE: Good heavens, how awful. Who's Eddie?

MEG: Eddie. *(He looks blank.)* Edwin. You have to go on for him.

GEORGE: On for him.

MEG: Well, he can't go on. He's been in a car accident.

GEORGE: Yes I understood that part. But what do you mean "go on for him"?

MEG: You play the part. Now I know you haven't had a chance to rehearse it exactly, but presumably you know your lines, and you've certainly seen it enough.

GEORGE: I don't understand. Do I know you?

MEG: George, we really don't have time for this kind of joshing. Half-hour. *(Exits.)*

GEORGE: My name isn't George, it's . . . well, I don't know what it is, but it isn't George. *(Enter Sarah Siddons, a glamorous actress, perhaps in a sweeping cape.)*

SARAH: My God, did you hear about Eddie?

GEORGE: Yes I did.

SARAH: It's just too, too awful. Now good luck tonight, George darling, we're all counting on you. Of course, you're a little too young for the part, and you are shorter than Edwin so we'll cut all the lines about bumping your head on the ceiling. And don't forget when I cough three times, that's your cue to unzip the back of my dress and then I'll slap you. We changed it from last night. *(She starts to exit.)*

GEORGE: Wait, please. What play are we doing exactly?

SARAH *(stares at him)*: What?

GEORGE: What is the play, please?

SARAH: Coward.

GEORGE: Pardon?

SARAH: Coward. *(Looks at him as if he's crazy.)* It's the Coward. Noel Coward. *(Suddenly relaxing.)* George, don't do that. For a second, I thought you were serious. Break a leg, darling. *(Exits.)*

GEORGE *(to himself)*:   Coward. I wonder if it's *Private Lives*. At least I've seen that one. I don't remember rehearsing it exactly. And am I an actor? I thought I was an accountant. And why does everyone call me George? *(Enter Dame Ellen Terry, younger than Sarah, a bit less grand.)*

ELLEN: Hello, Stanley. I heard about Edwin. Good luck tonight. We're counting on you.

GEORGE: Wait. What play are we doing?

ELLEN: Very funny, Stanley.

GEORGE: No really. I've forgotten.

ELLEN: *Checkmate.*

GEORGE: *Checkmate?*

ELLEN: By Samuel Beckett. You know, in the garbage cans. You always play these jokes, Stanley, just don't do it onstage. Well, good luck tonight. I mean, break a leg. Did you hear? Edwin broke *both* legs. *(Exits.)*

GEORGE: I've never heard of *Checkmate*. *(Reenter Meg.)*

MEG: George, get into costume. We have 15 minutes. *(Exits.)* *(Enter Henry Irving, age 28 to 33, also somewhat grand.)*

HENRY: Good God, I'm late. Hi, Eddie. Oh you're not Eddie. Who are you?

GEORGE: You've never seen me before?

HENRY: Who the devil are you?

GEORGE: I don't really know. George, I think. Maybe Stanley, but probably George. I think I'm an accountant.

HENRY: Look, no one's allowed backstage before a performance. So you'll have to leave, or I'll be forced to report you to the stage manager.

GEORGE: Oh she knows I'm here already.

HENRY: Oh. Well, if Meg knows you're here it must be all right I suppose. It's not my affair. I'm late enough already. (Exits.)

MEG (off-stage):   Ten minutes, everybody. The call is 10 minutes.

GEORGE: I better just go home. (Takes off his pants.) Oh dear, I didn't mean to do that. (Enter Meg.)

MEG: George, stop that. Go into the dressing room to change. Really, you keep this up and we'll bring you up on charges.

GEORGE: But where is the dressing room?

MEG: George, you're not amusing. It's that way. And give me those. (Takes his pants.) I'll go soak them for you.

GEORGE: Please don't soak them.

MEG: Don't tell me my job. Now go get changed. The call is 5 minutes. (Pushes him off to dressing room; crosses back the other way, calling out:) 5 minutes, everyone. 5 minutes. Places. (A curtain closes on the stage. Darkness. Lights come up on the curtain. A voice is heard.)

VOICE: Ladies and gentlemen, may I have your attention please? At this evening's performance, the role of Elyot, normally played by Edwin Booth, will be played by George Spelvin. (Sound of audience moans.) The role of Amanda, normally played by Sarah Bernhardt, will be played by Sarah Siddons. The role of Kitty the bar maid will be played by Mrs. Patrick Campbell. Dr. Crippin will play himself. The management wishes to remind the audience that the taking of photographs is strictly forbidden by law, and is dangerous as it may disorient the actor. Thank you.

(The curtain opens. There is very little set, but probably a small set piece to indicate the railing of a terrace balcony. Some other set piece {a chair, a table, a cocktail bar} might be used to indicate wealth, elegance, French Riviera.

Sarah Siddons is present when the curtain opens. She is in a glamorous evening gown, and is holding a cocktail glass and standing behind the terrace railing, staring out above the audience's head. There is the recorded sound of applause.

After a moment George arrives onstage, fairly pushed on. He is dressed as Hamlet—black leotard and large gold medallion around his neck. As soon as he enters, several flash photos are taken, which disorient him greatly. When he can, he looks out and sees the audience and is very taken aback. We hear music.)

SARAH: Extraordinary how potent cheap music is.

GEORGE: What?

SARAH: Extraordinary how potent cheap music is.

GEORGE: Yes, that's true. Am I supposed to be Hamlet?

SARAH *(Alarmed; then going on.)*: Whose yacht do you think that is?

GEORGE: Where?

SARAH: The duke of Westminster, I expect. It always is.

GEORGE: Ah, well, perhaps. To be or not to be. I don't know any more of it. *(She looks irritated at him; then she coughs three times. He remembers and unzips her dress; she slaps him.)*

SARAH: Elyot, please. We are on our honeymoons.

GEORGE: Are we?

SARAH: Yes. *(Irritated, being over-explicit.)* Me with Victor, and you with Sibyl.

GEORGE: Ah.

SARAH: Tell me about Sibyl.

GEORGE: I've never met her.

SARAH: Ah, Elyot, you're so amusing. You're married to Sibyl. Tell me about her.

GEORGE: Nothing much to tell really. She's sort of nondescript, I'd say.

SARAH: I bet you were going to say that she's just like Lady Bundle, and that she has several chins, and one blue eye and one brown eye, and a third eye in the center of her forehead. Weren't you?

GEORGE: Yes. I think so.

SARAH: Victor's like that too. *(Long pause.)* I bet you were just about to tell me that you travelled around the world.

GEORGE: Yes I was. I travelled around the world.

SARAH: How was it?

GEORGE: The world?

SARAH: Yes.

GEORGE: Oh, very nice.

SARAH: I always feared the Taj Mahal would look like a biscuit box. Did it?

GEORGE: Not really.

SARAH *(She's going to give him the cue again.)*: I always feared the Taj Mahal would look like a biscuit box. Did it?

GEORGE: I guess it did.

SARAH *(Again.)*:   I always feared the Taj Mahal would look like a biscuit box. Did it?

GEORGE: Hard to say. What brand biscuit box?

SARAH: I always feared the Taj Mahal would look like a biscuit box. Did it? *(Pause.)* Did it? Did it?

GEORGE: I wonder whose yacht that is out there.

SARAH: Did it? Did it? Did it? Did it? *(Enter Meg. She's put on an apron and maid's hat and carries a duster, but is otherwise still in her stage manager's garb.)*

MEG: My, this balcony looks dusty. I think I'll just clean it up a little. *(Dusts and goes to George and whispers in his ear; exits.)*

GEORGE: Not only did the Taj Mahal look like a biscuit box, but women should be struck regularly like gongs. *(Applause.)*

SARAH: Extraordinary how potent cheap music is.

GEORGE: Yes. Quite extraordinary.

SARAH: How was China?

GEORGE: China?

SARAH: You travelled around the world. How was China?

GEORGE: I liked it, but I felt homesick.

SARAH *(Again this is happening; gives him cue again.)*: How was China?

GEORGE: Lots of rice. The women bind their feet.

SARAH: How was China?

GEORGE: I hated it. I missed you.

SARAH: How was China?

GEORGE: I hated it. I missed . . . Sibyl.

SARAH: How was China?

GEORGE: I . . . miss the maid. Oh, maid!

SARAH: *How was China?*

GEORGE: Just wait a moment please. Oh, maid! *(Enter Meg.)* Ah, there you are. I think you missed a spot here. *(She crosses, dusts, and whispers in his ear; exits.)*

SARAH: How was China?

GEORGE *(With authority.)*: Very large, China.

SARAH: And Japan?

GEORGE *(Doesn't know, but makes a guess.)*: Very . . . small, Japan.

SARAH: And Ireland?

GEORGE: Very . . . green.

SARAH: And Iceland?

GEORGE: Very white.

SARAH: And Italy?

GEORGE: Very . . . Neapolitan.

SARAH: And Copenhagen?

GEORGE: Very . . . cosmopolitan.

SARAH: And Florida?

GEORGE: Very . . . condominium.

SARAH: And Perth Amboy?

GEORGE: Very . . . mobile home, I don't know.

SARAH: And Sibyl?

GEORGE: What?

SARAH: Do you love Sibyl?

GEORGE: Who's Sibyl?

SARAH: Your new wife, who you married after you and I got our divorce.

GEORGE: Oh were we married? Oh yes, I forgot that part.

SARAH: Elyot, you're so amusing. You make me laugh all the time. (*Laughs.*) So, do you love Sibyl?

GEORGE: Probably. I married her. (*Pause. She coughs three times, he unzips her dress, she slaps him.*)

SARAH: Oh, Elyot, darling, I'm sorry. We were mad to have left each other. Kiss me. (*They kiss. Enter Dame Ellen Terry as Sibyl, in an evening gown.*)

ELLEN: Oh, how ghastly.

SARAH: Oh dear. And this must be Sibyl.

ELLEN: Oh how ghastly. What shall we do?

SARAH: We must all speak in very low voices and attempt to be civilized.

ELLEN: Is this Amanda? Oh, Elyot, I think she's simply obnoxious.

SARAH: How very rude.

ELLEN: Oh, Elyot, how can you treat me like this?

GEORGE: Hello, Sibyl.

ELLEN: Well, since you ask, I'm very upset. I was inside writing a letter to your mother and wanted to know how to spell apothecary.

SARAH: A-P-O-T-H-E-C-A-R-Y.

ELLEN (*icy*): Thank you. (*Writes it down; Sarah looks over her shoulder.*)

SARAH: Don't scribble, Sibyl.

ELLEN: Did my eyes deceive me, or were you kissing my husband a moment ago?

SARAH: We must all speak in very low voices and attempt to be civilized.

ELLEN: I was speaking in a low voice.

SARAH: Yes, but I could still hear you.

ELLEN: Oh. Sorry. (*Speaks too low to be heard.*)

SARAH (*speaks inaudibly also*)

ELLEN (*speaks inaudibly*)

SARAH (*speaks inaudibly*)

ELLEN (*speaks inaudibly*)

SARAH: I can't hear a bloody word she's saying. The woman's a nincompoop. Say something, Elyot.

GEORGE: I couldn't hear her either.

ELLEN: Elyot, you have to choose between us immediately—do you love this creature, or do you love me?

GEORGE: I wonder where the maid is.

ELLEN & SARAH *(together, furious)*: Forget about the maid, Elyot! *(They look embarrassed.)* You could never have a lasting relationship with a maid. Choose between the two of us.

GEORGE: I choose . . . oh God, I don't know my lines. I don't know how I got here. I wish I *weren't* here. I wish I had joined the monastery like I almost did right after high school. I almost joined, but then I didn't.

SARAH *(trying to cover)*: Oh, Elyot, your malaria is acting up again and you're ranting. Come, come, who do you choose, me or that baggage over there.

ELLEN: You're the baggage, not I. Yes, Elyot, who do you choose?

GEORGE: I choose . . . *(To Sarah.)* I'm sorry, what is your name?

SARAH: Amanda.

GEORGE: I choose Amanda. I think that's what he does in the play.

ELLEN: Very well. I can accept defeat gracefully. I don't think I'll send this letter to your mother. She has a loud voice and an overbearing manner and I don't like her taste in tea china. I hope, Elyot, that when you find me hanging from the hotel lobby chandelier with my eyes all bulged out and my tongue hanging out, that you'll be very, very sorry. Goodbye. *(Exits.)*

SARAH: What a dreadful sport she is.

GEORGE *(doing his best to say something his character might)*:   Poor Sibyl. She's going to hang herself.

SARAH: Some women should be hung regularly like tapestries. Oh who cares? Whose yacht do you think that is?

GEORGE *(remembering)*:   The Duke of Westminster, I exp—

SARAH *(furious)*:   How dare you mention that time in Mozambique? *(Slaps him.)* Oh, darling, I'm sorry. *(Moving her cigarette grandly.)* I love you madly!

GEORGE *(gasps)*:   I've inhaled your cigarette ash. *(He coughs three times. Sarah looks confused, then unzips the front of his Hamlet doublet. He looks confused, then slaps her. She slaps him back with a vengeance. They both look confused.)*

SARAH: There, we're not angry anymore, are we? Oh, Elyot, wait for me here and I'll pack my things and we'll run away together before Victor gets back. Oh, darling, isn't it extraordinary how potent cheap music can be?

(She exits; recorded applause on her exit. George sort of follows a bit, but then turns back to face the audience. Flash photos are taken again; George blinks and is disoriented. Lights change, the sound of trumpets is heard, and Henry Irving, dressed in Shakespearean garb, enters and bows grandly to George.)

HENRY: Hail to your Lordship!

GEORGE: Oh hello. Are you Victor?

HENRY: The same, my Lord, and your poor servant ever.

GEORGE: This doesn't sound like Noel Coward.

HENRY: A truant disposition, good my Lord.

GEORGE: You're not Victor, are you?

HENRY: My Lord, I came to see your father's funeral.

GEORGE: Oh yes? And how was it?

HENRY: Indeed, my Lord, it followed hard upon.

GEORGE: Hard upon? Yes, I see. *(Enter Meg.)* Oh, good, the maid. *(She whispers to him.)* Thrift, thrift, Horatio. The funeral baked meats did coldly furnish forth the marriage tables. What does that mean? *(Meg exits.)* Ah, she's gone already.

HENRY: My Lord, I think I saw him yesternight.

GEORGE: Did you? Who?

HENRY: My Lord, the king your father.

GEORGE: The king my father?

HENRY: Season your admiration for a while with an attent ear till I may deliver upon the witness of these gentlemen this marvel to you.

GEORGE: I see. I'm Hamlet now, right?

HENRY: *Sssssh! (Rattling this off in a very Shakespearean way)*:
Two nights together had these gentlemen,
Marcellus and Bernardo, on their watch
In the dead waste and middle of the night
Been thus encountered. A figure like your father,
Arméd at point exactly, cap-a-pe,
Appears before them and with solemn march
Goes slow and stately by them. Thrice he walked
By their oppressed and fear-surprised eyes
Within his truncheon's length, whilst they, distilled
Almost to jelly with the act of fear,
Stand dumb and speak not to him. This to me
In dreadful secrecy impart they did,
And I with them the third night kept the watch,
Where, as they had delivered, both in time,
Form of the thing, each word made true and good,

The apparition comes. I knew your father.

These hands are not more like.

GEORGE: Oh, my turn? Most strange and wondrous tale you tell, Horatio. It doth turn my ear into a very . . . (*At a loss.*) Merry . . . bare bodkin.

HENRY: As I do live, my honored lord, tis true,

and we did think it writ down in our duty

To let you know of it.

GEORGE: Well, thank you very much. (*Pause.*)

HENRY: Oh yes, my Lord. He wore his beaver up.

GEORGE: His beaver up. He wore his beaver up. And does he usually wear it down?

HENRY: A countenance more in sorrow than in anger.

GEORGE: Well I am sorry to hear that. My father was a king of much renown. A favorite amongst all in London town. (*Pause.*) And in Denmark.

HENRY: I war'nt it will.

GEORGE: I war'nt it will also.

HENRY: Our duty to your honor. (*Exits.*)

GEORGE: Where are you going? Don't go. (*Smiles out at audience. Enter Sarah dressed as Queen Gertrude.*) Oh, Amanda, good to see you. Whose yacht do you think that is?

SARAH: O Hamlet, speak no more.

Thou turn'st mine eyes into my very soul,

And there I see such black and grainéd spots

As will not leave their tinct.

GEORGE: I haven't seen Victor. Someone was here who I thought might have been him, but it wasn't.

SARAH: Oh speak to me no more.

These words like daggers enter in mine ears.

No more, sweet Hamlet.

GEORGE: Very well. What do you want to talk about?

SARAH: No more! (*Exits.*)

GEORGE: Oh don't go. (*Pause; smiles uncomfortably at the audience.*) Maybe someone else will come out in a minute. (*Pause.*) Of course, sometimes people have soliloquies in Shakespeare. Let's just wait a moment more and maybe someone will come. (*The lights suddenly change to a dim blue background and one bright, white spot center stage. George is not standing in the spot.*) Oh dear. (*He moves somewhat awkwardly into the spot, decides to do his best to live up to the requirements of the moment.*) To be or not to be, that is the question. (*Doesn't know any more.*) Oh maid! (*No response; remembers that actors call for "line."*) Line. Line! Ohhhh. Oh, what a rogue and peasant slave am I. Whether tis nobler in the mind's eye to kill oneself, or not killing oneself, to sleep a great deal. We are such stuff as dreams are made on; and our lives are rounded by a little sleep. *(The lights change. The spot goes out, and another one comes up stage right. George moves into it.)* Uh, thrift, thrift, Horatio. Neither a borrower nor a lender be. But to thine own self be true. There is a special providence in the fall of a sparrow. Extraordinary how potent cheap music can be. Out, out, damn spot! I come to wive it wealthily in Padua; if wealthily, then happily in Padua. *(Sings.)* Brush up your Shakespeare; start quoting him now; Da da . . . *(Lights change again. That spot goes off; another one comes on, center stage, though closer to audience. George moves into that.)* I wonder whose yacht that is. How was China? Very large, China. How was Japan? Very small, Japan. I pledge allegiance to the flag of the United States of America and to the republic for which it stands, one nation, under God, indivisible with liberty and justice for all. Line! Line! Oh my God. *(Gets idea.)* O my God, I am heartily sorry for having offended thee, and I detest all my sins because I dread the loss of heaven and the pains of hell. But most of all because they offend thee, my God, who art all good and deserving of all my love. And I resolve to confess my sins, to do penance, and to amend my life, Amen. *(Friendly.)* That's the act of contrition that Catholic school children say in confession in order to be forgiven their sins. Catholic adults say it too, I imagine. I don't know any Catholic adults. Line! *(Explaining.)* When you call for a line, the stage manager normally gives you your next line, to refresh your memory. Line! The quality of mercy is not strained. It droppeth as the gentle rain upon the place below, when we have shuffled off this mortal coil. Alas, poor Yorick. I knew him well. Get thee to a nunnery. Line. Nunnery. As a child, I was taught by nuns, and then in high school I was taught by Benedictine priests. I really rather liked the nuns, they were sort of warm, though they were fairly crazy too. Line. I liked the priests also. The school was on the grounds of the monastery, and my junior and senior years I spent a few weekends joining in the daily routine of the monastery—prayers, then breakfast, then prayers, then lunch, then prayers, then dinner, then prayers, then sleep. I found the predictability quite attractive. And the food was good. I was going to join the monastery after high school, but they said I was too young and should wait. And then I just stopped believing in all those things, so I never did join the monastery. I became an accountant. I've studied logarithms, and cosine and tangent . . . *(Irritated.)* Line! *(Apologetic.)* I'm sorry. This is supposed to be *Hamlet* or *Private Lives* or something, and

I keep rattling on like a maniac. I really do apologize. I just don't recall attending a single rehearsal. I can't imagine what I was doing. And also you came expecting to see Edwin Booth and you get me. I really am very embarrassed. Sorry. *Line!* It's a far, far better thing I do than I have ever done before. It's a far, far better place I go to than I have ever been before. *(Sings the alphabet song.)* a,b,c,d,e,f,g,h,i,j,k,l,m,n,o,p,q,r,s,t . . . *(As he starts to sing, enter Ellen Terry, dragging two large garbage cans. She puts them side by side, gets in one.)* Oh, good. Are you Ophelia? Get thee to a nunnery. *(She points to the other garbage can, indicating he should get in it.)* Get in? Okay. *(He does.)* This must be one of those modern Hamlets. *(Lights change abruptly to "Beckett lighting.")*

ELLEN: Nothing to be done. Pause. Pause. Wrinkle nose. *(Wrinkles nose.)* Nothing to be done.

GEORGE: I guess you're not Ophelia.

ELLEN: We'll just wait. Pause. Either he'll come, pause pause pause, or he won't.

GEORGE: That's a reasonable attitude. Are we, on a guess, waiting for Godot?

ELLEN: No, Willie. He came already and was an awful bore. Yesterday he came. Garlic on his breath, telling a lot of unpleasant jokes about Jews and Polacks and stewardesses. He was just dreadful, pause, rolls her eyes upward. *(She rolls her eyes.)*

GEORGE: Well, I am sorry to hear that. Pause. So who are we waiting for?

ELLEN: We're waiting for Lefty.

GEORGE: Ah. And is he a political organizer or something. I seem to recall?

ELLEN: Yes, dear, he is a political organizer. He's always coming around saying get involved, get off your behinds and organize, fight the system, do this, do that, uh, he's exhausting, he's worse than Jane Fonda. And he has garlic breath just like Godot, I don't know which of them is worse, and I hope neither of them ever comes here again. Blinks left eye, blinks right eye, closes eyes, opens them. *(Does this.)*

GEORGE: So we're really not waiting for anyone, are we?

ELLEN: No, dear, we're not. It's just another happy day, pause, smile, pause, picks nit from head. *(Picks nit from head.)*

GEORGE: Do you smell something?

ELLEN: That's not your line. Willie doesn't have that many lines. *(Louder.)* Oh, Willie, how talkative you are this morning!

GEORGE: There seems to be some sort of muck at the bottom of this garbage can.

ELLEN: Mustn't complain, Willie. There's muck at the bottom of everyone's garbage can. Count your blessings, Willie. I do. *(Counts to herself, eyes closed.)* One. Two. Three. Are you counting, Willie?

GEORGE: I guess so.

ELLEN: I'm up to three. Three is my eyesight. *(Opens her eyes.)* Oh my God, I've gone blind. I can't see, Willie. Oh my God. Oh what a terrible day. Oh dear. Oh my. *(Suddenly very cheerful again.)* Oh well. Not so bad really. I only used my eyes occasionally. When I wanted to see something. But no more!

GEORGE: I really don't know this play at all.

ELLEN: Count your blessings, Willie. Let me hear you count them.

GEORGE: Alright. One. Two. Three. That's my eyesight. Four. That's my hearing. Five, that's my . . . Master Charge. Six, that's . . .

ELLEN: Did you say God, Willie?

GEORGE: No.

ELLEN: Why did you leave the monastery, Willie? Was it the same reason I left the opera?

GEORGE: I have no idea.

ELLEN: I left the opera because I couldn't sing. They were mad to have hired me. Certifiable. And they were certified shortly afterward, the entire staff. They reside now at the Rigoletto Home for the Mentally Incapacitated. In Turin. Pause. Tries to touch her nose with her tongue. *(Does this.)*

GEORGE: The duke of Westminster, I expect.

VOICE: Ladies and gentlemen, may I have your attention please?

ELLEN: Oh, Willie, listen. A voice. Perhaps there is a God.

VOICE: At this evening's performance, the role of Sir Thomas More, the man for all seasons, normally played by Edwin Booth, will be played by George Spelvin. The role of Lady Alice, normally played by Sarah Bernhardt, will be played by Sarah Siddons. The role of Lady Margaret, normally played by Eleanora Duse, will be read by the stage manager. And at this evening's performance the executioner will play himself.

GEORGE: What did he say?

ELLEN: The executioner will play himself.

GEORGE: What does he mean, "the executioner will play himself"? *(Lights change to* Man for All Seasons *general lighting. Enter Sarah as Lady Alice {Sir Thomas More's wife}, and Meg with a few costumed touches but otherwise in her stage manager's garb and carrying a script as Lady Margaret {Sir Thomas More's daughter.})**

---

* *Note*: Though Meg starts by referring to her script, quite quickly it becomes clear that she knows the lines and does her best to play Sir Thomas's daughter with appropriate passion and seriousness.

MEG: Oh father, why have they locked you up in this dreadful dungeon, it's more than I can bear.

SARAH: I've brought you a custard, Thomas.

MEG: Mother's brought you a custard, father.

GEORGE: Yes, thank you.

MEG: Oh father, if you don't give in to King Henry, they're going to cut your head off.

SARAH: Aren't you going to eat the custard I brought you, Thomas?

GEORGE: I'm not hungry, thank you. (*Sudden alarming crash of cymbals, or something similarly startling musically occurs. The Executioner appears upstage. He is dressed as the traditional headsman—the black mask, bare chest and arms, the large axe. The more legitimately alarming he looks, the better. He can be played by the same actor who plays Henry Irving if his build and demeanor are appropriate. If not, it is possible to have a different actor play this role.*) Oh my God, I've got to get out of here.

MEG: He's over here. And he'll never give in to the King.

GEORGE: No, no, I might. Quick, is this all about Anne Boleyn and everything?

MEG: Yes, and you won't give in because you believe in the Catholic Church and the infallibility of the Pope and the everlasting life of the soul.

GEORGE: I don't necessarily believe in any of that. (*To Executioner.*) Oh, sir, there's been an error. I think it's fine if the King marries Anne Boleyn. I just want to wake up.

MEG: Oh don't deny God, father, just to spare our feelings. Mother and I are willing to have you dead if it's a question of principle.

SARAH: The first batch of custard didn't come out all that well, Thomas. This is the second batch. But it has a piece of hair in it, I think.

GEORGE: Oh shut up about your custard, would you? I don't think the Pope is infallible at all. I think he's a normal man with normal capabilities who wears gold slippers. I thought about joining the monastery when I was younger, but I didn't do it.

ELLEN (*waking up from a brief doze*): Oh I was having such a pleasant dream, Willie. Go ahead, let him cut your head off, it'll be a nice change of pace. (*The Executioner, who has been motionless, now moves. In a sudden gesture, he reveals the cutting block that waits for George's head.*

Note: In the Playwrights Horizons production, our set designer constructed a square furniture piece that doubled as a settee and/or small cocktail table during the Private Lives section. However, when the Executioner kicked *the top of it, the piece fell open, revealing itself to contain a bloodied cutting block.)*

GEORGE: That blade looks very real to me. I want to wake up now. Or change plays. I wonder whose yacht that is out there. *(Sarah offers him the custard again.)* No, thank you. A horse, a horse! My kingdom for a horse!

EXECUTIONER: Sir Thomas More, you have been found guilty of the charge of High Treason. The sentence of the court is that you be taken to the Tower of London, thence to the place of execution, and there your head shall be stricken from your body, and may God have mercy on your soul. *(Meg helps George out of the garbage can.)*

GEORGE: All this talk about God. All right, I'm sorry I didn't go to the monastery, maybe I should have, and I'm sorry I giggled during Mass in third grade, but I see no reason to be killed for it.

ELLEN: Nothing to be done. That's what I find so wonderful. *(Meg puts George's head on the block.)*

GEORGE: No!

EXECUTIONER: Do I understand you right? You wish to reverse your previous stand on King Henry's marriage to Anne and to deny the Bishop of Rome?

GEORGE: Yes, yes, God, yes. I could care less. Let him marry eight wives.

EXECUTIONER: That's a terrible legacy of cowardice for Sir Thomas More to leave behind.

GEORGE: I don't care.

EXECUTIONER: I'm going to ignore what you've said and cut your head off anyway, and then we'll all pretend you went to your death nobly. The Church needs its saints, and school children have got to have heroes to look up to, don't you all agree?

ELLEN: I agree. I know I need someone to look up to. Pause smile picks her nose. *(Does this.)*

GEORGE: Yes, yes, I can feel myself waking up now. The covers have fallen off the bed, and I'm cold, and I'm going to wake up so that I can reach down and pull them up again.

EXECUTIONER: Sir Thomas, prepare to meet your death.

GEORGE: Be quiet, I'm about to wake up.

EXECUTIONER: Sir Thomas, prepare to meet your death.

GEORGE: I'm awake! *(Looks around him. Sarah offers him custard again.)* No, I'm not.

SARAH: He doesn't know his lines.

EXECUTIONER: Sir Thomas, prepare to meet your death.

GEORGE: Line! Line!

MEG: You turn to the executioner and say, "Friend, be not afraid of your office. You send me to God."

GEORGE: I don't like that line. Give me another.

MEG: That's the line in the script, George. Say it.

GEORGE: I don't want to.

MEG: Say it.

ELLEN: Say it, Willie. It'll mean a lot to me and to generations of school children to come.

SARAH: O Hamlet, speak the speech, I pray you, trippingly on the tongue.

EXECUTIONER: Say it!

GEORGE: Friend, be not afraid of your office. You send me . . . Extraordinary how potent cheap music is.

MEG: That's not the line.

GEORGE: Women should be struck regularly like gongs.

MEG: George, say the line right.

GEORGE: They say you can never dream your own death, so I expect I'll wake up just as soon as he starts to bring the blade down. So perhaps I should get it over with.

MEG: Say the proper line, George. *(George breaks down.)*

GEORGE: Friend, be not afraid of your office. *(Executioner raises his axe.)*

ELLEN: Goodbye, Willie.

SARAH: Goodbye, Hamlet.

MEG: Goodbye, George.

EXECUTIONER: Goodbye, Sir Thomas.

GEORGE: You send me to God. *(Executioner raises the axe to bring it down. Blackout. Sound of the axe coming down.)*

EXECUTIONER *(in darkness)*: Behold the head of Sir Thomas More.

ELLEN *((in darkness)*: Oh I wish I weren't blind and could see that, Willie. Oh well, no matter. It's still been another happy day. Pause, smile, wrinkles nose, pause, picks nit from head, pause, pause, wiggles ears, all in darkness, utterly useless, no one can see her. She stares ahead. Count two. End of play. *(Music plays. Maybe canned applause. Lights come up for curtain calls. The four take their bows {if Henry Irving does not play the Executioner, he comes out for his bow as well}. Sarah and Ellen have fairly elaborate bows, perhaps receiving flowers from the Executioner. They gesture for George to take his bow, but he seems to be dead. They applaud him, and then bow again, and lights out.)*

THE CONDUCT OF LIFE

MARIA IRENE FORNES

To Julian Beck
in memory of his courageous life
(1925–1985)

THE CONDUCT OF LIFE was first produced at Theater for the New City, 162 2nd Avenue, New York City, on February 21, 1985. It was directed by the author; set design by T. Owen Baumgartner; lighting by Anne E. Militello; costume by Sally Lesser, with the following cast:

ORLANDO	Pedro Garrido
LETICIA	Crystal Field
ALEJO	Hermann Lademann
OLIMPIA	Alba Oms
NENA	Sheila Dabney

Characters
ORLANDO, an army lieutenant at the start of the play; a lieutenant commander soon after
LETICIA, his wife, ten years his elder
ALEJO, a lieutenant commander; their friend
NENA, a destitute girl of twelve
OLIMPIA, a servant

Setting
A Latin American country. The present.

■ ■

The floor is divided in four horizontal planes. Downstage is the living room, which is about ten feet deep. Center stage, eighteen inches high, is the dining room, which is about ten feet deep. Further upstage, eighteen inches high, is a hallway which is about four feet deep. At each end of the hallway there is a door. The one to the right leads to the servants' quarters, the one to the left to the basement. Upstage, three feet lower than the hallway (same level as the living room), is the cellar, which is about sixteen feet deep. Most of the cellar is occupied by two platforms which are eight feet wide, eight feet deep, and three feet high. Upstage of the cellar are steps that lead up. Approximately ten feet above the cellar is another level, extending from the extreme left to the extreme right, which represents a warehouse. There is a door on the left of the warehouse. On the left and the right of the living room there are archways that lead to hallways or antechambers, the floors of these hallways are the same level as the dining room. On the left and the right of the dining room there is a second set of archways that lead to hallways or antechambers, the floors of which are the same level as the hallways. All along the edge of each level there is a step that leads to the next level. All floors and steps are black marble. In the living room there are two chairs. One is to the left, next to a table with a telephone. The other is to the right. In the dining room there are a large green marble table and three chairs. On the cellar floor there is a mattress to the right and a chair to the left. In the warehouse there is a table and a chair to the left, and a chair and some boxes and crates to the right.

Scene 1

Orlando is doing jumping-jacks in the upper left corner of the dining room in the dark. A light, slowly, comes up on him. He wears military breeches held by suspenders, and riding boots. He does jumping-jacks as long as it can be endured. He stops, the center area starts to become visible. There is a chair upstage of the table. There is a linen towel on the left side of the table. Orlando dries his face with the towel and sits as he puts the towel around his neck.

ORLANDO: Thirty three and I'm still a lieutenant. In two years I'll receive a promotion or I'll leave the military. I promise I will not spend time feeling sorry for myself.—Instead I will study the situation and draw an effective plan of action. I must eliminate all obstacles.—I will make the acquaintance of people in high power. If I cannot achieve this on my own merit, I will marry a woman in high circles. Leticia must not be an obstacle.—Man must have an ideal, mine is to achieve maximum power. That is my destiny.—No other interest will deter me from this.—My sexual drive is detrimental to my ideals. I must no longer be overwhelmed by sexual passion or I will be degraded beyond hope of recovery. *(Lights fade to black.)*

Scene 2

Alejo sits to the right of the dining room table. Orlando stands to Alejo's left. He is now a lieutenant commander. He wears an army tunic, breeches, and boots. Leticia stands to the left. She wears a dress that suggests 1940s fashion.

LETICIA: What! Me go hunting? Do you think I'm going to shoot a deer, the most beautiful animal in the world? Do you think I'm going to destroy a deer? On the contrary, I would run in the field and scream and wave my arms like a mad woman and try to scare them away so the hunters could not reach them. I'd run in front of the bullets and let the mad hunters kill me—stand in the way of the bullets—stop the bullets with my body. I don't see how anyone can shoot a deer.

ORLANDO *(to Alejo)*: Do you understand that? You, who are her friend, can you understand that? You don't think that is madness? She's mad. Tell her that—she'll think it's you who's mad. *(To Leticia.)* Hunting is a sport! A skill! Don't talk about something you know nothing about. Must you have an opinion about every damn thing! Can't you keep your mouth shut when you don't know what you're talking about? *(Orlando exits right.)*

LETICIA: He told me that he didn't love me, and that his sole relationship to me was simply a marital one. What he means is that I am to keep this house, and he is to provide for it. That's what he said. That explains why he treats me the way he treats me. I never understood why he did, but now it's clear. He doesn't love me. I thought he loved me and that he stayed with me because he loved me and that's why I didn't understand his behavior. But now I know, because he told me that he sees me as a person who runs the house. I never understood that because I would have never—if he had said, "Would you marry me to run my house even if I don't love you." I would have never—I would have never believed what I was hearing. I would have never believed that these words were coming out of his mouth. Because I loved him. *(Orlando has entered. Leticia sees him and exits left. Orlando enters and sits center.)*

ORLANDO: I didn't say any of that. I told her that she's not my heir. That's what I said. I told her that she's not in my will, and she will not receive a penny of my money if I die. That's what I said. I didn't say anything about running the house. I said she will not inherit a penny from me because I didn't want to be humiliated. She is capable of foolishness beyond anyone's imagination. Ask her what she would do if she were rich and could do anything she wants with her money. *(Leticia enters.)*

LETICIA: I would distribute it among the poor.

ORLANDO: She has no respect for money.

LETICIA: That is not true. If I had money I would give it to those who need it. I know what money is, what money can do. It can feed people, it can put a roof over their heads. Money can do that. It can clothe them. What do you know about money? What does it mean to you? What do you do with money? Buy rifles? To shoot deer?

ORLANDO: You're foolish!—You're foolish! You're a foolish woman! *(Orlando exits. He speaks from offstage.)* Foolish. . . . Foolish. . . .

LETICIA: He has no respect for me. He is insensitive. He doesn't listen. You cannot reach him. He is deaf. He is an animal. Nothing touches him except sensuality. He responds to food, to the flesh. To music sometimes, if it is romantic. To the moon. He is romantic but he is not aware of what you are feeling. I can't change him. —I'll tell you why I asked you to come. Because I want something from you.—I want you to educate me. I want to study. I want to study so I am not an ignorant person. I want to go to the university. I want to be knowledgeable. I'm tired of being ignored. I want to study political science. Is political science what diplomats study? Is that what it is? You have to teach me elemental things because I never finished grammar school. I would have to study a great deal. A great deal so I could enter the university. I would have to go through all the subjects. I would like to be a woman who speaks in a group and have others listen.

ALEJO: Why do you want to worry about any of that? What's the use? Do you think you can change anything? Do you think anyone can change anything?

LETICIA: Why not? *(Pause.)* Do you think I'm crazy?—He can't help it.—Do you think I'm crazy?—Because I love him? *(He looks away from her. Lights fade to black.)*

Scene 3

Orlando enters the warehouse holding Nena close to him. She wears a gray over-large uniform. She is barefoot. She resists him. She is tearful and frightened. She pulls away and runs to the right wall. He follows her.

ORLANDO *(softly)*: You called me a snake.

NENA: No, I didn't. *(He tries to reach her. She pushes his hands away from her.)* I was kidding.—I swear I was kidding.

(He grabs her and pushes her against the wall. He pushes his pelvis against her. He moves to the chair dragging her with him. She crawls to the left, pushes the table aside, and stands behind it. He walks around the table. She goes under it. He grabs her foot and pulls her out toward

the downstage side. He opens his fly and pushes his pelvis against her. Lights fade to black.)

Scene 4

Olimpia is wiping crumbs off the dining room table. She wears a plain gray uniform. Leticia sits to the left of the table facing front. She wears a dressing gown. She writes in a notebook. There is some silverware on the table. Olimpia has a speech defect.

LETICIA: Let's do this.

OLIMPIA: O.K. *(She continues wiping the table.)*

LETICIA *(still writing)*: What are you doing?

OLIMPIA: I'm doing what I always do.

LETICIA: Let's do this.

OLIMPIA *(in a mumble)*: As soon as I finish doing this. You can't just ask me to do what you want me to do, and interrupt what I'm doing. I don't stop from the time I wake up in the morning to the time I go to sleep. You can't interrupt me whenever you want, not if you want me to get to the end of my work. I wake up at 5:30. I wash. I put on my clothes and make my bed. I go to the kitchen. I get the milk and the bread from outside and I put them on the counter. I open the icebox. I put one bottle in and take the butter out. I leave the other bottle on the counter. I shut the refrigerator door. I take the pan that I use for water and put water in it. I know how much. I put the pan on the stove, light the stove, cover it. I take the top off the milk and pour it in the milk pan except for a little. *(Indicating with her finger.)* Like this. For the cat. I put the pan on the stove, light the stove. I put coffee in the thing. I know how much. I light the oven and put bread in it. I come here, get the tablecloth and I lay it on the table. I shout "Breakfast." I get the napkins. I take the cups, the saucers, and the silver out and set the table. I go to the kitchen. I put the tray on the counter, put the butter on the tray. The water and the milk are getting hot. I pick up the cat's dish. I wash it. I pour the milk I left in the bottle in the milk dish. I put it on the floor for the cat. I shout "Breakfast." The water boils. I pour it in the thing. When the milk boils I turn off the gas and cover the milk. I get the bread from the oven. I slice it down the middle and butter it. Then I cut it in pieces *(indicating)* this big. I set a piece aside for me. I put the rest of the bread in the bread dish and shout "Breakfast." I pour the coffee in the coffee pot and the milk in the milk pitcher, except I leave *(indicating)* this much for me. I put them on the tray and bring them here. If you're not in the dining room I call again. "Breakfast." I go to the kitchen, I fill the milk pan with water and let it soak. I pour my coffee, sit at the counter and eat my breakfast. I go upstairs to make your bed and clean your bathroom. I come down here to meet you and figure out what you want for lunch and dinner. And try to get you to think quickly so I can run to the market and get it bought before all the fresh stuff is bought up. Then, I start the day.

LETICIA: So?

OLIMPIA: So I need a steam pot.

LETICIA: What is a steam pot?

OLIMPIA: A pressure cooker.

LETICIA: And you want a steam pot? Don't you have enough pots?

OLIMPIA: No.

LETICIA: Why do you want a steam pot?

OLIMPIA: It cooks faster.

LETICIA: How much is it?

OLIMPIA: Expensive.

LETICIA: How much?

OLIMPIA: Twenty.

LETICIA: Too expensive. (*Olimpia throws the silver on the floor. Leticia turns her eyes up to the ceiling.*) Why do you want one more pot?

OLIMPIA: I don't have a steam pot.

LETICIA: A pressure cooker.

OLIMPIA: A pressure cooker.

LETICIA: You have too many pots. (*Olimpia goes to the kitchen and returns with an aluminum pan. She shows it to Leticia.*)

OLIMPIA: Look at this. (*Leticia looks at it.*)

LETICIA: What? (*Olimpia hits the pan against the back of a chair, breaking off a piece of the bottom.*)

OLIMPIA: It's no good.

LETICIA: All right! (*She takes money from her pocket and gives it to Olimpia.*) Here. Buy it!—What are we having for lunch?

OLIMPIA: Fish.

LETICIA: I don't like fish.—What else?

OLIMPIA: Boiled plantains.

LETICIA: Make something I like.

OLIMPIA: Avocados. (*Leticia gives a look of resentment to Olimpia.*)

LETICIA: Why can't you make something I like?

OLIMPIA: Avocados.

LETICIA: Something that needs cooking.

OLIMPIA: Bread pudding.

LETICIA: And for dinner?

OLIMPIA: Pot roast.

LETICIA: What else?

OLIMPIA: Rice.

LETICIA: What else?

OLIMPIA: Salad.

LETICIA: What kind?

OLIMPIA: Avocado.

LETICIA: Again. *(Olimpia looks at Leticia.)*

OLIMPIA: You like avocados.

LETICIA: Not again.—Tomatoes. *(Olimpia mumbles.)* What's wrong with tomatoes besides that you don't like them? *(Olimpia mumbles.)* Get some. *(Olimpia mumbles.)* What does that mean? *(Olimpia doesn't answer.)* Buy tomatoes.—What else?

OLIMPIA: That's all.

LETICIA: We need a green.

OLIMPIA: Watercress.

LETICIA: What else?

OLIMPIA: Nothing.

LETICIA: For dessert.

OLIMPIA: Bread pudding.

LETICIA: Again.

OLIMPIA: Why not?

LETICIA: Make a flan.

OLIMPIA: No flan.

LETICIA: Why not?

OLIMPIA: No good.

LETICIA: Why no good!—Buy some fruit then.

OLIMPIA: What kind?

LETICIA: Pineapple. *(Olimpia shakes her head.)* Why not? *(Olimpia shakes her head.)* Mango.

OLIMPIA: No mango.

LETICIA: Buy some fruit! That's all. Don't forget bread. *(Leticia hands Olimpia some bills. Olimpia holds it and waits for more. Leticia hands her one more bill. Lights fade to black.)*

Scene 5

The warehouse table is propped against the door. The chair on the left faces right. The door is pushed and the table falls to the floor. Orlando enters. He wears an undershirt with short sleeves, breeches with suspenders and boots. He looks around the room for Nena. Believing she has escaped, he becomes still and downcast. He turns to the door and stands there for a moment. He takes a few steps to the right and stands there for a moment staring fixedly. He hears a sound from behind the boxes, walks to them and takes a box off. Nena is there. Her head is covered with a blanket. He pulls the blanket off. Nena is motionless and staring into space. He looks at her for a while, then walks to the chair and sits facing right staring into space. A few moments pass. Lights fade to black.

Scene 6

Leticia speaks on the telephone to Mona.

LETICIA: Since they moved him to the new department he's different. *(Brief pause.)* He's distracted. I don't know where he goes in his mind. He doesn't listen to me. He worries. When I talk to him he doesn't listen. He's thinking about the job. He says he worries. What is there to worry about? Do you think there is anything to worry about? *(Brief pause.)* What meeting? *(Brief pause.)* Oh, sure. When is it? *(Brief pause.)* At what time? What do you mean I knew? No one told me.—I don't remember. Would you pick me up? *(Brief pause.)* At one? Isn't one early? *(Brief pause.)* Orlando may still be home at one. Sometimes he's here a little longer than usual. After lunch he sits and smokes. Don't you think one thirty will give us enough time? *(Brief pause.)* No. I can't leave while he's smoking . . . I'd rather not. I'd rather wait till he leaves. *(Brief pause.)* . . . One thirty, then. Thank you, Mona. *(Brief pause.)* See you then. Bye. *(Leticia puts down the receiver and walks to stage right area. Orlando's voice is heard offstage left. He and Alejo enter halfway through the following speech.)*

ORLANDO: He made loud sounds not high-pitched like a horse. He sounded like a whale, like a wounded whale. He was pouring liquid from everywhere, his mouth, his nose, his eyes. He was not a horse but a sexual organ.—Helpless. A viscera.—Screaming. Making strange sounds. He collapsed on top of her. She wanted him off but he collapsed on top of her and stayed there on top of her. Like gum. He looked more like a whale than a horse. A seal. His muscles were soft. What does it feel like to be without shape like that. Without pride. She was indifferent. He stayed there for a while and then lifted himself off her and to the ground. *(Pause.)* He looked like a horse again.

LETICIA: Alejo, how are you? *(Alejo kisses Leticia's hand.)*

ORLANDO *(as he walks to the living room)*: Alejo is staying for dinner. *(He sits left facing front.)*

LETICIA: Would you like some coffee?

ALEJO: Yes, thank you.

LETICIA: Would you like some coffee, Orlando?

ORLANDO: Yes, thank you.

LETICIA *(in a loud voice toward the kitchen)*:   Olimpia . . .

OLIMPIA: What?

LETICIA: Coffee . . . *(Leticia sits to the right of the table. Alejo sits center.)*

ALEJO: Have you heard?

LETICIA: Yes, he's dead and I'm glad he's dead. An evil man. I knew he'd be killed. Who killed him?

ALEJO: Someone who knew him.

LETICIA: What is there to gain? So he's murdered. Someone else will do the job. Nothing will change. To destroy them all is to say we destroy us all.

ALEJO: Do you think we're all rotten?

LETICIA: Yes.

ORLANDO: A bad germ?

LETICIA: Yes.

ORLANDO: In our hearts?

LETICIA: Yes.—In our eyes.

ORLANDO: You're silly.

LETICIA: We're blind. We can't see beyond an arm's reach. We don't believe our life will last beyond the day. We only know what we have in our hand to put in our mouth, to put in our stomach, and to put in our pocket. We take care of our pocket, but not of our country. We take care of our stomachs but not of our hungry. We are primitive. We don't believe in the future. Each night when the sun goes down we think that's the end of life—so we have one last fling. We don't think we have a future. We don't think we have a country. Ask anybody, "Do you have a country?" They'll say, "Yes." Ask them, "What is your country?" They'll say, "My bed, my dinner plate." But, things can change. They can. I have changed. You have changed. He has changed.

ALEJO: Look at me. I used to be an idealist. Now I don't have any feeling for anything. I used to be strong, healthy, I looked at the future with hope.

LETICIA: Now you don't?

ALEJO: Now I don't. I know what viciousness is.

ORLANDO: What is viciousness?

ALEJO: You.

ORLANDO: Me?

ALEJO: The way you tortured Felo.

ORLANDO: I never tortured Felo.

ALEJO: You did.

ORLANDO: Boys play that way. You did too.

ALEJO: I didn't.

ORLANDO: He was repulsive to us.

ALEJO: I never hurt him.

ORLANDO: Well, you never stopped me.

ALEJO: I didn't know how to stop you. I didn't know anyone could behave the way you did. It frightened me. It changed me. I became hopeless. *(Orlando walks to the dining room.)*

ORLANDO: You were always hopeless. *(He exits. Olimpia enters carrying three demitasse coffees on a tray. She places them on the table and exits.)*

ALEJO: I am sexually impotent. I have no feelings. Things pass through me which resemble feelings but I know they are not. I'm impotent.

LETICIA: Nonsense.

ALEJO: It's not nonsense. How can you say it's nonsense?—How can one live in a world that festers the way ours does and take any pleasure in life? *(Lights fade to black.)*

Scene 7

Nena and Orlando stand against the wall in the warehouse. She is fully dressed. He is barebreasted. He pushes his pelvis against her gently. His lips touch her face as he speaks. The words are inaudible to the audience. On the table there is a tin plate with food and a tin cup with milk.

ORLANDO: Look this way. I'm going to do something to you. *(She makes a move away from him.)* Don't do that. Don't move away. *(As he slides his hand along her side.)* I just want to put my hand here like this. *(He puts his lips on hers softly and speaks at the same time.)* Don't hold your lips so tight. Make them soft. Let them loose. So I can do this. *(She whimpers.)* Don't cry. I won't hurt you. This is all I'm going to do to you. Just hold your lips soft. Be nice. Be a nice girl. *(He pushes against her and reaches an orgasm. He remains motionless for a moment, then steps away from her still leaning his hand on the wall.)* Go eat. I brought you food. *(She goes to the table. He sits on the floor and watches her eat. She eats voraciously. She looks at the milk.)* Drink it. It's milk. It's good for you. *(She drinks the milk, then continues eating. Lights fade to black.)*

Scene 8

Leticia stands left of the dining room table. She speaks words she has memorized. Olimpia sits to the left of the table. She holds a book close to her eyes. Her head moves from left to right along the written words as she mumbles the sound of imaginary words. She continues doing this through the rest of the scene.

LETICIA: The impact of war is felt particularly in the economic realm. The destruction of property, private as well as public may paralyze the country. Foreign investment is virtually . . . *(To Olimpia.)* Is that right? *(Pause.)* Is that right!

OLIMPIA: Wait a moment. *(She continues mumbling and moving her head.)*

LETICIA: What for? *(Pause.)* You can't read. *(Pause.)* You can't read!

OLIMPIA: Wait a moment. *(She continues mumbling and moving her head.)*

LETICIA *(slapping the book off Olimpia's hand)*:   Why are you pretending you can read? *(Olimpia slaps Leticia's hands. They slap each other's hands. Lights fade to black.)*

Scene 9

Orlando sits in the living room. He smokes. He faces front and is thoughtful. Leticia and Olimpia are in the dining room. Leticia wears a hat and jacket. She tries to put a leather strap through the loops of a suitcase. There is a smaller piece of luggage on the floor.

LETICIA: This strap is too wide. It doesn't fit through the loop. *(Orlando doesn't reply.)* Is this the right strap? Is this the strap that came with this suitcase? Did the strap that came with the suitcase break? If so, where is it? And when did it break? Why doesn't this strap fit the suitcase and how did it get here? Did you buy this strap, Orlando?

ORLANDO: I may have.

LETICIA: It doesn't fit.

ORLANDO: Hm.

LETICIA: It doesn't fit through the loops.

ORLANDO: Just strap it outside the loops. *(Leticia stands. Olimpia tries to put the strap through the loop.)*

LETICIA: No. You're supposed to put it through the loops. That's what the loops are for. What happened to the other strap?

ORLANDO: It broke.

LETICIA: How?

ORLANDO: I used it for something.

LETICIA: What! *(He looks at her.)* You should have gotten me one that fit. What did you use it for?—Look at that.

ORLANDO: Strap it outside the loops.

LETICIA: That wouldn't look right.

ORLANDO *(going to look at the suitcase)*:   Why do you need the straps?

LETICIA: Because they come with it.

ORLANDO: You don't need them.

LETICIA: And travel like this?

ORLANDO: Use another suitcase.

LETICIA: What other suitcase. I don't have another. *(Orlando looks at his watch.)*

ORLANDO: You're going to miss your plane.

LETICIA: I'm not going. I'm not traveling like this.

ORLANDO: Go without it. I'll send it to you.

LETICIA: You'll get new luggage, repack it and send it to me?— All right. *(She starts to exit left.)* It's nice to travel light. *(Off stage.)* Do I have everything?—Come, Olimpia.

(Olimpia follows with the suitcases. Orlando takes the larger suitcase from Olimpia. She exits. Orlando goes up the hallway and exits through the left door. A moment later he enters holding Nena close to him. She is pale, disheveled and has black circles around her eyes. She has a high fever and is almost unconscious. Her dress is torn and soiled. She is barefoot. He carries a new cotton dress on his arm. He takes her to the chair in the living room. He takes off the soiled dress and puts the new dress on her over a soiled slip.)

ORLANDO: That's nice. You look nice. *(Leticia's voice is heard. He hurriedly takes Nena out the door, closes it, and leans on it.)*

LETICIA *(offstage)*: It would take but a second. You run to the garage and get the little suitcase and I'll take out the things I need. *(Leticia and Olimpia enter left. Olimpia exits right.)* Hurry. Hurry. It would take but a second. *(Seeing Orlando.)* Orlando, I came back because I couldn't leave without anything at all. I came to get a few things because I have a smaller suitcase where I can take a few things. *(She puts the suitcase on the table, opens it and takes out the things she mentions.)* A pair of shoes . . . *(Olimpia enters right with a small suitcase.)*

OLIMPIA: Here.

LETICIA:	OLIMPIA:
A nightgown,	A robe,
a robe,	a dress,
underwear,	a nightgown,
a dress,	underwear,
a sweater.	a sweater,
	a pair of shoes.

(Leticia closes the large suitcase. Olimpia closes the smaller suitcase.)

LETICIA *(starting to exit)*: Goodbye.

OLIMPIA *(following Leticia)*: Goodbye.

ORLANDO: Goodbye. *(Lights fade to black.)*

Scene 10

Nena is curled on the extreme right of the mattress. Orlando sits on the mattress using Nena as a back support. Alejo sits on the chair. He holds a green paper in his hand. Olimpia sweeps the floor.

ORLANDO: Tell them to check him. See if there's a scratch on him. There's not a scratch on that body. Why the fuss! Who was he and who's making a fuss? Why is he so important.

ALEJO: He was in deep. He knew names.

ORLANDO: I was never told that. But it wouldn't have mattered if they had because he died before I touched him.

ALEJO: You have to go to headquarters. They want you there.

ORLANDO: He came in screaming and he wouldn't stop. I had to wait for him to stop screaming before I could even pose a question to him. He wouldn't stop. I had put the poker to his neck to see if he would stop. Just to see if he would shut up. He just opened his eyes wide and started shaking and screamed even louder and fell over dead. Maybe he took something. I didn't do anything to him. If I didn't get anything from him it's because he died before I could get to him. He died of fear, not from anything I did to him. Tell them to do an autopsy. I'm telling you the truth. That's the truth. Why the fuss.

ALEJO *(starting to put the paper in his pocket)*:   I'll tell them what you said.

ORLANDO: Let me see that. *(Alejo takes it to him. Orlando looks at it and puts it back in Alejo's hands.)* O.K. so it's a trap. So what side are you on? *(Pause. Alejo says nothing.)* So what do they want? *(Pause.)* Who's going to question me? That's funny. That's very funny. They want to question me. They want to punch my eyes out? I knew something was wrong because they were getting nervous. Antonio was getting nervous. I went to him and I asked him if something was wrong. He said, no, nothing was wrong. But I could tell something was wrong. He looked at Velez and Velez looked back at him. They are stupid. They want to conceal something from me and they look at each other right in front of me, as if I'm blind, as if I can't tell that they are worried about something. As if there's something happening right in front of my nose but I'm blind and I can't see it. *(He grabs the paper from Alejo's hand.)* You understand? *(He goes up the steps.)*

OLIMPIA: Like an alligator, big mouth and no brains. Lots of teeth but no brains. All tongue. *(Orlando enters through the left hallway door, and sits at the dining room table. Alejo enters a few moments later. He stands to the right.)*

ORLANDO: What kind of way is this to treat me?—After what I've done for them?—Is this a way to treat me?—I'll come up . . . as soon as I can—I haven't been well.—O.K. I'll come up. I get depressed because things are bad and they are not going to improve. There's something malignant in the world. Destructiveness, aggressiveness.—Greed. People take what is not theirs. There is greed. I am depressed, disillusioned . . . with life . . . with work . . . family. I don't see hope. (*He sits. He speaks more to himself than to Alejo.*) Some people get a cut in a finger and die. Because their veins are right next to their skin. There are people who, if you punch them in their stomach the skin around the stomach bursts and the bowels fall out. Other people, you cut them open and you don't see any veins. You can't find their intestines. There are people who don't even bleed. There are people who bleed like pigs. There are people who have the nerves right on their skins. You touch them and they scream. They have their vital organs close to the surface. You hit them and they burst an organ. I didn't even touch this one and he died. He died of fear. (*Lights fade to black.*)

Scene 11

Nena, Alejo and Olimpia sit cross-legged on the mattress in the basement. Nena sits right, Alejo center, Olimpia left. Nena and Olimpia play pattycake. Orlando enters. He goes close to them.

ORLANDO: What are you doing?

OLIMPIA: I'm playing with her.

ORLANDO (*to Alejo*): What are you doing here? (*Alejo looks at Orlando as a reply. Orlando speaks sarcastically.*) They're playing pattycake. (*He goes near Nena.*) So? (*Short pause. Nena giggles.*) Stop laughing! (*Nena is frightened. Olimpia holds her.*)

OLIMPIA: Why do you have to spoil everything. We were having a good time.

ORLANDO: Shut up! (*Nena whimpers.*) Stop whimpering. I can't stand your whimpering. I can't stand it. (*Timidly, she tries to speak words as she whimpers.*) Speak up. I can't hear you! She's crazy! Take her to the crazy house!

OLIMPIA: She's not crazy! She's a baby!

ORLANDO: She's not a baby! She's crazy! You think she's a baby? She's older than you think! How old do you think she is—Don't tell me that.

OLIMPIA: She's sick. Don't you see she's sick? Let her cry! (*To Nena.*) Cry!

ORLANDO: You drive me crazy too with your . . . *(He imitates her speech defect. She punches him repeatedly.)*

OLIMPIA: You drive me crazy! *(He pushes her off.)* You drive me crazy! You are a bastard! One day I'm going to kill you when you're asleep! I'm going to open you up and cut your entrails and feed them to the snakes. *(She tries to strangle him.)* I'm going to tear your heart out and feed it to the dogs! I'm going to cut your head open and have the cats eat your brain! *(Reaching for his fly.)* I'm going to cut your peepee and hang it on a tree and feed it to the birds!

ORLANDO: Get off me! I'm getting tired of you too! *(He starts to exit.)* I can't stand you!

OLIMPIA: Oh, yeah! I'm getting rid of you.

ORLANDO: I can't stand you!

OLIMPIA: I can't stand you!

ORLANDO: Meddler! *(To Alejo.)* I can't stand you either.

OLIMPIA *(going to the stairs)*:   Tell the boss! Tell her! She won't get rid of me! She'll get rid of you! What good are you! Tell her! *(She goes to Nena.)* Don't pay any attention to him. He's a coward.— You're pretty. *(Orlando enters through the hallway left door. He sits center at the dining room table and leans his head on it. Leticia enters. He turns to look at her.)*

LETICIA: You didn't send it. *(Lights fade to black.)*

Scene 12

Leticia sits next to the phone. She speaks to Mona in her mind.

LETICIA: I walk through the house and I know where he's made love to her I think I hear his voice making love to her. Saying the same things he says to me, the same words.—*(There is a pause.)* There is someone here. He keeps someone here in the house. *(Pause.)* I don't dare look. *(Pause.)* No, there's nothing I can do. I can't do anything.

(She walks to the hallway. She hears footsteps. She moves rapidly to left and hides behind a pillar. Olimpia enters from right. She takes a few steps down the hallway. She carries a plate of food. She sees Leticia and stops. She takes a few steps in various directions, then stops.)

OLIMPIA: Here kitty, kitty. *(Leticia walks to Olimpia, looks closely at the plate, then up at Olimpia.)*

LETICIA: What is it?

OLIMPIA: Food.

LETICIA: Who is it for? *(Olimpia turns her eyes away and doesn't*

answer. Leticia decides to go to the cellar door. She stops halfway there.)
Who is it?

OLIMPIA: A cat. *(Leticia opens the cellar door.)*

LETICIA: It's not a cat. I'm going down. *(She opens the door to the cellar and starts to go down.)* I want to see who is there.

ORLANDO *(offstage from the cellar)*:   What is it you want? *(Lights fade to black.)*

Scene 13

Orlando leans back on the chair in the basement. His legs are outstretched. His eyes are bloodshot and leery. His tunic is open. Nena is curled on the floor. Orlando speaks quietly. He is deeply absorbed.

ORLANDO: What I do to you is out of love. Out of want. It's not what you think. I wish you didn't have to be hurt. I don't do it out of hatred. It is not out of rage. It is love. It is a quiet feeling. It's a pleasure. It is quiet and it pierces my insides in the most internal way. It is my most private self. And this I give to you.— Don't be afraid.—It is a desire to destroy and to see things destroyed and to see the inside of them.—It's my nature. I must hide this from others. But I don't feel remorse. I was born this way and I must have this.—I need love. I wish you did not feel hurt and recoil from me. *(Lights fade to black.)*

Scene 14

Orlando sits to the right and Leticia sits to the left of the table.

LETICIA: Don't make her scream. *(There is a pause.)*

ORLANDO: You're crazy.

LETICIA: Don't I give you enough?

ORLANDO *(calm)*:   Don't start.

LETICIA: How long is she going to be here?

ORLANDO: Not long.

LETICIA: Don't make her cry. *(He looks at her.)* I can't stand it. *(Pause.)* Why do you make her scream?

ORLANDO: I don't make her scream.

LETICIA: She screams.

ORLANDO: I can't help it. *(Pause.)*

LETICIA: I tell you I can't stand it. I'm going to ask Mona to come and stay with me.

ORLANDO: No.

LETICIA: I want someone here with me.

ORLANDO: I don't want her here.

LETICIA: Why not?

ORLANDO: I don't.

LETICIA: I need someone here with me.

ORLANDO: Not now.

LETICIA: When?

ORLANDO: Soon enough.—She's going to stay here for a while. She's going to work for us. She'll be a servant here.

LETICIA: . . . No.

ORLANDO: She's going to be a servant here. *(Lights fade to black.)*

Scene 15

Olimpia and Nena are sitting at the dining room table. They are separating stones and other matter from dry beans.

NENA: I used to clean beans when I was in the home. And also string beans. I also pressed clothes. The days were long. Some girls did hand sewing. They spent the day doing that. I didn't like it. When I did that, the day was even longer and there were times when I couldn't move even if I tried. And they said I couldn't go there anymore, that I had to stay in the yard. I didn't mind sitting in the yard looking at the birds. I went to the laundry room and watched the women work. They let me go in and sit there. And they showed me how to press. I like to press because my mind wanders and I find satisfaction. I can iron all day. I like the way the wrinkles come out and things look nice. It's a miracle isn't it? I could earn a living pressing clothes. And I could find my grandpa and take care of him.

OLIMPIA: Where is your grandpa?

NENA: I don't know. *(They work a little in silence.)* He sleeps in the streets. Because he's too old to remember where he lives. He needs a person to take care of him. And I can take care of him. But I don't know where he is.—He doesn't know where I am.— He doesn't know who he is. He's too old. He doesn't know anything about himself. He only knows how to beg. And he knows that, only because he's hungry. He walks around and begs for food. He forgets to go home. He lives in the camp for the homeless and he has his own box. It's not an ugly box like the others. It is a real box. I used to live there with him. He took me with him when my mother died till they took me to the home. It is a big box. It's big enough for two. I could sleep in the front where it's cold. And he could sleep in the back where it's warmer. And he could lean on me. The floor is hard for him because he's skinny and it's hard on his poor bones. He could sleep on top of me if that would make him feel comfortable. I wouldn't mind. Except that he may pee on me because he pees in his pants. He doesn't know not to. He is incontinent. He can't hold it. His box was a little smelly. But that doesn't matter because I could clean it. All I would need is some soap. I could get plenty of water from the public faucet. And I could borrow a brush. You know how clean I could get it? As clean as new. You know what I would do? I would make holes in the floor so the pee would go down to the ground. And you know what else I would do?

OLIMPIA: What?

NENA: I would get straw and put it on the floor for him and for me and it would make it comfortable and clean and warm. How do you like that? Just as I did for my goat.

OLIMPIA: You have a goat?

NENA: . . . I did.

OLIMPIA: What happened to him?

NENA: He died. They killed him and ate him. Just like they did Christ.

OLIMPIA: Nobody ate Christ.

NENA: . . . I thought they did. My goat was eaten though.—In the home we had clean sheets. But that doesn't help. You can't sleep on clean sheets, not if there isn't someone watching over you while you sleep. And since my ma died there just wasn't anyone watching over me. Except you.—Aren't you? In the home they said guardian angels watch your sleep, but I didn't see any there. There weren't any. One day I heard my grandpa calling me and I went to look for him. And I didn't find him. I got tired and I slept in the street, and I was hungry and I was crying. And then he came to me and he spoke to me very softly so as not to scare me and he said he would give me something to eat and he said he would help me look for my grandpa. And he put me in the back of his van . . . And he took me to a place. And he hurt me. I fought with him but I stopped fighting—because I couldn't fight anymore and he did things to me. And he locked me in. And sometimes he brought me food and sometimes he didn't. And he did things to me. And he beat me. And he hung me on the wall. And I got sick. And sometimes he brought me medicine. And then he said he had to take me somewhere. And he brought me here. And I am glad to be here because you are here. I only wish my grandpa were here too. He doesn't beat me so much anymore.

OLIMPIA: Why does he beat you? I hear him at night. He goes down the steps and I hear you cry. Why does he beat you?

NENA: Because I'm dirty.

OLIMPIA: You are not dirty.

NENA: I am. That's why he beats me. The dirt won't go away from inside me.—He comes downstairs when I'm sleeping and I hear him coming and it frightens me. And he takes the covers off me and I don't move because I'm frightened and because I feel cold and I think I'm going to die. And he puts his hand on me and he recites poetry. And he is almost naked. He wears a robe but he leaves it open and he feels himself as he recites. He touches himself and he touches his stomach and his breasts and his behind. He puts his fingers in my parts and he keeps reciting. Then he turns me on my stomach and puts himself inside me. And he says I belong to him. (*There is a pause.*) I want to conduct each day of my life in the best possible way. I should value the things I have. And I should value all those who are near me. And I should value the kindness that others bestow upon me. And if someone should treat me unkindly, I should not blind myself with rage, but I should see them and receive them, since maybe they are in worse pain than me. (*Lights fade to black.*)

Scene 16

Leticia speaks on the telephone with Mona. She speaks rapidly.

LETICIA: He is violent. He has become more so. I sense it. I feel it in him.—I understand his thoughts. I know what he thinks.—I raised him. I practically did. He was a boy when I met him. I saw him grow. I was the first woman he loved. That's how young he was. I have to look after him, make sure he doesn't get into trouble. He's not wise. He's trusting. They are changing him.—He tortures people. I know he does. He tells me he doesn't but I know he does. I know it. How could I not. Sometimes he comes from headquarters and his hands are shaking. Why should he shake? What do they do there?—He should transfer. Why do that? He says he doesn't do it himself. That the officers don't do it. He says that people are not being tortured. That that is questionable.—Everybody knows it. How could he not know it when everybody knows it. Sometimes you see blood in the streets. Haven't you seen it? Why do they leave the bodies in the streets,—how evil, to frighten people? They tear their fingernails off and their poor hands are bloody and destroyed. And they mangle their genitals and expose them and they tear their eyes out and you can see the empty eyesockets in the skull. How awful, Mona. He mustn't do it. I don't care if I don't have anything! What's money! I don't need a house as big as this! He's doing it for money! What other reason could he have! What other reason could he have!! He shouldn't do it. I cannot look at him without thinking of it. He's doing it. I know he's doing it.—Shhhh! I hear steps. I'll call you later. Bye, Mona. I'll talk to you. (*She hangs up the receiver. Lights fade to black.*)

Scene 17

The living room. Olimpia sits to the right, Nena to the left.

OLIMPIA: I don't wear high heels because they hurt my feet. I used to have a pair but they hurt my feet and also (*pointing to her calf*) here in my legs. So I don't wear them anymore even if they were pretty. Did you ever wear high heels? (*Nena shakes her head.*) Do you have ingrown nails? (*Nena looks at her questioningly.*) Nails that grow twisted into the flesh. (*Nena shakes her head.*) I don't either. Do you have sugar in the blood? (*Nena shakes her head.*) My mother had sugar in the blood and that's what she died of but she lived to be eighty-six which is very old even if she had many things wrong with her. She had glaucoma and high blood pressure. (*Leticia enters and sits center at the table. Nena starts to get up. Olimpia signals her to be still. Leticia is not concerned with them.*)

LETICIA: So, what are you talking about?

OLIMPIA: Ingrown nails. (*Nena turns to Leticia to make sure she may remain seated there. Leticia is involved with her own thoughts. Nena turns front. Lights fade to black.*)

Scene 18

Orlando is sleeping on the dining room table. The telephone rings. He speaks as someone having a nightmare.

ORLANDO: Ah! Ah! Ah! Get off me! Get off! I said get off! (*Leticia enters.*)

LETICIA (*going to him*):   Orlando! What's the matter! What are you doing here!

ORLANDO: Get off me! Ah! Ah! Ah! Get off me!

LETICIA: Why are you sleeping here! On the table. (*Holding him close to her.*) Wake up.

ORLANDO: Let go of me. (*He slaps her hands as she tries to reach him.*) Get away from me. (*He goes to the floor on his knees and staggers to the telephone.*) Yes. Yes, it's me.—You did?—So?—It's true then.—What's the name?—Yes, sure.—Thanks.—Sure. (*He hangs up the receiver. He turns to look at Leticia. Lights fade to black.*)

Scene 19

Two chairs are placed side by side facing front in the center of the living room. Leticia sits on the right. Orlando stands on the down left corner. Nena sits to the left of the dining room table facing front. She covers her face. Olimpia stands behind her, holding Nena and leaning her head on her.

ORLANDO: Talk.

LETICIA: I can't talk like this.

ORLANDO: Why not?

LETICIA: In front of everyone.

ORLANDO: Why not?

LETICIA: It is personal. I don't need the whole world to know.

ORLANDO: Why not?

LETICIA: Because it's private. My life is private.

ORLANDO: Are you ashamed?

LETICIA: Yes, I am ashamed!

ORLANDO: What of . . . ? What of . . . ?—I want you to tell us—about your lover.

LETICIA: I don't have a lover. *(He grabs her by the hair. Olimpia holds on to Nena and hides her face. Nena covers her face.)*

ORLANDO: You have a lover.

LETICIA: That's a lie.

ORLANDO *(moving closer to her)*:   It's not a lie. *(To Leticia.)* Come on tell us. *(He pulls harder.)* What's his name? *(She emits a sound of pain. He pulls harder, leans toward her and speaks in a low tone.)* What's his name?

LETICIA: Albertico. *(He takes a moment to release her.)*

ORLANDO: Tell us about it. *(There is silence. He pulls her hair.)*

LETICIA: All right. *(He releases her.)*

ORLANDO: What's his name?

LETICIA: Albertico.

ORLANDO: Go on. *(Pause.)* Sit up! *(She does.)* Albertico what?

LETICIA: Estevez. *(Orlando sits next to her.)*

ORLANDO: Go on. *(Silence.)* Where did you first meet him?

LETICIA: At . . . I . . .

ORLANDO *(grabs her by the hair)*:   In my office.

LETICIA: Yes.

ORLANDO: Don't lie.—When?

LETICIA: You know when.

ORLANDO: When! *(Silence.)* How did you meet him?

LETICIA: You introduced him to me. *(He lets her go.)*

ORLANDO: What else? *(Silence.)* Who is he!

LETICIA: He's a lieutenant.

ORLANDO (*stands*):   When did you meet with him?

LETICIA: Last week.

ORLANDO: When!

LETICIA: Last week.

ORLANDO: When!

LETICIA: Last week. I said last week.

ORLANDO: Where did you meet him?

LETICIA: . . . In a house of rendez-vous . . .

ORLANDO: How did you arrange it?

LETICIA: . . . I wrote to him . . . !

ORLANDO: Did he approach you?

LETICIA: No.

ORLANDO: Did he!

LETICIA: No.

ORLANDO (*grabs her hair again*):   He did! How!

LETICIA: *I* approached him.

ORLANDO: How!

LETICIA (*aggressively*):   I looked at him! I looked at him! I looked at him! (*He lets her go.*)

ORLANDO: When did you look at him?

LETICIA: Please stop . . . !

ORLANDO: Where! When!

LETICIA: In your office!

ORLANDO: When?

LETICIA: I asked him to meet me!

ORLANDO: What did he say?

LETICIA (*aggressively*):   He walked away. He walked away! He walked away! I asked him to meet me.

ORLANDO: What was he like?

LETICIA: . . . Oh . . .

ORLANDO: Was he tender? Was he tender to you!

(*She doesn't answer. He puts his hand inside her blouse. She lets out an excruciating scream. He lets her go and walks to the right of the dining room. She goes to the telephone table, opens the drawer, takes a gun, and shoots Orlando. Orlando falls dead. Nena runs to downstage of the table. Leticia is disconcerted, then puts the revolver in Nena's hand and steps away from her.*)

LETICIA: Please . . .

(*Nena is in a state of terror and numb acceptance. She looks at the gun. Then, up. The lights fade.*)

STATEMENTS AFTER AN ARREST UNDER THE IMMORALITY ACT

ATHOL FUGARD

This play was given its first performance on January 22, 1974, at the Royal Court Theatre, London, and was directed by Athol Fugard with the following cast:

FRIEDA JOUBERT	Yvonne Bryceland
ERROL PHILANDER	Ben Kingsley
DETECTIVE-SERGEANT J. DU PREEZ	Wilson Dunster

Characters
A WHITE WOMAN (Frieda Joubert)
A COLORED MAN (Errol Philander)
A POLICEMAN (Detective-Sergeant J. du Preez)

Note The following words appear in the play:
brak: mongrel dog
ja: yes
spruit: spring, stream

■ ■

A Man and a Woman on a blanket on the floor. Both of them are naked. He is caressing her hair.
Dim light.

WOMAN (*shyly*): I dried it in the sun. Just sat there, on a chair in the back yard, feeling the warmth of it on my head. Every strand felt separate and my head very light. . . . The texture of the hair changes as it dries. And then the smell of it when it falls over my face . . . the smell of clean hair and shampoo. The warmer it gets the more you smell it. And if there's a breeze, even a small one, the way it lifts and floats. Also . . . the color of the strands, specially when they hang close to your eyes. . . . The color seems to pulse. (*Pause.*) There's no sense of time. Everything very still. Just the sounds of a warm afternoon . . . warm sounds, warm smells . . . specially the fig tree. A lot of the fruit has fallen now and burst, rotting on the ground . . . almost like wine! The leaves also have a very strong smell when it's hot. *(Pause.)* What else? . . . Doves . . . a locust flying suddenly . . . bees . . . Just sat there. . . . Quiet Saturday afternoon . . . hearing and smelling it all quietly, being very lazy and thinking all sorts of things. *(Turning to the man.)* And you?

MAN: Oh . . . another day. Nothing special . . . until now.

WOMAN: I don't care. Tell me.

MAN: There's nothing to tell. I did a bit of work at the school. . . . No! Of course! I know what happened today.

WOMAN: Tell me.

MAN: I built a five-roomed house. *(She laughs.)* I did! Lunchtime. On the way home I passed a little boy . . . Izak . . . his older brother Henry started school this year . . . Izak Tobias . . . anyway Izak was playing there in the sand with some old bricks and things. I stopped and watched him. Building himself a house he said. Told me all about it. His mother and his father and his baby brother sleep, in one room, and he and his sister and his granny in the other. Two rooms. It's the house he lives in. I know. I've been in it. It's a Bontrug house. *(Pause.)* You know what I made him do? Build a separate room for his granny. Then I explained that when his sister got big she would need a room for herself. So he built another one for her. When I left him he had a five-roomed house and a garage. . . . That's what it's all about, hey.

WOMAN: Yes.

MAN: If you're going to dream, give yourself five rooms, man. *(Silence.)*

WOMAN: I love you. *(Pause.)* What's the matter? What are you doing?

(A match flares in the darkness. She scrambles away.)

WOMAN: No!

MAN: Please.

WOMAN: No!!

(The match dies. Darkness.)

MAN: Is it me or you?

WOMAN: You don't understand.

MAN: Understand what? There is seeing, and being seen. Which one are you frightened of? Me or you?

WOMAN: It's not as simple as that!

MAN: Yes, it is! It's got to be . . . sometimes. That last book you lent me ends off a chapter with a paragraph, and the paragraph ends off his speculation about the origin of life . . . conclusions . . . vague. Nobody will ever know. . . . "These questions cannot be answered at this point and are perhaps unanswerable." But we do know that the difference between life and even the most complex of chemical processes are four-fold . . . metabolic processes of a wide but not unlimited variety; a degree of independence from the environment; sexual reproduction; and, finally, a susceptibility to death. Because life lives, life must die. Simple. (*Pause.*) Moon's nearly full out there tonight, you know. Toringberg will be splendid when I walk back. Hell, Frieda, if we could have opened those curtains . . . !

WOMAN: Don't! Please. . . .

MAN: Why? What about me? I want to be seen. I want you to see me. (*Moves suddenly into a faint patch of light from the curtained window.*) The brightest spot in our world. Here I am. Me. Can you see me?

WOMAN: Yes.

MAN: And?

WOMAN: I see you.

MAN: Frieda! Frieda! Life . . . is three billion years old. Fact. This little piece of the earth, the few miserable square feet of this room . . . this stupid little town, this desert . . . was a sea, millions and millions of years ago. Dinosaurs wallowed here! Truly. That last book mentions us: "The richest deposits . . . Permian and Triassic periods . . . are to be found in the Graaff Reinet district of the Cape Province of South Africa." Us. Our world. Are you listening?

WOMAN: Yes.

MAN: You *can* see me?

WOMAN: Yes.

MAN: You want to hear more?

WOMAN: Yes.

MAN (*thinks . . . then*):   There was a point . . . a billion or so years after the beginning of the earth, when the surface cooled sufficiently to permit water to accumulate in liquid form. Up until then it had just been gaseous, remember. But when this stage was reached . . . (*Pause.*) It rained continuously for millions of years.
    Rain . . . water . . . on and on. . . . (*Pause.*) Frieda? (*Holds out his hand. She moves to him, but remains shy and reticent.*) What are you frightened of?

WOMAN: Everything. Me . . . you . . . them. . . .

MAN: Them?

WOMAN: No. That as well of course. But I wasn't thinking about them now. (*Pause.*) The dinosaurs and those hairy . . . missing links . . . that look like baboons, stand like men, and could almost smile.

MAN: Australopithecus. Fossilized skull in a limestone quarry in Taung, Bechuanaland. Raymond Dart. 1930.

WOMAN: Is that the one . . . ?

MAN: Yes. That's the one you don't like.

WOMAN: With the females and their babies . . . looking so . . .

MAN: Yes. (*Laughing.*) You're frightened of him! You know who I am frightened of? Bishop Ussher. God created the world . . . the act of creation took place on October the twenty-sixth, four thousand and four B.C., at nine a.m.

WOMAN: You shouldn't . . .

MAN: He worked it out. From the Bible. (*Pause.*) Come.

WOMAN: Try . . . please try to understand.

MAN: No. You understand. Do you think I just want to *see* you? Do you think I just want to look? (*Pause.*) I do. (*Pause.*) Listen to this one: ". . . no vestige of a beginning and no prospect of an end. . . ." Did you hear that?

WOMAN: Yes.

MAN: And? Listen again. ". . . no vestige of a beginning and no prospect of an end." The conclusion of Charles Lyell after a good look at what was happening on the surface of the earth. *Principles of Geology*, 1830. What does that do to you?

WOMAN: Nothing.

(*Pause. He laughs quietly.*)

MAN: You're wrong. You're so wrong. If it wasn't for that sentence . . . I don't think we should have ever met. Hey, when did . . . ?

WOMAN: Almost a year ago. January the twenty-sixth.

MAN: Then it was the night of January the twenty-fifth. My family were already asleep. It was quiet . . . the best time to read or study. . . . The lamp on the table, me, one of Bontrug's mongrels barking outside in the dark. . . . Anyway, I was reading, understanding everything clearly . . . fact after fact . . . the time it all took. . . . So slow . . . God is so lazy, Frieda! . . . and then suddenly those words: ". . . no vestige of a beginning, no prospect of an end. . . ." I stopped. I had to. I couldn't go further. They weren't just words, it wasn't just that I understood that somebody had said . . . I'm expressing myself badly. It's hard to describe. It was almost like having a . . . No! . . . it was a "comprehension"—*ja*, of life and time . . . and there in the middle of it . . . at that precise moment . . . in Bontrug, was me. Being me, just being me there in that little room was . . . (*choosing his words carefully*) . . . the most exciting thing that had ever happened to me. I wanted that moment to last forever! It was so intense it almost hurt. I couldn't sit still.

    I just left the book . . . didn't look at it again . . . I didn't want to see another word, read another fact. . . . *Ja!* It wasn't a question of facts anymore, something else, something bigger. I went outside. Walking round Bontrug. I looked at the Bontrug *braks* with their tails between their legs. . . . Dogs. . . . I stopped in front of old Tobias's little place with the five of them inside at that moment sleeping on the floor. . . . I looked at it and said "House" . . . at the stars. . . . My hands were cold . . . but ten fingers, Frieda. . . . If I was the first man I could have started to count the stars.

    There was nothing I was frightened to see.

WOMAN: You've never told me about that before. *(Pause.)*

MAN *(as if he hadn't heard her)*:   So, the next morning there I was on . . . what did you say it was . . . the twenty-sixth . . . January the twenty-sixth . . . asking if you had—

WOMAN: Julian Huxley's *Principles of Evolution.* *(Pause.)* Why . . . why have you waited, almost a year . . . to tell me about that?

MAN: I've told no one.

WOMAN: I'm not no one. I'm also me. I'm the older person on the floor. With you. *(Pause.)* I'm jealous. You can make me so jealous. And I'm frightened. Yes. And there are things I don't want to see. . . . They found two snakes in my neighbor's backyard yesterday . . . Mr. van Wyk. . . .

MAN: What were they?

WOMAN: Somebody said they were rinkhals.

MAN: Rinkhals, the drought's bringing them out. We've had no trouble in Bontrug.

WOMAN: They killed them.

MAN: Well, if they were rinkhals . . . old people say, if they sit up in your footpath, they can spit you blind.

WOMAN: Mr. van Wyk . . . said they were mating at the time. Their . . . the pieces kept moving . . . for a long time afterwards.

MAN: *Ja* . . . it's the nervous system. . . . I think they die later or something. *(Pause. He feels around in the darkness for his trousers.)* What's the time?

WOMAN: No . . . not yet. I'm sorry. Please. Say it again.

MAN: What?

WOMAN: Those words . . . that sentence. . . .

MAN: ". . . no vestige of a beginning and no prospect of an end."

WOMAN: Did it work?

MAN: *Ja.*

WOMAN: Good. *(She draws closer to him out of the darkness.)* It's so quiet. Just those dogs.

(Pause. He listens.)

MAN: Town dogs.

WOMAN: What makes you so sure?

MAN: I've walked past them. *(He has removed a few coins from his trouser pocket and is idly trying to count them in the dark.)* Which ones have got the ridges round them?

WOMAN: What?

MAN: Coins. Which ones have got those little ridges?

WOMAN: Two cents and one cent.

MAN *(counting)*: Five . . . seven . . . seventeen.

WOMAN: About two years ago I thought of leaving here. Going back to Cradock.

MAN: Why didn't you?

WOMAN: Too much bother I suppose.

MAN: What was it like?

WOMAN: Cradock?

MAN: Yes.

WOMAN: You've been there.

MAN: I mean . . . were you happy there?

WOMAN *(after a pause)*: My first memory is being very small and sitting on the floor of the long passageway in our house. The shutters must have been closed because it was all dark and quiet. Then somebody opened the front door at the other end and suddenly I saw all the sunlight and noise of the street outside. I started to walk towards it, but before I could get there the door closed. I was so upset! I sat down and cried and cried. *(Pause.)* My last memory of Cradock is locking that same door from the outside, and taking the keys to the estate agent.

MAN: You sold the house.

WOMAN: Yes . . . after my mother died, and I got the job here.

MAN: What else?

WOMAN: That's all.

MAN *(the coins in his hand)*: Forty-three.

WOMAN: What?

MAN: Forty-three cents.

WOMAN: Are you sure you are happy?

MAN: Of course. It was good, man. Wasn't it?

WOMAN: Yes.

MAN: Do you ever do that? Imagine that what you've got in your pockets is all you've got, but really all you've got. No family, no place to go, nothing to do, just standing suddenly in Church Street with forty-three cents . . . and then try to work out what you would do with it.

WOMAN: No.

MAN: Ten cents for bread . . . that would last the whole day . . . ten cents for cooldrink.

WOMAN: Buy milk.

MAN: No. When we're thirsty we drink cooldrink. Twenty-three cents left. What would you do? What do you think you'd want? You got something to eat, you're not thirsty.

WOMAN: Save something for tomorrow.

MAN: No. There's no tomorrow. Just today.

WOMAN: Why not?

MAN: Just part of the game.

WOMAN: I don't like the game.

MAN *(in vacant fascination with the thought of himself, one day, and twenty-three cents)*:   Could buy a newspaper. Read what happened in the world yesterday. Seventeen cents left. Place like Cape Town that could be bus fare. Go and look at the sea. Here you could only spend it in the shops.
        Buy a stamp, post a letter!

WOMAN: Envelope and writing-paper?

MAN: That's true. Could you send a telegram for twenty-three cents?

WOMAN: If the address and message was short enough.

MAN: How short?

WOMAN: I don't know.

MAN: Let's say ten words. *(Counting them on his fingers.)* "Give us this day our daily bread." Three left for my name and His address. What's your message?

WOMAN: "Forgive us our trespasses as we forgive those who . . ."

MAN: You haven't even got enough for the message! I still haven't spent the twenty-three cents. Shops close at six. *Ja!* That's what would do it. Twenty-three cents and the shops closing. That's how I'd make my mistake. I'd be too late for anything except twenty-three cents of sweets, or six stale cakes. Eat them all and be sick. What would you do?

WOMAN: Am I alone?

MAN: What do you mean?

WOMAN: Do I have you?

MAN: No. I haven't got you. You haven't got me. All you've got is forty-three cents, and one day. *(Feels for her hand in the dark and gives her the money.)* What would you do with it?

WOMAN: Nothing.

MAN: Nothing! You wouldn't . . .

WOMAN: No, I wouldn't. I wouldn't even have bought bread. *(Pause.)*

MAN: The only reason I bought it was because . . .

WOMAN: You had nothing except forty-three cents and one day.

MAN: *Ja.* I'm a *brak*, hey!

WOMAN: No.

MAN: It's true. I'm hungry enough to make every mistake . . . even bark. *(Pause.)* But if that one day also had a real chance to start again—you know, to make everything different—and forty-three cents would buy me even just the first brick for a five-roomed house . . . I'd spend it on that and go hungry. *(Pause.)* Anyway listen. I'm going to try hard now to look after things. Okay? Give me one more chance, man.

WOMAN: Don't ask for that. You are my chance. I don't want to lose it.

MAN: It all goes wrong because I don't! Like my correspondence course. Three assignments unopened. In my drawer. Twenty-five rand. That's no good. I must finish it. I've got all the time until school starts. And this year . . . I'm really going to teach. You watch.

And stop hurting you. I don't do it on purpose. I don't want to hurt you. I love you. But hell, it's just so useless at times I can't help it. And then that makes me feel even worse. Some of those walks back have been hard. Specially when I wanted to turn round and come back and say I'm sorry . . . but you know you can't. *(Pause.)* Hey. You know what I was thinking coming here? I must try and buy a car this year. Good second-hand car.

(A sudden noise startles them. They scramble apart, the woman grabbing the blanket and covering herself.)

Ssssh!! *(Pause.)* Sure you locked it?

WOMAN *(nodding)*: Back door?

MAN: Yes. *(Tense, motionless pause as they listen in silence for a few seconds longer. The man moves to his clothes on the floor.)* Hot tonight, hey.

WOMAN: Do you want the towel?

MAN: *Ja*, okay. I'm sweating. *(The woman finds a towel, takes it to him.)* There's no water left in Bontrug.

WOMAN: We're going to have prayers for rain next week. Wednesday.

MAN: The location dam is empty. Little mud left for the goats. They're going to start bringing in for us on Monday. Got to be ready with our buckets at twelve. Two for each house.

WOMAN: Then why won't you let me send you some of mine? The borehole is still very strong. Please! It would be so easy.

MAN: Thanks, but I'll go along with Bontrug.

WOMAN: Don't thank me for something you won't take.

MAN: For the thought, then.

WOMAN: To hell with the thought! I'm not trying to be kind. It's only water, and you need it.

MAN: We all do.

WOMAN: Exactly! So your family must suffer because of your pride.

MAN *(disbelief)*: Pride?

WOMAN: It sounds like it.

MAN: Pride doesn't use back doors!

WOMAN: Sssh, please!

MAN: Or wait until it's dark. You don't walk the way I do between the location and town with pride.

WOMAN: Please don't let's argue tonight.

MAN: Okay. *(Defeated by her apparent lack of understanding, he turns away from her to his clothes. For a few seconds he tries to sort them out, then stops. He confronts her again.)* Water. Water, man. You know . . . water!

I wanted to wash before I came here tonight.

Your water. You want to send me some of *your* water. Is it so hard to understand? Because if you can't . . . ! Why do you think it's easy? Is that what I look like? Is that why they're so nice to me out there? Because I'm easy? But when for once I get so . . . I feel so buggered-up inside that I say "No" instead of "Yes" . . . I'm proud! Proud! I teach children how to spell that word. I say to them: "Proud as a Peacock!" Me? Holding my breath and sweating, really sweating, man, because suddenly we heard something and I thought: "They've found us! Run!" Coming here to-night I heard a car coming, from the location. . . . I hid under that little bridge over the *spruit* . . . people relieve themselves there! . . . I was on my hands and knees among the shit, waiting for that car to pass, so that Bontrug won't start asking, "Why is the Meester walking into town every night?" *(Stopping her from moving away.)* No! Please listen. I must talk. When I take that same walk just now . . . back . . . out there in the dark where the tar and the light ends, where the stones start. I'm going to sit down and say to myself: "Back home again!" . . . and hate it. *Ja.* Hate it! Bontrug. The *braks* that run out at me when I get there. My school. The children I teach. My home. The same world I looked at that night a year ago and said "Mine!!" and was excited that I was there, in it! Easy to hate, man, when you suddenly find you're always walking back to it . . . and I am. Whatever happens I'm going to be there walking back to it. So I say to myself: "Careful, Philander. It's yours. It's all you can ever really have. Love it. You've got to." Sometimes that's easy too. But you see, even when I do . . . there's still you. I'm in the shit, hey. That's how I walk now between Bontrug and the town . . . one way guilty, back with . . . *(Pause.)* I'll tell you something else. Coming here once . . . in the "old" days . . . I passed a man and a woman and their child . . . little boy . . . going back to the location. They got names, but it doesn't matter. You don't know them. They had stopped halfway up the hill to rest. It's hard walking up there with the sun on your back. All three of them . . . hot and unwashed. They smell. Because I was coming to you, you know what I saw? Rags. I don't mean their clothes. The people inside looked like rags. The man drinks too much, he's a useless rag. The woman's an old rag. Their child is going to be somebody's good rag, until . . . What do you do with yours? I was looking at my feet when I walked past them. Frieda! . . . *(shaking his head)* . . . when I realized that . . . when I realized what I . . . I wanted to call them and bring them with me to the library. I wanted to knock on that back door and stand there with them when you opened it. I wanted you to see me with them! What would you have done? Asked them in? Called them Miester and Miesies? Would you have given them tea in your cups? How long before you would have started waiting for them to go? You understand now. The reason I don't want your water is just because Bontrug is thirsty.

WOMAN: And that is not pride.

MAN: No. Exactly the opposite. Shame.

WOMAN: I don't understand . . . anything.

MAN: Then you can't. Don't even try. *(He turns away from her back to his clothes and puts on his vest.)*

WOMAN: It really would be better if you could wait until it's darker. *(He stops. Pause.)* Old Mrs. Buys is still staring and being strange. She changed her books again today. I might be wrong but . . . She's taken out more books this month than she did the whole of last year.

MAN: And you think I'm proud.

WOMAN: You should be . . . of some things. *(Pause.)* I didn't think you were going to come.

MAN: I couldn't help myself.

WOMAN: Didn't you want to?

MAN: No, I wanted to. But I thought maybe you'd had enough of me for a while. . . .

WOMAN: That's not true.

MAN: I haven't been cheerful company lately. *(Pause.)*

WOMAN: What must I do? Please tell me.

MAN: Don't say that.

WOMAN: I've got to. What will make you happy?

MAN: Something that doesn't hurt anybody.

WOMAN: We do?

MAN: Yes.

WOMAN: Your family?

MAN: Not we. I do.

WOMAN: It's the holiday, isn't it?

MAN: That's one thing.

WOMAN: Listen. Stop worrying about it. Take your family. I promise I'll understand. We won't talk about it again.

MAN: I don't want to go. I decided to settle it last night after supper. Be firm with them, I said to myself. Explain you need the time for the course. Before I could bring up the subject, they started talking. When must they start packing? How much they were looking forward to it! Selina hasn't seen her mother for three years. I couldn't even open my mouth. I'm so bloody sick of my lies.

WOMAN: How much do you think your wife . . . ?

MAN: I don't know. I can't tell. I can't see or do anything properly any more, except come here, and even that I do thinking it's a mistake. *(Pause.)* No, she knows nothing. How can she? She doesn't have tea with your old Mrs. Buys. She thinks I'm tired! Been studying too hard. All I need is a good holiday. Jesus, they're so innocent.

WOMAN: Even if you could, you would never leave them.

MAN: I don't know.

WOMAN: No! Tell the truth, please. Even if you could you would never leave them. *(Pause.)*

MAN: No. I would never leave them. I'm not . . . strong enough to hurt them, for something I wanted. What would happen to them if I did?

WOMAN: Go home. Take your conscience and your guilt and go back to Bontrug and look after your family. I've also got problems. I can't add your adultery to them. If you haven't got the courage to say No . . . to anybody . . . me or her . . . I'll do it for you. Go home.

MAN *(viciously)*:   It would be better if I waited until it's dark . . . remember! *(Pause.)* My adultery? And yours? *Ja.* Yours! If that's true of me because of you and my wife, then just as much for you because of me and your white skin. Maybe you are married to that the way I am to Bontrug. You sneak out of it the way I sneak out of my house to come here. Let me see you choose!!

WOMAN: I will. Take me with you. Now.

(Silence.)

MAN: You're right. I'm a coward.

WOMAN: Is there nothing we can do any more except hurt each other?

MAN: One day when I was a boy, my father came home after work to our hut on the farm. He brought with him a jackal's foot. The animal had escaped that way . . . chewed off the foot caught in the trap. For a long time I waited for the story of the dogs that had caught and killed a jackal with only three legs. You see, I could only think about how much it must have hurt to do that. I didn't know anything yet about being so frightened of something else, that you would do that to yourself. *(Pause.)* That's what we're doing . . . chewing away, chewing away. And if we're frightened enough . . . we'll escape . . . but . . . *(Pause.)* What's the time?

WOMAN: Too dark. I can't see the clock. Or you.

MAN: I'm here.

WOMAN: What are you doing?

MAN: Nothing. And you?

WOMAN: Waiting. . . . *(Pause.)*

MAN: For what?

WOMAN: I don't know. I suppose the dogs.

MAN: Frieda. *(Holding out a hand in the dark.)* Frieda!

(A moment's hesitation and then they impulsively come together and embrace. Against this image of the two lovers, a plain-clothes policeman, Detective-Sergeant J. du Preez, walks on. He carries a police dossier and notebook. His statement is dictated to the audience.)

POLICEMAN: Frieda Joubert. Ten, Conradie Street. European. Errol Philander. Bontrug Location. Coloured. Charge: Immorality Act.

Joubert runs the library in the town. Been living here for six years. Unmarried. No previous convictions.

Errol Philander is Principal of the location school. Born here. Wife and one child. No previous convictions.

My suspicions were first aroused by a report from Mrs. Tienie Buys.

(Abandoning "dictation," he takes a statement out of the police dossier and reads it aloud.)

Statement to Detective-Sergeant J. du Preez at the Noupoort Police Station on December the seventeenth: "My attention was first drawn to the behaviour of Joubert and Philander on a night in June last year. Late that afternoon I was down at the bottom of my garden when I saw Philander arrive at the back door of the library and without knocking, go in. A few moments later, the light in the back room of the library was put on. Some time later Joubert herself came out and emptied some rubbish in the dirt bin. At about eight o'clock that night I was down at the bottom of my garden again and I noticed that the light was still on. I'd no sooner noticed this when it was switched off. No other lights were on in the library. I waited to see what would happen next. After some time—about forty-five minutes of darkness—the back door opened and Philander came out.

He closed the door behind him, locked it with a key which he put in his trouser pocket, and walked away. This pattern of events—Philander's arrival followed by a period of darkness until he left—was repeated on many occasions between that night and today . . . December the seventeenth. I also noticed that his movements became more and more secretive over the six months. I am prepared to repeat this statement under oath in Court.

Signed: Mrs. Tienie Buys, 2 Riebeeck Street, Noupoort."

(Replaces the statement in the dossier. He continues his "dictation" to the audience.)

Mrs. Buys's back garden is immediately behind the library. On her side there is now a row of quince trees. The back entrance to the library—which leads directly into the room Joubert uses as an office, and in which the two of them were arrested tonight—can be clearly seen from under these trees. I asked Mrs. Buys to contact me the next time Philander arrived at the library. She did this the very next afternoon, the twenty-ninth. I watched the library back entrance from under the trees at the bottom of Mrs. Buys's garden. After at least an hour of darkness, Philander came out of the back door, locked it behind him, put the key in his pocket, and walked away. I went round quickly to the corner of Church and Conradie Streets. I was just in time to see Joubert leaving by the front door. I decided that these events warranted a thorough investigation of the whole matter. The library was kept under observation. Philander visited it every day. On a further three occasions the pattern of events was suspicious. After discussion with Warrant Officer Pieterse it was decided that Joubert and Philander should be apprehended at the next opportunity. It was also decided that a camera should be used to obtain photographic evidence of the suspected offence. On the twelfth of January, Constable Harvey, who had been keeping a watch on the library reported in the late afternoon that Philander had arrived and was in the building with Joubert. Together with Harvey and Sergeant Smit, we went to Mrs. Buys's back garden. We waited from six o'clock to eight o'clock. Constable Harvey reported that nobody had left through the front door. We climbed over the fence, and in the dark made our way to the back door. Even though it and the window was closed, we could clearly hear voices whispering inside. On a sign from me the window was forced open, and a torch shone into the room. I saw Joubert and Philander lying side by side on a blanket on the floor. She was naked and he appeared to be wearing a vest. Sergeant Smit started to take photographs.

(A blackout, during which the policeman exists. A sequence of camera flashes in the darkness exposes the man and the woman tearing apart from their embrace; the man then scrambling for his trousers, finding them, and trying to put them on; the woman, naked, crawling around on the floor, looking for the man. As she finds him, and tries to hide behind his back, the flashes stop and torches are shone on them. The woman scrambles away, finds the blanket, and covers herself. The torches are relentless, but we never see anything of the men behind them. These "flash-sequences" are nightmare excursions into the split second of exposure and must be approached as "sub-text" rather than "reality.")

MAN *(Terrified. Covering his genitals with his trousers he talks desperately to the torch shining on him.)*:   Look . . . look—before you make up your mind let me tell you something. . . . I'm . . . I'm Principal. . . . I . . . I won't do it again. . . . I'm frightened. *Ja*, I'm frightened.

(Blinking back at the torch with terror he tries to get into his trousers without exposing himself. He can't manage it. The operation becomes a nightmare. For a few seconds the woman watches him with vacant horror. Then she scrambles forward and, using her blanket, tries to shield him while she talks compulsively to the torches. Her first words are an almost incoherent babble. As she moves around, the torches follow her. Finding himself in darkness, the man gets slowly to his feet, retrieves his hat, and then tries—carefully and quietly—to get away.)

WOMAN: Tennis biscuits! Only one. In the afternoons I have my tea at four. I like to make it myself. The tea things are kept in my office, nice and neat on a tray under a clean drying-up cloth. I can see the library clock from my desk. I was . . . *(Pause.)* I was waiting for him. I was always waiting for him. I tried as long as I could to think he might still come. Then at half-past five I thought to myself . . . No, he's not going to . . . and suddenly . . . nothing. There was . . . nothing. Just lock up and go home, have supper, go to bed, try to sleep so that tomorrow and its chance of seeing him would come.

   I locked the library door—I was hating myself for having waited—walked back into the office, and there he was. He looked tired, hot, his shoes were dusty. We talked a bit. But I didn't really listen to him because . . . he wasn't really talking to me. I could see something was wrong, that he was still unhappy, so I went to the desk—I was carrying a pile of books. . . . The new books have come! . . .

I was trying to work out what I could expect. I knew he was going to hurt me . . . I mean, not on purpose, but it just seems we can't avoid it. So, I waited for it. It came. He said he supposed he shouldn't have come.

(Pause.)

I didn't want to stay there then, in the office I mean, so I took the books I had sorted out and went into the library. But I didn't want to be there either! I had to go back because I couldn't leave it like that. When I did he said he was sorry and that he hadn't meant it. I was at the desk again stamping books and just wishing he would stop saying and doing all the things that always made him feel so sorry! It was getting dark and I had that hopeless feeling inside. He tried to explain, again. Said it was because of the way he was neglecting things—me, his family, his correspondence course, his school—all the things that really mattered in his life because they all still did, only he felt he'd become so useless at looking after them. I told him . . . I said, he wasn't neglecting me and that even if he did I would understand so he shouldn't worry about it, but he said he did, because he loved us all—me, his family, his school. . . . *(Pause.)* I was feeling terribly lonely again. We seemed so far away from each other and I didn't know why, or what to do. It was dark. I couldn't see properly where to stamp the books any more. I should have put on the light. But I just went on stamping and wishing it would get still darker so that everything would disappear—him, me, the room, what I was feeling—just disappear. . . . *(Frightened of what she had just said; very loudly)* No. No!

(One of the torches leaves her abruptly and picks up the man still trying to get away. He drops his trousers with fright and shields his genitals with his hat. He listens carefully to what the woman is saying.)

He stopped talking suddenly, and stood up. I had given him a fright. He asked me what was wrong. I just said . . . "Nothing." We were whispering. Whispering makes you sweat. He loosened his tie and said . . .

(The man realizes he must stop, and correct, this vein of intimate confession. With a sign to the torch he puts his hat on, then steps forward and faces her, and then takes his hat off in the correct and respectful manner.)

MAN: Miss Frieda Joubert?

(The woman stops talking, turns, and looks at him. She can't believe what she sees. She laughs with bewildered innocence. The man accepts her amusement. He handles his hat with a suggestion of nervousness as he starts to talk, respectfully.)

There's no water left in Bontrug. The dam's empty. Little mud left for the goats. They're going to start bringing in for us on Monday. We've been told to be ready with our buckets at twelve. Two for each house.

(The woman has watched his performance with growing bewilderment. At the end of it she tries to cope with the situation with another laugh. Pause. The man, under pressure, tries again, now more desperately.)

Miss Frieda Joubert! There's no water left . . .
WOMAN: I know.
MAN: There's no water left in Bontrug. Dam's empty.
WOMAN: I know! You told me.
MAN: Little mud left for the goats. They're going to start bringing in for us on Monday. We've got to be ready with our buckets at twelve. Two for each . . .
WOMAN: You've already told me! Don't you remember . . . ? *(Her desperation now growing. A move to him. He backs away from it. He is hanging on.)*
MAN: Miss Frieda Joubert. There's no water left in . . .
WOMAN: Why are you . . . ?
MAN: There's no water left in Bontrug!
WOMAN: What are you doing?

(Her bewilderment now edged by anxiety. Equivalently his performance degenerates more and more.)

MAN: Please listen, Miss Frieda! There's no water left in Bontrug, man. Dam's empty. Little mud left. For the goats. They're going to start bringing in for us . . .
WOMAN *(her desperation mounting)*:   You've already said that!
MAN: Miss Frieda . . . they're going to start bring for us . . .
WOMAN *(hanging on to herself)*:   And I said . . . I said I'd send you some of mine and you . . .
MAN: I got to be ready with my buckets at twelve.
WOMAN: You got angry!
MAN: Two buckets, lady. Got to be ready with my buckets at twelve. 'Cause they sending to us . . . me and my buckets . . . two for each . . .

(The woman now starts to lose control. The man's "performance" has now degenerated into a grotesque parody of the servile, cringing "Coloured.")

WOMAN: Sit down!

MAN: Bontrug's dry. Little mud in the dam.

WOMAN: Come!

MAN: Water, Miesies. Please, Miesies . . . water . . .

WOMAN: The way you . . .

MAN: Just a little . . . We're thirsty . . . please, Miesies. . . .

(The woman, now almost hysterical, looks around wildly for an affirmative action.)

WOMAN: Sit down . . . here . . . and read . . .

MAN: Water, Miesies, water, Miesies.

WOMAN: No, no . . . stop it . . . *(knocking the hat out of his hand.)* STOP IT!

MAN: I'll . . . I'll just go. I'll use the back door.

(Camera flashes and finally torches as in the previous sequence. This time, however, the torches trap the man against a wall and the woman on the floor looking down at the man's jumbled pile of clothing. To start with she is completely unaware of the torch shining on her.)

WOMAN: I don't understand. . . . You can't. Don't even try. *(Carefully examines one of his shoes.)* Dust on his shoes. Him. His feet. His thoughts. A man . . . walking, from Bontrug to here, the town, to me . . . and then back again. *(Pause.)* One night I watched him through the window, walk away, quietly, quickly, and disappear down the street. I tried to imagine. . . *(Pause.)* I can't. *(Very carefully replaces the shoe as she found it. His clothes. She is trying hard to understand.)* There is no water in Bontrug! . . . I'm not thirsty. . . . I don't understand. . . . He uses the back door. He can't come to me any other way. When I heard the knock and opened it, the first time, wondering who it was . . . and saw him. . . . No! I didn't. I saw a coloured man. . . . I was not surprised. Because it was the back door.

MAN: I needed a book. I knew I couldn't be a subscriber. But it was my third assignment. . . .

WOMAN: . . . . Julian Huxley's . . . *Principles of Evolution*. . . .

MAN: . . . . and I didn't have any of the books on their list. It had happened with the first two as well.

(Both talk to the torches, and each other, in a frank and eager manner.)

WOMAN: He was very serious about it. Explained what he was doing.

MAN: You were interested, hey.

WOMAN: Oh yes! Very. I could see it was important to him. I didn't have any of the books he mentioned . . . but I knew what he wanted and I found something else that I thought would help him. I said if there was anything I could do to help he must just tell me.

MAN: I could see she really meant it. So I didn't worry too much about going back again.

WOMAN: He always used my office. It started to seem so silly. Nobody was reading the books he needed. Only a few people ever went to that side of the library.

MAN: It made a big difference . . . being able to go there and use the encyclopedias, and read.

WOMAN: I found myself seeing books and articles in newspapers which I thought would help him. He's a very fast reader . . . and shy . . . at first . . . but once we started talking it was almost hard to keep up with him. And exciting. For me too. Even going home after I'd closed the library began to be different. I had something to do, and think about at night. You see, the library is not very busy . . . there's not all that much to look after.

MAN: We talked about lots of things, didn't we?

WOMAN: Oh yes! Not just the course. That's how we came to know each other. (*Pause as they both wait innocently and eagerly for a response to what they have said. Nothing. The silence slowly becomes a threat.*) Say something. (*Mounting hysteria.*) SAY SOMETHING! . . . Yes, we have made love. I switched off the light. Yes. Yes. Guilty. No doubt about it. Guilty of taking my chance and finding him. Hands, eyes, ears, nose, tongue . . . totally guilty. Nothing is innocent.

MAN: *Ja*, she put off the light. I mean . . . suppose I had made a mistake. Hey? And she wasn't feeling the way I did. Or even thinking about it. You know what I'm saying? I couldn't move. Just sat there looking at what I was thinking, and I couldn't move. It wasn't the first time I realized what was happening to us. We knew all right what we were doing. But that night I knew, it can happen now! If I was right about her, and did the right thing, it was going to happen. But suppose I was wrong. Suppose she screamed.

(*Camera flashes and finally torches as in the previous sequences. This time the torches trap the woman alone, naked. Once again she is unaware of the light shining on her. She studies herself, quietly, privately.*)

WOMAN: Ugly feet. The soles have got hard patches. My legs are bandy. Good calf muscles . . . probably got them riding to school on my bicycle up a very steep hill each day. Skin around my knees is just starting to get a little slack. I enjoy making the muscles in my thighs move. Hair is very mousy . . . very sparse. . . . I think the area around my waist is quite nice. Few soft and feminine contours around my hips. My breasts are slacker than I would like them to be. My neck is unattractive. My face is quite interesting but can be very plain sometimes. Lines around my mouth are starting to worry me. Hair causes me concern. I think it's going off. Ashamed of my hands. Nail-polish has come off in patches. Skin looks very old.

I think there is a lot of me in my hands somehow.

My favourite colour is blue. . . .

My favourite flower is . . .

You say you have no previous experience of men. That you were a virgin, and yet you took the initiative. What would you have done if Philander had rejected you?

Hated him.

Would the fact that a coloured man had rejected you have humiliated you more than if a white man had done so?

By the time it happened his colour did not mean anything to me any more.

Did you encourage Philander?

Yes.

Why?

I wanted him.

Would you say that you encouraged him against his will?

No. I think that he felt almost as strongly about me as I did about him.

Did it ever occur to you that he might have accepted a physical relationship with you out of respect for your feelings?

Yes. It did occur to me sometimes.

You are older than Philander?

Yes.

By how many years?

Six.

Do you think it possible that Philander thought you provided him with an easy opportunity to have intercourse with a white woman? Because as a Coloured man the law forbids it.

No.

What makes you so sure?

He was a man who had too strong a feeling of responsibility towards his family to take that chance for that reason.

Did you feel any responsibilities towards his family?

I did think about them for a time.

After you put out the light did he then initiate the physical encounter?

No.

What did you do. Describe what happened until you are told to stop.

I . . . I put off the light. . . .

Well . . .

Yes . . . *ja* . . . I stood there. . . . I knew why I had put off the light. . . . But once I had put it off . . . I was . . . hesitant . . . I was nervous . . . I wasn't sure what to do next. . . . Well . . . he . . . he didn't move or do or say anything. . . . I knew it was so hard for him that if I didn't do something . . . nothing would happen . . . so I . . .

(Pause.)

I knew where he was. . . . So I took a few . . . paces . . . towards him. . . . My hand came in contact with his . . . coat or jacket. . . . There was another moment of hesitation. . . . I had found him. And then . . .

(Pause.)

I moved in close to him. I knew that the response coming from him was the same. I wouldn't have had the courage if I didn't know that he felt . . . that he . . . So I leant against him . . . his shoulder. . . .

(Pause.)

He put his arms around me. . . . It felt like he . . . there was . . . his lips . . . yes. Then his lips touched the top of my head . . . it's very hard to remember anything.

(Pause.)

I know that we finally did kiss each other. Please, do I have to . . . please, it's very hard for me.

(Pause.)

So . . . so then . . . yes. . . . So then we made love. . . . I don't know how . . . but we were on the floor . . . the floor of the library. . . . And he . . . And me . . . We . . .

(Another sequence of flashes during which the woman scrambles around looking for the man and finally finds him—standing against a wall, protecting his genitals with his hands. This time the sequence does not end with torches, but harsh, directionless, white light. The image is sugges-

tive of one of the photographs handed in in the Court as evidence and it is with this as a background that the policeman finally completes his statement.)

MAN: There was nothing left to say. I had thought there would be. That if it ever happened, and we had known it could, that there would be something left to say, to her, to myself. Something to say to them. But when the light went on, it burnt out all the words I had left. Nothing to say. Nothing to do. –

(The policeman, still carrying his dossier and notebook, enters and completes his statement.)

POLICEMAN: Exhibit A. We gained entry to the room by forcing the door, and put on the light. By this time Joubert had covered herself with a blanket. Exhibit B. I immediately arrested them, and asked them whether they wished to make a statement warning them, at the same time, that anything they said would be taken down in writing and could be used in evidence against them. Full stop. Joubert's response to this was: quote "I'm not ashamed of myself" unquote. I asked her if she was prepared to repeat the statement in front of a magistrate. She said quote "Anyone" unquote. She then turned to Philander and said quote "I'm sorry" unquote. Philander said nothing. On being searched a key was found in Philander's trouser pocket. I asked him to identify it, and he said it was a key to the back door of the library. When I asked him where he had got it, he did not reply. Joubert then interrupted and said quote "I gave it to him" unquote. The key is attached to the statement as exhibit C. I finally asked them to get dressed and to accompany me to the police station, where they were formally charged.
Signed: Detective-Sergeant J. du Preez . . . South African Police. Noupoort.

(Exit. A short pause and then the man leaves the pool of light in which he and the woman had been standing. The woman is totally isolated in her last speech, as will also be the case with the man.)

WOMAN: I am here. You are not here. I know that without even trying to find you, as I did once, because nothing can be here except me. That doesn't mean I don't want you. But you are gone from other places. The pain will come. I'm holding it far away. But just now I will have to let it go and it will come. It will not take any time to find me. Because it's mine. That pain is going to be me. I don't want to see myself. But I know that will also happen. I must be my hands again, my eyes, my ears . . . all of me but now without you. All of me that found you must now lose you. My hands still have the sweat of your body on them, but I'll have to wash them . . . sometime. If I don't, they will. Nothing can stop me losing that little bit of you. In every corner of being myself there is a little of you left and now I must start to lose it. I must be very still, because if I do anything, except think nothing, it will all start to happen, I won't be able to stop it.

MAN: Frieda! *(He discovers himself alone . . . with his clothes.)* Now I must understand it.

> If they take away your eyes you can't see.
> If they take away your tongue you can't taste.
> If they take away your hands you can't feel.
> If they take away your nose you can't smell.
> If they take away your ears you can't hear.
> I can see.
> I can taste.
> I can feel.
> I can smell.
> I can hear.
> I can't love.
>
> I must understand it.
> If they take away your legs you can't walk.
> If they take away your arms you can't work.
> If they take away your head you can't think.
> I can walk.
> I can work.
> I can think.
> I can't love.
>
> I must understand it.
> When you are hungry you eat.
> When you are thirsty you drink.
> When you are tired you sleep.
> I will eat.
> I will drink.
> I will sleep.
> I won't love.
>
> I must understand it again.
> If they take away your soul, you can't go to Heaven.
> I can go to Heaven.
> I can't love.

And then I'm running away very fast, from everything but especially God, because he mustn't know. But the street doesn't work any more. Because when I reach the end where the stones and the darkness should start, the light goes on, and I come out of the back door of the library and I've got to start running again. But I can't run very fast. My hands get in the way because I don't want them to see. So I'm crawling instead and she is not surprised. Nobody is surprised. They still greet me.

> But I know you see.
> An arm without a hand.
> A leg without a foot.
> A head without a body.
> A man without his name.

And I'm terribly frightened they will find out. That the dogs will tell them. Because they can see. And then I'm sitting just past the lamppost where my shadow always turns into the night and she asks me, "What do you want?"

I don't know.
Yes, you do.
Everything.
You can't have it. Choose.
I can't.
You're a coward.
I know.
You realize it's useless.
Yes.
What will you do if they find out about us?
I don't know. So she tells me.
Nothing. You do nothing. They do it all.
Trust them. They know what to do.
They find you.
They put on the light.
They take the picture.
They take your name.
And then they take you.
And then they take your belt and your tie and your shoelaces.
They lock the door.
They will ask questions.
They will try you.
And then at the end as at the beginning, they will find you
    again.
Guilty.

That frightens me. I get up and I start running. And I can't understand why she doesn't call me back, because I'm only running home.

And then I'm in Bontrug. And the dogs don't bark at me, they laugh. They're all standing up and walking around on their back legs to show me theirs.

And then I reach my house. But I don't find anyone there, only God, waiting in the dark. And now I'm too tired to run away any more. I just think he must have driven there by car because otherwise how could he have got there before me. He lives in the town.

And it's a court case. That on the night of January the twelfth, 1966, I . . . who had been made in his image . . . did lose a part of me. They did it I say. They dug a hole and buried it. Ask the dogs. And then Frieda comes in to give evidence. It's very dark. God shines a torch to see what she looks like. Did he have it, he asks her. Yes, she says. Then he asks me: "Why did you let them do it?"

So I tell God I don't smoke and I don't drink and I know the price of bread. But he says it makes no difference and that he wants back what is left. And then I start to give him the other parts. I give him my feet and my legs, I give him my head and body, I give him my arms, until at last there is nothing left, just my hands, and they are empty. But he takes them back too. And then there is only the emptiness left. But he doesn't want that. Because it's me. It's all that is left of me.

They arrest it all the same.

Now I'm here.

There is nothing here.

They can't interfere with God any more.

VIVIEN

PERCY GRANGER

VIVIEN was first presented in New York, at the Ensemble Studio Theater, in May of 1979. It was directed by Peter Lownds, with the following cast:

VIVIEN	Paul Austin
PAUL	Kelly Monaghan
MRS. TENDESCO	Marilyn Rockafellow

Production Notes

VIVIEN has been performed with both modular units and realistic set pieces. A definitive stage design has yet to be found, thus future designers are hereby granted some latitude.

As to the style of performance, it should be almost, but not quite completely, realistic. VIVIEN in reality has been on thorazine and other drugs for thirty years. Clearly the actor cannot play this with total verisimilitude nor can he ignore it. A style must be found that balances reality with theatrical necessity.

PAUL is high-strung, self-centered, and obsessed by time—at least at the outset of the play. As written, his reaction to his father's refusal to recognize and accept him is an overreaction. There are moments of absurdity, leaps of logic, particularly in the first two scenes. These are intentional; go with them. Later he settles down.

There is also something slightly askew in MRS. TENDESCO. At first she seems merely affable and competent, but gradually we begin to suspect one of her buttons might be missing. She responds to PAUL'S growing frustration and anger with a consistent pleasantness that leaves him wondering if he is dreaming. Perhaps this is her way of surviving the irrationality of mental patients and their families, or perhaps she is a closet rhapsodic, as her final speech seems to indicate. Whatever cause one assigns, the important thing is for the actress to find the special and private place the character inhabits. Her unRatchette-like strangeness might be signaled by some small aberration in her appearance: perhaps a uniform that is too short or tight, a hairstyle that is too youthful, or bobbysocks, or a spray of flowers on her breast. Whatever it is, it should not be flagrant; she is not a clown.

■ ■

Lights up.

A man sits on a bench, his mouth is slack and his eyes are glazed. There is a trace of a deep anger nestled in his brow, the impression is that of a slumbering violence. He is a large man with massive shoulders. He wears a white shirt, yellowed with age; gray work pants held up by suspenders and a garrison belt outside and below the belt loops; and a shabby car coat. His black work shoes are scuffed and his thin white socks are bunched down below his ankles. An old tie protrudes from one pocket. No movement.

After a long moment he rocks slightly. He stops. No movement.

A younger man enters. He is fashionably dressed in sports jacket, tie, slacks and a smart new raincoat with belt and epaulets. He stops and peers at the seated figure.

PAUL: Dad? *(No response; the man does not look at him.)* Dad? It's Paul. *(No response.)* Dad . . . Mr. Howard . . . Vivien? *(Vivien looks at him.)*

PAUL: Hi. *(No response.)* You been waiting long? *(No response.)* I'm sorry about the rain.

VIVIEN *(looking away)*: Weather doesn't bother me.

PAUL: Are you all set to go? *(No response. Paul takes a step forward.)* Can I give you a hand?

VIVIEN: Keep your distance.

PAUL: What's the matter?

VIVIEN: I'm not going with you.

PAUL: What?

VIVIEN: You're not Paul.

PAUL: Yes I am. It's Paul. *(Vivien begins to tremble slightly.)* Are you cold? Should we get in the car?

VIVIEN: I'm not getting in your car.

PAUL: Why not?

VIVIEN: You're not Paul.

PAUL: Sure I'm Paul. Of course I'm Paul. It's me. Who else would I be?

VIVIEN: That's your problem.

PAUL: Are you Vivien Howard?

VIVIEN: Yes.

PAUL: I'm Paul Howard, I'm your son. *(No response.)* I know it's been a long time; I'm just grown up now. It's still me. *(No response.)* Norristown, you remember? It was just like today, it was raining. We sat in the parking lot. Mom went in and got you. You sat in the back seat. You stared at me, do you remember that? It was 1955, I was ten. I was just ten.

VIVIEN: Everyone I know is dead.

PAUL: I spoke to—Mrs. Tendesco is it?

VIVIEN: Yes.

PAUL: She said you were very excited.

VIVIEN: I'm all right.

PAUL: I mean we made all the arrangements. She said you wanted to go out. *(No response.)* You want me to get her?

VIVIEN: You can get her if you want.

PAUL: What should I tell her's the matter?

VIVIEN: You're not Paul.

PAUL: What are you doing out here then?

VIVIEN: Waiting for Paul.

PAUL *(gestures)*:   You got 'im. *(Beat.)* Look, it's starting to rain again, let's get in the car okay?

VIVIEN: No.

PAUL: It's right over there—

VIVIEN: No.

PAUL: Dad, it's after twelve, we've got to go.

VIVIEN: You go on.

PAUL: What about you?

VIVIEN: I'm sorry you drove all this way for nothing.

PAUL *(taking out his wallet)*:   I can prove I'm Paul. There's my driver's license, there's my picture and my name. *(Vivien won't look.)* Look—I've got credit cards, union cards—I've got identification coming out of my ears!

VIVIEN: Don't show me your private property.

PAUL: Look for yourself.

VIVIEN: Don't show me your private property! *(Pause.)*

PAUL: Can I sit down?

VIVIEN: It's a free country.

PAUL *(sits next to him)*:   Paulie? Po? Pooh? I don't remember, what did you call me? *(No response.)* How are you?

VIVIEN: I can't complain.

PAUL: You look terrific.

VIVIEN: You're not Paul.

PAUL: I am Paul! Why else would I be here?

VIVIEN: I'm supposed to meet Paul here.

PAUL: Okay—here, right? At the bus stop?

VIVIEN: Yes.

PAUL: In front of the buildings?

VIVIEN: Yes.

PAUL: On the bench?

VIVIEN: Yes.

PAUL: Okay, so here we are.

VIVIEN: Here we are.

PAUL: I'm your son.

VIVIEN: Go away.

PAUL: Didn't Mrs. Tendesco tell you who I was?

VIVIEN: You don't know her.

PAUL: Do you want to go talk to her?

VIVIEN: No.

PAUL: Why don't we go see her?

VIVIEN: No.

PAUL: Alright, we won't. Look, could we start over?

VIVIEN: He's late.

PAUL: It's only twelve-fifteen.

VIVIEN: Late! There's going to be hell to pay. You stick around if you want to see some fireworks, mister. When he sees this son of his there's going to be hell to pay! He won't stand for it—he doesn't have to. He's got other recourses. He knows the score. There's a worm of truth there, you don't think so by your expression? You think he's just free?

PAUL: I didn't know where you were, all right? I had to fight with Mom to get her to tell me. I told her I had a right to know.

VIVIEN: I'm sure you're very busy.

PAUL *(in a frenzy)*:   I rented a car, you want to see the papers? Here—see?—that's my signature! That's my handwriting! And look here, I got a letter from my wife, see? It's addressed to me! What else do you want? I know I'm Paul Howard, I paid a lot of money to an analyst to establish that fact! *(Vivien looks at him.)*

VIVIEN: You ever make a basket? *(Pause.)*

PAUL: No. So what I hear you saying is you don't want to come with me.

VIVIEN: I'm going to wait for Paul.

PAUL: Well, he won't come because that's me!

VIVIEN: Go away.

PAUL: We were supposed to spend the day together!

VIVIEN *(rising, advancing on Paul)*:   Go away! Scat!

PAUL: Dad—

VIVIEN: Shoo!

PAUL *(backing up, frightened)*:   Hey Dad, come on, okay?

VIVIEN: Sssss!

PAUL: Take it easy—

VIVIEN *(makes a large gesture with his arms; roars)*:   Aaaaaaaah! *(He turns and walks off with a jerky, stiff-legged stride.)*

PAUL *(angry)*:   Why'd you say yes then if you didn't want to come? Why'd you make me rent a car and drive all the way down here? Why'd you make me come?! *(Beat.)* I thought you'd enjoy this!

(Lights change: The lights on the bench crossfade with a harsher fluorescent light. Paul steps into this light, lights a cigarette, and waits impatiently. He glances at his watch. Sound: A soft bell dings three times and a soft

voice comes over a loudspeaker: "Dr. Craig, Dr. Craig." Mrs. Tendesco enters pushing a cart filled with files, medicine bottles and small paper cups. She stops and begins to put pills in the cups, making a mark in each file as she does so. She is any age over forty and wears a nurse's uniform. Paul waits for her to see him; when she does not, he speaks.)

PAUL: Miss Tendesco?

MRS. TENDESCO: Ah! Mr. Nystrum.

PAUL: I'm Paul Howard.

MRS. TENDESCO: Who?

PAUL *(beginning to think he's in Never Land)*:   I'm Paul Howard. I'm Vivien Howard's son.

MRS. TENDESCO: Oh yes, yes of course—from New York.

PAUL: Yes.

MRS. TENDESCO: We spoke over the phone.

PAUL: Yes.

MRS. TENDESCO: Yes. *(She glances at her watch.)* But you shouldn't be here. Vivien wanted you to meet him at the bus stop.

PAUL: I know—

MRS. TENDESCO: He was very definite about that.

PAUL: We met. I'm going back to Seattle without him.

MRS. TENDESCO *(concerned)*:   Oh? What happened?

PAUL: It seems he doesn't want to come with me.

MRS. TENDESCO: But I know he was looking forward to it.

PAUL: He was extremely hostile. He refused to recognize me.

MRS. TENDESCO: Perhaps he was embarrassed.

PAUL: By me?

MRS. TENDESCO: By himself.

PAUL: Oh. Then maybe it's just as well then, huh? Don't you think so?

MRS. TENDESCO: Shall we go find him?

PAUL: No skip it, I've got to go. I just wanted to let you know he got away from me.

MRS. TENDESCO: You were only interested in taking him out for the day?

PAUL: Yes. Didn't I make that clear over the phone?

MRS. TENDESCO *(smiles)*:   Well no harm in trying. I'm sure he'll be sorry. *(She goes back to her work. Paul hesitates; he seems unable to leave.)*

PAUL: I mean there's no inherent reason why he'd want to come with me is there.

MRS. TENDESCO: You haven't seen him in quite a while.

PAUL: Hey look I'm here, okay? Whatever happened happened a long time before I was any part of it. I'm just here. My mother wouldn't tell me where he was. She got remarried. I never even saw a picture for Christ's sake. I mean it was kind of a shock for me too.

MRS. TENDESCO: It usually is.

PAUL *(calmer)*:   It's just—you see my wife and I just had a kid ourselves. It's started me thinking—I just thought it might be important to see him.

MRS. TENDESCO *(smiles)*:   That was a nice thought, it's too bad it didn't work out. *(Pause. Paul glances at his watch. Paces.)*

PAUL: Did he remember who I was when you told him I'd called?

MRS. TENDESCO: Oh yes.

PAUL: What did he say?

MRS. TENDESCO: Oh I don't remember.

PAUL: Could you try?

MRS. TENDESCO: He said, "Paul can come if he wants to."

PAUL: He remembered my name?

MRS. TENDESCO: I'd said it first.

PAUL: So what—he just changed his mind, is that what happened?

MRS. TENDESCO: I don't know. *(She goes back to work.)*

PAUL: I don't know how the hell I thought I could squeeze this in anyway. We have our final preview this afternoon and we open tonight and I'm flying out first thing in the morning.

MRS. TENDESCO: You were going to take him to a play?

PAUL: Yeah. He'd have been bored stiff, huh.

MRS. TENDESCO: You never know. *(She gives Paul an ambiguous smile.)* What play was it?

PAUL: *The Seagull.*

MRS. TENDESCO: You wrote it?

PAUL: No. Anton Chekov. I directed it, I'm a director. I only took the job in the first place so I could come see him. I mean it's not helping my career any to direct the three millionth production of *The Seagull* in some second-rate regional—*(Mrs. Tendesco bursts out laughing.)* What's so funny?

MRS. TENDESCO: I just got it. *(Her laughter increases.)*

PAUL: Got what?

MRS. TENDESCO *(She puts a notepad on the counter.)*:   It's a memo pad. It says Chekov, like the playwright, and Liszt, like the composer. "Check-off list." *(More laughter as Paul stares at her.)* One of the social workers gave it to me.

PAUL: I thought I'd anticipated all the possible scenarios for today, y'know? But I never thought he just wouldn't recognize me.

MRS. TENDESCO: Well they're full of surprises this crew. *(A final burst of laughter.)*

PAUL: I don't understand why I do this to myself. I deliberately create stress situations and put myself right in the middle of them. It's an obsession, I'm sure it's a pattern. Why do you suppose I do that?

MRS. TENDESCO: Would you like to wait and try again?

PAUL: No, it's too depressing.

MRS. TENDESCO: I know. Well you'd better be off if you're going to make your show.

PAUL: What are you going to do?

MRS. TENDESCO: About what?

PAUL: Finding him.

MRS. TENDESCO: Where is he?

PAUL: I don't know. I told you he got away from me.

MRS. TENDESCO: Oh they never go far. Excuse me, I have to go look for Mr. Nystrum.

PAUL: What's Nystrum, a patient?

MRS. TENDESCO: Yes.

PAUL: You thought I was a patient?

MRS. TENDESCO: I'm sorry, I didn't really look.

PAUL: Did you try to force him to go with me? Is that why he wouldn't come?

MRS. TENDESCO: No.

PAUL: Well I wish you'd told me this might happen. It cost a small fortune to rent a car. I have critics coming.

MRS. TENDESCO: We had no way of knowing this is how he'd react.

PAUL: But he's in your care!

MRS. TENDESCO (*promptly and pleasantly amending her statement*):   We had no way of knowing for certain this is how he'd react. Believe me, Mr. Howard, we're as sorry as you are. This was going to be a trial run for Vivien.

PAUL: What do you mean?

MRS. TENDESCO: We hoped he might be ready for removal from maximum security.

PAUL: Maximum—! And I was going to be the guinea pig?

MRS. TENDESCO: It was perfectly safe.

PAUL: But we'd have been gone all day!

MRS. TENDESCO: So long as you had him back by curfew.

PAUL: I'm a layman!

MRS. TENDESCO: He's medicated.

PAUL: What if it wore off? What if he'd gotten violent? He looked damn angry to me.

MRS. TENDESCO: That's a very misleading look.

PAUL: We had a fifty-mile drive ahead of us! Just how was I supposed to act with him?

MRS. TENDESCO: Normally. Excuse me. (*She starts out.*)

PAUL: Wait, please, I'm sorry. I'm going. I'm sorry if I upset him by coming here, it was just an impulse. I didn't stop to think, I just thought—Damn it! *(Pause.)* Anyway thanks. Better to find out now than out on the highway at sixty miles an hour, huh. Thank you. Thanks. *(She exits. Paul lingers as:)*

(Light change: Hospital light crossfades with lights that illuminate yet another area on the stage and reveal the front seat of a car. Vivien enters and lingers near the car. Paul circles out of the hospital area and approaches the car. As he starts to get in:)

VIVIEN: Hello. *(Paul looks up. Pause.)*

PAUL *(sullenly)*: I'm going.

VIVIEN: Okay.

PAUL: I'm sorry it didn't work out.

VIVIEN: You were right about the rain. I'm soaked to the marrow. You look dank too.

PAUL *(grudgingly)*: Do you want a lift back to your building? *(Beat.)*

VIVIEN: That should be all right. *(They get in the car. Vivien first dusts off the seat with great energy; Paul watches this uneasily. Paul takes out a small ornate pillbox and pops a pill. Vivien watches this with great interest.)* What do you take?

PAUL: Just Valium.

VIVIEN: What's that?

PAUL: A tranquilizer.

VIVIEN *(grins)*: Ah. *(Paul starts to pocket the box, Vivien takes it from him.)* It's a nice box. *(Paul watches nervously as Vivien opens it.)*

PAUL: It's a present from my wife.

VIVIEN: What else have you got here?

PAUL: Just some B-12, aspirin, Dexedrine. . . . *(Vivien inspects the contents with great interest before handing it back. He watches closely to see which pocket Paul puts it in. Paul mimes starting the engine and putting the car in gear. He puts his arm on the back of Vivien's seat and looks over his shoulder to back out.)*

VIVIEN: I've changed my mind.

PAUL *(looks at him; freezes)*: What?

VIVIEN: I've decided it will be all right to go with you.

PAUL: You have? Do you think you should?

VIVIEN: I think I can trust you.

PAUL: It's a long drive.

VIVIEN *(taking a pass from his pocket)*: Here's my pass. We need to show it to the guard at the gate. They have dogs running wild here. Discretion is the better part of valor.

PAUL: This rain's going to make it tough.

VIVIEN: So much the better. *(Paul, not knowing what else to do, takes the pass and puts the car in motion. After a few awkward moments of silence he nods out the window.)*

PAUL *(in a forced conversational tone)*:   Ah. You've got a lake here. That's something we miss in the city.

VIVIEN: There's killer whales in there'll bite your cock off.

PAUL: . . . Well it's a trade-off I guess.

VIVIEN *(to himself)*:   The Indians put them there to outlive them. . . . Nothing as fast as an Indian . . . fleet of foot, ate berries . . . The poisoned ones killed the weaker ones. . . .

PAUL: You interested in Indians? *(No response.)* They treating you okay here?

VIVIEN: Not the way they think I'd like to be treated if they had the money. *(A beat.)*

PAUL *(trying again)*:   Do they ever take you out?

VIVIEN: They took us to a county fair last year. The Pierce County Fair. In Puyallup. The Daffodil Capital of the World.

PAUL: Fun?

VIVIEN: What?

PAUL: Fun? *(Vivien doesn't seem to understand the word.)* Was it fun?

VIVIEN: Oh. No, too many people. They stare at you. I managed to have a productive time but it was a lot of trouble. I was just as glad they didn't make us go again. I'm wanted back in Pennsylvania by an institution so I have to be careful about my movements.

PAUL: Look, are you sure you feel up to this?

VIVIEN *(excitedly)*:   There's the gate! *(In a conspiratorial tone.)* Act normal. Don't worry about me, I'll sit still so they can't see me. I'm still pretty good at that. *(Paul, more nervous than ever, brings the car to a halt by the gate, rolls down the window and shows the pass. Vivien sits rigidly but his face is fairly bursting with excitement; out of the side of his mouth to Paul:)* Go! go! *(Startled, Paul accelerates. Vivien clenches his fists and rocks slightly.)*

VIVIEN: You see? As long as they don't catch my smell. I used to smell of semen but that's all over since I contracted syphilis. *(Paul rolls up the window.)*

PAUL: It's just that I'm a little nervous. The critics are coming tonight. They don't count for much out here but still—*(He breaks off because Vivien has taken the pass and is slowly, triumphantly, tearing it up.)*

VIVIEN: Paul will sure be surprised when he shows up and I'm not there. *(Paul stops the car abruptly.)* What's the matter?

PAUL: Who am I?

VIVIEN: We met at the bus stop.

PAUL: What's my name?

VIVIEN: We had a long talk.

PAUL: We're not going anywhere until you admit who I am.

VIVIEN: You want me to get out?

PAUL: No! Who am I?

VIVIEN: The little lost sheep.

PAUL: Dad—

VIVIEN (*fiercely*):   Let's make tracks, mister! (*Pause. Vivien begins to tremble violently and just as violently struggles to keep it under control. Paul, angry, takes scant notice. He glances back toward the hospital and then at his watch. Vivien presses his knees together and cups his hand over his mouth. He drools. Paul impatiently puts the car in gear and drives on.*)

PAUL (*mutters*):   God damn rain, can't see a thing. (*Vivien's trembling gradually subsides.*)

VIVIEN (*apologetically*):   They put stuff in your food and make you eat it. (*Paul takes out his handkerchief, bunches it, and wipes the fog from the windshield.*)

PAUL: Look at this, we're never going to make it on time. (*He puts the handkerchief in his lap. Vivien reaches over and takes it.*) What are you doing?

VIVIEN: I'll help you.

PAUL: It's okay—(*Vivien spreads the cloth in his lap and carefully folds it.*)

VIVIEN: I had a shop instructor at Norristown, Mr. Adolphus McPherson. He said always make a pad . . . make a pad. . . . (*He suddenly lunges across Paul and wipes the windshield with broad energetic strokes.*)

PAUL (*swerving*):   Watch out! Really it's—

VIVIEN (*raising his voice*):   How's that? Can you see better?

PAUL: Yes, thank you. Just—

VIVIEN: I'll keep it wiped for you.

PAUL: That's okay, really you don't have to—

VIVIEN: A nice view is very restful.

PAUL: Just sit there, okay? Just relax, don't do anything. I'll get us there. (*They drive in silence.*)

VIVIEN: We're going to a play, is that right?

PAUL: Yes.

VIVIEN: Good. I'll need my tie then. (*He takes the tie from his pocket and turns the rear-view mirror toward himself. He clumsily puts it on.*)

PAUL (*finally*):   I need the mirror.

VIVIEN: Just a minute. It needs to be straight. (*After another moment Paul reaches for the mirror.*)

PAUL: Okay?

VIVIEN: Is it straight?

PAUL (*without looking*):   Yeah. (*He readjusts the mirror.*)

VIVIEN (*continues to fret with it*):   It doesn't feel straight.

PAUL: It's straight.

VIVIEN: It doesn't feel right.

PAUL: It's fine, leave it alone.

VIVIEN: No. (*He takes the mirror back.*)

PAUL: I need the mirror.

VIVIEN (*frustrated*):   Just a minute! (*They struggle for the mirror.*)

PAUL: Stop it! Stop! Relax! (*Paul breaks Vivien's grip on the mirror then lets go of him. Pause. Paul readjusts the mirror. Pause. Vivien removes the tie.*)

VIVIEN: There. That's better. (*They drive in silence.*) I've been to a play before. They did a lopped-off Shakespeare for our benefit once.

PAUL: You want me to tell you about it?

VIVIEN: I remember it pretty well.

PAUL: I mean the one we're going to now.

VIVIEN: Oh. Just a little bit.

PAUL: It's called—

VIVIEN: But not the ending.

PAUL: It's called *The Seagull*. It's about a group of people living in a summer house in Russia about 1890.

VIVIEN: You've lost me.

PAUL (*after a beat*):   Well—there's a mother; she's a famous actress, and she's in love with a successful hack writer—not hack really, just second rate—and she has a son who is older than she cares to admit. (*Relaxing a bit.*) And the plot thickens. The son is in love—

VIVIEN: Are there any animals in the play?

PAUL: There's some animal imagery, hence the title—

VIVIEN: Last night two of the regular patients and I had a very happy little evening. The grounds crew said they had seen a fox on the road to the fishing dock so we went down to try to trap a glimpse of it. On the way we saw the broken sewer drain it uses as an escape route, but no fox. So we sat on the benches on the dock and watched the boats and the water skiers. Their bathing suits were very colorful. So were the boat hulls for that matter. We waved to each one and they waved back. It made for a long-to-be-remembered picture. When the sun was to the tops of the trees we had to start back. We walked very stealthily to increase our chance of success. We passed the sewer hole. Nothing. So we relaxed all caution and kicked the rocks on the road in disappointment. About a hundred yards up the road there was a garter snake. Its head was crushed but its tail was still moving. We gathered around to watch. Then I looked back down the road and there was the fox we'd been stalking. It was trotting after us like a little dog. When it saw us looking it stopped and sat down in the middle of the road and scratched its ear with its hindpaw just like a dog. Then it disappeared into the bushes. *(Silence.)*

PAUL: The son is in love with a young girl who wants to be an actress. But the hack—the successful—writer is also in love with her.

VIVIEN *(angrily, perhaps because his story got no response)*: I have to go to the bathroom.

PAUL: What? *(No response; Vivien's face contorts.)* You do? *(No response.)* Badly?

VIVIEN: I don't know yet.

PAUL: Can you hold it? If we stop we'll be late.

VIVIEN: I think I can do something with it. *(He lifts off the seat slightly and grunts ambiguously. Then he sits back. Pause.)*

PAUL: Wha—ah, what'd you do?

VIVIEN: I got it, don't worry.

PAUL: What do you mean?

VIVIEN *(to himself)*: I'm not going to drop my trousers on an Interstate.

PAUL *(glances at his watch)*: Look if you really want me to pull off, I can.

VIVIEN: *(no longer concerned, glances out the window)*: There's a motel.

PAUL: How am I on that side—any cars?

VIVIEN: No . . . Big semi, though.

PAUL *(jerking the wheel back)*: Jesus! Look, why don't I just turn on the radio, okay? You can listen to some music, would you like that?

VIVIEN: If you think it would help. *(Paul, chagrined, does not turn it on. They drive in silence several moments.)* There's another motel. Are we going to check into a motel tonight?

PAUL: No.

VIVIEN: I want to get some fresh food. I'll be better then.

PAUL: We'll have a quick bite after the show if you want, before I take you back.

VIVIEN: I'm not going back.

PAUL: What?

VIVIEN: I'm not going back.

PAUL: Of course you are.

VIVIEN: Who told you I was going back?

PAUL: You have to be back by—

VIVIEN: I don't have to do anything, you got that, mister?

PAUL: But I promised I'd bring you back, that was the deal.

VIVIEN: You can't. There'd be reprisals.

PAUL: Reprisals?

VIVIEN: Yes.

PAUL: What do you mean?

VIVIEN: There would.

PAUL: Against whom?

VIVIEN: Me.

PAUL: Why?

VIVIEN: I was trying to change doctors; they don't like that. My current doctor is old and cynical, he doesn't have anything to lose anymore. I'd written three letters to a new Jamaican doctor named Sohkey. He acts like he hasn't received them. If he's been forced to show them to the authorities it's curtains.

PAUL: Can't you talk to Miss Tendesco?

VIVIEN: No.

PAUL: She seems reasonable.

VIVIEN: She puts on a good show for the outsiders because we're her bread and butter, but in her heart of hearts she's a leopard.

PAUL: How would you live?

VIVIEN: I'll forage.

PAUL: What about your medication?

VIVIEN: I don't need it. I'm always okay once I get away from that place.

PAUL: Where would you go?

VIVIEN: Back to veterinary school. I'll get some clothing to improve my appearance. Professor Milton Dornhoffer said there'd always be a place for me.

PAUL: Have you written to him? *(Beat.)*

VIVIEN: I don't want to talk about it with you. *(He begins to rock back and forth violently; Paul clutches the steering wheel with both hands.)* I'm tired of being in this car with you. I don't have enough room. Stop.

PAUL: I can't.

VIVIEN: I want to get out.

PAUL: It's raining.

VIVIEN: I'll be all right.

PAUL: We're going too fast.

VIVIEN: I want to get out.

PAUL: No. This is our day together.

VIVIEN: I don't make deals, mister.

PAUL: I'm not letting you out of this car.

VIVIEN: Just drop me at a clothing store.

PAUL: I'm not letting you out of this car! You're my father and I've got you in here and you're not getting out! We're going to Seattle, you got that? So just sit there! *(Vivien looks at him.)*

VIVIEN: Are you all right?

PAUL: We can talk about it later, okay? We can talk about it at dinner. *(Pause. Vivien looks away. Pause.)*

VIVIEN: If you love me you won't take me back. *(Pause.)*

(Blackout. Sound: Applause. Out. Lights up on a restaurant table: dessert plate and beer bottle and glass at Vivien's place; coffee cup and credit card slip at Paul's. Paul is smoking a cigarette. He watches his father busily finishing up his dessert. His mood is subdued, as if the final line of the previous scene still rings in his ears. Vivien stops eating, looks up.)

VIVIEN: Tasty, wholesome food, it makes a difference. It's nice to have things arrive on your plate hermetically sealed.

PAUL: You almost done?

VIVIEN: Um. *(He takes the last bite of his pie.)* There. *(He wipes off his silverware as Paul takes out a pen to total the bill and figure the tip.)*

PAUL: It's just the opening's in two hours. *(Vivien pockets the silverware.)* What're you doing?

VIVIEN: I'll need 'em for the open road.

PAUL: You can't do that.

VIVIEN: You take too many pills.

PAUL: Only when I'm under stress.

VIVIEN: Oh, here's your program back.

PAUL: Don't you want to keep it?

VIVIEN: You take it. You can use it again.

PAUL: You didn't enjoy it?

VIVIEN: I enjoyed it but I didn't like it. Everyone was so miserable. Of course that's Communism for you.

PAUL: It happened before the Communists took over.

VIVIEN: Can I have another beer?

PAUL: I don't think you should, do you?

VIVIEN: Okay. We can go to a bar later and watch t.v. You need a stronger plot. It was too hard to keep tabs on so many people at once. That wasn't a real dead bird was it? I didn't like that part.

PAUL: No.

VIVIEN: Why did that one fellow kill himself at the end just before he took his bow?

PAUL: He was—he didn't have his medication.

VIVIEN *(surprised)*:   He was sick? He didn't look very sick to me, just long-winded.

PAUL: He was sick in his soul. His mother had no time for him and the girl he loved didn't love him back. He was an artist without an audience—

VIVIEN: My mother had no use for me either, but you'd never catch me drinking two ounces of gin and a half bottle of Carbona, even if I knew it no longer contained carbon tet.

PAUL: That isn't what he did, Dad, he— (*In the midst of writing in the tip, he stops and looks up, realizing the implication of what Vivien has said.*)

VIVIEN: After a while you realize suicide hasn't taken care of anything either. The best thing is just to let them help you. (*Brief pause.*) Are you all right? Aren't the critics going to like your play?

PAUL: I just don't feel so good I guess.

VIVIEN (*grins*):   There are times when I don't feel so good myself.

PAUL: (*rousing himself*):   Look, if we're finished we should—

VIVIEN: You'd better reconsider your decision to make a career of the theater.

PAUL: What?

VIVIEN: There isn't much future in it. This play for example, it looked like it was written a long time ago.

PAUL: Yes?

VIVIEN: So its frosting of attractiveness has rubbed off. I don't think it will be much in demand.

PAUL: But that's the beauty of it, it is in demand. It—

VIVIEN: Besides there are so many classical play productions given in secret—at the Walnut Street Theater, for example. Yours won't be able to stand the competition.

PAUL: Chekov will always be in demand because he's timeless.

VIVIEN (*frowning*):   You have to be careful of that.

PAUL: I mean good art creates its own necessity.

VIVIEN: So does the medical profession.

PAUL: Yes, but art creates value and nothing else does that. A doctor can save your life, but he can't make it worth living.

VIVIEN: Yes, I know. (*Brief pause.*)

PAUL: I'm happy in the theater, Dad. It's my whole life. You don't have to worry about me.

VIVIEN: Are you a success? (*For a long moment, Paul does not respond. Finally he shrugs.*)

PAUL: I'm going to Hollywood.

VIVIEN: That's a nice place.

PAUL: No it isn't, but anyway there it is. I directed a soap last year and a lot of people are beginning to know who I am. (*He smiles wryly.*) The nice thing about fame is they return your phone calls.

VIVIEN (*frowns*):   Who does?

PAUL: Anyone. So I'm doing okay, I guess. I'm screwed up in other ways, but who isn't. It's a trade-off.

VIVIEN: Just remember, fame and fortune are short-lived. Phyllis Diller lives in Tacoma now and nobody likes her very much. And you look like you're past the age to stand the sexual stress the theater puts on one.

PAUL: Well, I'm married so that's not really a problem anymore.

VIVIEN: Is your wife a woman?

PAUL: Yes.

VIVIEN: Heterosexual marriage in the theater isn't very stable is it?

PAUL: Harriet's not an actress. She has a degree in English and another in Sociology. She's an interior decorator with a side interest in art placement.

VIVIEN: So she's got a lot of options.

PAUL: Well not anymore; we just had a baby. I don't know how it happened—I mean, we'd made a decision against having children because we have our careers to think of. And there's a lot of different things we want to do. We knew we'd resent the responsibility. Harriet was afraid she would put too much pressure on a kid because she's such an achiever herself, and I figured it would be tough to relate to someone so much younger than I. Anyway, now that he's here we're both trying to regard it as a positive event. If you have a kid you're just going to miss out on some things, but if you don't have 'em you miss something too. So it's a trade-off. One thing's for certain, we're going to have to change our lifestyle.

VIVIEN: You must be happy about that.

PAUL: Well in fact we are thinking about a separation. I'll be making enough money now to support them, so—for the first time in our marriage divorce is a possibility. But I feel guilty about it too so I guess I'm not completely lost. *(Pause.)* Oh—Harriet just sent me some picture of the kid this morning. You want to see them? *(He digs the envelope out of his pocket. Vivien regards the pictures for a long moment, then drops them.)*

VIVIEN: People oughtn't to take pictures of babies. *(Paul picks the pictures up, gazes at them.)*

PAUL: He is kind of cute. He looks like—*(He breaks off.)* His name is Dougal. *(The mood reverts; he puts the pictures away.)* I don't know, sometimes I get so depressed. I mean it's okay. I just used to think—I had this idea once. Oh not really, I just thought I did without really thinking about it. I've decided I don't have any creativity at all. I thought if I started drinking it would help. I know what I should be doing but it doesn't work. And now I'm

going to Hollywood? I'm fine. *(Beat. A final protest.)* But I know
I'm *good*.

VIVIEN: You ever try to commit suicide?

PAUL: I don't know, it's hard to tell; everything's so relative. *(He looks up.)* Why'd you ask that?

VIVIEN: That's the first thing the doctors want to know. *(Brief pause.)* If you've got a family to support you should go into horse-shoeing. It's a good money-making trade and it's well respected. Get in touch with Philip Ewing at 1016 South 45th Street in Philadelphia. He doesn't have a zip code.

PAUL: All right, I'll look into it.

VIVIEN: I'll send you some fresh fruit.

PAUL *(deeply moved; smiles)*:   Thanks. I'll eat it. *(Pause.)* We have to go, Dad.

VIVIEN: Okay. Can we go to a clothing store now?

PAUL: It's late. I think everything's closed.

VIVIEN: . . . Tomorrow?

PAUL: Let's just go for a ride, okay?

VIVIEN: Where?

PAUL: We'll just drive around, digest our food. *(Long pause. They look at each other.)*

(Lights change: Down on restaurant and seconds later up on car. Paul and Vivien seated there as before, Paul driving. They drive in silence for several moments, then Vivien becomes aware of the direction they are taking.)

VIVIEN: Where are we going?

PAUL: I have to take you back. I'm sorry . . . *(Pause.)*

VIVIEN: You can turn on the radio if you want.

PAUL *(smiles)*:   You got your pad? My window could use a good wipe. *(Vivien obliges in the same energetic manner as before, then sits back.)* Thanks.

VIVIEN: It's stopped raining. *(Paul nods. Vivien leans forward and gazes up at the sky.)* I bet you don't see stars in the city.

PAUL: No.

VIVIEN: This is a good place to be for rainbows too. *(Brief pause; Vivien indicates the pad and the windshield.)* I used to do that for my father. He let me sit beside him in the front seat and keep the windshield clean.

PAUL: Were you close to him?

VIVIEN *(grins)*:   "Cheek by jowl." He used to take me on long trips. We went to the Chicago World's Fair—"The Century of Progress" they were still calling it then—and Florida, and Michigan. Ocean

Boulevard . . . Once we drove all the way to New Mexico. My mother had to sit in the back seat.

PAUL: What did he do for a living?

VIVIEN: He operated a steam shovel, dredged the Mississippi.

PAUL: Yeah?

VIVIEN: Oh yeah. We were river rats. Played poker, ate ice cream, drank whiskey, rented rooms. . . . He took us everywhere.

PAUL: What was his name?

VIVIEN: Edgar.

PAUL: What was your mother's name? (*Pause. Vivien's brow furrows. He does not want to talk about her.*)

VIVIEN: Dougal. (*Beat.*)

PAUL: It's just that Mom never told me anything about you. The only thing I ever remember her saying was once that you liked the out-of-doors.

VIVIEN: That's right. I could disappear for days into the mountains and no one would know where I was. Bang! I'm gone.

PAUL: Yeah?

VIVIEN: I was alone on a mountain one day when I made a discovery. If I stared long enough at the landscape and sat very still, I could blend in with it. I could disappear. The forest animals would go on about their business as if I wasn't there. And the birds would sing different songs, not the ones they sang when people were around. I was no one and that made me special.

PAUL: . . . Sounds wonderful.

VIVIEN: The trouble was when I started doing it around the house. (*Pause.*) I don't do it anymore now. You get more conservative with age.

PAUL: Were you really studying to be a veterinarian? (*No response.*) How—how did you and Mom meet?

VIVIEN: . . . I was in charge of the pets at the college. There weren't supposed to be any. She had a cat. (*Pause. A look of pain crosses his face.*) The confiscated animals were sent to the labs. (*Pause.*) She never told you even that?

PAUL (*shakes his head; inaudibly*): No.

VIVIEN: She's very strong-minded, isn't she? (*Paul, unable to speak, just nods.*) Well I let her keep that cat I'll tell you. The next thing you know she invited me home to meet her father. He was pretty imposing too, ate good food. She hoped he wouldn't approve but he took a shine to me because of my prospects which weren't bad. So I went along with it. (*Pause.*) Recently I've been interested in suspended animation, freezing people until you can find a cure for them. I think that's a good idea. (*Pause.*)

PAUL: Was it Mom—Was she the one who took you to Norristown?

VIVIEN *(with great difficulty)*:   . . . No. I went of my own free will.

PAUL: Why? *(Vivien tries to respond; cannot.)* I wish you'd tried, you know? I wish you'd tried harder. *(Long silence. Finally Vivien looks out the window.)*

VIVIEN: We're here. *(Paul brings the car to a stop, turns to Vivien.)*

PAUL: There was a lot more I wanted to ask you.

VIVIEN: I had a good time.

PAUL: Is there anything I can send you?

VIVIEN *(getting out of the car)*:   Don't bother.

PAUL *(getting out quickly to stop him)*:   Do you want me to buy you some clothes?

VIVIEN: What I have fits well enough.

PAUL: I could send you some food, some fruits or nuts, something that's fresh.

VIVIEN: They feed us very well.

PAUL: Isn't there anything I can—

VIVIEN: I'd better go in.

PAUL: That doctor you said you wanted, Dr. Sohkey, you want me to arrange that?

VIVIEN: You're going to miss your opening night.

PAUL: It doesn't matter. Dad—it doesn't matter.

VIVIEN: I've got everything I need.

PAUL: They want me to come back next year and direct another show. I'll bring Harriet and our son. I want them to meet you. *(Pause.)*

VIVIEN: I won't be disappointed if you don't. *(A moment, then Mrs. Tendesco enters wearing an overcoat and carrying her purse, just going off duty.)*

MRS. TENDESCO: Good evening! *(To Vivien.)* So you went after all.

VIVIEN: Yes ma'am.

MRS. TENDESCO: Good for you. And did you have a nice time?

VIVIEN: Very nice. This is Paul. He's my son. He's a general theatrical director.

MRS. TENDESCO *(with a smile to Paul)*:   Oh. *(Back to Vivien.)* Did you let them know at the office that you're back? *(Vivien immediately goes off in a direction different from the one in which he was headed.)*

MRS. TENDESCO: So, he recognized you after all.

PAUL *(impulsively)*:   I—I want to do something to help him. He told me he wanted to change doctors. I'd like to see that's taken care of.

MRS. TENDESCO: He and Dr. Braden get along famously.

PAUL: If it would make him happy I'd like to see it done.

MRS. TENDESCO: Did he say who he wanted?

PAUL: Yes, a Dr. Sohkey.

MRS. TENDESCO: Dr. Sohkey?

PAUL: If there's any expense or legal problem involved I'll pay for it, money's no object.

MRS. TENDESCO (*smiling*):   Mr. Howard, Jimmi Sohkey is a ward attendant.

PAUL: He's not a doctor?

MRS. TENDESCO: He's a student at the local junior college.

PAUL: Oh. Well I guess there's no problem then.

MRS. TENDESCO: No, no problem at all.

PAUL: But he seemed to get better as the day went on.

MRS. TENDESCO: Because he was enjoying himself. I've always believed that if every patient had one person who would devote himself exclusively to him, this kind of illness would melt into the shadows.

PAUL: You think Dad could get better?

MRS. TENDESCO: No.

PAUL: But you just said—

MRS. TENDESCO: I know. (*She smiles at him and goes. After a moment Vivien re-enters and crosses toward his ward without looking at Paul and without slowing his stride. Paul makes a movement as if to speak, but something in Vivien's manner tells him not to. Vivien disappears.*)

THE AUTHOR'S VOICE

RICHARD GREENBERG

For Kevin, Patti, David, and Evan.

THE AUTHOR'S VOICE was presented as part of Marathon '87 at the Ensemble Studio Theatre (Curt Dempster, Artistic Director; Erik Murkoff, Managing Director) in New York City on May 13, 1987. It was directed by Evan Yionoulis; the stage manager was Judith Ann Chew; and the assistant director was Christopher Ashley. The producers of the marathon were John McCormack and Jamie Mendlovitz; the scenic design was by Lewis Folden; the lighting design was by Greg MacPherson; the costume design was by Deborah Shaw; the sound design was by Bruce Ellman; the production stage manager was Nicholas Dunn; and the associate scenic design was by Elizabeth Kellehere. The cast, in order of appearance, was as follows:

PORTIA	Patricia Clarkson
TODD	Kevin Bacon
GENE	David Pierce

■ ■

Scene One

Todd's apartment. Strangely shadowed. A door in the back wall. A bed obliquely angled into the room. Two chairs and a table—both dark wood.

Lights up on Todd and Portia. They are both young and beautiful and dressy.

PORTIA: The author's lair . . .
TODD: All right, you've seen it, let's go.
PORTIA: You're joking.
TODD: I—
PORTIA: You're serious?
TODD: Well—
PORTIA: What? What are you?
TODD: Portia.
PORTIA: I'm looking for clues.

TODD: . . . Hm.

PORTIA: Tips.

TODD: Yes.

PORTIA: Leads.

TODD: None here.

PORTIA: It's not . . . exactly . . .

TODD: No—

PORTIA: . . . *forthcoming* . . .

TODD: This—

PORTIA: —room.

TODD (*sighs with relief*):   No.

PORTIA: You're strange, Todd.

TODD: I'm not, not at all.

PORTIA: What's behind that door?

TODD: Another apartment. Neighbors.

PORTIA: Really?

TODD: Railroad flat. Tenement.

PORTIA: Curious smell.

TODD: The neighbors.

PORTIA: Food become flesh, somehow, you know?

TODD (*stymied*):   Of course.

PORTIA: Well, you know those people who trap cooking odors? In their hair—in their down vests—in their—all over, all over themselves?

TODD: They're sloppy people, the neighbors.

PORTIA: Do you know them?

TODD: We've never met.

PORTIA: They *must* be sloppy people.

TODD: Yes. (*He looks puzzled.*)

PORTIA: This isn't what I expected, I must say.

TODD: What did you—?

PORTIA: Something cleaner, more pared down, geometric, somehow, I don't know, I can't say. But not this . . . I don't know . . . House of Usher. Do you like living here?

TODD (*curiously mechanical*):   Sometimes the walls feel like predators, they roam and idle, grow mouths and tongues, close in and bare their teeth; this is what loneliness is to me—living beasts.

PORTIA (*beat*):   I've noticed you quote from yourself an awful lot.

TODD: What?

PORTIA: That, just now, that was a quotation, wasn't it?

TODD: . . . Yes.

PORTIA: From this book of ours, wasn't it?

TODD: . . . Yes.

PORTIA: Well, of course I'd realize that, wouldn't I?

TODD: . . . Yes. Look, why don't you just go home now, I need—

PORTIA: I've also noticed that, in general, when you're not quoting from yourself, your conversation tends towards the . . .

TODD: . . . Towards the . . . ?

PORTIA: Bland.

TODD: Ah, the bland, yes.

PORTIA: You're not one of our *glib* authors.

TODD: Perhaps . . . *(searches for the word)* not.

PORTIA: You're beautiful, though.

TODD: So are you.

PORTIA: And you write like an angel. How do you write so beautifully?

TODD: My writing—

PORTIA: Yes?

TODD: It . . . burns in the smithy of my . . . in my smithy.

PORTIA: The torment, I love it. Beauty and pain, what a parlay! Tell me the truth—those aren't the neighbors behind that door. Behind that door, there's some horribly twisted gnome who does all your writing for you—

TODD: You had too much to drink tonight . . .

PORTIA: I'm celebrating!

TODD: Celebrating what?

PORTIA: Us . . . this teaming, this partnership. Success is absolutely assured, Todd, no, I want you to know that. Those pages you've shown us . . . God, they're incredible. And the jacket photograph *alone* will be a classic. No, I'm sincere. I think you have something important to contribute to literature.

TODD: Thank you.

PORTIA: Why are you so nervous?

TODD: I'm embarrassed by the smell.

PORTIA: . . . I don't mind.

TODD: It embarrasses me.

PORTIA: I think it's sexy.

TODD: It's not.

PORTIA: It is—

TODD: No—

PORTIA: I swear—

TODD: Tonight it's not.

PORTIA *(beat)*: You want me to go.

TODD: You've noticed.

PORTIA: You're the fevered type.

TODD: A little.

PORTIA: And tomorrow you must rise early and have your jog and your protein shake and then spill your pain at the typewriter.

Hours and hours of wiggling the loosened tooth of your despair.

TODD: I guess.

PORTIA: I'm sorry I've invaded your territory. I needed to see, though. I'm not one of those casual editors. I can't just tighten your syntax. I need to *see*, to *know*, to *absorb*, to *live through*, to *live with*, to *contemplate*, to *understand*. To *understand*. (*She kisses him passionately.*) Good night. (*She exits. Todd sits at the table for a long moment. The door in the back creaks opens. A horribly twisted gnome emerges, carrying a sheaf of papers. He goes to Todd and hands him the pages. Todd accepts them. They look at each other. Fadeout.*)

Scene Two

Todd reading. The gnome, Gene, watches.

GENE: You *balked.*

TODD: This is wonderful. Is it?

GENE: The moment came—the decisive moment—and you let it slip by. That's unforgivable.

TODD: The pain, the sheer . . . *pain*; it's painful, right?

GENE: Was it because of me?

TODD: I'll send this off first thing tomorrow. Portia will think she inspired me. Will she like it?

GENE: What?

TODD: The chapter.

GENE: Yes. She will.

TODD: You're sure?

GENE: I'm sure . . .

TODD: Because I can't tell—

GENE: I'm sure—

TODD: Because I don't seem to have a feel for—

GENE: I'M SURE!

TODD: Touchy, touchy, touchy.

GENE: She was beautiful, wasn't she?

TODD: Who?

GENE: The girl.

TODD: Which . . . ?

GENE: Tonight.

TODD: Portia.

GENE: Yes.

TODD (*thinks a moment*): Yes. I think so. Yes.

GENE: You *think* so?

TODD: I wasn't paying close attention. That sort of thing gets stale.

GENE (*lets out a strangled howl*): You *appall* me.

TODD: She was beautiful.

GENE: I saw.

TODD: *What?*

GENE: There's a keyhole, you know. A slit at the bottom of the door. Slants of light. This room made visible. I moved, I watched, I saw—

TODD: Son-of-a-bitch—

GENE: Not the whole picture, but . . . hair and . . .

TODD: Son-of-a-bitch—

GENE: —calves and ankles and once, I think—

TODD: I told you—

GENE: —an elbow—

TODD: I told you not to move when she was here. I told you to act like a churchmouse.

GENE: I *am* a churchmouse—

TODD: She was curious enough without hearing sounds—

GENE: She was curious, you—

TODD: Don't you know how fragile this whole deal is—

GENE: You nipped that curiosity in the bud, I noticed—the *neighbors!*

TODD: She can't find out about this, Gene, or it's over, all over, we're through.

GENE: Is that a *bad* thing?

TODD: Not again, please. Not again. That damned . . . what is it called, something you say over and over?

GENE: Litany.

TODD: That damned litany, over and over! Yes, it would be a bad thing. What we have, this is a good thing. If it ended, it would be a bad thing.

GENE: Not for me.

TODD: Oh, please . . .

GENE: Despised, sequestered, denied even the standard compensations, I would relish the termination of all—

TODD: Do you want me to put you back where I found you? *(Beat.)*

GENE *(quietly):* No.

TODD: In the gutter.

GENE: In the gutter! What a cliché. I was in an alley.

TODD: Starving and crying—

GENE: And carrying pages of precious material which you promptly sold to the highest—

TODD: I took you in!

GENE: You took me for everything I had; it was not Nightingale in the Crimea.

TODD: I brought the pages to a party—could you have done that?

I met Portia there—could you have done that? She said, "This is a work of . . . this is a work of . . ."

GENE: Genius—

TODD: Genius! Yes! I let her take me to lunch, I worked my charm, I finessed her into a contract—

GENE: Thus began my stellar career!

TODD: And it's good! *(Gene stares at him fiercely, then lets out a beastly roar. Beat.)* That sort of thing has got to stop.

GENE: Why did you let her go tonight?

TODD: I wasn't interested.

GENE: How can you not be interested?

TODD: These things repeat themselves.

GENE: *They—!*

TODD: —get dull—

GENE: *I—*

TODD: My libido wavers.

GENE: *Use mine!*

TODD: I'm going to bed.

GENE: You never bring anyone home! Some nights you don't come home yourself! I wait. I sit. I don't move. It hurts to move anyway. My body is sore. My muscles ache from disuse and misshapenness. I sit in that patch of darkness, that cupboard that has been allotted me, and stare out at an airshaft and wait for some noise from the hallway, some stirring, for *you* . . . and you don't come. Why don't you bring one home? I'd be still as a churchmouse. I'd hold my breath. I want to hear it, to peek through the keyhole and see it. Live. Unrehearsed. The whole event. I would be so grateful.

TODD: Please stop talking and go to sleep before I say something true that will hurt you.

GENE: I *wash*. Hour after hour, I scrub, I pumice! I'm meticulously clean. The smell comes from *airlessness*. From being alone with myself in a dark room. It's the smell of *imprisonment*, let me out and it will go away!

TODD: You can't go out!

GENE: You don't let me.

TODD: Don't dare.

GENE: Just for a stroll. A walk on the street. I need books! If I'm to live in a purely verbal universe, I must have my vocabulary replenished every now and then, let me buy books and I'll come right back and be happy—

TODD: I get you whatever books you need, you know that—

GENE: I need to see people walking on the street—

TODD: No fits, tonight, I'm too tired.

GENE: My needs are not being attended to!

TODD: You don't want to go out, you know you don't, you know it—

GENE: Just for an afternoon—

TODD: They *laugh* at you on the street.

GENE: *Not always.*

TODD: *Mostly they do! (Beat.)*

GENE *(softly)*:   Mostly they do. *(He goes quietly to his room, closes the door. Todd lies down on bed. A knocking starts from behind the door. Pauses. Starts again. Pauses. From behind the closed door.)* Todd—?

TODD: Yes—?

GENE: What's in it for you? *(Todd puts pillow over his head and turns over. Fadeout.)*

Scene Three

A flash goes off in the dark. Lights up. Portia is taking Polaroids of Todd.

PORTIA: Now, don't get offended!

TODD: I'm not offended.

PORTIA: The higher-ups simply think—and in a way I agree with them—they simply think—here, hold this. *(She hands him photo.)* They simply think the book, as it stands, is a little *spineless*, that's all—Pose. *(He poses.)*

TODD: Spineless?

PORTIA: Lacking a spine.

TODD: Ah!

PORTIA: The quality of the—of the what?—of the *feeling*, of the emotional, you know, *milieu*—is immaculately rendered, but there seems to be no, no thrust, no action, no event. Right now it's sort of lumpy, sort of pudding-y, a kind of *mousse* of despair, if you know what I—Not that that's *bad*—we're all agreed despair is due for a revival. Here, hold this. *(She hands him photo.)* We're simply suggesting you incorporate more of the, you know, you make it less *endoscopic*, if you know what I—Pose. *(He poses.)*

TODD: I don't know how to do that.

PORTIA: Oh, Todd, oh, Todd . . .

TODD: What does that mean, "Oh, Todd, oh Todd"?

PORTIA: I know your nightlife.

TODD: That's irrelevant.

PORTIA: It's superficial; it's not irrelevant.

TODD: I could never possibly . . . write . . . I could never possibly write that.

PORTIA: Hold this. *(She hands him photo.)*

TODD: These are grotesque.

PORTIA: They're just jacket ideas, they're not the real thing.

TODD: Do I look like this?

PORTIA: Of course not.

TODD: How do I look?

PORTIA: Like Todd.

TODD: I mean, how do I look to *you*? *(Portia sits on him.)*

PORTIA: Nice.

TODD: Portia—

PORTIA: Todd.

TODD: Please get off me.

PORTIA: Aren't you attracted to me?

TODD: I don't remember.

PORTIA: What?

TODD: I sometimes empty out.

PORTIA: What?

TODD: I can't muster enthusiasm. I forget. My body remembers but I forget.

PORTIA: Is that, what, is that some sort of Zen *koan* or something, what is that?

TODD: Please.

PORTIA: What is it with you, Todd?

TODD: Portia—

PORTIA: Don't hide from me, Todd. There's no need. Don't you know? There is nothing about you too dark, too hideous, no single thing too ugly for me to accept, embrace, and love. *(She moves to kiss him.)*

TODD: I need to do rewrites.

PORTIA: It's come over you?

TODD: What—?

PORTIA: Inspiration?

TODD: Yes!

PORTIA: I'll go. *(Dismounts him.)* Now, remember: a story, a spine, facts! Bring in your club days, bring in your sex life! Make me a book I can sell!

TODD: Yes.

PORTIA: Wait a second.

TODD: What?

PORTIA: Have the neighbors moved?

TODD: . . . Why?

PORTIA: The smell is gone. *(She kisses two fingers, waves with them, and exits.)*

TODD: . . . Gene? *(He approaches Gene's room.)* Gene! *(He opens the door, bangs violently around in the room.)* GENE! *(Blackout.)*

Scene Four

Todd is seated at the table. Gene wears a long coat, dark glasses, a fedora. By his side, there is a package of books.

GENE: It came to me: Why not? *(Beat.)* You were gone and I wasn't physically restrained. The outside world might be a painful place but every place is a painful one, so why not? *(Beat.)* I put on your greatcoat and your glasses and your fedora and looked almost hardly abnormal at all. I was careful, Todd, don't look at me like that, I was so careful, no neighbor saw, not the super, no one, I walked in shadows *exclusively*. *(He smiles hopefully.)* I know you've taken me on at great financial and personal sacrifice to yourself, I know I've altered your life completely, I know with me on your hands no sane life is possible, I'm grateful, I truly am, I'm not an ingrate, *don't look at me like that! (Beat. He picks up the books.)* I got these at a used-book store, a place, I swear to you, as musty as myself. I fit right in. *(Beat.)* Todd, I had to do this for both of us. I was forgetting things; words lost their attachments. Without this little trip, this one, one-time-only little trip, you would have had a book full of nonsense, a mere *crunch* of syllables. *(Beat.)* It's not a place I want to go to anymore, the world. I promise. *(Beat.) This isn't fair! (Beat.)* Look: burn this coat, buy another on our royalties! Another hat, too, and new glasses, I know I'm an infection, I won't be insulted! Please, please talk! I'm sure I must have been laughed at on the street, you don't have to worry . . . *(Beat.)* Please . . . *(Beat.)*

TODD *(quietly)*:   Come here . . .

GENE: Why?

TODD: Come here . . .

GENE: Why?

TODD: I want to hug you. *(Pause.)*

GENE: . . . Todd?

TODD: Please. *(Gene approaches gingerly as Todd stretches out his arms. Gene is about to enter them when Todd grabs his wrist and wrestles him to the ground, getting him in a hammerlock. Gene howls, tries to twist his way out of the lock, rolls. Todd rolls with him, gets him into the lock again.)* SON-OF-A-BITCH! *(Gene cries out in blinding pain.)* NEVER DO THAT AGAIN! *(Gene cries out.)* DO YOU HEAR ME? *(Gene cries out again.)* DO YOU HEAR ME! *(Gene utters a strangled, rattling cry, manages to dodge out of Todd's grip and crawl a few inches away. Todd leaps on top of him, lies flat on him, crushing him into the ground.)* Do you hear me?

GENE: Y-E-E-E-E-E-S!!!!!!!!!!!!!! *(Todd springs off him, falls panting onto the bed. Gene crawls to his room, as quickly as he can from fear, but still haltingly, jerkily. He kicks the door shut. A long moment.)*

TODD: Gene . . . ? *(Beat.)* Gene . . . ? *(Beat.)* Gene . . . ?

GENE: We're over. *(Fadeout.)*

Scene Five

Todd stands at the door, a liquor bottle in his hand. From Gene's room, an incessant keening, a mournful, animal sound. Todd knocks his palm against the door. Again. Again. Again. Again.

TODD: Christ, I'm sorry! *(Beat.)* I didn't mean to hurt you. Please come out. *(Beat.)* Please come out. *(Beat.)* I'm not a cruel person. I'm not . . . I don't . . . *(Beat. The keening subsides.)* Gene? *(It starts again.)* Gene, I'm sorry, I'm sorry, I'm sorry, I'm sorry, I'm . . . *(He is now almost climbing the door, almost caressing it, pacifying.)* Listen . . . Listen . . . Listen . . . Gene? Gene? . . . Gene? . . . *(The keening subsides again.)* Gene, are you all right, now? *(Beat. Still quiet.)* Are you better? *(Still quiet.)* Are you better? *(Still quiet.)* You sound better . . . Gene, what can we do? Can we be friends? Can we . . . ? *(Beat.)* Gene, listen, I'm going to do like we used to, okay? Remember? I'm going to tell you something that happened to me and you can tell me what it means, remember? Okay? *(Beat.)* Is that okay? *(Beat.)* Is that okay? *(Beat.)* Okay. *(He sits with his back against the door.)* This happened the other day at the Health Club. You know, where I go? *(Beat.)* Right. Well, I was going to take a swim. I'd never used the pool there before but I wanted to swim. So I was getting suited up when a man at the row of lockers across from me started talking to his friend. This man, he was balding, but he seemed pretty fit, and he was pleased with himself, you could tell, like he didn't even mind being bald, and I thought, well, if I feel like that at his age, I won't be doing half-bad. And his friend looked pretty good, too, and it sort of cheered me up. Anyway, they went to the pool. I finished getting ready, and then I went to the pool. It was just the three of us and an attendant. The attendant yelled at me, "No trunks!" I didn't understand. Then I looked at the two men swimming in the pool. They were naked. It was policy. When they were naked like that, they didn't look so good. They looked fat. They looked like fish—large . . . extinct . . . fish . . . I bent to take off my trunks. As I did, the bald man came up for air. For a second, he was completely still, frozen solid in the water. He looked at me and kept looking. I dove in, a perfect dive with a flip and a spin. When I came up for air, the bald man wasn't in the pool anymore. He was standing by the poolside, crying hysterically. His friend was next to him, trying to calm him down, but the bald-headed man wouldn't stop crying. "Why are you crying?" his friend kept asking. "It was the dive." he said. "It was the dive." *(Beat.)* Gene . . . ? *(Beat.)* Gene, why did that make him cry? *(Beat.)* Why? . . . Why did that make him cry? *(Beat.)* Gene . . . ? Gene . . . ? Why?

GENE *(from the bedroom; braying)*:   BECAUSE IT WAS *SAD!* *(Beat.)*

TODD: Oh. *(Beat.)* I need you to tell me these sort of things, Gene. I can't figure them out on my own. *(Beat.)* My life isn't good. You think it is, but it's not. Once it was, but it's not anymore. *(Beat.)* I used to be made happy by . . . stupid things. Parties! People around me. I was vain. I was a peacock. I looked in the mirror. I looked so hard I didn't recognize myself. I didn't recognize anything. I forgot why I did things. I got scared, Gene! I got scared outside, I got scared in my room. I didn't know where I was half the time. I wanted to drown, I wanted to be covered over. . . . Then I found you. *(Beat.)* Make me famous, Gene. I want to be famous. People will photograph me and write about me. I'll study how they see me and live inside it. . . . Fame will be a kind of home. But I need you to get it for me. Only they can't know it's you, they can't know it's *you;* if they ever see you, it will die like *that. (Snaps his fingers. Beat.)* It panics me when you leave and it panics me when you're here. You're the whole problem of my life, but without you I don't have any life. *(Beat.)* I'll give you what you want. I won't deny you anymore. Anything I can, I'll give you. *(Beat. Gene emerges from the room. He embraces Todd. Todd moans. Fadeout.)*

Scene Six

Todd and Gene. Todd dressing for the evening.

GENE: The scene must be played beautifully.

TODD: I don't know if I can do this.

GENE: You don't have a choice. I'll stop writing if you don't. I'll go back to the streets, find another benefactor. Or die, I don't care which.

TODD: All right. But what do I say? It's been a long time . . .

GENE: I'll write the scene for you. You simply play it out.

TODD: Jesus.

GENE: You come up behind Portia . . .

TODD: Yes . . .

GENE: Fling an arm across her chest—

TODD: That's melodramatic—

GENE: *You fling an arm across her chest*—

TODD: Yes, yes, all right, fine—

GENE: And you say, "Darling, I want you." *(Beat.)*

TODD: I say, what?

GENE: "Darling, I want you."

TODD: I don't say that.

GENE: You do.

TODD: She'd laugh in my face.

GENE: Never.

TODD: You're insane.

GENE *(insistently)*: "Darling, I want you."

TODD: The only words I could possibly get away with in that whole sentence are "I" and "you."

GENE: You will say this! You will say, "Darling, I want you." She will be moved by the poetic simplicity of your expression! *(Beat.)*

TODD: Fine.

GENE: Then—you will turn her towards you, kiss each shoulder, her neck, then rise ever so slowly till your lips meet hers. You will kiss her, and say, "Be mine." *(Beat. Todd looks at him skeptically.)* Then—

TODD: Wait a minute—

GENE: What?

TODD: That won't work.

GENE: It will work like a *dream*—

TODD: Trust me on this—

GENE: Like a *dream*—

TODD: She will be out of here in fourteen seconds flat.

GENE: Nonsense.

TODD: I promise you.

GENE: Nonsense.

TODD: I *promise* you. *(Beat.)*

GENE: What would you say—what *do* you say, then, in circumstances like these? There's a woman, there's a bed, you're alone, you're enchanted, what do you say? *(Beat.)*

TODD: Do you want to sleep with me?

GENE: A-A-A-R-G-H!!!!

TODD: I'm sorry.

GENE: You don't understand.

TODD: I do—

GENE: You don't understand the situation.

TODD: Inform me.

GENE: You are *enraptured*. You are . . . *transported*. This is no common *lay*. This is no cheap *one-nighter*. The finest fibers of your being quiver in expectancy. Poetry floods your soul. "Do you want to sleep with me?" simply will not suffice, not this night. What do you say, then? When all the beauty of the universe churns inside you. *(Beat. Todd thinks.)*

TODD: Are you staying?

GENE: A-A-A-R-G-H!!!!!!

TODD: Gene—

GENE: A-A-A-R-G-H!!!!!

TODD: Gene—

GENE: The world *requires* me—

TODD: Gene—

GENE: —to rewrite its wretched *dialogue!*

TODD: Gene—

GENE: You will make it beautiful. You will proceed as I describe. You will *say,* "Darling, I want you." You will say, "Be mine," you will be tender and slow and romantic. You will *make it work!* *(Beat.)*

TODD: Not a word from you.

GENE: . . . I know.

TODD: Not a peep.

GENE: I promise.

TODD: For your own good as well as mine. You know I act for both of us, don't you? You know I want the best for both of us?

GENE: . . . Yes.

TODD: I'll be back soon. *(He exits. Gene looks after him, waits until he's sure he's gone. Then he approaches Todd's bed. He touches it carefully.)*

GENE: Todd . . . ? *(Gene runs his hands across the bed, feeling the smooth, silky textures.)* Todd . . . it wouldn't be bad if she saw me. Not so bad. *(He climbs onto the bed.)* Often beautiful women come upon hideous men and love them. They uncover an inner beauty, oh, and crowns of light weave into canopies over their heads and the carbuncles and the cicatrices, the humps and wens miraculously disappear. The beasts are replaced by angels. She'll see me, Todd, she'll see. And you'll be loved for me. *(Fadeout.)*

Scene Seven

Todd's room in half-light—a golden shaft spilled across the floor. Todd and Portia enter. The picture they make in this light is burnished and lovely. Lights come up slightly fuller.

PORTIA: You were brilliant tonight. You didn't even have to *speak* is how brilliant you were. I loved when we went to that place

with the flashing lights and your face came floating up at me in
patches, it was poetry, truly poetry. I was speaking to the big boys
today, Todd. They want to take you to lunch; they're very excited,
really thrilled. Everything's mapped out, your whole itinerary. The
book jacket's designed, there are display cases ready, and we're
putting your photograph on billboards all over the city. All we
need now is a book. . . .

TODD: I'm working slowly.

PORTIA: No matter. I have faith in you. I believe in you. *(Beat.)*
This night has been sensational. You actually invited me in. *(Beat.)*
Todd?

TODD *(grabbing her from behind)*:   Darling, I want you . . .

PORTIA: What? *(Beat.)*

TODD: Darling, I want you. *(She turns, laughs in his face, and in one
blindingly quick motion, whips her dress off over her head.)* Hey—
(She starts undressing him.)

PORTIA: This will have to be quick; I have an early day tomorrow.

TODD: Wait! I have to kiss you slowly, I have to—

PORTIA: I've been wondering what your problem was—

TODD: Portia, I— *(She has his shirt off, is starting on his pants.)*

PORTIA: I was beginning to think you were gay—

TODD: Turn around—

PORTIA: You always wonder about that. Could you shrug out of
these? *(He shrugs out of his pants. Portia lies on the bed.)* Thank
you. Now be careful, I'm getting my period, I'm a little
sensitive—

TODD: Wait—

PORTIA: I know this is not the best time to start some sort of blazing
romance, but you were just so damned *slow.*

TODD *(kneels on bed, grabs her hand)*:   Be mine! *(Beat. She laughs in
his face.)*

PORTIA: Christ, Todd, where are you getting these lines? Come
on. *(She starts to pull off his underpants; he stops her, moves away
from her.)*

TODD: Wait!

PORTIA: What?

TODD: This is not going well. . . .

PORTIA: I think it's going pretty well. I think most people would
think it was going pretty well . . .

TODD *(pulling her off the bed)*:   You don't understand.

PORTIA: What?

TODD: Turn around . . .

PORTIA: Todd . . .

TODD: *Turn around. (Beat. She turns around. He puts his arm across her chest.)* Be mine.

PORTIA: Look, do you want to sleep with me?

TODD: Portia—

PORTIA: Am I staying?

TODD: You're doing everything wrong!

PORTIA: What are you talking about?

GENE *(from his room):*   IT'S SUPPOSED TO BE BEAUTIFUL! *(A deathless pause.)*

PORTIA: Todd . . .

TODD: Oh, Jesus . . .

PORTIA: What was that, Todd?

TODD: Nothing.

PORTIA: That wasn't nothing. That was a voice, saying—

GENE *(from bedroom):* IT'S SUPPOSED TO BE BEAUTIFUL!

PORTIA: Jesus Christ, what's the deal here? *(Gene flings open the door.)*

GENE: Am I the only one left with a sense of loveliness? *(Portia stares at him in horror.)*

PORTIA: Oh my God . . . oh my God . . .

TODD: Gene . . .

GENE *(coming out of the room):*   Look at the two of you. . . . You are . . . trustees of beauty. . . . You shine with grace. . . . How have you managed to avoid a minimal interior fineness?

PORTIA: Todd . . .

GENE *(approaches her):*   Don't you know what you're supposed to do now? Don't know your part?

PORTIA: Todd . . .

TODD: Oh, Jesus . . .

GENE: You see me and you are not repelled. You draw in. You come closer and closer. The closer you get, the handsomer I become. You touch me. You kiss me. *(He kisses her.)* I stand tall. *(She faints. Todd catches her.)* No. You don't know your part at all. *(He closes his eyes. Fadeout.)*

Scene Eight

Gene is bent half on a chair, half on the table, hands spread flat before him almost in an attitude of supplication. He is moaning softly, his eyes closed. Todd laces into him.

TODD: I *lied.* I *finessed* the situation. I said you were an *intruder.* The crazed, hideous neighbor breaking down the door between us. I *calmed* her down. I said this was an *unprecedented* event. I said

I was contacting the authorities *immediately*. I said it would *never* happen again.

GENE: O-o-o-o-h-h . . .

TODD: And it's not going to, either. There aren't going to be any more little jaunts, Gene. No more charming trips into the street. No more expeditions into the living room. From now on, you lock yourself in that room, and you don't come out until there's a book, a goddamn publishable item! *Do you understand me!*

GENE: I can't . . .

TODD: What are you talking about?

GENE: I can't go on . . .

TODD: *What are you talking about!*

GENE: . . . She fainted . . .

TODD: Oh, Jesus . . .

GENE: I lived for the moment when I would blossom at a kiss and she fainted!

TODD: I don't want to hear this, now!

GENE: I can't, I can't possibly go on. . . .

TODD: *Listen to me!* You *will* go on. You will . . . do what I demand of you! You will find a story and . . . pick the words you need and . . . get a *spine* and *make me a book!* Do you *understand?*

GENE: . . . I can't . . .

TODD: You will *do it! Do you understand! (He slaps him.) Do you understand! (He slaps him again.)*

GENE *(Roaring it out)*:   YES! *(Todd pulls Gene up out of the chair.)*

TODD: Then *start! (Todd throws Gene toward his room. He lands hunched in the doorway, his back to us. Todd sits, controls himself.)* Gene . . . ?

GENE: . . . What?

TODD: I didn't mean to be harsh.

GENE: . . . Ah.

TODD: I just wanted you to know that. *(Gene turns sharply; looks at Todd. Fadeout.)*

Scene Nine

Gene sits at the table, smiling. A small gift-wrapped package is on the table. Todd bursts in, effusive.

TODD: I just got word! We're already into a second printing. That's extremely unusual on a publication day.

GENE: Ah!

TODD: And three reviews came out—all raves!

GENE: Lovely.

TODD (*reading*):   "When a book receives as much hype as *Drift* has, and when, in addition, its author looks more like a model for cologne than like Herman Melville, this critic is naturally inclined to skepticism. That proves unfounded here, however, because *Drift* is a knockout, far and away the best first novel of the season, perhaps the decade." Do you believe it?

GENE: Very nice.

TODD: I have to thank you.

GENE: Oh, no . . .

TODD: No, I do. I know things weren't always . . . pleasant . . . between us, but look what it got you to do! Gene, I can say it now. I was amazed how you worked! Once you got started, it took you, what, three weeks? And that from scratch! You ditched all the material you had before and just started. I used to listen, I can tell you this now, I listened at the door to the typewriter clattering away, nonstop, it just *thundered* out of you!

GENE: Yes.

TODD: When I go on talk shows, Gene—I want you to know this—I'm always asked, "How do you write?" And do you know what I say? I say, "A demon lives with me." I mean, you. I want you to know that. For vanity's sake . . .

GENE: You're very kind.

TODD: This review starts by quoting the entire opening paragraph! "I live alone. There are no neighbors. There is no neighborhood. Brick has vanished. Tree and sky, too. When I peer through the narrow, grimy shaft that is my window, I see horizon and murk." He says it's the most memorable opening since, "Call me Ishmael."

GENE (*indicating package*):   This is for you.

TODD: What?

GENE: For you.

TODD: What?

GENE: A present.

TODD (*touched*):   . . . Gene!

GENE: Open it.

TODD: I don't know what to say . . .

GENE: I wanted to give you this for publication day. A memento.

TODD (*unwraps it*):   A book. *Layaway*. Thank you.

GENE: I found it that day I was a bad boy . . . remember. . . . It's very obscure. Canadian. It was out-of-print but it called to me. I used the phone when you were out. I was so moved, I tracked the author down and spoke to him.

TODD: Really?

GENE: I hope you don't mind.

TODD: Of course not. I'm very touched that you'd think of me.

GENE: Read some.

TODD: Now?

GENE: Yes, please. It's one of my favorite books, ever. I think I'm the only one who's ever read it, but it may gain shortly in prestige.

TODD (*reads*): "I live alone. There are no neighbors. There is no neighborhood. . . ."

GENE: That resonates, doesn't it?

TODD (*reading on in horror*): "Brick has vanished. Tree and sky, too. When I peer through the narrow, grimy shaft that is my window . . ."

GENE: So Canadian . . .

TODD: ". . . I see horizon and murk. . . ."

GENE: Do you like it?

TODD (*flipping in horror through the book*): Every word . . . You stole every word!

GENE: The author has such a strong voice, don't you think? Truly distinctive. It comes right out of him. He's sickly, he told me. Stooped and scarred. Unpleasant looking. He should be calling any minute. Be kind to him. (*Todd doubles over, clutches himself, lets out an almost silent cry.*) I hear he's in tremendous pain. (*Gene looks at Todd. Fadeout.*)

STORY IN HARLEM SLANG

(from SPUNK)

ZORA NEALE HURSTON

Adapted by George C. Wolfe
Music by Chic Street Man

Production History

SPUNK was originally developed under the auspices of the Center Theatre Group of Los Angeles at the Mark Taper Forum, Gordon Davidson, Artistic Director. It was funded in part by the Rockefeller Foundation.

SPUNK had its world premiere at the Crossroads Theatre Company on November 2, 1989. Rick Khan was the Producing Artistic Director. George C. Wolfe directed the following cast:

GUITAR MAN	Chic Street Man
BLUES SPEAK WOMAN	Betty K. Bynum
THE FOLKS	Danitra Vance, Reggie Montgomery, Kevin Jackson, Tico Wells

Characters
BLUES SPEAK WOMAN
GUITAR MAN
THE FOLK, an acting ensemble of three men and a woman

Time
"Round about long 'go"

Place
"O, way down nearby"

Acting Style
It is suggested that the rhythms of the dialect be played, instead of the dialect itself. A subtle but important distinction: The former will give you Zora. The latter, Amos and Andy.

The emotional states of the characters should not be sacrificed for "style." Nor should style be sacrificed because it gets in the way of the emotions. The preferred blend is one in which stylized gesture and speech are fueled by the emotional states.

Setting

The setting is a playing arena, as stark as a Japanese woodcut and as elegant as the blues. The set piece should be kept to a minimum so that gesture, lighting, music and the audience's imagination make the picture complete.

Note

"Story in Harlem Slang" is excerpted here as one of three tales, which along with "Sweat" and "The Gilded Six-Bits" comprise "Spunk."

■ ■

Lights reveal Slang Talk Man: his attire, very debonair; his manner of speaking, very smooth.

SLANG TALK MAN: Wait till I light up my coal-pot and tell you about this Zigaboo called Jelly.

(On Slang Talk Man's signal, lights reveal Jelly, a hick trying to pass himself off as slick. He wears a stocking cap and underneath his "street" bravado is a boyish charm.)

JELLY: Well all right now!

SLANG TALK MAN: He was sealskin brown and papa-tree-top tall.

JELLY: Skinny in the hips and solid built for speed.

SLANG TALK MAN: He was born with this rough-dried hair, but when he laid on the grease and pressed it down overnight with his stocking cap . . .

JELLY *(pulls off the cap to admire his "do")*:   It looked just like righteous moss.

SLANG TALK MAN: Had so many waves, you got seasick from lookin'.

JELLY: Solid man solid.

SLANG TALK MAN: His mama named him Marvel, but after a month on Lenox Avenue . . .

(On Slang Talk Man's signal, a zoot-suit jacket and hat magically appear.)

SLANG TALK MAN: He changed all that to—

JELLY *(getting dressed)*:   Jelly.

SLANG TALK MAN: How come? Well he put it in the street that when it comes to filling that long-felt need . . .

JELLY: Sugar-curing the ladies' feelings . . .

SLANG TALK MAN: He was in a class by himself. And nobody knew his name, so he had to tell 'em.

JELLY: It must be Jelly cause jam don't shake!

SLANG TALK MAN: That was what was on his sign. The stuff was there and it was mellow. N' whenever he was challenged by a hard-head or a frail eel on the right of his title, he would eyeball the idol-breaker with a slice of ice and say—

JELLY: Youse just dumb to the fact, baby. If you don't know what you talking 'bout, you better ask Granny Grunt. I wouldn't mislead you baby. I don't need to. Not with the help I got.

SLANG TALK MAN: Then he would give the pimp's sign . . .

(Jelly/Slang Talk Man adopt an exaggerated "street" pose; for Slang Talk Man it's empty posturing; for Jelly it's the real deal.)

SLANG TALK MAN: And percolate on down the Avenue.

(On Slang Talk Man's signal, the Footnote Voice is heard. As the Voice speaks, Jelly practices a series of poses.)

FOOTNOTE VOICE: Please note. In Harlemese, pimp has a different meaning than its ordinary definition. The Harlem pimp is a man whose amatory talents are for sale to any woman who will support him, either with a free meal or on a common-law basis; in this sense, he is actually a male prostitute.

SLANG TALK MAN: So this day he was airing out on the Avenue. It had to be late afternoon, or he would not have been out of bed.

JELLY: Shoot, all you did by rolling out early was to stir your stomach up. *(Confidentially.)* That made you hunt for more dishes to dirty. The longer you slept, the less you had to eat.

SLANG TALK MAN: But you can't collar nods all day. So Jelly . . .

(Music underscore.)

SLANG TALK MAN: Got into his zoot suit with the reet pleats and got out to skivver around and do himself some good.

(The transformation from "Jelly the Hick" into "Jelly the Slick" is now complete. He struts and poses like a tiger on the prowl; his moves suggestive, arrogant, mocking.
Lights reveal Blues Speak Woman and Guitar Man, sitting outside the playing arena, scatting vocalise which accents Jelly's moves.)

JELLY: No matter how long you stay in bed, and how quiet you keep, sooner or later that big guts is going to reach over and grab that little one and start to gnaw. That's confidential from the Bible. You got to get out on the beat and collar yourself a hot!

SLANG TALK MAN: At 132nd Street, he spied one of his colleagues, Sweet Back! Standing on the opposite sidewalk, in front of a café.

(Lights reveal Sweet Back, older than Jelly; the wear and tear of the street is starting to reveal itself in Sweet Back's face. Nonetheless, he moves with

*complete finesse as he and Jelly stalk each other, each trying to outdo the
other as they strut, pose and lean.)*

SLANG TALK MAN: Jelly figured that if he bull-skated just right, he
might confidence Sweet Back out of a thousand on a plate. Maybe
a shot of scrap-iron or a reefer. Therefore, they both took a quick
backward look at the soles of their shoes to see how their leather
was holding out. They then stanched out into the street and made
the crossing.

(Music underscore ends.)

JELLY: Hey there, Sweet Back. Gimme some skin!

SWEET BACK: Lay the skin on me pal. Ain't seen you since the last
time, Jelly. What's cookin'?

JELLY: Oh, just like the bear, I ain't no where. Like the bear's
brother, I ain't no further. Like the bear's daughter, ain't got a
quarter.

SLANG TALK MAN: Right away he wished he had not been so honest.
Sweet Back gave him a—

SWEET BACK: Top-superior, cut-eye look.

SLANG TALK MAN: Looked at Jelly just like—

SWEET BACK: A showman looks at an ape.

SLANG TALK MAN: Just as far above Jelly as fried chicken is over
branch water.

SWEET BACK: Cold in the hand huh? A red hot pimp like you say
you is ain't got no business in the barrel. Last night when I left
you, you was beating up your gums and broadcasting about how
hot you was. Just as hot as July jam, you told me. What you doin'
cold in hand?

JELLY: Aw man, can't you take a joke? I was just beating up my
gums when I said I was broke. How can I be broke when I got
the best woman in Harlem? If I ask her for a dime, she'll give me
a ten-dollar bill. Ask her for a drink of likker, and she'll buy me
a whiskey still. If I'm lyin' I'm flyin'!

SWEET BACK: Man, don't hang out that dirty washing in my back
yard. Didn't I see you last night with that beat chick, scoffing a
hot dog? That chick you had was beat to the heels. Boy, you ain't
no good for what you live. And you ain't got nickel one. *(As if
to a passing woman.)* Hey baby!

SLANG TALK MAN: Jelly—

JELLY: Threw back the long skirt of his coat.

SLANG TALK MAN: And rammed his hand into his pants pocket.
Sweet Back—

SWEET BACK: Made the same gesture . . .

SLANG TALK MAN: Of hauling out nonexistent money.

JELLY: Put your money where your mouth is. Back yo' crap with your money. I bet you five dollars.

SWEET BACK: Oh yeah!

JELLY: Yeah.

(Jelly/Sweet Back move toward each other, wagging their pants pockets at each other.)

SWEET BACK *(Playfully)*:   Jelly-Jelly-Jelly. I been raised in the church. I don't bet. But I'll doubt you. Five rocks!

JELLY: I thought so. *(Loud talking.)* I knowed he'd back up when I drawed my roll on him.

SWEET BACK: You ain't drawed no roll on me, Jelly. You ain't drawed nothing but your pocket. *(With an edge.)* You better stop that boogerbooing. Next time I'm liable to make you do it.

SLANG TALK MAN: There was a splinter of regret in Sweet Back's voice. If Jelly really had had some money, he might have staked him to a hot.

SWEET BACK: Good Southern cornbread with a piano on a platter.

SLANG TALK MAN: Oh well! The right broad would . . . might come along.

JELLY: Who boogerbooing? Jig, I don't have to. Talkin' about me with a beat chick scoffing a hot dog? Man you musta not seen me, 'cause last night I was riding 'round in a Yellow Cab, with a yellow gal, drinking yellow likker, and spending yellow money. *(To the audience.)* Tell 'em 'bout me. You was there. Tell 'em!

SWEET BACK: Git out of my face Jelly! That broad I seen you with wasn't no pe-ola. She was one of them coal-scuttle blondes with hair just as close to her head as ninety-nine to hundred. She look-ted like she had seventy-five pounds of clear bosom, and she look-ted like six months in front and nine months behind. Buy you a whiskey still! That broad couldn't make the down payment on a pair of sox.

JELLY: Naw-naw-naw-now Sweet Back, long as you been knowing me, you ain't never seen me with nothing but pe-olas. I can get any frail eel I wants to. How come I'm up here in New York? Huh-huh-huh? You don't know, do you? Since youse dumb to the fact, I reckon I'll have to make you hep. I had to leave from down south cause Miss Anne used to worry me so bad to go with her. Who me? Man, I don't deal in no coal.

SWEET BACK: Aww man, you trying to show your grandma how to milk ducks. Best you can do is confidence some kitchen-mechanic out of a dime or two. Me, I knocks the pad with them cackbroads up on Sugar Hill and fills 'em full of melody. Man, I'm quick death 'n' easy judgment. You just a home-boy, Jelly. Don't try to follow me.

JELLY: Me follow you! Man, I come on like the Gang Busters and go off like The March of Time. If that ain't so, God is gone to Jersey City and you know He wouldn't be messing 'round a place like that.

SLANG TALK MAN: Looka there!

(Sweet Back/Jelly scurry and look.)

SLANG TALK MAN: Oh well, the right broad might come along.

JELLY: Know what my woman done? We hauled off and went to church last Sunday. And when they passed 'round the plate for the penny collection, I throwed in a dollar. The man looked at me real hard for that. That made my woman mad, so she called him back and throwed in a twenty-dollar bill. Told him to take that and go! That's what he got for looking at me 'cause I throwed in a dollar.

SWEET BACK: Jelly . . .

> The wind may blow
> And the door may slam.
> That what you shooting
> Ain't worth a damn!

JELLY: Sweet Back you fixing to talk out of place.

SWEET BACK: If you tryin' to jump salty Jelly, that's yo' mammy.

JELLY: Don't play in the family Sweet Back. I don't play the dozens. I done told you.

SLANG TALK MAN: Jelly—

JELLY: Slammed his hand in his bosom as if to draw a gun.

SLANG TALK MAN: Sweet Back—

SWEET BACK: Did the same.

JELLY: If you wants to fight, Sweet Back, the favor is in me.

(Jelly/Sweet Back begin to circle one another, each waiting on the other to "strike" first.)

SWEET BACK: I was deep-thinking then, Jelly. It's a good thing I ain't short-tempered. Tain't nothing to you nohow.

JELLY: Oh yeah. Well, come on.

SWEET BACK: No you come on.

SWEET BACK/JELLY *(overlapping)*:   Come on! Come on! Come on! Come on!

(They are now in each other's face, grimacing, snarling, ready to fight, when Sweet Back throws Jelly a look.)

SWEET BACK: You ain't hit me yet.

(They both begin to laugh, which grows, until they are falling all over each other: the best of friends.)

SWEET BACK: Don't get too yaller on me Jelly. You liable to get hurt some day.

JELLY: You over-sports your hand yo' ownself. Too blamed astor-perious. I just don't pay you no mind. Lay the skin on me man.

SLANG TALK MAN: They broke their handshake hurriedly, because both of them looked up the Avenue and saw the same thing.

SWEET BACK/JELLY: It was a girl.

(Music underscore as lights reveal the girl, busily posing and preening.)

SLANG TALK MAN: And they both remembered that it was Wednesday afternoon. All the domestics off for the afternoon with their pay in their pockets.

SWEET BACK/JELLY: Some of them bound to be hungry for love.

SLANG TALK MAN: That meant . . .

SWEET BACK: Dinner!

JELLY: A shot of scrap-iron!

SWEET BACK: Maybe room rent!

JELLY: A reefer or two!

SLANG TALK MAN: They both . . .

SWEET BACK: Went into the pose.

JELLY: And put on the look. *(Loud talking.)* Big stars falling.

SLANG TALK MAN: Jelly said out loud when the girl was in hearing distance.

JELLY: It must be just before day!

SWEET BACK: Yeah man. Must be recess in Heaven, pretty angel like that out on the ground.

SLANG TALK MAN: The girl drew abreast of them, reeling and rocking her hips.

(Blues Speak Woman scats as the girl struts, her hips working to the beat of the music. Jelly and Sweet Back swoop in and begin their moves.)

JELLY: I'd walk clear to Diddy-Wah-Diddy to get a chance to speak to a pretty li'l ground-angel like that.

SWEET BACK: Aw, man you ain't willing to go very far. Me, I'd go slap to Ginny-Gall, where they eat cow-rump, skin and all.

SLANG TALK MAN: The girl smiled, so Jelly set his hat and took the plunge.

JELLY: Ba-by, what's on de rail for de lizard?

SLANG TALK MAN: The girl halted and braced her hips with her hands.

(Music underscore stops.)

GIRL: A Zigaboo down in Georgy, where I come from, asked a woman that one time and the judge told him ninety days.

(Music underscore continues.)

SWEET BACK: Georgy! Where 'bouts in Georgy you from? Delaware?

JELLY: Delaware? My people! My people! Man, how you going to put Delaware in Georgy. You ought to know that's in Maryland.

(Music underscore stops.)

GIRL: Oh, don't try to make out youse no northerner, you! Youse from right down in 'Bam your ownself.

JELLY: Yeah, I'm *from* there and I aims to stay from there.

GIRL: One of them Russians, eh? Rushed up here to get away from a job of work.

(Music underscore continues.)

SLANG TALK MAN: That kind of talk was not leading towards the dinner table.

JELLY: But baby! That shape you got on you! I bet the Coca-Cola company is paying you good money for the patent!

SLANG TALK MAN: The girl smiled with pleasure at this, so Sweet Back jumped in.

SWEET BACK: I know youse somebody swell to know. Youse real people. There's dickty jigs 'round here tries to smile. You grins like a regular fellow.

SLANG TALK MAN: He gave her his most killing look and let it simmer.

SWEET BACK: S'pose you and me go inside the café here and grab a hot.

(Music underscore ends.)

GIRL: You got any money?

SLANG TALK MAN: The girl asked and stiffed like a ramrod.

GIRL: Nobody ain't pimping on me. You dig me?

SWEET BACK/JELLY: Aww now baby!

GIRL: I seen you two mullet-heads before. I was uptown when Joe Brown had you all in the go-long last night. That cop sure hates a pimp. All he needs to see is the pimps' salute and he'll out with his night-stick and ship your head to the red. Beat your head just as flat as a dime.

(The girls sounds off like a siren. Sweet Back and Jelly rush to silence her.)

SWEET BACK: Ah-ah-ah, let's us don't talk about the law. Let's talk about us. About you goin' inside with me to holler, "Let one come flopping! One come grunting! Snatch one from the rear!"

GIRL: Naw indeed. You skillets is trying to promote a meal on me. But it'll never happen, brother. You barking up the wrong tree. I wouldn't give you air if you was stopped up in a jug. I'm not putting out a thing. I'm just like the cemetery. I'm not putting out, I'm takin' in. Dig. I'll tell you like the farmer told the potato—plant you now and dig you later.

(Music underscore.)

SLANG TALK MAN: The girl made a movement to switch off. Sweet Back had not dirtied a plate since the day before. He made a weak but desperate gesture.

(Just as Sweet Back places his hand on her purse, the girl turns to stare him down. Music underscore ends.)

GIRL: Trying to snatch my pocketbook, eh?

SLANG TALK MAN: Instead of running . . .

GIRL *(grabs Sweet Back's zoot-suit jacket)*:   How much split you want back here? If your feets don't hurry up and take you 'way from here, you'll ride away. I'll spread my lungs all over New York and call the law. *(Jelly moves in to try and calm her.)* Go ahead. Bedbug! Touch me! I'll holler like a pretty white woman! *(The girl lets out three "pretty white woman" screams and then struts off. Music underscores her exit.)*

SLANG TALK MAN: She turned suddenly and rocked on off, her earring snapping and her heels popping.

SWEET BACK: My people, my people.

SLANG TALK MAN: Jelly made an effort to appear that he had no part in the fiasco.

JELLY: I know you feel chewed.

SWEET BACK: Oh let her go. When I see people without the periodical principles they's supposed to have, I just don't fool with 'em. *(Calling out after her.)* What I want to steal her old pocketbook with all the money I got? I could buy a beat chick like you and give you away. I got money's mammy and Grandma's change. One of my women, and not the best one I got neither, is buying me ten shag suits at one time.

He glanced sidewise at Jelly to see if he was convincing.

JELLY: But Jelly's thoughts were far away.

(Music underscore.)

SLANG TALK MAN: He was remembering those full hot meals he had left back in Alabama to seek wealth and splendor in Harlem without working. He had even forgotten to look cocky and rich.

The lights slowly fade.

Glossary for "Story in Harlem Slang"

AIR OUT: leave, flee, stroll

ASTORPERIOUS: haughty, biggity

'BAM, DOWN IN 'BAM: down South

BEATING UP YOUR GUMS: talking to no purpose

BULL-SKATING: bragging

COLLAR A NOD: sleep

COAL-SCUTTLE BLONDE: black woman

CUT: doing something well

DIDDY-WAH-DIDDY: (1) a far place, a measure of distance; (2) another suburb of Hell, built since way before Hell wasn't no bigger than Baltimore. The folks in Hell go there for a big time.

DUMB TO THE FACT: "You don't know what you're talking about."

FRAIL EEL: pretty girl

GINNY GALL: a suburb of Hell, a long way off

GRANNY GRUNT: a mythical character to whom most questions may be referred

I DON'T DEAL IN COAL: "I don't keep company with black women."

JIG: Negro, a corrupted shortening of Zigaboo

JELLY: sex

JULY JAM: something very hot

JUMP SALTY: get angry

KITCHEN MECHANIC: a domestic

MANNY: a term of insult; never used in any other way by Negroes

MISS ANNE: a white woman

MY PEOPLE! MY PEOPLE!:   sad and satiric expression in the Negro language; sad when a Negro comments on the backwardness of some members of his race; at other times, used for satiric or comic effect.

PE-OLA: a very white Negro girl

PIANO: spareribs (white rib bones suggest piano keys)

PLAYING THE DOZENS: low-rating the ancestors of your opponent

REEFER: a marijuana cigarette, also a drag

RIGHTEOUS MOSS OR GRASS: good hair

RUSSIAN: a southern Negro up North. "Rushed up here," hence a Russian

SCRAP-IRON: cheap liquor

SOLID: perfect

STANCH or STANCH OUT: to begin, commence, step out

SUGAR HILL: northwest sector of Harlem, near Washington Heights; site of the newest apartment houses, mostly occupied by professional people. (The expression has been distorted in the South to mean a Negro red-light district.)

THE BEAR: confession of poverty

THOUSAND ON A PLATE: beans

WHAT'S ON DE RAIL FOR THE LIZARD?:   suggestion for moral turpitude

ZIGABOO: a Negro

ZOOT SUIT WITH THE REET PLEAT: Harlem-style suit with padded shoulders, 43-inch trousers at the knee with cuff so small it needs a zipper to get into, high waistline, fancy lapels, bushels of buttons, etc.

THE SOUND OF
A VOICE

DAVID HENRY HWANG

THE SOUND OF A VOICE (on a double bill with "The House of Sleeping Beauties" and under the omnibus title of *Sound and Beauty*) was presented by Joseph Papp at the New York Shakespeare Festival Public Theater, in New York City, where it opened on November 6, 1983. Direction was by John Lone, assisted by Lenore Kletter; scenery by Andrew Jackness; lighting by John Giscondi; costumes by Lydia Tanii; wigs and makeup by Marlies Vallant. Jason Steven Cohen was associate producer; with the following cast:

MAN	John Lone
WOMAN	Natsuko Ohama

(Movement by Ching Valdes and Elizabeth Fong Sung)

Characters
MAN, fifties, Japanese
WOMAN, fifties, Japanese

Setting
WOMAN's house, in a remote corner of a forest

Note on Incidental Music
Incidental music composed by Lucia Hwong for the New York productions of THE SOUND OF A VOICE is available in reel to reel or cassette tape format. For rental please contact: Harold Orenstein P.C., 157 West 57th Street, Room 500, New York, N.Y. 10019, (212) 247-6460

■ ■

Scene One

Evening. Woman pours tea for Man. Man rubs himself, trying to get warm.

MAN: You're very kind to take me in.
WOMAN: This is a remote corner of the world. Guests are rare.
MAN: The tea—you pour it well.
WOMAN: No.
MAN: The sound it makes—in the cup—very soothing.

WOMAN: That is the tea's skill, not mine. *(She hands the cup to him.)* May I get you something else? Rice, perhaps?

MAN: No.

WOMAN: And some vegetables?

MAN: No, thank you.

WOMAN: Fish? *(Pause.)* It is at least two days' walk to the nearest village. I saw no horse. You must be very hungry. You would do a great honor to dine with me. Guests are rare.

MAN: Thank you.

(Woman gets up, leaves. Man holds the cup in his hands, using it to warm himself. He gets up, walks around the room. It is sparsely furnished, drab, except for one shelf on which stands a vase of brightly colored flowers. The flowers stand out in sharp contrast to the starkness of the room. Slowly, he reaches out towards them. He touches them. Quickly, he takes one of the flowers from the vase, hides it in his clothes. He returns to where he had sat previously. He waits. Woman reenters. She carries a tray with food.)

WOMAN: Please eat. It will give me great pleasure.

MAN: This—this is magnificent.

WOMAN: Eat.

MAN: Thank you. *(He motions for Woman to join him.)*

WOMAN: No, thank you.

MAN: This is wonderful. The best I've tasted.

WOMAN: You are reckless in your flattery. But anything you say, I will enjoy hearing. It's not even the words. It's the sound of a voice, the way it moves through the air.

MAN: How long has it been since you last had a visitor? *(Pause.)*

WOMAN: I don't know.

MAN: Oh?

WOMAN: I lose track. Perhaps five months ago, perhaps ten years, perhaps yesterday. I don't consider time when there is no voice in the air. It's pointless. Time begins with the entrance of a visitor, and ends with his exit.

MAN: And in between? You don't keep track of the days? You can't help but notice—

WOMAN: Of course I notice.

MAN: Oh.

WOMAN: I notice, but I don't keep track. *(Pause.)* May I bring out more?

MAN: More? No. No. This was wonderful.

WOMAN: I have more.

MAN: Really—the best I've had.

WOMAN: You must be tired. Did you sleep in the forest last night?

MAN: Yes.

WOMAN: Or did you not sleep at all?

MAN: I slept.

WOMAN: Where?

MAN: By a waterfall. The sound of the water put me to sleep. It rumbled like the sounds of a city. You see, I can't sleep in too much silence. It scares me. It makes me feel that I have no control over what is about to happen.

WOMAN: I feel the same way.

MAN: But you live here—alone?

WOMAN: Yes.

MAN: It's so quiet here. How can you sleep?

WOMAN: Tonight, I'll sleep. I'll lie down in the next room, and hear your breathing through the wall, and fall asleep shamelessly. There will be no silence.

MAN: You're very kind to let me stay here.

WOMAN: This is yours. (*She unrolls a mat; there is a beautiful design of a flower on the mat. The flower looks exactly like the flowers in the vase.*)

MAN: Did you make it yourself?

WOMAN: Yes. There is a place to wash outside.

MAN: Thank you.

WOMAN: Goodnight.

MAN: Goodnight. (*Man starts to leave.*)

WOMAN: May I know your name?

MAN: No. I mean, I would rather not say. If I gave you a name, it would only be made-up. Why should I deceive you? You are too kind for that.

WOMAN: Then what should I call you? Perhaps—"Man Who Fears Silence"?

MAN: How about, "Man Who Fears Women"?

WOMAN: That name is much too common.

MAN: And you?

WOMAN: Yokiko.

MAN: That's your name?

WOMAN: It's what you may call me.

MAN: Goodnight, Yokiko. You are very kind.

WOMAN: You are very smart. Goodnight.

(*Man exits. Hanako goes to the mat. She tidies it, brushes it off. She goes to the vase. She picks up the flowers, studies them. She carries them out of the room with her. Man reenters. He takes off his outer clothing. He glimpses the spot where the vase used to sit. He reaches into his clothing, pulls out the stolen flower. He studies it. He puts it underneath his head*) *as he lies down to sleep, like a pillow. He starts to fall asleep. Suddenly, a start. He picks up his head. He listens.)*

Scene Two

Dawn. Man is getting dressed. Woman enters with food.

WOMAN: Good morning.

MAN: Good morning, Yokiko.

WOMAN: You weren't planning to leave?

MAN: I have quite a distance to travel today.

WOMAN: Please. *(She offers him food.)*

MAN: Thank you.

WOMAN: May I ask where you're traveling to?

MAN: It's far.

WOMAN: I know this region well.

MAN: Oh? Do you leave the house often?

WOMAN: I used to. I used to travel a great deal. I know the region from those days.

MAN: You probably wouldn't know the place I'm headed.

WOMAN: Why not?

MAN: It's new. A new village. It didn't exist in "those days." *(Pause.)*

WOMAN: I thought you said you wouldn't deceive me.

MAN: I didn't. You don't believe me, do you?

WOMAN: No.

MAN: Then I didn't deceive you. I'm traveling. That much is true.

WOMAN: Are you in such a hurry?

MAN: Traveling is a matter of timing. Catching the light. *(Woman exits; Man finishes eating, puts down his bowl. Woman reenters with the vase of flowers.)* Where did you find those? They don't grow native around these parts, do they?

WOMAN: No; they've all been brought in. They were brought in by visitors. Such as yourself. They were left here. In my custody.

MAN: But—they look so fresh, so alive.

WOMAN: I take care of them. They remind me of the people and places outside this house.

MAN: May I touch them?

WOMAN: Certainly.

MAN: These have just blossomed.

WOMAN: No; they were in bloom yesterday. If you'd noticed them before, you would know that.

MAN: You must have received these very recently. I would guess —within five days.

WOMAN: I don't know. But I wouldn't trust your estimate. It's all in the amount of care you show to them. I create a world which is outside the realm of what you know.

MAN: What do you do?

WOMAN: I can't explain. Words are too inefficient. It takes hundreds of words to describe a single act of caring. With hundreds of acts, words become irrelevant. *(Pause.)* But perhaps you can stay.

MAN: How long?

WOMAN: As long as you'd like.

MAN: Why?

WOMAN: To see how I care for them.

MAN: I *am* tired.

WOMAN: Rest.

MAN: The light?

WOMAN: It will return.

Scene Three

Day. Man is carrying chopped wood. He is stripped to the waist. Woman enters.

WOMAN: You're very kind to do that for me.

MAN: I enjoy it, you know. Chopping wood. It's clean. No questions. You take your axe, you stand up the log, you aim—pow! —you either hit it or you don't. Success or failure.

WOMAN: You seem to have been very successful today.

MAN: Why shouldn't I be? It's a beautiful day. I can see to those hills. The trees are cool. The sun is gentle. Ideal. If a man can't be successful on a day like this, he might as well kick the dust up into his own face. *(Man notices Woman staring at him. Man pats his belly, looks at her.)* Protection from falls.

WOMAN: What? *(Man pinches his belly, showing some fat.)* Oh. Don't be silly. *(Man begins slapping the fat on his belly to a rhythm.)*

MAN: Listen—I can make music—see?—that wasn't always possible. But now—that I've developed this—whenever I need entertainment.

WOMAN: You shouldn't make fun of your body.

MAN: Why not? I saw you. You were staring.

WOMAN: I wasn't making fun. *(Man inflates his cheeks.)* I was just —stop that!

MAN: Then why were you staring?

WOMAN: I was—

MAN: Laughing?

WOMAN: No.

MAN: Well?

WOMAN: I was—Your body. It's . . . strong. *(Pause.)*

MAN: People say that. But they don't know. I've heard that age brings wisdom. That's a laugh. The years don't accumulate here. They accumulate here. *(Pause; he pinches his belly.)* But today is a day to be happy, right? The woods. The sun. Blue. It's a happy day. I'm going to chop wood.

WOMAN: There's nothing left to chop. Look.

MAN: Oh. I guess . . . that's it.

WOMAN: Sit. Here.

MAN: But—

WOMAN: There's nothing left. *(Man sits; Woman stares at his belly.)* Learn to love it.

MAN: Don't be ridiculous.

WOMAN: Touch it.

MAN: It's flabby.

WOMAN: It's strong.

MAN: It's weak.

WOMAN: And smooth.

MAN: Do you mind if I put on my shirt?

WOMAN: Of course not. Shall I get it for you?

MAN: No. No. Just sit there. *(Man starts to put on his shirt. He pauses, studies his body.)* You think it's cute, huh?

WOMAN: I think you should learn to love it. *(Man pats his belly, talks to it.)*

MAN *(to belly)*:   You're okay, sir. You hang onto my body like a great horseman.

WOMAN: Not like that.

MAN *(ibid.)*:   You're also faithful. You'll never leave me for another man.

WOMAN: No.

MAN: What do you want me to say? *(Woman walks over to Man. She touches his belly with her hand. They look at each other.)*

Scene Four

Night. Man is alone. Flowers are gone from stand. Mat is unrolled. Man lies on it, sleeping. Suddenly, he starts. He lifts up his head. He listens. Silence. He goes back to sleep. Another start. He lifts up his head, strains to hear. Slowly, we begin to make out the strains of a single shakuhachi playing a haunting line. It is very soft. He strains to hear it. The instrument slowly fades out. He waits for it to return, but it does not. He takes out the stolen flower. He stares into it.

Scene Five

Day. Woman is cleaning, while Man relaxes. She is on her hands and knees, scrubbing. She is dressed in a simple outfit, for working. Her hair is tied back. Man is sweating. He has not, however, removed his shirt.

MAN: I heard your playing last night.

WOMAN: My playing?

MAN: Shakuhachi.

WOMAN: Oh.

MAN: You played very softly. I had to strain to hear it. Next time, don't be afraid. Play out. Fully. Clear. It must've been very beautiful, if only I could've heard it clearly. Why don't you play for me sometime?

WOMAN: I'm very shy about it.

MAN: Why?

WOMAN: I play for my own satisfaction. That's all. It's something I developed on my own. I don't know if it's at all acceptable by outside standards.

MAN: Play for me. I'll tell you.

WOMAN: No; I'm sure you're too knowledgeable in the arts.

MAN: Who? Me?

WOMAN: You being from the city and all.

MAN: I'm ignorant, believe me.

WOMAN: I'd play, and you'd probably bite your cheek.

MAN: Ask me a question about music. Any question. I'll answer incorrectly. I guarantee it.

WOMAN: Look at this.

MAN: What?

WOMAN: A stain.

MAN: Where?

WOMAN: Here. See? I can't get it out.

MAN: Oh. I hadn't noticed it before.

WOMAN: I notice it every time I clean.

MAN: Here. Let me try.

WOMAN: Thank you.

MAN: Ugh. It's tough.

WOMAN: I know.

MAN: How did it get here?

WOMAN: It's been there as long as I've lived here.

MAN: I hardly stand a chance. *(Pause.)* But I'll try. Uh—one—two—three—four! One—two—three—four! See, you set up . . . gotta set up . . . a rhythm—two—three—four. Like fighting! Like battle! One—two—three—four! Used to practice with a rhythm

. . . beat . . . battle! Yes! *(The stain starts to fade away.)* Look—
it's—yes!—whoo!—there it goes—got the sides—the edges—
yes!—fading quick—fading away—ooo—here we come—
towards the center—to the heart—two—three—four—slow—
slow death—tough—dead! *(Man rolls over in triumphant laughter.)*

WOMAN: Dead.

MAN: I got it! I got it! Whoo! A little rhythm! All it took! Four!
Four!

WOMAN: Thank you.

MAN: I didn't think I could do it—but there—it's gone—I did it!

WOMAN: Yes. You did.

MAN: And you—you were great.

WOMAN: No—I was carried away.

MAN: We were a team! You and me!

WOMAN: I only provided encouragement.

MAN: You were great! You were! *(Man grabs Woman. Pause.)*

WOMAN: It's gone. Thank you. Would you like to hear me play
shakuhachi?

MAN: Yes I would.

WOMAN: I don't usually play for visitors. It's so . . . I'm not sure.
I developed it—all by myself—in times when I was alone. I heard
nothing—no human voice. So I learned to play shakuhachi. I tried
to make these sounds resemble the human voice. The shakuhachi
became my weapon. To ward off the air. It kept me from choking
on many a silent evening.

MAN: I'm here. You can hear my voice.

WOMAN: Speak again.

MAN: I will.

Scene Six

*Night. Man is sleeping. Suddenly, a start. He lifts his head up. He
listens. Silence. He strains to hear. The shakuhachi melody rises up once
more. This time, however, it becomes louder and clearer than before. He
gets up. He cannot tell from what direction the music is coming. He walks
around the room, putting his ear to different places in the wall, but he
cannot locate the sound. It seems to come from all directions at once, as
omnipresent as the air. Slowly, he moves towards the wall with the sliding
panel through which the Woman enters and exits. He puts his ear against
it, thinking the music may be coming from there. Slowly, he slides the
door open just a crack, ever so carefully. He peeks through the crack. As
he peeks through, the upstage wall of the set becomes transparent, and
through the scrim, we are able to see what he sees. Woman is upstage of
the scrim. She is tending a room filled with potted and vased flowers of*

all variety. The lushness and beauty of the room upstage of the scrim stands out in stark contrast to the barrenness of the main set. She is also transformed. She is a young woman. She is beautiful. She wears a brightly colored kimono. Man observes this scene for a long time. He then slides the door shut. The scrim returns to opaque. The music continues. He returns to his mat. He picks up the stolen flower. It is brown and wilted, dead. He looks at it. The music slowly fades out.

Scene Seven

Morning. Man is half-dressed. He is practicing sword maneuvers. He practices with the feel of a man whose spirit is willing, but the flesh is inept. He tries to execute deft movements, but is dissatisfied with his efforts. He curses himself, and returns to basic exercises. Suddenly, he feels something buzzing around his neck—a mosquito. He slaps his neck, but misses it. He sees it flying near him. He swipes at it with his sword. He keeps missing. Finally, he thinks he's hit it. He runs over, kneels down to recover the fallen insect. He picks up two halves of a mosquito on two different fingers. Woman enters the room. She looks as she normally does. She is carrying a vase of flowers, which she places on its shelf.

MAN: Look.

WOMAN: I'm sorry?

MAN: Look.

WOMAN: What? *(He brings over the two halves of mosquito to show her.)*

MAN: See?

WOMAN: Oh.

MAN: I hit it—chop!

WOMAN: These are new forms of target practice?

MAN: Huh? Well—yes—in a way.

WOMAN: You seem to do well at it.

MAN: Thank you. For last night. I heard your shakuhachi. It was very loud, strong—good tone.

WOMAN: Did you enjoy it? I wanted you to enjoy it. If you wish, I'll play it for you every night.

MAN: Every night!

WOMAN: If you wish.

MAN: No—I don't—I don't want you to treat me like a baby.

WOMAN: What? I'm not.

MAN: Oh, yes. Like a baby. Who you must feed in the middle of the night or he cries. Waaah! Waaah!

WOMAN: Stop that!

MAN: You need your sleep.

WOMAN: I don't mind getting up for you. *(Pause.)* I would enjoy playing for you. Every night. While you sleep. It will make me feel—like I'm shaping your dreams. I go through long stretches when there is no one in my dreams. It's terrible. During those times, I avoid my bed as much as possible. I paint. I weave. I play shakuhachi. I sit on mats and rub powder into my face. Anything to keep from facing a bed with no dreams. It is like sleeping on ice.

MAN: What do you dream of now?

WOMAN: Last night—I dreamt of you. I don't remember what happened. But you were very funny. Not in a mocking way. I wasn't laughing at you. But you made me laugh. And you were very warm. I remember that. *(Pause.)* What do you remember about last night?

MAN: Just your playing. That's all. I got up, listened to it, and went back to sleep. *(Man gets up, resumes practicing with his sword.)*

WOMAN: Another mosquito bothering you?

MAN: Just practicing. Ah! Weak! Too weak! I tell you, it wasn't always like this. I'm telling you, there were days when I could chop the fruit from a tree without ever taking my eyes off the ground. *(He continues practicing.)* You ever use one of these?

WOMAN: I've had to pick one up, yes.

MAN: Oh?

WOMAN: You forget—I live alone—out here—there is . . . not much to sustain me but what I manage to learn myself. It wasn't really a matter of choice.

MAN: I used to be very good, you know. Perhaps I can give you some pointers.

WOMAN: I'd really rather not.

MAN: C'mon—a woman like you—you're absolutely right. You need to know how to defend yourself.

WOMAN: As you wish.

MAN: Do you have something to practice with?

WOMAN: Yes. Excuse me. *(She exits. He practices more. She reenters with two wooden sticks. He takes one of them.)* Will these do?

MAN: Nice. Now, show me what you can do.

WOMAN: I'm sorry?

MAN: Run up and hit me.

WOMAN: Please.

MAN: Go on—I'll block it.

WOMAN: I feel so . . . undignified.

MAN: Go on. *(She hits him playfully with stick.)* Not like that!

WOMAN: I'll try to be gentle.

MAN: What?

WOMAN: I don't want to hurt you.

MAN: You won't—Hit me! *(Woman charges at Man, quickly, deftly. She scores a hit.)* Oh!

WOMAN: Did I hurt you?

MAN: No—you were—let's try that again. *(They square off again. Woman rushes forward. She appears to attempt a strike. He blocks that apparent strike, which turns out to be a feint. She scores.)* Huh?

WOMAN: Did I hurt you? I'm sorry.

MAN: No.

WOMAN: I hurt you.

MAN: No.

WOMAN: Do you wish to hit me?

MAN: No.

WOMAN: Do you want me to try again?

MAN: No.

WOMAN: Thank you.

MAN: Just practice there—by yourself—let me see you run through some maneuvers.

WOMAN: Must I?

MAN: Yes! Go! *(She goes to an open area.)* My greatest strength was always as a teacher. *(Woman executes a series of deft movements. Her whole manner is transformed. Man watches with increasing amazement. Her movements end. She regains her submissive manner.)*

WOMAN: I'm so embarrassed. My skills—they're so—inappropriate. I look like a man.

MAN: Where did you learn that?

WOMAN: There is much time to practice here.

MAN: But you—the techniques.

WOMAN: I don't know what's fashionable in the outside world. *(Pause.)* Are you unhappy?

MAN: No.

WOMAN: Really?

MAN: I'm just . . . surprised.

WOMAN: You think it's unbecoming for a woman.

MAN: No, no. Not at all.

WOMAN: You want to leave.

MAN: No!

WOMAN: All visitors do. I know. I've met many. They say they'll stay. And they do. For a while. Until they see too much. Or they learn something new. There are boundaries outside of which visitors do not want to see me step. Only who knows what those boundaries are? Not I. They change with every visitor. You have to be careful not to cross them, but you never know where they are. And one day, inevitably, you step outside the lines. The visitor knows. You don't. You didn't know that you'd done anything different. You thought it was just another part of you. The visitor sneaks away. The next day, you learn that you had stepped outside his heart. I'm afraid you've seen too much.

MAN: There are stories.

WOMAN: What?

MAN: People talk.

WOMAN: Where? We're two days from the nearest village.

MAN: Word travels.

WOMAN: What are you talking about?

MAN: There are stories about you. I heard them. They say that your visitors never leave this house.

WOMAN: That's what you heard?

MAN: They say you imprison them.

WOMAN: Then you were a fool to come here.

MAN: Listen.

WOMAN: Me? Listen? You. Look! Where are the prisoners? Have you seen any?

MAN: They told me you were very beautiful.

WOMAN: Then they are blind as well as ignorant.

MAN: You are.

WOMAN: What?

MAN: Beautiful.

WOMAN: Stop that! My skin feels like seaweed.

MAN: I didn't realize it at first. I must confess—I didn't. But over these few days—your face has changed for me. The shape of it. The feel of it. The color. All changed. I look at you now, and I'm no longer sure you are the same woman who had poured tea for me just a week ago. And because of that I remembered—how little I know about a face that changes in the night. *(Pause.)* Have you heard those stories?

WOMAN: I don't listen to old wives' tales.

MAN: But have you heard them?

WOMAN: Yes. I've heard them. From other visitors—young—hot-blooded—or old—who came here because they were told great glory was to be had by killing the witch in the woods.

MAN: I was told that no man could spend time in this house without falling in love.

WOMAN: Oh? So why did you come? Did you wager gold that you could come out untouched? The outside world is so flattering to me. And you—are you like the rest? Passion passing through your heart so powerfully that you can't hold onto it?

MAN: No! I'm afraid!

WOMAN: Of what?

MAN: Sometimes—when I look into the flowers, I think I hear a voice—from inside—a voice beneath the petals. A human voice.

WOMAN: What does it say? "Let me out"?

MAN: No. Listen. It hums. It hums with the peacefulness of one who is completely imprisoned.

WOMAN: I understand that if you listen closely enough, you can hear the ocean.

MAN: No. Wait. Look at it. See the layers? Each petal—hiding the next. Try and see where they end. You can't. Follow them down, further down, around—and as you come down—faster and faster—the breeze picks up. The breeze becomes a wail. And in that rush of air—in the silent midst of it—you can hear a voice.

WOMAN (*grabs flower from Man*):   So, you believe I water and prune my lovers? How can you be so foolish? (*She snaps the flower in half, at the stem. She throws it to the ground.*) Do you come only to leave again? To take a chunk of my heart, then leave with your booty on your belt, like a prize? You say that I imprison hearts in these flowers? Well, bits of my heart are trapped with travelers across this land. I can't even keep track. So kill me. If you came here to destroy a witch, kill me now. I can't stand to have it happen again.

MAN: I won't leave you.

WOMAN: I believe you. (*She looks at the flower that she has broken, bends to pick it up. He touches her. They embrace.*)

Scene Eight

Day. Woman wears a simple undergarment, over which she is donning a brightly colored kimono, the same one we saw her wearing upstage of the scrim. Man stands apart.

WOMAN: I can't cry. I don't have the capacity. Right from birth, I didn't cry. My mother and father were shocked. They thought they'd given birth to a ghost, a demon. Sometimes I've thought myself that. When great sadness has welled up inside me, I've prayed for a means to release the pain from my body. But my prayers went unanswered. The grief remained inside me. It would sit like water, still. (*Pause; she models her kimono.*) Do you like it?

MAN: Yes, it's beautiful.

WOMAN: I wanted to wear something special today.

MAN: It's beautiful. Excuse me. I must practice.

WOMAN: Shall I get you something?

MAN: No.

WOMAN: Some tea, maybe?

MAN: No. (*Man resumes swordplay.*)

WOMAN: Perhaps later today—perhaps we can go out—just around here. We can look for flowers.

MAN: All right.

WOMAN: We don't have to.

MAN: No. Let's.

WOMAN: I just thought if—

MAN: Fine. Where do you want to go?

WOMAN: There are very few recreational activities around here, I know.

MAN: All right. We'll go this afternoon. (*Pause.*)

WOMAN: Can I get you something?

MAN (*turning around*):   What?

WOMAN: You might be—

MAN: I'm not hungry or thirsty or cold or hot.

WOMAN: Then what are you?

MAN: Practicing.

(*Man resumes practicing; Woman exits. As soon as she exits, he rests. He sits down. He examines his sword. He runs his finger along the edge of it. He takes the tip, runs it against the soft skin under his chin. He places the sword on the ground with the tip pointed directly upwards. He keeps it from falling by placing the tip under his chin. He experiments with different degrees of pressure. Woman reenters. She sees him in this precarious position. She jerks his head upward; the sword falls.*)

WOMAN: Don't do that!

MAN: What?

WOMAN: You can hurt yourself!

MAN: I was practicing!

WOMAN: You were playing!

MAN: I was practicing!

WOMAN: It's dangerous.

MAN: What do you take me for—a child?

WOMAN: Sometimes wise men do childish things.

MAN: I knew what I was doing!

WOMAN: It scares me.

MAN: Don't be ridiculous. (*He reaches for the sword again.*)

WOMAN: Don't! Don't do that!

MAN: Get back! (*He places the sword back in its previous position, suspended between the floor and his chin, upright.*)

WOMAN: But—

MAN: Sssssh!

WOMAN: I wish—

MAN: Listen to me! The slightest shock, you know—the slightest shock—surprise—it might make me jerk or—something—and then . . . so you must be perfectly still and quiet.

WOMAN: But I—

MAN: Sssssh! *(Silence.)* I learned this exercise from a friend—I can't even remember his name—good swordsman—many years ago. He called it his meditation position. He said, like this, he could feel the line between this world and the others because he rested on it. If he saw something in another world that he liked better, all he would have to do is let his head drop, and he'd be there. Simple. No fuss. One day, they found him with the tip of his sword run clean out the back of his neck. He was smiling. I guess he saw something he liked. Or else he'd fallen asleep.

WOMAN: Stop that.

MAN: Stop what?

WOMAN: Tormenting me.

MAN: I'm not.

WOMAN: Take it away!

MAN: You don't have to watch, you know.

WOMAN: Do you want to die that way—an accident?

MAN: I was doing this before you came in.

WOMAN: If you do, all you need to do is tell me.

MAN: What?

WOMAN: I can walk right over. Lean on the back of your head.

MAN: Don't try to threaten—

WOMAN: Or jerk your sword up.

MAN: Or scare me. You can't threaten—

WOMAN: I'm not. But if that's what you want.

MAN: You can't threaten me. You wouldn't do it.

WOMAN: Oh?

MAN: Then I'd be gone. You wouldn't let me leave that easily.

WOMAN: Yes, I would.

MAN: You'd be alone.

WOMAN: No. I'd follow you. Forever. *(Pause.)* Now, let's stop this nonsense.

MAN: No! I can do what I want! Don't come any closer!

WOMAN: Then release your sword.

MAN: Come any closer and I'll drop my head.

WOMAN *(Woman slowly approaches Man. She grabs the hilt of the sword. She looks into his eyes. She pulls it out from under his chin.)*:   There will be no more of this. *(She exits with the sword. He starts to follow her, then stops. He touches under his chin. On his finger, he finds a drop of blood.)*

Scene Nine

Night. Man is leaving the house. He is just about out, when he hears a shakuhachi playing. He looks around, trying to locate the sound. Woman appears in the doorway to the outside. Shakuhachi slowly fades out.

WOMAN: It's time for you to go?

MAN: Yes. I'm sorry.

WOMAN: You're just going to sneak out? A thief in the night? A frightened child?

MAN: I care about you.

WOMAN: You express it strangely.

MAN: I leave in shame because it is proper. *(Pause.)* I came seeking glory.

WOMAN: To kill me? You can say it. You'll be surprised at how little I blanche. As if you'd said, "I came for a bowl of rice," or "I came seeking love" or "I came to kill you."

MAN: Weakness. All weakness. Too weak to kill you. Too weak to kill myself. Too weak to do anything but sneak away in shame. *(Woman brings out Man's sword.)*

WOMAN: Were you even planning to leave without this? *(He takes sword.)* Why not stay here?

MAN: I can't live with someone who's defeated me.

WOMAN: I never thought of defeating you. I only wanted to take care of you. To make you happy. Because that made me happy and I was no longer alone.

MAN: You defeated me.

WOMAN: Why do you think that way?

MAN: I came here with a purpose. The world was clear. You changed the shape of your face, the shape of my heart—rearranged everything—created a world where I could do nothing.

WOMAN: I only tried to care for you.

MAN: I guess that was all it took. *(Pause.)*

WOMAN: You still think I'm a witch. Just because old women gossip. You are so cruel. Once you arrived, there were only two possibilities: I would die or you would leave. *(Pause.)* If you believe I'm a witch, then kill me. Rid the province of one more evil.

MAN: I can't—

WOMAN: Why not? If you believe that about me, then it's the right thing to do.

MAN: You know I can't.

WOMAN: Then stay.

MAN: Don't try and force me.

WOMAN: I won't force you to do anything. *(Pause.)* All I wanted

was an escape—for both of us. The sound of a human voice—
the simplest thing to find, and the hardest to hold onto. This
house—my loneliness is etched into the walls. Kill me, but don't
leave. Even in death, my spirit would rest here and be comforted
by your presence.

MAN: Force me to stay.

WOMAN: I won't. *(Man starts to leave.)* Beware.

MAN: What?

WOMAN: The ground on which you walk is weak. It could give way
at any moment. The crevice beneath is dark.

MAN: Are you talking about death? I'm ready to die.

WOMAN: Fear for what is worse than death.

MAN: What?

WOMAN: Falling. Falling through the darkness. Waiting to hit the
ground. Picking up speed. Waiting for the ground. Falling faster.
Falling alone. Waiting. Falling. Waiting. Falling.

*(Woman wails and runs out through the door to her room. Man stands,
confused, not knowing what to do. He starts to follow her, then hesitates,
and rushes out the door to the outside. Silence. Slowly, he reenters from
the outside. He looks for her in the main room. He goes slowly towards
the panel to her room. He throws down his sword. He opens the panel.
He goes inside. He comes out. He unrolls his mat. He sits on it, cross-
legged. He looks out into space. He notices near him a shakuhachi. He
picks it up. He begins to blow into it. He tries to make sounds. He continues
trying through the end of the play. The upstage scrim lights up. Upstage,
we see the Woman. She is young. She is hanging from a rope suspended
from the roof. She has hung herself. Around her are scores of vases with
flowers in them whose blossoms have been blown off. Only the stems remain
in the vases. Around her swirl the thousands of petals from the flowers.
They fill the upstage scrim area like a blizzard of color. Man continues
to attempt to play. Lights fade to black.)*

SURE THING

DAVID IVES

This play is for Jason Buzas,
who conducted perfectly

SURE THING was presented by the Manhattan Punch Line Theatre, in
New York City, in February 1988. The production was directed by Jason
McConnell Buzas; costumes were by Michael S. Schler; scenery was by
Stanley A. Meyer; lighting was by Joseph R. Morley; sound was by Duncan
Edwards; and the stage manager was Carl Gonzalez. The cast was as follows:

BILL	Robert Stanton
BETTY	Nancy Opel

Characters
BILL and BETTY, both in their late twenties

Setting
A café table, with a couple of chairs

■ ■

Betty, reading at the table. An empty chair opposite her. Bill enters.

BILL: Excuse me. Is this chair taken?
BETTY: Excuse me?
BILL: Is this taken?
BETTY: Yes it is.
BILL: Oh. Sorry.
BETTY: Sure thing. *(A bell rings softly.)*
BILL: Excuse me. Is this chair taken?
BETTY: Excuse me?
BILL: Is this taken?
BETTY: No, but I'm expecting somebody in a minute.
BILL: Oh. Thanks anyway.
BETTY: Sure thing. *(A bell rings softly.)*
BILL: Excuse me. Is this chair taken?
BETTY: No, but I'm expecting somebody very shortly.
BILL: Would you mind if I sit here till he or she or it comes?
BETTY *(glances at her watch)*:   They seem to be pretty late. . . .

BILL: You never know who you might be turning down.

BETTY: Sorry. Nice try, though.

BILL: Sure thing. *(Bell.)* Is this seat taken?

BETTY: No it's not.

BILL: Would you mind if I sit here?

BETTY: Yes I would.

BILL: Oh. *(Bell.)* Is this chair taken?

BETTY: No it's not.

BILL: Would you mind if I sit here?

BETTY: No. Go ahead.

BILL: Thanks. *(He sits. She continues reading.)* Everyplace else seems to be taken.

BETTY: Mm-hm.

BILL: Great place.

BETTY: Mm-hm.

BILL: What's the book?

BETTY: I just wanted to read in quiet, if you don't mind.

BILL: No. Sure thing. *(Bell.)*

BILL: Everyplace else seems to be taken.

BETTY: Mm-hm.

BILL: Great place for reading.

BETTY: Yes, I like it.

BILL: What's the book?

BETTY: *The Sound and the Fury.*

BILL: Oh. Hemingway. *(Bell.)* What's the book?

BETTY: *The Sound and the Fury.*

BILL: Oh. Faulkner.

BETTY: Have you read it?

BILL: Not . . . actually. I've sure read *about* . . . it, though. It's supposed to be great.

BETTY: It is great.

BILL: I hear it's great. *(Small pause.)* Waiter? *(Bell.)* What's the book?

BETTY: *The Sound and the Fury.*

BILL: Oh. Faulkner.

BETTY: Have you read it?

BILL: I'm a Mets fan, myself. *(Bell.)*

BETTY: Have you read it?

BILL: Yeah, I read it in college.

BETTY: Where was college?

BILL: I went to Oral Roberts University. *(Bell.)*

BETTY: Where was college?

BILL: I was lying. I never really went to college. I just like to party. *(Bell.)*

BETTY: Where was college?

BILL: Harvard.

BETTY: Do you like Faulkner?

BILL: I love Faulkner. I spent a whole winter reading him once.

BETTY: I've just started.

BILL: I was so excited after ten pages that I went out and bought everything else he wrote. One of the greatest reading experiences of my life. I mean, all that incredible psychological understanding. Page after page of gorgeous prose. His profound grasp of the mystery of time and human existence. The smells of the earth . . . What do you think?

BETTY: I think it's pretty boring. *(Bell.)*

BILL: What's the book?

BETTY: *The Sound and the Fury*.

BILL: Oh! Faulkner!

BETTY: Do you like Faulkner?

BILL: I love Faulkner.

BETTY: He's incredible.

BILL: I spent a whole winter reading him once.

BETTY: I was so excited after ten pages that I went out and bought everything else he wrote.

BILL: All that incredible psychological understanding.

BETTY: And the prose is so gorgeous.

BILL: And the way he's grasped the mystery of time—

BETTY: —and human existence. I can't believe I've waited this long to read him.

BILL: You never know. You might not have liked him before.

BETTY: That's true.

BILL: You might not have been ready for him. You have to hit these things at the right moment or it's no good.

BETTY: That's happened to me.

BILL: It's all in the timing. *(Small pause.)* My name's Bill, by the way.

BETTY: I'm Betty.

BILL: Hi.

BETTY: Hi. *(Small pause.)*

BILL: Yes I thought reading Faulkner was . . . a great experience.

BETTY: Yes. *(Small pause.)*

BILL: *The Sound and the Fury* . . . *(Another small pause.)*

BETTY: Well. Onwards and upwards. *(She goes back to her book.)*

BILL: Waiter—? *(Bell.)* You have to hit these things at the right moment or it's no good.

BETTY: That's happened to me.

BILL: It's all in the timing. My name's Bill, by the way.

BETTY: I'm Betty.

BILL: Hi.

BETTY: Hi.

BILL: Do you come in here a lot?

BETTY: Actually I'm just in town for two days from Pakistan.

BILL: Oh. Pakistan. *(Bell.)* My name's Bill, by the way.

BETTY: I'm Betty.

BILL: Hi.

BETTY: Hi.

BILL: Do you come in here a lot?

BETTY: Every once in a while. Do you?

BILL: Not much anymore. Not as much as I used to. Before my nervous breakdown. *(Bell.)* Do you come in here a lot?

BETTY: Why are you asking?

BILL: Just interested.

BETTY: Are you really interested, or do you just want to pick me up?

BILL: No, I'm really interested.

BETTY: Why would you be interested in whether I come in here a lot?

BILL: Just . . . getting acquainted.

BETTY: Maybe you're only interested for the sake of making small talk long enough to ask me back to your place to listen to some music, or because you've just rented some great tape for your VCR, or because you've got some terrific unknown Django Reinhardt record, only all you'll really want to do is fuck—which you won't do very well—after which you'll go into the bathroom and pee very loudly, then pad into the kitchen and get yourself a beer from the refrigerator without asking me whether I'd like anything, and then you'll proceed to lie back down beside me and confess that you've got a girlfriend named Stephanie who's away at medical school in Belgium for a year, and that you've been involved with her—*off and on*—in what you'll call a very "intricate" relationship, for about *seven YEARS*. None of which *interests* me, mister!

BILL: Okay. *(Bell.)* Do you come in here a lot?

BETTY: Every other day, I think.

BILL: I come in here quite a lot and I don't remember seeing you.

BETTY: I guess we must be on different schedules.

BILL: Missed connections.

BETTY: Yes. Different time zones.

BILL: Amazing how you can live right next door to somebody in this town and never even know it.

BETTY: I know.

BILL: City life.

BETTY: It's crazy.

BILL: We probably pass each other in the street every day. Right in front of this place, probably.

BETTY: Yep.

BILL *(looks around)*:   Well, the waiters here sure seem to be in some different time zone. I can't seem to locate one anywhere . . . Waiter! *(He looks back.)* So what do you—*(He sees that she's gone back to her book.)*

BETTY: I beg pardon?

BILL: Nothing. Sorry. *(Bell.)*

BETTY: I guess we must be on different schedules.

BILL: Missed connections.

BETTY: Yes. Different time zones.

BILL: Amazing how you can live right next door to somebody in this town and never even know it.

BETTY: I know.

BILL: City life.

BETTY: It's crazy.

BILL: You weren't waiting for somebody when I came in, were you?

BETTY: Actually I was.

BILL: Oh. Boyfriend?

BETTY: Sort of.

BILL: What's a sort-of boyfriend?

BETTY: My husband.

BILL: Ah-ha. *(Bell.)* You weren't waiting for somebody when I came in, were you?

BETTY: Actually I was.

BILL: Oh. Boyfriend?

BETTY: Sort of.

BILL: What's a sort-of boyfriend?

BETTY: We were meeting here to break up.

BILL: Mm-hm . . . *(Bell.)* What's a sort-of boyfriend?

BETTY: My lover. Here she comes right now! *(Bell.)*

BILL: You weren't waiting for somebody when I came in, were you?

BETTY: No, just reading.

BILL: Sort of a sad occupation for a Friday night, isn't it? Reading here, all by yourself?

BETTY: Do you think so?

BILL: Well sure. I mean, what's a good-looking woman like you doing out alone on a Friday night?

BETTY: Trying to keep away from lines like that.

BILL: No, listen—*(Bell.)* You weren't waiting for somebody when I came in, were you?

BETTY: No, just reading.

BILL: Sort of a sad occupation for a Friday night, isn't it? Reading here all by yourself?

BETTY: I guess it is, in a way.

BILL: What's a good-looking women like you doing out alone on a Friday night anyway? No offense, but . . .

BETTY: I'm out alone on a Friday night for the first time in a very long time.

BILL: Oh.

BETTY: You see, I just recently ended a relationship.

BILL: Oh.

BETTY: Of rather long standing.

BILL: I'm sorry. *(Small pause.)* Well listen, since reading by yourself *is* such a sad occupation for a Friday night, would you like to go elsewhere?

BETTY: No . . .

BILL: Do something else?

BETTY: No thanks.

BILL: I was headed out to the movies in a while anyway.

BETTY: I don't think so.

BILL: Big chance to let Faulkner catch his breath. All those long sentences get him pretty tired.

BETTY: Thanks anyway.

BILL: Okay.

BETTY: I appreciate the invitation.

BILL: Sure thing. *(Bell.)* You weren't waiting for somebody when I came in, were you?

BETTY: No, just reading.

BILL: Sort of a sad occupation for a Friday night, isn't it? Reading here all by yourself?

BETTY: I guess I was trying to think of it as existentially romantic. You know—cappuccino, great literature, rainy night . . .

BILL: That only works in Paris. We *could* hop the late plane to Paris. Get on a Concorde. Find a café . . .

BETTY: I'm a little short on planefare tonight.

BILL: Darn it, so am I.

BETTY: To tell you the truth, I was headed to the movies after I finished this section. Would you like to come along? Since you can't locate a waiter?

BILL: That's a very nice offer, but . . .

BETTY: Uh-huh. Girlfriend?

BILL: Two, actually. One of them's pregnant, and Stephanie— *(Bell.)*

BETTY: Girlfriend?

BILL: No, I don't have a girlfriend. Not if you mean the castrating bitch I dumped last night. *(Bell.)*

BETTY: Girlfriend?

BILL: Sort of. Sort of.

BETTY: What's a sort-of girlfriend?

BILL: My mother. *(Bell.)* I just ended a relationship, actually.

BETTY: Oh.

BILL: Of rather long standing.

BETTY: I'm sorry to hear it.

BILL: This is my first night out alone in a long time. I feel a little bit at sea, to tell you the truth.

BETTY: So you didn't stop to talk because you're a Moonie, or you have some weird political affiliation—?

BILL: Nope. Straight-down-the-ticket Republican. *(Bell.)* Straight-down-the-ticket Democrat. *(Bell.)* Can I tell you something about politics? *(Bell.)* I like to think of myself as a citizen of the universe. *(Bell.)* I'm unaffiliated.

BETTY: That's a relief. So am I.

BILL: I vote my beliefs.

BETTY: Labels are not important.

BILL: Labels are not important, exactly. Like me, for example. I mean, what does it matter if I had a two-point at—*(bell)*—three-point at—*(bell)*—four-point at college, or if I did come from Pittsburgh—*(bell)*—Cleveland—*(bell)*—Westchester County?

BETTY: Sure.

BILL: I believe that a man is what he is. *(Bell.)* A person is what he is. *(Bell.)* A person is . . . what they are.

BETTY: I think so too.

BILL: So what if I admire Trotsky? *(Bell.)* So what if I once had a total-body liposuction? *(Bell.)* So what if I don't have a penis? *(Bell.)* So what if I once spent a year in the Peace Corps? I was acting on my convictions.

BETTY: Sure.

BILL: You can't just hang a sign on a person.

BETTY: Absolutely. I'll bet you're a Scorpio. *(Many bells ring.)* Listen, I was headed to the movies after I finished this section. Would you like to come along?

BILL: That sounds like fun. What's playing?

BETTY: A couple of the really early Woody Allen movies.

BILL: Oh.

BETTY: Don't you like Woody Allen?

BILL: Sure. I like Woody Allen.

BETTY: But you're not crazy about Woody Allen.

BILL: Those early ones kind of get on my nerves.

BETTY: Uh-huh. *(Bell.)*

BILL: —*(simultaneously)*—   BETTY:
Y'know I was   I was thinking
headed to the—   about—

BILL: I'm sorry.

BETTY: No, go ahead.

BILL: I was going to say that I was headed to the movies in a little while, and . . .

BETTY: So was I.

BILL: The Woody Allen festival?

BETTY: Just up the street.

BILL: Do you like the early ones?

BETTY: I think anybody who doesn't ought to be run off the planet.

BILL: How many times have you seen *Bananas*?

BETTY: Eight times.

BILL: Twelve. So are you still interested? *(Long pause.)*

BETTY: Do you like Entenmann's crumb cake . . . ?

BILL: Last night I went out at two in the morning to get one. *(Small pause.)* Did you have an Etch-a-Sketch as a child?

BETTY: Yes! And do you like Brussels sprouts? *(Small pause.)*

BILL: I think they're gross.

BETTY: They *are* gross!

BILL: Do you still believe in marriage in spite of current sentiments against it?

BETTY: Yes.

BILL: And children?

BETTY: Three of them.

BILL: Two girls and a boy.

BETTY: Harvard, Vassar and Brown.

BILL: And will you love me?

BETTY: Yes.

BILL: And cherish me forever?

BETTY: Yes.

BILL: Do you still want to go to the movies?

BETTY: Sure thing.

BILL & BETTY *(together)*:   *Waiter!*

(Blackout.)

FUN

HOWARD KORDER

FUN was originally presented as part of the Eleventh Annual Humana Festival of New American Plays at the Actors Theatre of Louisville (Jon Jory, Producing Director) in Louisville, Kentucky, from February 18 through March 22, 1987. It was directed by Jon Jory; the set designer was Paul Owen; the lighting designer was Ralph Dressler; the sound designer was David A. Strang; the property master was Charles J. Kilian, Jr.; and the fight director was Steve Rankin. The cast, in order of appearance, was as follows:

CASPER	Doug Hutchison
DENNY	Tim Ransom
SECURITY GUARD	Nick Bakay
WAITRESS	Lili Taylor
MATTHEW	David Bottrell
LARRY	Dana Mills
WORKMAN	Andy Backer

Characters
DENNY, a fifteen-year-old boy
CASPER, his friend, also fifteen
LARRY, a salesman, late twenties
MATTHEW, a movie usher, nineteen
WAITRESS, fourteen
WORKMAN, forties
SECURITY GUARD

Time
The present. An evening in spring.

Place
The outskirts of Roberson City, an industrial town in the northeastern United States

A Note on the Set
The set should be suggestive of the various locales mentioned in the text, conveyed through minimal means. The overall impression of the design should be that of a contemporary industrial landscape.

A Note on the Characters

In both dress and manner, Denny and Casper should present the image of two normal teenagers, not hardcore punks, heavy metal freaks, or confirmed sociopaths.

■ ■

Scene One

Casper sitting on the front steps of a house with a boom box playing. Denny enters.

DENNY: Dickwad.

CASPER: Hey Denny.

DENNY: How's it going.

CASPER: I don't know.

DENNY: Uh-huh.

CASPER: You know.

DENNY: Right.

CASPER: How's it going with you.

DENNY: Sucks.

CASPER: Yeah.

DENNY *(indicating box)*:   Motley *Crüe*.

CASPER: The best.

DENNY: New album?

CASPER: No. *(Pause.)*

DENNY: So what I miss today?

CASPER: Nothing. Exponents.

DENNY: Shit.

CASPER: Little numbers.

DENNY: You take notes?

CASPER: Uh-huh.

DENNY: Thanks.

CASPER: Sure.

DENNY: Thursday, you know? I just couldn't get into it. My head hurt all morning.

CASPER: Yeah, smoke's coming in off the Monsanto plant. *(Pause.)*

DENNY: So you doing anything?

CASPER: Nope.

DENNY: Wanna do something?

CASPER: I don't know. My mom's out, I'm supposed to hang around.

DENNY: Where's she out?

CASPER: On a date.

DENNY: Same dude?

CASPER: No. *(Pause.)* What were you gonna do?

DENNY: Have some fun. I don't know.

CASPER: Well . . .

DENNY: You wanna?

CASPER: Sure, I don't know. I gotta be back soon.

DENNY: Okay, so let's go. *(They exit.)*

Scene Two

The railing of a bridge. Roar of cars. Casper with boom box.

DENNY: This sucks.

CASPER: Yeah.

DENNY: Shit people throw outta cars . . .

CASPER: It's disgusting.

DENNY: PICK UP YOUR FUCKING GARBAGE, ASSHOLES!

CASPER: WOULD YOU DO THAT AT HOME? *(Pause.)* They got the windows up.

DENNY: They got the A.C. on. The *cruise* control . . . they got dinner on the table . . . *(Mimicking a driver.)* "Thank God *we* don't have to *live* here . . ."

CASPER: Yup.

DENNY: Fuck *them*. *(Pause. He looks over the railing.)* I mean lookit that *water*.

CASPER: Okay.

DENNY: You ever look what's in this river?

CASPER: No.

DENNY: You know what I *found* in there once?

CASPER: What.

DENNY: A finger.

CASPER: No.

DENNY: Yes.

CASPER: No way.

DENNY: I did.

CASPER: A whole finger?

DENNY: Most of a finger.

CASPER: Did you pick it *up*?

DENNY: Uh-huh.

CASPER: You didn't.

DENNY: Fuck you, I did.

CASPER: No way.

DENNY: Don't believe me.

CASPER: Whose finger was it?

DENNY: Jesus, the fuck would I know? It wasn't *autographed*.

CASPER: Okay.

DENNY: Some *dead* guy. Some guy jumped off drowned himself in the river.

CASPER: If he drowned himself, how'd he cut off his finger?

DENNY: How?

CASPER: Yeah. *(Pause.)*

DENNY: Casper, watch out.

CASPER: What?

DENNY: There's something on your neck.

CASPER: Where, get it off!

DENNY: Right . . . there. *(He flicks Casper's Adam's apple with his finger.)*

CASPER: Ah, shit!

DENNY: You wad.

CASPER: That hurt.

DENNY: *Supposed* to hurt.

CASPER: You could of killed me. You could of broke my wind thing.

DENNY: You'd be dead.

CASPER: I *would* be.

DENNY: Then I could just dump you in the water.

CASPER *(feeling his throat)*: I'm practically numb.

DENNY: Bye-bye. *(He picks up a stone and throws it in the water. Casper does the same. Pause.)*

CASPER: How far you think we could get on this river?

DENNY: *On* it.

CASPER: Like a raft or something.

DENNY: Who are you, Huckleberry Pinhead?

CASPER: I'm just saying.

DENNY: Jeez, bring your camera, you can get great pictures of old refrigerators. *(Pause.)* So what do you want to do?

CASPER: I don't know. You wanna go to the mall?

DENNY: God, no.

CASPER: You wanna find a party?

DENNY: Who's having a party?

CASPER: I don't know, you wanna see a movie?

DENNY: *What* movie? *(Pause.)*

CASPER: You wanna find some girls? *(Pause.)*

DENNY: Let's check out the mall.

Scene Three

The Mall. A bench with a large potted plant behind it. Muzak playing in the background.

DENNY: This is fucking *stupid*.

CASPER: Yeah.

DENNY: I hate this place. You know how much time we spend in this place?

CASPER: A lot of time.

DENNY: It's like we grew up in here.

CASPER: They got everything, all right. Anything you can think of, it's right in front of you.

DENNY: People dressing themselves up to look at *shoes*. You count the number of shoe stores in this mall? Lookit Thom McCann, and Kinney, and Florsheim, Fayva, National Shoes. . . .

CASPER: Sears.

DENNY: Shoe stores, you hole.

CASPER: They sell shoes at Sears. I got my Ponys there.

DENNY: You know who shops at Sears? Zombies in plaid shirts. They go in there and price band saws.

CASPER: My mother shops at Sears.

DENNY: Mine does too. Is that tasteless or what? She wants me to wear that shirt, I told her to go fuck herself.

CASPER: You told her that?

DENNY: I would. I will. Her and my father. Right before I take off.

CASPER: Where you going? *(Pause.)*

DENNY: Check out that car.

CASPER: Excellent car.

DENNY: Gimme *that* car, man.

CASPER: Is that a Camaro?

DENNY: Looks it. '88 Camaro.

CASPER: How'd they get it in here?

DENNY: They *drive* it.

CASPER: Camaro's a bitching car.

DENNY: Camaro's the best. *(Pause.)* Know what we could do?

CASPER: What?

DENNY: Get in that car, jump start her, tear ass off that platform all through this mall. Mow these fuckers down in their Hush Puppies.

CASPER: Except the girls.

DENNY: Crash it through the plate glass, man, bam through the GNC, bam through the Hickory Farms—

CASPER: Smoked *cheese*—

DENNY: Bam through the Radio Shack, the fucking Walden-books—

CASPER: Bam!

DENNY: Then we ditch it in the fountain, right, we break some forty-fours outta Monty Wards, a couple of hunting knives, ammo, and we head upstairs, way up in the mall where no one ever goes, and there is this dude up there, okay, this fat asshole in a control room, all these screens and shit, and he runs the place, he plays all the Muzak and makes the people walk around and smile and buy things only they don't even *know* it, and we shove him down on the counter and blow his fucking brains out.

CASPER (*making machine-gun noises*):   Chaka-chaka-chaka!

DENNY: *Except* when we turn around, da-dum . . . there's like eighty security guards standing there with sawed-offs. (*He makes the sound of a safety clicking.*)

CASPER: We got out the window!

DENNY: There's no *window*.

CASPER: Trap door?

DENNY: Forget it.

CASPER: Okay, but behind *them*—

DENNY: Uh-uh. We are on our own. (*Pause.*)

CASPER: What happens?

DENNY: They open up and spray us across the wall. (*Pause.*)

CASPER (*solemnly*):   In slo-mo.

DENNY: *Definitely* slo-mo. (*They do their slo-mo death scenes with sound effects. Pause.*)

CASPER (*tapping a plant leaf above his head*):   This is rubber or something, you know? All this time I thought it was real, but it's not. (*Pause. A security guard walks by and looks at them.*)

GUARD: Evening.

DENNY: How's it going.

GUARD: It's going. (*He stands there for a moment, then continues on. Denny and Casper watch him go.*)

DENNY: Let's lose this place.

CASPER: Where do you wanna go?

DENNY: I don't know.

CASPER: Okay.

Scene Four

A "Big Boy's" restaurant. Denny and Casper in a booth with menus.

CASPER: What are you gonna have, Denny?

DENNY: I don't know. Something that's less than three dollars 'cause that's all I got.

CASPER: I'm gonna have a hamburger.

DENNY: So *have* a hamburger.

CASPER: Only I had a hamburger for lunch.

DENNY: So *don't* have a hamburger. Jesus.

CASPER: But that was a Whopper. This is a Big Boy's burger. I don't know.

DENNY: It's the same cow, wad. *(Pause.)*

CASPER: What are you gonna have, Denny?

DENNY: *Ice* cream, okay? A sundae or something.

CASPER: No, I don't think I want that. *(The waitress, high school age, enters.)*

WAITRESS: Hi.

DENNY: How ya doing.

WAITRESS: Okay.

DENNY: Okay.

WAITRESS: You ready to order?

CASPER: You go first, Denny.

DENNY: Yeah, gimme a chocolate sundae.

WAITRESS: What kind of ice cream?

DENNY: Chocolate.

WAITRESS: You want hot fudge?

DENNY: Yeah, chocolate fudge.

WAITRESS: Sprinkles?

DENNY: Chocolate. Chocolate everything. Make the whole thing chocolate.

WAITRESS: You're into chocolate, huh?

DENNY: I like it, I wouldn't kill somebody for it.

WAITRESS: I would.

DENNY: Yeah?

WAITRESS: When you eat chocolate you're supposed to feel like you're in love.

DENNY: No kidding.

WAITRESS: I read that somewhere.

DENNY: Love is like chocolate, huh?

WAITRESS: That's what it said.

DENNY: Well. Hmm. Yeah. *(Pause. To Casper.)* You know what you want?

CASPER: Ah . . . oh boy . . . gimme, um, a stack of blueberry—no, no, give me a hamburger. A well-done burger.

WAITRESS: You want that on a platter?

CASPER: Yeah, actually, are the burgers good here?

WAITRESS: They're okay.

CASPER: Compared like to Burger King?

WAITRESS: Well, they're okay. Is that what you want?

CASPER: Yeah, why not. Gimme that. No, actually, miss, can I have a sundae?

WAITRESS: Chocolate?

CASPER: Okay, yeah, chocolate.

WAITRESS: You sure?

CASPER *(looking at menu)*: Actually—

DENNY *(taking the menu away from Casper)*: He's sure. He's very very sure.

WAITRESS: Okay, two sundaes. *(She exits. Denny looks at Casper.)*

CASPER: What? Should I get something else? *(Denny turns away. Pause. Casper drinks his water and begins chewing the ice cubes.)* Who you looking at, Denny?

DENNY: Nobody.

CASPER: You looking at those guys from Saunders? I don't like those guys.

DENNY: I'm not looking at anyone.

CASPER: Remember we bought those Iron Maiden tee's, and they ripped us off right at the bus stop?

DENNY: Uh-huh.

CASPER: I never even got to *wear* mine. How come that stuff always happens to us?

DENNY: Two kinds of people, Casper.

CASPER: Yeah? Which are we?

DENNY: The other ones. *(He looks away again. Casper chews his ice cubes. Pause.)*

CASPER: So ask her out, Denny.

DENNY: Ask who.

CASPER: The waitress.

DENNY: Get fucked.

CASPER: I don't know, she's kinda cute.

DENNY: You're cute. *(Pause.)* You think I should?

CASPER: I don't know.

DENNY: You think she's cute?

CASPER: She's kinda cute.

DENNY: You think I should ask her out *tonight*?

CASPER: I don't mind.

DENNY: Where you think I should take her?

CASPER: You could take her to a restaurant.

DENNY: She's *in* a restaurant, you bone.

CASPER: You could go miniature golf.

DENNY: Geez, won't *that* be fun.

CASPER: I don't know, you could go walk on the bridge.

DENNY: What are we gonna do on a bridge?

CASPER: I'm just saying you could go for a walk and wind up on the bridge. *(Pause.)*

DENNY: Yeah, we could do that. We could go to the bridge.

CASPER: I don't mind, Denny.

DENNY: Yeah, that would be pretty decent.

CASPER: I gotta get back anyway. (*Waitress enters with two sundaes.*)

WAITRESS: Here we go.

CASPER: Wow, check this out.

WAITRESS: You want chocolate, you get chocolate.

DENNY: Great.

WAITRESS: Listen, I gave you nuts, okay? I didn't charge you so don't tell anybody.

DENNY: Okay.

WAITRESS: I mean I just felt like it.

DENNY: Thanks. (*She shrugs. Pause.*) So . . .

WAITRESS: Yeah.

DENNY: You like working here or what?

WAITRESS: It's okay.

DENNY: They make you buy that uniform?

WAITRESS: No, they give it to you.

DENNY: That's good.

WAITRESS: Yeah. (*Pause.*)

DENNY: Umm, how long do you usually work?

WAITRESS: Another half hour. Ten-thirty.

DENNY: No kidding.

WAITRESS: Yeah.

DENNY: Hmm. (*Pause. She puts down the check.*)

WAITRESS: Have a good night.

DENNY: Oh yeah, you too. (*She exits. Casper begins eating his sundae. Denny picks up his spoon and sticks it in the ice cream.*) Let's go. This place fucking sucks. (*He stands, throws some money down, and leaves. Casper watches him and follows after a moment.*)

Scene Five

The bridge. Roar of cars. Casper throwing bits of junk into the river. Denny carving on rail post with a house key. Boom box playing.

CASPER: I don't know, I'm not doing so good in math. Actually I think he's gonna clip me.

DENNY: Fuck him.

CASPER: Yeah. But it's cool 'cause I'm thinking I could go to trade school.

DENNY: Toolbox U.

CASPER: Yeah, I could learn to do something with my hands. (*Denny snorts.*) That's what they teach!

DENNY: "Boys, today we're going to show how to *do* something with your *hands*."

CASPER: It's only an idea. I gotta do something, don't I? I mean
     . . . I don't know. I don't think much is going to happen to me.
     It's just a feeling I get.

DENNY: Break outta this dump.

CASPER: Yeah, I could always join the army.

DENNY: Right.

CASPER: You wanna join the army, Denny?

DENNY: Sure, we're in the army.

CASPER: We'd fight, wouldn't we? I'd fight, I would. Right?

DENNY: Jesus, Casper, talk about something important.

CASPER: Like what? *(Denny says nothing.)* What you doing, Denny?

DENNY: Carving.

CASPER: What's that, a Hitler thing?

DENNY: It's called a swastika.

CASPER: How come you're doing that?

DENNY: 'Cause I feel like it, Goldberg.

CASPER: My name's not Goldberg.

DENNY: Put another tape on, why dontcha.

CASPER: I don't got another.

DENNY: Then turn on the *radio*.

CASPER: The antenna's broke.

DENNY: Let's go riding.

CASPER: How we gonna—

DENNY: Oh, let's just get wasted!

CASPER: You got proof? I don't think— *(Denny leaps up and screams
     wordlessly over the bridge. Pause.)* You okay, Denny? *(Pause.)*
     Denny? *(Pause.)*

DENNY: Do you have any shit on you?

CASPER: Geez, I don't.

DENNY: I am going to score some shit.

CASPER: How?

DENNY: I'm going to find a *guy* he owes me a *favor* and we're going
     to fuck ourselves up. That's what I *want*. That's what's going to
     happen. (He starts off.)

CASPER: Where we going, Denny?

DENNY *(exiting)*:   We're going to the *mall*. (Casper takes the boom box
     and follows him off.)

Scene Six

*A parking lot outside the movie theater in the mall. A dumpster sits
overflowing with garbage, including several large plastic bags of popcorn.
Casper, with boom box, rests on one of the bags. Denny leans against the
dumpster.*

CASPER (*looking out; after a moment*):   You know, the parking lot looks really beautiful this time of night. I mean without a lot of cars all over it.

DENNY: It's a poem, Casper.

CASPER: Yeah, I guess so. (*Pause.*) What are we waiting for, Denny?

DENNY: He's gonna come around and meet us.

CASPER: You got any money? I only got like eighty cents.

DENNY: It's cool, I *know* this guy. He owes me. (*Casper starts eating popcorn out of a torn bag.*) Don't eat that, it's garbage.

CASPER: It's just popcorn. You can't do anything to popcorn. (*He finds a discarded movie poster.*) Hey, Rambo, remember Rambo? Check out this gun, Denny. Man, that is *wicked.* (*Imitating a bazooka.*) Ba-doom! Suck on this, slope, we're coming back!

DENNY: You're the slope.

CASPER: Ba-doom! (*Denny picks up a bag of popcorn and throws it at Casper. He misses.*)

CASPER: Missed me! You missed you— (*Denny clubs him with another bag.*)

DENNY: Stop acting like a child. (*He drops the bag on Casper's head. Casper "dies." Matthew enters in usher's uniform.*)

MATTHEW: Yo, man, don't fuck around with the popcorn.

DENNY: It's in the garbage.

MATTHEW: No, no, my buddy's coming with a van, we're gonna sell it to this porno movie on South Washington. (*He picks some popcorn off the ground.*) That look clean?

DENNY: Yeah. (*Matthew puts it in the bag.*) Matt, you know Casper?

MATTHEW: The friendly ghost. (*Casper laughs.*) How's your brother?

CASPER: I don't have a brother.

MATTHEW: How's your sister?

CASPER: She's okay.

MATTHEW: Oh yeah? (*He laughs. Pause. Casper laughs.*) Pretty funny, huh? Listen, that's not for free. (*He takes the poster out of Casper's hand. Pause.*)

DENNY: So, Matty.

MATTHEW: Yo.

DENNY: How's college?

MATTHEW: I'm outta there, man.

DENNY: Seriously?

MATTHEW: Waste of my abilities. I'm into venture capital now. Very into the idea of thirty, forty million bucks, my own island, lots of barbed wire, babes, armored Mercedes fleet. I wanna get myself situated before the dark ages start blowing back. Won't be too hard. I got a good growth plan.

DENNY: No kidding.

MATTHEW: Yeah, I'll have that in ten years, tops.

DENNY: That's really excellent.

MATTHEW: It *is* excellent. What can I do for you?

DENNY: We're looking for some shit.

MATTHEW: You check the toilet? *(He looks as Casper. Casper laughs.)* This man has a sick sense of humor. *(Casper laughs again.)*

DENNY: Yeah, well, I thought you could help us out.

MATTHEW: Uh-huh, okay. *(Pause.)*

DENNY: Remember Christmas, I did some drops with you, you said come by I wanted anything.

MATTHEW: Huh.

DENNY: Yeah, up in Port Dickinson, I sat in the car.

MATTHEW: *Christmas.*

DENNY: Yeah. *(Pause.)*

MATTHEW: Okay, so what can I sell you?

DENNY: Well—

MATTHEW: You wanna check out some sess? You want a little marching powder?

DENNY: I thought maybe you could help us out here.

MATTHEW: How you want me to help you? Yo, Friendly, don't sit on the bags. Hmmm? *(Pause.)* You want me to give it to you?

DENNY: You said at Christmas—

MATTHEW: I didn't say I'd *give* it to you. I don't hand out free samples. I'd said I'd sell to you, I don't remember saying anything to you. Most guys, a fifteen-year-old-kid—

DENNY: I'm not fifteen—

MATTHEW: I'm developing a select clientele, you're lucky I—

DENNY: We went up to Port *Dick*inson—

MATTHEW: I don't deal up there.

DENNY: Ah, *shit,* man—

MATTHEW: *Hey.* You *control* yourself. People are watching a *movie* in there, they don't want to hear about your problems. The world does *not* turn around your navel. No. No, I'm sorry. *(He goes. Silence.)*

CASPER: Denny, you wanna go home? It's getting late, maybe it's time. *(Denny attacks the dumpster, flinging garbage out of it with his hands. Matthew reenters.)*

MATTHEW: YO! *(He grabs Denny and bangs him against the dumpster, holding him there.)* The *fuck* is wrong with you? Where'd you grow up, in a cage? Kids, fucking kids, waste my time you don't know *what's* going on. You don't do business this way. Never. This is not how you *conduct* yourself. *(He smacks Denny in the head with the back of his hand.)*

MANAGER *(offstage)*: Pauling!

MATTHEW: Yes sir!

MANAGER *(off)*: You wanna let the people outta the theater?

MATTHEW: Yeah, okay, sorry! *(Pause. To Denny.)* You're furious, right? Look at me. Furious little kid. You gotta do something about that. You can't go spilling it all over the place. Keep it behind your eyes and don't let anyone see it. You know how a killer thinks?

DENNY: How?

MATTHEW: He doesn't get excited. *(Pause.)* All right. I got some dealing up on Chenango later, you meet me there. Ten-twelve Chenango, across from the sausage factory. Maybe I'll have something for you, maybe I won't. I can't make promises. *(Pause.)*

DENNY: When.

MATTHEW: A couple hours. Two, three hours.

DENNY: Okay.

MATTHEW: You wanna check out a movie?

DENNY: Huh?

MATTHEW: A movie, I'll walk you in. There's a midnight show.

DENNY: What's playing?

MATTHEW: E.T. II.

DENNY: What else?

MATTHEW: That's it. All six movies.

DENNY: No.

MATTHEW: Suit yourself. Hey, give me your radio. Come on.

CASPER: Why?

MATTHEW: Just give it. An exchange. Let's make a deal here. *(Casper does not move.)* No, okay, it's a favor. Overhead. Remember that. *(He starts to exit. He stops and turns to Denny.)* How's your father doing.

DENNY: Looking for a job. Waxing the car a lot. Drinking without a glass.

MATTHEW: Huh.

DENNY: Yup.

MATTHEW: Yeah, my dad was talking about him. Tell him . . . he says hello.

DENNY: Right.

MATTHEW: Okay, catch you later. *(Matthew exits. Pause.)*

CASPER: I don't know, I kinda liked the first E.T.

DENNY: It was a fucking *puppet*, you wad.

CASPER: Yeah, I guess. *(Pause.)* What do you wanna do now, Denny?

DENNY: Go meet Matty.

CASPER: What do you wanna do in the meantime? I got eighty cents. You wanna do the Arcade?

DENNY: No.

CASPER: You wanna hang out at the Trailways station?

DENNY: Bunch of alkies waiting for a morning bus.

CASPER: You wanna go to Food World? It's open twenty-four hours. We could look at the magazines. *(Denny just stares at him.)* What do you wanna do?

DENNY: I want . . . to blow up a freight train. I want to hijack a jet. I want Madonna to jump off a poster and come sit on my dick. I want them to drop every bomb there is and be the only person left alive. I wanna be famous, and rich, and I want everybody to be scared of me. That's what I wanna do. *(Pause.)*

CASPER: Okay, but what do you wanna do *now*?

Scene Seven

A small concrete patio behind a house. Chinese lanterns overhead on a string. Card table piled with party rubbish: bottles, potato chip bags, cups, etc. A folding chaise longue, draped by a plastic tablecloth. Portable phonograph with a stuck record playing at low volume. A child's "Big Wheel" tricycle off to one side. Denny and Casper standing center.

CASPER: You sure this is it, Denny?

DENNY: It's the address he said.

CASPER: There's nobody here. Must of been a party or something, huh?

DENNY: No, it's a car wash. What time did they kick us out of the Food World?

CASPER: I don't know. One-thirty. Around one-thirty. Actually it was more like two.

DENNY: Bastards. Who wants to watch some pimply geek stack oranges anyway. *(He begins looking around.)*

CASPER: Maybe we shouldn't be in this guy's back yard.

DENNY: What are you scared of?

CASPER: I'm not scared.

DENNY: Then don't be. *(He looks at record on the phonograph.)* Jesus, "Frampton Comes Alive." *(He shuts it off.)* Let's have a drink.

CASPER: What if somebody sees us?

DENNY: We're here on business, drain. We got an appointment. Hey, Cutty my man! *(He picks up a bottle from the table, takes a long swig, and offers it to Casper. Casper shakes his head.)* Come on, don't pussy out. *(Casper takes the bottle without drinking. He sits on the tricycle and slowly pedals it backward and forward.)*

CASPER: If we join the army, Denny, you think we'd have to—

DENNY *(listening to something)*: Quiet! *(Sound of a woman's laughter from offstage, followed by a man murmuring indistinctly. Laughter from both.)*

CASPER: Where are they? *(Denny points toward the house.)* Can they see us?

DENNY: They're not looking at us. *(More laughter, voices.)*

CASPER: Well, *they're* having fun.

DENNY: You know what they're doing?

CASPER: What?

DENNY: What do you *think*? *(Pause.)*

CASPER: You think so?

DENNY: I bet they're down on the floor.

CASPER: Yeah?

DENNY: With a . . . with a *ski jacket* under her ass . . . and her . . .

CASPER: Her *legs* . . .

DENNY: . . . Her legs are open, and she's saying *please* . . .

CASPER: She's not . . .

DENNY: Please give it to me, *please* . . .

CASPER: She's *begging* him . . .

DENNY: No panties, and he's looking down at her . . .

CASPER: Oh God . . .

DENNY: And he says . . .

CASPER: He says . . .

DENNY: He says . . . *(Pause.)* Ah, shit. Who knows what he says. *(He walks over to the bottle and drinks. More laughter.)* Shut the fuck up.

CASPER: Maybe it's just the TV.

DENNY *(indicating tricycle)*: Doing that with kids around. That is disgusting.

CASPER: It is.

DENNY: A little kid sees something like that, he doesn't know what to think. He's fucked up for life. And then you know what, *he* has kids . . .

CASPER: And they're fucked up.

DENNY: And their kids . . .

CASPER: And *those* kids . . .

DENNY: Then *they* . . .

CASPER: It's like a disease.

DENNY: It's like a movie.

CASPER: It's a mess.

DENNY: They probably *are* fucking on the floor. (*More laughter. Pause.*)

CASPER: I don't think he's coming, Denny. Or else he already did. Or something.

DENNY: Yah. (*A man's voice comes from beneath the cover of the lawn chair.*)

VOICE: Jesus Christ, who shut off the *music*? (*Denny and Casper look at each other. Denny pulls the tablecloth off the chair. Underneath is Larry, dressed in a rumpled suit and tie.*)

DENNY: Hi . . . ah, we . . . we were supposed to meet—

LARRY (*as Elmer Fudd*):   Shh. Be verrry quiet, I'm hunting wabbits. (*He gets up, walks to a corner, and starts to urinate.*) This is one of the greatest pleasures known to man. I'm not lying. (*He buttons his fly and turns around.*) Am I right? Now don't *brood* about it.

DENNY: Sure.

LARRY: A *great* pleasure. Pleasure everywhere you look. That's life in a nutshell. And I think you'd probably agree with me, yes? Am I talking English? Hmmm? Am I?

DENNY: Uh-huh.

LARRY: Then why are you *looking* at me like that? Why are you— okay, okay, I know. I've been a bad boy. A bad, bad . . . (*Pause.*) Where is everybody?

DENNY: They're gone.

LARRY: Gone . . . where? Home? Did they go home? They can't go home. You can't go home again, didn't they prove that? I mean, scientifically? Look, I'm sorry, don't listen to anything I say. Just tell me—no, but listen to this—did she go? She didn't. She did. Did she?

DENNY: Who?

LARRY: Who, who I'm *saying*. Sandy. Sandra. The beautiful . . . (*Pause.*) She's gone.

DENNY: Yeah.

LARRY: All right. All right. I'm . . . sure. (*Pause.*)

DENNY: She left with some guy.

LARRY: Who?

DENNY: Just some guy.

LARRY: *Curse* him. *Kill* him. *Goddamn* that guy. Yeah. (*Pause.*) Hey. Hey, let's have fun. Let's all just do that. Simon says . . . open up that bottle there. Come on. (*Denny opens a bottle of Scotch.*) Simon says . . . pour three cups. (*Denny pours three paper cups.*) Now drink. (*He drinks his cup.*)

DENNY: You didn't say Simon says.

LARRY: Listen, we're all friends here. Drink up. WAIT. How old are you guys?

DENNY: Nineteen.

LARRY: Nineteen. Great age. Beautiful age.

DENNY: Yeah, I'm nineteen, he's eighteen.

LARRY: Eighteen, a great age.

DENNY: The best.

LARRY: He doesn't *say* much.

DENNY: He likes to think.

LARRY: Who doesn't. What it *is*, man.

CASPER: Hi.

LARRY: So here we *are*, three really *happening* dudes, we're young, we're—*(Pause. He looks at them closely.)* Oh boy, I'm sorry. I can't believe the way I'm acting. Look at you two. Of *course* you are. I can't *believe* it. *(Pause.)* You don't remember me, do you?

DENNY: Ah . . .

LARRY: You don't, you don't! I can't believe it. I remember *you*. You're Michael and you're um . . . Jeffrey.

CASPER: Casper.

LARRY: Casper, sure, sure. *Look* at you guys. You must be what, eighteen, nineteen by now, right?

DENNY: Right.

LARRY: And you don't remember Larry? I'm hurt, I'm hurt!

DENNY: You know, I think . . .

LARRY: Oh, come on, remember me and Sandy? Remember, I used to come around when you guys lived over on, what, Murray Street, geez, must be ten years.

DENNY *(with a look to Casper)*:   Larry, sure.

LARRY: Oh, fellas, your sister, your sister, I can't apologize eno— you *know* me, I wouldn't . . . but God she looked great tonight, she really . . . she left with some guy, you know that?

DENNY: No.

LARRY: She did, some guy. I had a little drinks, I admit it, but I mean Sandy, ten years, I just *remembered* . . . *(Pause.)* Yeah. Little Mikey and Jeffy. Little kids. How come you guys grew up, and I'm not any older?

DENNY: I don't know, Larry, it's hard to say.

LARRY: It is, it's hard. It really is. *(Pause.)* Well, fuck it. Let's have some fun. Let's just do that.

DENNY: Okay.

LARRY: I mean what are we here for anyway. The night *beckons*. It's just out there beckoning away, huh? What do you wanna do?

DENNY: Us three?

LARRY: Damn straight. These bozos don't know the meaning of party. What do you want?

DENNY: Ah . . .

LARRY: You name it. Tell me. *Anything* you want to do.

DENNY: Anything?

LARRY: Anything. My little *buddies*. *(Pause.)*

DENNY: Well, frankly, Larry . . . we'd like to get laid.

LARRY: I also would like to get laid.

DENNY: So would we.

LARRY: The question is, how low are your standards?

DENNY: Pretty low.

LARRY: You guys been to Watsonville lately?

DENNY: Yeah.

LARRY: You been on Nanticoke Avenue?

DENNY: Uh-huh.

LARRY: You been in the whorehouse behind the Power Test?

DENNY: No.

LARRY: Then, gentlemen, Paradise awaits.

DENNY: Only we don't got any money, Larry.

LARRY: No no. No money. My treat. Mikey and Jeffy. Little buddies. You just tell Sandra I . . . you say your main man Larry . . .
you tell her . . . you just let her know.

DENNY: Okay.

LARRY: So . . . LET'S DO IT! *(He beats his chest, Tarzan-like, grabs
a bottle, and runs off. Denny starts to follow.)*

CASPER: Denny, I—

DENNY: Shut up. We're finally gonna have some *fun*! *(He exits.
Casper gets his boom box and follows.)*

Scene Eight

*Larry's car. Casper in back. Denny in front with Larry, who is driving
very fast. The opening chords of Springsteen's "Born to Run" boom out of
the car speakers.*

LARRY: BROOOO-OOCE! *(He sings along for a few lines, getting the
words wrong. He takes a drink from the bottle and passes it to Denny.)*
This is GREAT. Isn't it? Isn't this just GREAT? Gimme a car,
man! Gimme a *road!* (*Sticking his head out the window.*) Ba-
ROOOOOO-OOCE!

DENNY: Nice car, Larry.

LARRY: Isn't it? Isn't it GREAT? It's the greatest car! I *live* in this
car. I mean I *sleep* in motels but I live in *this car*. And it's not
even mine! It isn't! They *give* it to me! For my *job!* I could wreck
it if I want! Just squash it flat! *(He laughs and takes his hands off
the wheel.)* BROOO-OOCE! *(He puts his hands back. Pause.)* It's a
great country, fellas. Isn't it a great country?

DENNY: The greatest, Larry.

LARRY (*turning the music down slightly*):   No, no, I'm serious. I am.
  You can say what you want about it, but here it is, all of it, it's
  right here. The land . . . the people . . . the *garbage*. Our garbage
  is the best garbage in the world, I don't *care* what they say I love
  it. Now you *been* to California, Mikey.

DENNY: No.

LARRY: Oh, we all have to go to California, we have to! Everybody's
  young in California, it's not like here. There's *nothing* here, it's
  all worn out. I mean . . . you take a guy like me, huh? Right?

DENNY: Yeah.

LARRY: Let's take a guy who— (*He swerves the wheel suddenly.*) Whoa,
  that was a fucking bump, did you see that? You okay there,
  Jeff?

CASPER: I'm fine.

LARRY: All right, a guy who, let's be honest, I had opportunities,
  great opportunities, and I threw them *away*. I had—I did very
  well on my SATs, you know that, very well, the top of the
  percent—*experts* told me things and I just did not listen, because
  I thought . . . I thought I *deserved* . . . well, fuck what I *thought*.
  Here it is, right here. I'm selling industrial tubing out of a rented
  car. Is that a disgrace? Is it?

DENNY: Um . . .

LARRY: I make a lot of money, thank you, I do very well indeed.
  You march in there and turn it around, that's business. And there's
  no reason you can't—(*He swerves again.*) Whoa, sorry, sorry—
  you can't come back home and feel . . . something. Just . . .
  something. What I'm saying is . . . hey, guess how old I am.

DENNY: I don't know, Larry.

LARRY: Guess!

DENNY: You're, ah—

LARRY: No, no, not you. Jeffy, Jeffy!

CASPER: Thirty-five?

LARRY: What? Jesus, no! I'm twenty-nine—twenty-eight. I'm your
  age. Well, not—but you know. Rock and *roll!* Hey, remember I
  took you guys to go-karts, you, me, and Sandy? You were scared
  to get on? Does your sister ever talk about me? So who was that
  guy? No, don't tell me. (*Pause. They drive in silence.*)

DENNY: Where we going, Larry?

LARRY: Huh?

DENNY: We're going to Watsonville, right?

LARRY: Oh, we're gonna have fun.

DENNY: Isn't it the other way? (*Pause.*)

LARRY: Right, yeah . . . Oh, but we're going to the motel first. I need some cash. These ladies don't come cheap. Actually I don't think they come at all. But they fake it pretty good. Huh?

DENNY: Sure.

LARRY: You *know* what I'm saying.

DENNY: Ah, Larry—

LARRY: The sweet spot, boys, it's just like coming home.

DENNY: Larry—

LARRY: Hey, you think they take credit cards? Maybe I could—

CASPER *(covering his face)*:   WATCH OUT!

LARRY: What the— *(He swerves the car violently and slams the brakes. They plunge forward in their seats as the car stops. Silence.)*

DENNY: Jesus Christ.

LARRY: Son of a bitch.

DENNY: You okay?

CASPER: Uh-huh.

LARRY: Who put that asshole behind a wheel?

DENNY: You were on the wrong side of the *road*, Larry.

LARRY: No I wasn't. Was I?

DENNY: You almost got us killed! *(Pause.)*

LARRY: Ah . . . yeah . . . whoo. You know what it is, it's these rented cars. You take your life in your hands, they don't care. I tell you what, let's just, I just need to . . . *(He takes a drink from the bottle.)* Yeah, yeah, I'm just gonna take a second here and get my bearings, and then we'll—okay, I'm fine. I am. Actually I think I was supposed to be in Albany tonight, I don't know why I . . . *(He puts his head down and starts sobbing.)* Oh God . . . what am I doing here . . . my whole life . . . I want to be a baby, that's all . . . I just wanna be a baby. . . . *(He cries some more, then becomes quiet. Pause.)*

DENNY: Larry? You okay? *(He shakes him tentatively. Larry does not stir. Denny leans him against the seat. Larry's head drops back, mouth open.)*

CASPER: Is he dead?

DENNY: He's asleep. Do you believe this guy?

CASPER: He drank too much.

DENNY: He's a fucking *basket* case. No wonder that girl dumped him. God, I don't wanna get old. Yo, wake up! *(No response from Larry.)* Can you drive?

CASPER: I'm not allowed.

DENNY: *Can* you.

CASPER: Not a stick.

DENNY *(turning off the tape deck)*:   What *is* this shit? *(Pause.)*

CASPER: Are we having fun now, Denny? *(Denny pays him no attention. He is staring hard at Larry.)* What you looking at?

DENNY: Nothing much.

CASPER: So? *(Pause.)*

DENNY: You know what we could do?

CASPER: What.

DENNY: We could . . . just . . .

CASPER: What? *(Denny reaches over and puts his hand on Larry's exposed throat. He strokes it gently. He looks at Casper, smiling. Casper laughs briefly. Denny puts his thumb and forefinger over Larry's Adam's apple. He presses it slightly. Larry grunts. He wraps his hand around Larry's throat. Larry grunts again without waking. Reaching forward.)* Okay, Denny—*(Denny slaps him away with his other hand. He increases the pressure for several seconds. Suddenly Larry coughs and wakes. Denny takes his hand away. Larry looks at them, somewhat dazed. Pause.)*

LARRY: What happened?

DENNY: You fell asleep.

LARRY: I did?

DENNY: Yah. *(Pause. Larry clears his throat.)* You still wanna go to the motel?

LARRY: Motel?

DENNY: You said for money.

LARRY: Money, right. No problem. And we're going to . . .

DENNY: Watsonville.

LARRY: Right, Watsonville. *(Remembering.)* Watsonville, yeah! *(Pause.)* What's the car doing in a ditch? *(He looks at them and bursts out laughing. He turns on the tape deck, loud, and floors the pedal. They lurch forward in their seats.)* THIS IS FUCKING GREAT!

Scene Nine

The upper terrace of a motel off the highway. Denny and Casper in front of a door.

DENNY: You sure this is his room?

CASPER: I thought I saw him go up here.

DENNY *(looking along the terrace)*: Christ, this place is built like a *dog* kennel. *(He leans into the door.)* Larry . . . hey, Larry . . . What the fuck is he doing in there?

CASPER: He probably fell asleep.

DENNY: *Larry* . . . Shit, this isn't his room. Go down the office and ask the guy the room he's in.

CASPER: What should I ask him?

DENNY: Larry's fucking room!

CASPER: Larry *who*?

DENNY: Larry the fuck I don't know what his name is! *(Pause.)*

CASPER: There's nobody down there anyway, Denny. It's too late.

DENNY *(pounding on the doorway)*: WAKE UP! *(Pause.)* Where are we?

CASPER: I don't know. Up the Thruway somewhere. I wish I had like another shirt or something. It's getting kind of cold. It's weird, you know, in the daytime it's hot and then—

DENNY: He said he was going to get us *laid*.

CASPER: Yeah.

DENNY: He was gonna take us and he was gonna *pay* for it! He *promised*!

CASPER: Well, that would of been nice.

DENNY: *Nice?* Don't you *want* it?

CASPER: It just didn't work out.

DENNY: No. Shit. He *promised*. We could be getting ourselves blown right now—

CASPER: I don't—

DENNY: We could! Right now by some *whore* with *big* tits. She'd *have* to, whatever we want!

CASPER: No she wouldn't.

DENNY: Bull*shit* she would, it's her job. I'd say go down on me and she'd do it!

CASPER: Come on, stop.

DENNY: Like a fucking *tootsie* pop . . .

CASPER: Oh geez . . .

CASPER: Right on me the whole night! *(Pause.)* Ah, how come I got to feel all this shit when there's nothing I can do about it? I don't wanna *be* like this! I mean why can't I get just ONE FUCK-ING THING? *(Pause.)*

CASPER: We could . . . jerk off.

DENNY: What?

CASPER: You know. Like in the Scouts.

DENNY: Are you sick?

CASPER: There's no one around.

DENNY: Me! I'm around! I don't wanna watch you humping your knuckles!

CASPER: I was only saying.

DENNY: Fucking disgusting! *(Pause.)* All right. But don't look at me.

CASPER: Huh?

DENNY: Don't *look* at me! Turn around. Come on, let's just get it over with. *(They stand with their backs to each other, unzip their pants, and put their hands down their shorts. Denny does not move.*

Casper begins to masturbate and stops. Pause.) What the fuck am I doing?

CASPER: I don't know, Denny. *(They take their hands out of their pants.)* Have you done it yet? With a girl?

DENNY: Yeah.

CASPER: Is it fun?

DENNY: It's a riot. *(Pause.)* Let's get outta here.

CASPER: We don't know where we are.

DENNY: Then it doesn't matter where we go.

CASPER: I guess not. *(Denny looks at Casper. Pause. He takes off his jacket.)*

DENNY: Here. *(He throws him the jacket. Casper catches it. Denny exits.)*

Scene Ten

A concrete pillar beneath a highway overpass, covered with graffiti. Various kinds of junk shored up against the foot of the pillar, including a cushionless sofa, a broken armchair, and a discarded oven. Sound of steady rain mixed with the rumble of tractor-trailers passing by overhead. Denny and Casper stand with wet hair and rain-splattered clothes. They look out at the rain.

CASPER *(after a moment)*:   Well, maybe we *shoulda* walked the other way.

DENNY: Great idea.

CASPER: I just thought that gas station looked familiar . . . I don't know. At least it's dry under here.

DENNY: It's perfect.

CASPER: April showers bring . . . what do they bring, Denny?

DENNY: Earthworms. Earthworms coming up all over the sidewalks. *(Taking off his wet T-shirt.)* Yach! *(He throws it off to the side, leaving him bare-chested.)*

CASPER: Here, Denny, take your coat back.

DENNY: Uh-uh.

CASPER: Come on, you'll get froze.

DENNY: I don't *want* it. *(Pause.)*

CASPER: You know what the Indians up here used to do? When they were like out in the forest at night? They'd dig a hole in the ground, then they'd lie down and cover themselves with leaves. It kept them warm. Only I don't see any leaves around.

DENNY: You don't see many Indians either.

CASPER: No, you don't.

DENNY *(moving to sofa)*:   I'm gonna lie down.

CASPER: Smells of piss.

DENNY: All the comforts of home. *(He stretches himself out on the sofa. Casper looks inside the oven and takes out a pile of old magazines. He sits in the armchair and starts thumbing through them.)* What's that?

CASPER *(looking at cover)*: *Family Circle*. December 1979. *(Pause.)*

DENNY: Read me something.

CASPER: Like what?

DENNY: I don't care. Just read it out loud. *(Casper picks a page at random.)*

CASPER *(speaking haltingly, without punctuation)*: "One-oh-one ideas for Christmas fun holiday time is a time of family joy but today's mother can find her hands full when it comes to keeping the kids . . . okewped but with a little bit of—"

DENNY: What?

CASPER: "With a little—"

DENNY: Keeping them *what*?

CASPER: Okewped. *(Pause.)* Osapeed? *(Denny takes the magazine from him and looks at it.)*

CASPER: Jesus. *Occupied*. Keeping the kids *occupied*.

CASPER: Oh, yeah.

DENNY: Don't you *know* that word?

CASPER: Sure.

DENNY: That's not a hard word! It's right there! Occupied! Can't you read even?

CASPER: Yeah, I can read. I can read fine. I just need some time to . . . sound out the words. *(Pause.)* Should I do some more? *(Denny shakes his head and lies back down. A truck goes by overhead.)*

DENNY: Oh God will you shut UP! Somebody's trying to sleep!

CASPER: They're sixty feet up, Denny. They don't know we're here.

DENNY: But we are. Whether they like it or not. I'm here.

CASPER: Come on, Denny, take your jacket.

DENNY: Casper . . . are you real?

CASPER: Huh? Ah . . . I guess so. I'm real. Am I? *(Denny looks at him. Pause.)*

DENNY: Yeah. You're lucky. *(Sound of a man whistling in the distance. Denny leans forward and whispers.)* Cop?

CASPER: I don't know. *(He looks off.)* Doesn't look it.

DENNY: Alone?

CASPER: Uh-huh.

DENNY: Big dude?

CASPER: It's hard to tell. *(Pause.)* Should we . . . ask him for directions?

DENNY *(not listening)*: Huh?

CASPER: Directions home, Denny. I mean he doesn't look like a—

DENNY: Yeah. Yeah, good idea. You ask him for directions. I'll stash myself here. When he stops I'll yoke him up from the back.

CASPER: What?

DENNY: Like this. (*He demonstrates with his twisted-up T-shirt, miming wrapping it around someone's neck and pulling it taut.*) Right?

CASPER: Aw, Denny.

DENNY: We're not gonna hurt him. We're just gonna do him. We can take a taxi home!

CASPER: No, Denny, why?

DENNY: Because I *want* to, okay? Because I fucking feel like it!

CASPER: Oh boy. Oh no. Oh geez.

DENNY: You gonna help me or not? (*Casper does not answer.*) Then get outta here. I'm gonna bag this chump and you're a fucking chickenshit, you are. They won't *take* you in the army. Fuck off! (*Pause.*)

CASPER: What do I have to do.

DENNY: Okay. Okay. Ask him . . . what time it is. Go in for his wallet while I hold him. Don't act stupid. (*He ducks behind the sofa. Casper sits in the chair and waits. A workman in overalls and raincoat enters. Casper rises.*)

CASPER: Excuse me sir, can you tell me what's the time? (*Pause.*)

WORKMAN: It's around five-thirty.

CASPER: Okay, thanks. (*Pause.*) Does this lead back to town?

WORKMAN: Service road to the coal dump. (*Pause.*)

CASPER: Listen . . . I think you should—(*Denny comes up behind the workman and twists the T-shirt around his neck. The workman lurches forward. Denny tries to drag him back. They stand like this for a few seconds. Then the workman starts inching forward.*)

DENNY: His wallet! (*Casper does not move.*) The fucking wallet! What are you— (*The workman drops suddenly and tosses Denny over onto the ground. He kicks him twice. He looks at Casper, who remains still. He moves to kick Denny again. Denny cringes. The workman lowers his foot. Pause.*)

WORKMAN: Cocksucking little punks. Fence you off in a desert somewhere so you can all beat your own brains out. I worked all my life. You try it! (*He glares at them for a moment and stalks off. Casper watches him go, then comes over to Denny.*)

CASPER: You all right, Denny? Let me— (*Denny waves him away.*) We gotta go, Denny. He might call the police. (*Denny doesn't move.*) Can you walk?

DENNY (*in an even tone*): Where were you.

CASPER: I was here. I was standing.

DENNY: Why didn't you do something. *(Pause.)* You're not saying anything.

CASPER: I couldn't. I didn't want to.

DENNY: How come.

CASPER: It's wrong, Denny. It's just wrong to do.

DENNY: The *fuck* made you an expert.

CASPER *(coming up to him)*: Oh, I don't know, let's go before—

DENNY *(pushing him back)*: Stay . . . away . . . from me. 'Cause I swear to God I wanna kill some fucking thing. *(With a yell he lunges at the oven and yanks at its door until he tears it off. He charges up to the pillar and starts pounding the door against it.)* You, fucker! I want you to die, goddamn you! You fucking concrete . . . you fucking *highway* . . . you fucking *bridges* . . . and *cities* and houses and all the people crawling in 'em, I don't WANT you here! I don't want you in my HEAD! Get OUT! GET OUT GET OUT GET OUT! *(He throws down the door, nearly exhausted. He sees Casper's radio.)* And *this* . . . this is just *crap* . . . *(He picks it up and lifts it over his head.)*

CASPER: Don't break it, Denny.

DENNY: WHY NOT!

CASPER: 'Cause it's mine. 'Cause I need it. 'Cause we're friends. And 'cause . . . it's not gonna make any difference. *(Pause. Denny feigns tossing the radio against the pillar and throws it sharply at Casper, who catches it. He takes a last swipe at the sofa and collapses onto it. Pause. A police siren sounds in the distance, then fades away.)*

DENNY: Jesus, can't I even get arrested.

CASPER: Not this time I guess. *(He picks up the radio and wipes it clean with the edge of his shirt.)* It's getting light. I shoulda been back a while ago. It's a long walk home.

DENNY: Well . . . at least it's Saturday.

CASPER: It's Friday, Denny. Friday morning.

DENNY: Oh good. *(Pause.)*

CASPER: Hey, we had some fun tonight, didn't we? I mean . . . all the other stuff aside. We had a little fun.

DENNY: Yeah.

CASPER: Yeah, we had some fun. *(Pause.)* So, Denny . . . what do you wanna do now? *(Denny looks straight out. He draws in a long, slow breath and holds it. The lights fade to black.)*

DANCING ON CHECKERS' GRAVE

ERIC LANE

DANCING ON CHECKERS' GRAVE was originally produced by Orange Thoughts Theater Company at St. Mark's Church, New York City, in March 1988. Marc Helman directed the following cast:

DINA	Michelle Banks
LISA	Jennifer Aniston

Dancing on Checkers' Grave was awarded co-winner as best play in Love Creek Productions' annual Alternative Lifestyles Festival at the Nat Horne Theatre, New York City, in October 1992.

Characters
DINA, seventeen years old, black
LISA, also seventeen, white

Setting
A pet cemetery on Long Island, spring, noon

Note
Accents are not necessary; in speaking the lines, whatever rhythms should emerge naturally.

■ ■

A pet cemetery on Long Island. Noon.

The cemetery is basically like any other. A few trees. One or two benches. Some brown patches in the grass. Some real flowers: most geraniums. Some plastic, too.

The stones are arranged in horizontal rows and are unevenly spaced. Spacing depends on the size of the animal buried and amount the owner spends on the plot. Animals are not segregated. A dog may be buried next to a bird, a cat, etc. The placement is more dependent on the year of death than type of animal. Most of the graves in this area are from 1964 to the mid-70s.

The tombstones generally follow this pattern: name of the animal on top, year of birth/death below, family name on the bottom. A few have a poem or inspirational message. Others, an oval photo of the deceased covered by plastic and mounted directly on the stone.

The basic feel of the cemetery is either serene or kind of creepy, depending on how long you've been there. Usually, both.

It is next to the high school (unseen). Behind it is the expressway. Off-right is the woods.

Dina enters. She is black and a junior in high school. She is shy, hesitant, and a lot stronger than she lets herself realize. She is pretty, though not fashionably so. Her features are uneven and striking. She does not consider herself pretty. "Dina" rhymes with "Lena."

She walks along the outer edges of the graves, careful not to step on them. She reads the names, then moves on to the next, until she finds the one she is looking for. It reads:

CHECKERS
1952–1964

NIXON

DINA *(calls)*: Lisa. Lisa.
LISA *(off-stage)*: Yeah?
DINA: I found it.
LISA: You found it?
DINA: Yeah. Over here.

(Lisa enters. Also a junior. She is white, very pretty and takes great care in her appearance. While not intellectual, she is very quick. Tries to hide her insecurities by making sure her physical appearance is perfect. Even when it is, still feels something missing. Rather than take that in, keeps herself busy. She is very much out there. Though different, she and Dina like each other. She walks directly across the graves, heads to Dina.)

DINA *(points)*: Here.
LISA *(takes it in, sits)*: They moved it.
DINA: What?
LISA: They moved it.
DINA: How could they?
LISA *(reaches into her bag)*: You want a chicklet?
DINA *(shakes head "no")*: How could they?
LISA: What?
DINA: Move it, I mean.
LISA: They just did. You gonna sit down, or what?
DINA: Right. *(Sits, not on the grave.)*
LISA: They always do. Ask Jean.
DINA: Zirpelli?

LISA: Her brother. What's his name? Jan. He worked here. Said they used to do it all the time.

DINA: Move them.

LISA: That's what he said. Said they'd charge like a lot of money for a spot. Well, maybe like under a tree. And when they knew they weren't coming back anymore—like maybe after a few years.

DINA: Five.

LISA: Yeah. Like after five years, they'd move the dog, if it was a dog. They'd move the dog to someplace like not as nice. In the back maybe. And sell the one under the tree for a lot more money.

DINA: To somebody else.

LISA: Right. Dig it up and sell it again to somebody else.

DINA: That is so gross.

LISA: That's why he left.

DINA: Jean's brother.

LISA: He said it was really gross.

DINA: Sounds it.

LISA: You want a Life Saver? (*Dina shakes head "no."*) I got some Velamints if you want.

DINA: No thanks.

LISA: If you want them, they're here, so.

DINA: Thanks.

LISA: You know it's not gonna hurt him. Checkers. If you sit on him. It's not like it's gonna hurt.

DINA: I know, but—

LISA: I mean, he is dead.

DINA: I know. (*Takes a moment, decides. Moves over and sits on grave.*) It's not like it's any big deal.

LISA: No.

DINA: After all, he is dead.

LISA: Right. (*Dina looks very uneasy, tries to cover.*) Dee-na.

DINA: All right. All right.

LISA: You sure?

DINA: No.
　　Yeah, I'm fine.

LISA: God, I can't believe you never been here before.

DINA: I guess I never had any reason to.

LISA: You must've passed by.

DINA: Passed by, sure. (*Reads a stone.*)
　　　　　　　"He lived out his days
　　　　　　　Yet never our love.
　　　　　　　—Blackie."
　　That's kind of nice.

LISA: Yeah.

DINA: You think we better get started?

LISA: On our composition?

DINA: On *your* composition. Yeah.

LISA: We still got some time. *(Pulls nail polish from her bag.)* Raspberry. *(Dina nods. Lisa starts to give herself a manicure.)*

DINA: That was smart coming here.

LISA: That cafeteria is so gross.

DINA: No, I mean for that composition. In Social Studies.

LISA: Social Studies? God, that was almost two years ago.

DINA: Yeah, well.

LISA: I can't believe you remember that. I didn't even know you then.

DINA: Well, the same class.

LISA: Yeah, but it's not like we were friends or anything. How come you remember that?

DINA: I guess I just did. I don't know.

LISA: Historic Wantagh. Give me a break.

DINA: Right.

LISA: All those papers about that stupid train car. It's not like it's so old or anything. I mean, they take this train car, stick it in the middle of this park nobody can get to, except the Boy Scouts who paint it every other week.

DINA: I think they get a merit badge. For community service or something.

LISA: They want to do the community a service, they'll stop painting that car. *(Shows nail.)* What do you think?

DINA: I like it.

LISA: You don't think it's too red.

DINA: No.

LISA: Me, either.

God, all those papers. I can't believe Fogel made us read them all. How many times can you listen to that same paper over and over?

DINA: A few were different.

LISA: A few. Right.

DINA: Like yours. And Mara.

LISA: Mara. Please. Her father tells her McDonald's used to be a hotel George Washington slept at. Right. So she goes down and gets an "A" for eating a Big Mac.

DINA: I thought the two of you were friends.

LISA: Yeah, well.

DINA: I mean, you're always spending time together. Like in Bio.

LISA: You know it's her fault I gotta stay after. What was I doing? I was just looking for the dorsal exterdermis. It's not my fault my hand slipped.

DINA: I guess not.

LISA: No. But she has to make a big deal. "Mrs. Boone. Mrs. Boone. Lisa cut my worm in half." Like it was hers to begin with. So now I gotta stay after and I got a zero for lab.

DINA: Is she gonna let you make it over?

LISA: Boone? She gave me a zero. So? What do I care? It's only Bio.

DINA: She seemed really pissed. Mara, I mean.

LISA: *She* was pissed.

DINA: Like before you even started. Like, I don't know.

LISA: You want to pass me a tissue? *(Dina does.)*

DINA: Even before.

LISA: What?

DINA: Mara. Like before you started.

LISA: God, she is such an asshole.

DINA: I mean—

LISA: What?

DINA: Nothing. *(A beat.)*

LISA: You like these?

DINA: The stones?

LISA: The pictures on them. Photos. You like them?

DINA: I guess. I mean they are a little creepy.

LISA: Yeah. Like especially when they crack and the rain gets in, and the picture fades so it's like this ghost sitting there. Like you can't see it anymore, but it's still there. God, I hate that.

DINA: Yeah.

LISA: Me, too. *(Finishes polish on first hand.)* There. You like it, right?

DINA: Raspberry.

LISA: Yeah.

DINA: It's nice.

LISA: Yeah. I think so, too. Maybe later we'll do yours.

DINA: Mine?

LISA: Sure. Why not?

DINA: I don't know. Sure.

LISA: Later maybe.

DINA: Maybe.

LISA: God, what time is it? *(Dina shows her watch.)* We better get started. Look, I'll dictate. You can write it down. *(Off Dina's look.)* What?

DINA: He's gonna know you didn't write it.

LISA: Just put circles over the "i"s, he'll never know the difference.

DINA: Lisa—

LISA: I'm telling you. I do it all the time. It's no big deal. *(Dina writes Lisa's name.)* Slant the letters to the right more. *(Dina writes date.)* Yeah. Like that. Only rounder. *(Dina takes another piece, starts over.)* What'd you write about anyway?

DINA: Something I like to do.

LISA: Duh.

DINA: Well, that's the subject.

LISA: I know that's the subject. I mean like what?

DINA: Going to the city.

LISA *(completely foreign idea)*:   You mean like New York? *(Dina nods.)* For what?

DINA: I don't know. Just to walk around.

LISA: Round where?

DINA: I don't know. The village. Around St. Marks.

LISA: Oh.

DINA: Just to walk.

LISA: Right.

My brother went there once. He said he saw somebody get shot. It was really disgusting. That ever happen when you were there?

DINA: No.

LISA: I guess you must've gone a different day.

DINA: I guess.

LISA: Yeah.

He said the people there were like really weird.

DINA: I don't think I'd call them weird.

LISA: Well, what?

DINA: Different, I guess.

LISA: You mean like with mohawks and stuff?

DINA: Some. Or earrings through their nose.

LISA: That is so gross.

DINA: I don't know. It's like whatever you want to wear. Like that's who you are. And that's it. You know what I mean?

LISA: I'm sorry. But that is gross.

DINA: No. I mean, it's like—

LISA: What?

DINA: Never mind.

LISA: What were you gonna say?

DINA: I don't know. It's like just standing there. Like you're standing still and all these vocabulary words come flying at you. You ever felt like that? *(Lisa shakes head "no.")* Me either. I mean before. But—I don't know.

LISA: Why don't you read me it?

DINA: My paper?

LISA: Sure.

DINA: I left it in my locker.

LISA: Why'd you do that?

DINA: I figured I'd get it on the way to class. Anyway, I didn't finish it anyway.

LISA: It's next class. When are you gonna?

DINA: Well, I mean I used all the vocabulary words. I just couldn't figure how to end it.

LISA: "And then I woke up."

DINA *(laughs)*: What?

LISA: "And then I woke up." Sure. Like every paper. First grade to sixth. This happened. This. This. Da. Da. Da. Da. Da . . . And then I woke up. Like it was all a dream or something. What do they call that? You know.

DINA: A metaphor.

LISA: Yeah. Like a metaphor.

DINA: You really did that?

LISA: Worked every time. "And then I woke up." *(Picks gum wrapper from ground.)* You figure they'd have a little more respect. Anyway, I figured I'd write about munchkining.

DINA: Munchkining?

LISA: Yeah. You never done that? *(Dina shakes head "no.")* I can't believe. See, you get in a car. Buy a box of Dunkin' Munchkins. Then drive around town and throw them at people. I can't believe you never done that.

DINA: I guess, I just never thought to.

LISA: Well, the next time we go—

DINA: "We" who?

LISA: Huh?

DINA: The next time *we* go. Who?

LISA: I don't know. Whoever we ask. You'll come, right?

DINA: Sure.

LISA: I mean like it doesn't matter who we ask. Even if we went ourselves.

DINA: Right.
        Sounds like fun.

LISA: Sure. *(A beat.)*

DINA *(reads definition)*:   Abstemious. Sparing in food or drink. Not self-indulgent.

LISA: Let's skip it. What's next?

DINA: Antithesis. Direct contrast: opposition. You know my handwriting is nothing like this.

LISA: I'm telling you it's not a problem.

DINA: He's gonna know.

LISA: Look, I didn't write that anyway. So what difference does it make?

DINA: Who did then?

LISA: I just got them.

DINA: Oh.

LISA: I mean it's not like it makes any difference, you know.

DINA: I know.

LISA: Right.
  So?

DINA: Awesome. Adjective. Causing awe.

LISA: I mean, even if Mara did give me them she's still an asshole.

DINA: Yeah. Sure.

LISA: I mean, it's not like she looked them up or anything.

DINA: No?

LISA: No. She copied them off of Stephen. He got them off of Marco. So if there's anybody I should be thanking it's him.

DINA: Right.

LISA: Right.
  Awesome.

DINA: Causing awe.

LISA: Right. *(She thinks a minute.)*

DINA: Look, I have an idea. Why don't we just start and we'll use them?

LISA: The words?

DINA: Yeah. You just start and then we'll make them fit. We'll put them in. We'll jam them in. We'll just do it.

LISA: Okay. *(Quickly.)* "Something I like to do. By Lisa Steinman." *(Dina already has it.)* Munchkining is something I like to do. You got that?

DINA *(writes)*: Yeah.

LISA: To munchkin. To munchkin you need a car.

DINA: How about: The rules of some games are very *awesome*.

LISA: Awesome. Yeah. Good.

DINA: Very awesome. And the *bane* of one's existence, but—

LISA: But not so with munchkining.

DINA *(writes)*: But not so with munchkining. How's that?

LISA: You should slant your writing more. *(Dina shoots her a look.)* That's good. What's next?

DINA: Carouse.

LISA: Next.

DINA: Cheerfully.

LISA: Okay. Okay. One cheerfully asks your mother for the car.

DINA: One's mother.

LISA: One's mother for the car. *(Looks at list.)* And hopes she has not taken it to a choral recital. *(Dina laughs.)* What?

DINA: A choral recital?

LISA: What? I think that's good.

DINA: Okay.

LISA: Don't you?

DINA: Well, it's not something I would normally say—

LISA: Well, me either but—

DINA: Right.

LISA: Okay.

DINA: Gaunt.

LISA: You think my pocket's a little droopy?

DINA: What?

LISA: My pocket.

DINA: No.

LISA: What's next?

DINA: Gaunt.

LISA: Right. Gaunt. *(They think.)* Indigestible.

DINA: No. I know. . . . To a choral recital by the Gaunt Opera Company of Eastern Long Island.

LISA: Southeastern.

DINA *(writes)*: The Gaunt Opera Company of Southeastern Long Island.

LISA: Next you need a box, yeah. No. Two boxes of Dunkin' Munchkins. One box of which can be indigestible because we will ride around town and throw them at people.

DINA: At various people.

LISA: Various.

DINA: Ranging from—

LISA: Masons.

DINA: To noisome megalomaniacs.

LISA: To noisome megalomaniacs. That is so good.

DINA *(writes)*: Okay.

LISA: Right. What else?

DINA: I don't know.
How about that other box?

LISA: What?

DINA: You need *two* boxes.

LISA: That one you eat.

DINA: Right.
The other box you eat as you peruse the—what was that first one?

LISA: Abstemious.

DINA: Peruse the area.

LISA: Unless you are abstemious. Then you don't eat it.

DINA: Right.

LISA: God, you'd think they have some kind of flag or something.

DINA: What?

LISA *(points to grave)*:   Here. You'd think they would. Or something.

DINA: Right. *(Looks at vocabulary list.)*

LISA: I mean, that dog did save him the presidential nomination, right?

DINA: Vice-presidential.

LISA: Vice. Right.

DINA: Muse: to ponder.

LISA: How'd you remember that?

DINA: What?

LISA: Vice-presidential. How'd you remember?

DINA: Wasn't that in your composition? Nixon was in trouble for taking some money, some contributions. So he makes this speech about somebody giving his daughters a cocker spaniel, and he's not giving it back. So Eisenhower keeps him on. Like for Vice-President.

LISA: How'd you remember all that?

DINA: I don't know. I guess I just did. Muse.

LISA: I mean, I don't remember, and I wrote it.

DINA: I guess maybe it was just really good. Your composition, I mean.

LISA: Oh, please.

DINA: How else would I remember? What? Don't you think you're a good writer?

LISA: No.

DINA: Well, you are.

LISA: Tell that to Dunnbar.

DINA: Well, Dunnbar.

LISA: Yeah. *(A beat.)*

DINA: So before we start we muse over which direction to head—

LISA: You know my brother told me Mrs. Boone was a lesbian. You believe that?

DINA: I don't know.

LISA: He said he heard it someplace. Yeah. And the real reason she got married was so they could like what? Cover it over. You ever hear that?

DINA: No.
        Should we head toward the noxious raw sewage treatment plant—

LISA: That's what he said.

DINA: Or the less odorous part of town?

LISA: You believe that?

DINA (*writes*): Wait a minute.
    Um, I don't know. What about you?
LISA: I don't know. . . . Maybe.
DINA: Yeah. It is possible.
LISA: I mean, not that it would make any difference.
DINA: No.
    Maybe we could use something about that choral group.
LISA: What?
DINA: "Quintet." Maybe we could tie it in.
LISA: The Gaunt Opera Company.
DINA: Yeah. That's it. (*Looks.*)
LISA: I mean, like to her friends.
DINA: What?
LISA: Boone. Her friends. Maybe it'd make a difference to them.
DINA: Not if they were really her friends.
LISA: I guess not.
DINA: No. (*Overlapping.*) You think we could tie it in?
LISA (*overlapping*): You like the name Lassie?
DINA: I'm sorry.
LISA: No. What were you gonna say?
DINA: Nothing.
LISA: No, what?
DINA: Just. Well, quintet. You think we could tie it in?
LISA: Sure.
DINA: Right.
LISA: Like with choral.
DINA: Yeah.
    What about you?
LISA: What?
DINA: Saying. What were you gonna say?
LISA: Oh, right. (*Re: tombstone.*) Lassie. You like that name?
DINA: For a dog?
LISA: Yeah.
DINA: No. I mean, I don't know.
LISA: I don't. I mean, if I had a dog I wouldn't name it that.
DINA: No?
LISA: I mean, like if it's a collie, all the other collies are named
    Lassie. And if it's not, who wants to name it that anyway.
DINA: That makes sense.
LISA: It's not like I'd name my chihuahua Lassie.
DINA: Yeah.
LISA: No way. (*A beat.*)
DINA: What about rules? Anybody we're not allowed to throw
    Munchkins at.

LISA: Right. You are not allowed to throw Munchkins at choral quintets, especially—

DINA: Hold on.

LISA: Especially those with sinewy arms.

DINA (*laughs*): That's good.

LISA: Nor.

DINA: Nor.

LISA: Abstemious people.

DINA: We used it already.

LISA: Right. Rambunctious people in wheelchairs.

DINA: Wheelchairs?

LISA: Yeah. Dunnbar's big on handicapped. Maybe he'll give extra credit.

DINA (*writes*): In wheelchairs.

LISA: God, it's hot out here.

DINA: Yeah.

LISA: You hot?

DINA: A little.

LISA (*removing sweater*): You wouldn't think. This time of year. I mean, like one day I'm freezing, then the next—

DINA: Yeah.

LISA: You can take off your sweater if you want.

DINA: I know. I guess— Anyway, so you gotta stay after.

LISA: That Mara is such an asshole. Two days. Boone says I was defacing school property. God, it was only a fucking worm.

DINA: Right.

LISA (*show nails*): How do you like?

DINA: They're good.

LISA: Yeah. I like them.

DINA: Yeah. They're good. So you and Mara still friends or what?

LISA: No. I mean, I don't know. I mean, God, all I wanted to do was dance.

DINA: In Bio?

LISA: No. I mean, last night. It's like what? That's why she was so pissed.

DINA: 'Cause you wanted to dance.

LISA: Then her parents came home and— Anyway, it was stupid so—

DINA: I could tell you were pissed.

LISA: When?

DINA: At each other. Before Bio even started. I could tell.

LISA: Yeah, well. See, it's 'cause like every Tuesday night her parents go out to play cards. With their friends.

DINA (*knowingly*): Once a week.

LISA: Yeah. Well, unless it's their turn, then everybody comes over there. To Mara's. I mean, well, her parents. So when they go out, it's like we go over.

DINA: We?

LISA: Me. Stephen and Marco. We go over and we hang out for like the night. We watch T.V. Maybe Marco makes this hot fudge sauce. It is like so good.

DINA: Yeah.

LISA: You ever have it?

DINA: No. I mean, like yeah, I'm sure it is.

LISA: Yeah. Like with honey vanilla. That is so good. So we finish that and then we start dancing. Like every Tuesday. See Marco and Stephen, they dance together and like, well, Mara and me. And it's getting late. So, Cyndi Lauper's singing "True Colors" and what? Mara's parents pull up. And what we do is when we hear them it's like we switch. It's like automatic. Mara starts dancing with Stephen and me with Marco. I mean that's what we do. So like "True Colors," it's playing and I don't know why, but I don't. Switch, I mean. I mean, I hear their car, but it's like I just want to dance with her. And so her parents come in and they see us. Not like dancing. Well, dancing, but Mara pulling away from me and—I just wanted to dance with her. (A beat.)

DINA: That sucks.

LISA: Yeah, well. I mean, well, what did I expect.

DINA: I guess—

LISA: What?

DINA: Something different.

LISA: Yeah, well.

DINA: Right. I mean, you just wanted to dance with her.

LISA: Yeah, but— Oh, shit.

DINA: What?

LISA: My nail. Look at that. I smudged the— In my bag. A tissue.

DINA: Right. (Dina gives tissue. Lisa wipes excess polish from finger.)

LISA: Look at that. Jeez.
    So what's next?

DINA: What?

LISA: The word. What one?

DINA: Right. Refreshing.

LISA: Refreshing. Jeez.

DINA: You O.K.?

LISA: Yeah. No. I mean, I don't know. (Lisa starts to laugh slightly. So does Dina. Re: nail.) Look at this.

DINA: It's not so bad.

LISA: No.

DINA: Here. Give me. (*Takes Lisa's hand, applies polish.*)

LISA: It's like. I don't know—I mean, she is an asshole.

DINA: Mara?

LISA: It's like I wish I had a box of Munchkins right now. I'd throw them right at her.

DINA (*finishes nail*):   There.

LISA: Thanks.
You wanna?

DINA: What?

LISA (*reaches over, opens imaginary door*):   Get in.

DINA: What are you talking about?

LISA: Munchkining. You said you wanted to.

DINA: I know but—

LISA: But what?

DINA: You need a car. That's what you said.

LISA: So.

DINA: First thing. Rules of munchkining. One: You need a car.

LISA: I got one. My mother's. The Honda. It's even got a sunroof.

DINA: Lisa—

LISA: What?

LISA: This is too weird.

LISA: You know you want to. (*Dina shakes head "no."*) You know you do. Look, I even bought the Munchkins.

DINA: Right.

LISA: Two boxes. One to eat. The other to throw. You can hold them if you want.

DINA: Look, maybe sometime. Like some night. We'll borrow your mother's car—

LISA: I already did.

DINA: Lisa—

LISA: I can't wait here forever. (*A beat.*)

DINA: I get to hold them, right?

LISA: Lap or floor. Take your pick. (*Dina looks around to see if anyone is watching. She is about to get in car, stops.*) What?

DINA: There's somebody there.

LISA: Where?

DINA: Sitting next to you. I can see her.

LISA: Who?

DINA: This girl.

LISA: Dina, there's nobody there.

DINA: I see her.

LISA (*runs hand through space*):   Nobody.

DINA: You're sure?

LISA: Dee-na. (*A moment. Dina gets in.*)

DINA: This is too weird.

LISA: Your seatbelt on?

DINA: Right. So where we headed?

LISA: I figure we circle the neighborhood then head downtown.

DINA: And the donuts?

LISA *(indicates floor)*: Right in front of you. Help yourself. *(Dina tastes one. Doesn't really like it.)* What?

DINA: You like these?

LISA: Maybe you got a bad one. Try the chocolate.

DINA: That was the chocolate.

LISA: The coconut then. *(Dina does.)* So?

DINA: I'm sure they make very good ammunition.

LISA: Dina.

DINA: What can I tell you? They're too sweet.

LISA: Well, I like them.

DINA: You can eat them.

LISA: Fine. Stick it in.

DINA: What?

LISA: My mouth. Stick it in. *(Dina does.)* Refreshing.

DINA: Refreshing?

LISA: Yes. That is what we call word power.

DINA: Oh, come on. Where'd you come up with—

LISA *(cuts her off)*: Shhh.

DINA: What?

LISA: Over there.

DINA: Where?

LISA: Don't you see them? Those Boy Scouts. Painting that train car. 'Cause they still need like their merit badge.

DINA: For community service.

LISA: That's the one. Look at that color. Puce. It's supposed to be like historic. When was the last time you saw a puce railroad car? Well . . .

DINA: What?

LISA: You're in charge of the Munchkins.

DINA: Lisa—

LISA: Well are you or aren't you? *(Dina nods, reluctantly. Gives Lisa ammo, prepares to throw it herself.)* What're you doing? You're never gonna reach from here.

DINA: Well, what else am I supposed to do?

LISA: Lure them over here.

DINA: Lure them?

LISA: Yeah. Pretend like you need directions or something.

DINA: Excuse me.

LISA: Louder.

DINA: Excuse me. Can you tell me how to get to the library, please?
What's happening?

LISA: They're coming over.

DINA: How many?

LISA: Five. You ready? *(Overlapping.)* 5—4—3—2—1.

DINA *(overlapping)*:   Can you tell me where the library—?

LISA: Now! *(They throw the Munchkins. Lisa peels out.)* Woo! You
get them?

DINA: One.

LISA: Where?

DINA: On the arm. The left one. I was aiming for the chest but I
got his arm. You?

LISA: Right shoulder. And kneecap. You did good.

DINA: Well, the first time.

LISA: Even so.
They're not following, are they? *(Dina looks back, shakes head "no.")*
Probably too stunned.

DINA: Yeah.
Oh my God.

LISA: What?

DINA: Slow down.

LISA: What?

DINA: My sister. She's just getting outta the library. She's got her
dental hygiene midterm tomorrow, and she's been studying. Slow
down, I want to ask her something. *(Lisa slows down.)* Grace, how
come you always been such an asshole? *(Throws Munchkins.)* Peel
out.

LISA: You get her?

DINA: Right in her lower tricuspid. I always wanted to do that.

LISA: Well, now you did.

DINA: Right. That was so mint.

LISA: Yeah, it was.

DINA: Yeah.
So where we headed?

LISA: For somebody who didn't want to go munchkining—

DINA: Watch the road. *(Lisa swerves.)* So where we headed?

LISA: I figure we'd head over behind the high school.

DINA: The high school?

LISA: Yeah. This friend of my mother's. Charlene. It's like every
time I come into the room she asks, "How come a pretty girl like
you doesn't have a boyfriend?"

DINA *(points)*:   There's her husband.

LISA: You know him?

DINA: Every time I pass him on the way to school, it's like he checks his wallet to make sure it's still there.

LISA: He's doing it now?

DINA: Wait. He hasn't seen me yet.

Yeah. Now! *(They throw.)*

LISA: Right in the head.

DINA: Yeah. I saw.

LISA *(checks rearview mirror)*: Look. It's still caught in her hair.

DINA: God, I hate that. The way she has it piled up like that.

LISA: Yeah, that is gross.

DINA: And his.

LISA: Yeah.

DINA: Combed from the back.

LISA: I mean who are they trying to fool.

DINA: Right. *(Spots another.)* Let's nail this guy.

LISA: Who is he?

DINA: A father.

LISA: Yours?

DINA *(not answering)*: This little girl. She's in third grade, and runs to him with her report card. Twenty-seven marks. Twenty-six of them A's. He takes one look, asks her, "Why'd you get the B-plus?" *(They nail him.)*

LISA: Debbie DeSimone. I copy off of her in Spanish. She gets a 67. I get a 63.

DINA: Debbie DeSimone. She copies off of me in Bio. She gets a 95. I get an 87.

LISA: God, look at that.

DINA: What?

LISA: This girl walking home from her friend's. See, it's like her friend asked her to leave before her parents get home. 'Cause they started asking questions like why they're spending so much time together.

DINA: She looks kinda sad.

LISA: Yeah, well.

DINA: Slow down. We'll let her in. *(They do.)* Honk the horn.

LISA: She's already in.

DINA: No. Across the street. Walking home from the train. See that bracelet she's wearing. She's wearing it now 'cause in a few blocks she'll have to take it off. See, she bought it on St. Marks, and's hiding it 'cause her parents told her not to go into the city.

LISA: How come?

DINA: I don't know. It's like they think she's a baby and don't want her to be anything else.

LISA: She in? *(Dina nods.)* Why don't you give them the other box?

DINA: Right. *(Gives it to them.)* Ammunition.

LISA: Oh, my God.

DINA: What?

LISA: You're never gonna believe.

DINA: Tell me. What?

LISA: This convention of gym teachers coming out of the high school. Every one we ever had. *(Throw at each.)* Sheridan.

DINA: O'Hara.

LISA: Briggs.

DINA: Valentine.

LISA: Harper.

DINA: Lutz.

DINA/LISA: Miss Murray. *(They throw a whole load at them and laugh.)*

LISA: God, that was good. How we holding out? Supplies?

DINA: We still got half a box.

LISA: Good. 'Cause I see them heading at us right now.

DINA: What?

LISA: Like those words you were talking about flying at you. Only this time they're ones, well . . . You're just like your father.

DINA: Why can't you be more like your sister?

LISA: The maid's off today. Clean up your room.

DINA: You start out laughing. You end up crying.

LISA: No one ever said the world was fair.

DINA: Everyone else is going. Why aren't you?

LISA: I don't care what everyone else is doing. You're not going.

DINA: Dina, go to sleep.

LISA: Lisa, geh schlufen.*

DINA: Dina, get up.

LISA: Who are you, Pifke the Manager?**

DINA: I am not writing you another late note.

LISA: No, I will not write you a note out of gym.

DINA: This is the last time I am telling you.

LISA: What is this—a hotel?

DINA: Young lady, I am not in the habit of repeating myself.

LISA: You heard what I said.

DINA: I am not going to say it again.

LISA: Ugh, it is so hot. Just looking at you I am fainting.

DINA: Young lady.

LISA: You're not going outta the house dressed like that.

DINA: You're not going outta the house dressed like that. That hat.

---

* gā shluf'in. Yiddish: go to sleep

** pif'kē

LISA: That dress.

DINA: Those shoes.

LISA: That face.

DINA: That hair.

LISA: That hair. Ugh, noxious.

DINA: Noisome.

LISA: Odorous.

DINA: Indigestible.

LISA: Bane.

DINA: Gaunt.

LISA: Sinewy. *(They throw the rest of the box. A beat. "Hears" girl in back seat.)* What's that?

DINA: What?

LISA: The girl.

DINA: The one who's going home from her friend's.

LISA: Yeah. It's getting late. She's gotta get home.

DINA: Doesn't she want to drive around some more?

LISA: Well, she does. She's just gotta get home. Her parents.

DINA: Yeah. Right. *(They drive. Lisa stops.)* Is this it?

LISA: Second from the corner.

DINA: Right.
Well, so long.

LISA: "So long," she says.
I see her go up to the house. She lets herself in. Turns off the outside light.

DINA: Locks the door. I hear her going up to her room. Like real quiet so she doesn't wake her parents.

LISA: They're sleeping. Yeah.

DINA: I can hear her crying.

LISA: You hear it?

DINA: All these people around. She feels so—

LISA: Alone.

DINA: That's it. Alone. It's like she's tired of that. And doesn't want it anymore.

LISA: No.

DINA: No. *(A moment.)*

DINA: God, look at that.

LISA: What?

DINA: Across the street. Mara's house.

LISA: Mara?

DINA: Yeah. She's standing at the window. Looking out.

LISA: You see her?

DINA: Well, her shadow, against the window. She's looking out. You want to throw one?

LISA: A Munchkin?

DINA: Yeah. You want one?

LISA: I thought we were out.

DINA: From the floor. It must've fallen out of the box. You want? *(Raises as if to throw it.)*

LISA: Come on. Get back in.

DINA: What?

LISA: Get in the car. *(They drive in silence.)* This is it. *(Dina looks at her.)* Your house. God, you don't even recognize your own house.

DINA: I was just—
Right.
So. That was fun.

LISA: Yeah. I had a good time.

DINA: You did?

LISA: Yeah.

DINA: So did I.
Wait a minute. What about that girl?

LISA: What?

DINA: The one with the bracelet. That she was hiding.

LISA: Oh. She slipped out.

DINA: Of the car?

LISA: Yeah. I mean, not like she fell. But—When the other girl got out. She slipped out the other door.

DINA: Oh. Right.

LISA: Yeah.

DINA: So. I had a good time.

LISA: Yeah. Me, too.

DINA: You want to come in?

LISA: Inside? *(Dina nods.)* Well, it's getting kinda late.

DINA *(immediately)*: Yeah. I guess it is.

LISA: And anyways, your parents.

DINA: My parents.
What about them?

LISA: If they see us . . .

DINA: What if they do?

(A moment. Dina starts to hum "True Colors." She starts to sing, humming when she forgets the lyric. Lisa joins in.

They rise and begin to dance. Awkward. Tender. They move closer becoming more intimate. They kiss.

A sound. Lisa pushes Dina away.)

LISA: God, what was that?

DINA: What?

LISA: That sound. Didn't you hear it? It sounded like somebody—

DINA: In the grass?

LISA: Yeah.

DINA: No. It was just some jack rabbit or something.

LISA: No. It sounded like—God, look what time it is. I gotta get this done or shit. What were we up to?

DINA: What?

LISA: Word. What one were we—? *(Looks.)* Refreshing.

DINA: Right.

LISA: I thought we used that.

DINA: No, not yet.

LISA: I thought.

DINA: No.

LISA: You want to write this or what? *(Dina sits. Takes notebook.)* What?

DINA: It's just—
Never mind.

LISA: So we take a boxful of refreshing Munchkins—

DINA: It's just now I know. *(Lisa looks at her.)* How you felt. When Mara pushed you away.

LISA: That's not the same thing.

DINA: No?

LISA: No.
When Mara pushed me away it was like she was afraid of her parents seeing who she really was.

DINA: And just now. Who were you afraid of?

LISA: Mara.
That she would see us. Or someone would and like—I don't know. Maybe they'd tell her.

DINA: Then you still—

LISA: Yeah. I guess I do. *(A beat.)* Look, you want a cigarette or something. I—*(Dina shakes her head "no.")* God, we better get back.

DINA *(simply)*: You know, if you hurry you might be able to catch her before class.

LISA: Yeah, right.
You're coming, right?

DINA: Well, I still gotta finish my composition.

LISA: I thought you left it in your locker.

DINA: Yeah, well. Anyway.

LISA: You want me to tell him you're sick. Dunnbar, I mean.

DINA: Nah.

LISA: I mean, I'll tell him if you want.

DINA: I'll be there soon.

LISA (*nods*):   Anyway, thanks.

DINA: Right. (*Lisa moves to Dina, gives her a quick kiss.*) God, who'd want to name their dog Lassie?

(*She exits. Dina sits a moment. She takes out her composition. She had it with her. Reads.*)

DINA: I am standing on St. Marks, and this girl comes up. She is wearing this bracelet she just bought. It is silver and turquoise. She has never seen one like it before. (*Starts to write.*) She does not know the neighborhood and wants to know someplace good to eat. (*Takes out bracelet, puts it on.*) I take out my bracelet. The same one. And put it on. I reach out and take her hand, and we go out for iced coffee and tuna sandwiches. My treat.

(*Dina smiles. Lights fade.*)

THE COAL DIAMOND

SHIRLEY LAURO

THE COAL DIAMOND was presented by The Ensemble Studio Theatre, in New York City, in June 1979. It was directed by Peter Maloney; the setting was by Brian Martin; lighting was by Marie Louise Moreto; and the costumes were by Charles Schoonmaker. The cast was as follows:

INEZ	Melodie Somers
PEARL	Amelia Penland
BETTY JEAN	Kathy McKenna
LENA	Dolores Kenan

Characters

INEZ, mid-twenties to mid-thirties. Tall, thin, flat-chested. Nothing fits right although she drinks malts to GAIN WEIGHT! Wears a flowered chintz skirt and peasant blouse that won't stay in. Bare-legged, white sandals that she kicks off. She smokes Camels and chews a lot of gum.

LENA, middle-aged. Wears girdle, hose, rayon print dess, pumps. Little gold-rimmed glasses. Permanent in her hair. "The Boss."

BETTY JEAN, nineteen. Peroxided blond, dark at roots, in ponytail with pink ribbon. Noticeably pregnant, wears pink and white polka-dot maternity smock, flat white sandals. Toe-nails and fingernails are painted pink.

PEARL, mid-twenties to mid-thirties. Summer dress. Trying hard to look like the office girls here in Valley Center. She's just moved to town and it's a new town and a new job, and she doesn't feel as smart as the other girls. Especially the ones here in Research.

The Scene

The Insurance Office, Research Department of Southeastern Missouri Farm Insurance Co.; Valley Center, Missouri. August 1955. The hottest day of the year.

■ ■

A corner of the Research Office in the Insurance Company.
Where the "smart girls" work. Lunchtime.
   Two gray desks with typewriters on them. An old-fashioned ceiling fan, moving only in centimeters. If at all. A water cooler.
   One desk has been pushed up to the window to get whatever breeze there may be. There is one door, downstage right, to hall. Office is deserted except

for three typists who are bustling around, getting ready to eat lunch and play bridge. (Lena, Inez, and Betty Jean).
  In the dark we hear Inez typing. Lights up.

LENA *(telling punchline of joke)*:   And then, he said to her: "I said *bells*, lady, not *balls!*" *(Peals of laughter from Inez, Betty Jean and Lena.)*

BETTY JEAN: Oh, Lena, that's jist awful!

INEZ *(Makes mistake on typewriter)*:   Law! You got me laughin' so, I jist made a mistake!

LENA: You can fix it this afternoon. It's ten after twelve already! And both you girls have put in a terrible hard mornin' as it is!

BETTY JEAN: Isn't that the truth! Land! This hot ole mornin' seemed a thousand hours long!

LENA: Well, come on now, Betty Jean . . . let's us jist all relax our brains—and have us some *fun!* It's "Lunch Time" girls! *(Pearl enters, carrying her lunch, looking around, not immediately seeing the others, who are now setting up for bridge game and lunch. They put deck of cards and scorepad on desk, and take out brown paper bags with baloney and cheese sandwiches, apples, candy bars and Cokes. Inez puts a pack of Camels on the desk.)*

INEZ: Hey, Pearl: Honey; you jist come right along over here! We're jist about ready to start!

PEARL *(joining the group)*:   I'm jist terrible sorry to be late and all. I got stuck doin' this report? And I couldn't remember how she said to do it. Finally I jist give up!

INEZ *(rising, encircling Pearl's waist)*:   Jist never you mind, Pearl, honey. It's O.K. Why, we're all so tickled to git us a fourth, we're about to die! Now jist let me name you around. Everyone: this here's my friend, Pearl Brewster, like I said. Jist started to work here Monday. They stuck her in Underwriting.

BETTY JEAN: Oh Law!

INEZ: This here's Betty Jean McGaffee.

PEARL: Pleased to know you Betty Jean.

BETTY JEAN: Thanks.

INEZ: Her husband works out to the Firestone Plant. First Shift!!

BETTY JEAN: Shoot! Don't have to give her my family tree!

INEZ *(patting Betty Jean's stomach)*:   Somebody already gave you your family tree, girl! *(Everyone laughs.)* Anyhow, this little gold-haired honey jist graduated high school a year ago June, and already got herself this good job in Research, a husband on First Shift, and a kid almost due!

PEARL *(taking in the black roots on Betty Jean's hair)*:   Isn't that something now? *(Betty Jean takes her knitting {booties} from desk drawer.)*

INEZ: And finally . . . this is Lena Travis, Boss of the Research Section! (*Lena shakes Pearl's hand.*) Lena is terrible smart at Insurance and bridge. Only thing is—she can't get her a man! (*The other girls smile ever so sweetly at Lena.*)

LENA (*hitching up her glasses, a habit which she does very often, and then taking a bite out of her apple*): Never you mind what I got or ain't got, Inez Potter!

INEZ: Heck! I was only teasin', Lena! Truth is, Pearl, honey, Lena is jist too dang good for any old man! Why, Betty Jean and me, we never had such a wonderful girl to work for ever in our lives as Lena Travis. And that's a fact!

LENA (*touched*): Shoot! (*Lena sits, motions Pearl to sit. Betty Jean goes to window, opens it wide.*)

INEZ: Well, it's the Lord's truth, Lena, and you know it is. Why, we're jist crazy about workin' for you!

BETTY JEAN: She is jist terrible nice, Pearl. Heck! Everytime I get the backache, she give me this pass to the Lounge. And she sure has got a swell sense of humor, Lena has. Keeps us in stitches all the time! 'I—I said 'bells' lady, not 'balls!' '' (*Betty Jean, Lena and Inez laugh. Everyone settles down at table.*)

LENA: Aw go on! (*Begins to welcome Pearl, dealing cards as she does.*) Now, I mean to tell ya, Pearl, honey, we're proud to have ya come in like this of a Friday to be a fourth. Friday noons is terrible hard to get a fourth. Everybody goes on uptown, see, to make their deposits on account of we git paid about a quarter of. Why it's a positive chore gittin' someone up here of a Friday. Specially since we're the only Department hasn't got us our air-conditioner yet. Hot as this weather is . . .

PEARL (*kicking off sandals and spreading her toes over the cool linoleum. Opens lunch bag now, eating her jelly doughnut first. It drips on her dress.*): Oh, pshaw! Don't both me none about the air-conditioner. I'm jist glad to git out of Underwriting! All they do is play Pinochle! Got this mean ole Boss . . .

LENA: Jessie?

PEARL: . . . Jessie!! . . . always makes me do my reports over again!

INEZ: Well, don't worry. You'll catch on. Pearl just moved to town. From River Falls. You was cashierin' there weren't ya? Never tried office work before?

PEARL: Mmm. It's double the money! It's gonna be our break!

INEZ: That's where we two met. When I was livin' in River Falls.

PEARL (*confused*): It is? I thought we met at that company picnic when our husbands was workin' over at Atlas Movin' Outfit in Cherokee.

INEZ (*chuckles, wads up gum wrapper and shoots it at the waste-*

basket):   Pshaw! Pearl! You got a memory like a frog! It was over to River Falls we met. Before we was ever married. *(Others laugh.)* She can't even remember bird one!

PEARL: You're right! I remember it all now. It was at one a them Baptist Fellowship Picnics we met. And they had it right on the river bank . . . and there was these big ole horseflies around. And they bit Inez! And she started yellin' out—so I come over and . . .

INEZ *(anxious to get off the topic):*   We all set? *(Cards have been dealt. Lena and Betty Jean are partners, sitting opposite, and Pearl and Inez.)*

LENA: Mmm. Let's play cards. Here we go: One heart!

INEZ: Crime 'n Itly! I haven't got anything! Pass!

BETTY JEAN: Two hearts!

PEARL: Two spades.

LENA: Three hearts.

INEZ: I still haven't got piddly: pass.

PEARL: That's okay.

BETTY JEAN: Pass. My land! What a hot ole August day!

PEARL: You got it, Lena. It's yours.

LENA: Ain't that nice now. Three hearts. *(Inez leads out, Betty Jean lays down hand, gets up and goes around to look over Lena's shoulder at her hand.)*

PEARL *(taking the first trick):*   Hey . . . who's the fourth here the rest of the week?

INEZ: Wanda Sue Turner. Goes to the bank to deposit on Fridays regular. Puts away every cent she gits I guess!

LENA *(slapping her card down to take trick):*   I guess! *(Leads out.)*

PEARL: Tight, huh?

LENA *(taking next trick, winking at Betty Jean):*   Tight? Girl, I mean to tell you she puts Jack Benny to shame! Why she lives in a rented room over Ramsey's Auto Parts Store. Hasn't even got a hotplate to her name! She makes a complete diet outa soda crackers and skim milk, and she won't even chip in on the baby showers or birthday cards for the rest of the force!

PEARL *(stunned):*   She don't chip in?

LENA: Isn't that the limit though? Why, when she first came in here to work and I knew she was a stranger in town, yah know? I tried to find her a place to live. I told her about my apartment . . . the Glenview Arms? Them real swell apartments over by the river?

PEARL: Oh, I seen them . . . they're just awful nice.

LENA: So, anyhow, she says, how much do they cost, and I says I pay $60 a month, and . . .

PEARL: Oh, Law! You pay $60 a month? Jist for yourself?

LENA: Mmm. $65 now. That was three years ago. Anyhow. You shoulda seen ole Wanda's face when I told her. Flabbergasted is the only word to name the state of that girl's face. I figured her out then and there. *(Betty Jean goes back to the window.)*

INEZ: Aw, that ain't nice, Lena! She's not so tight! *(Inez takes a swig of her Coke.)* Truth of it is, Wanda Sue's hopin' to git married. She's savin' for her hope chest. Lena jist don't like her. She's got a chip on her shoulder about poor Wanda Sue.

PEARL: Oh?

LENA: She is too tight! . . . Among other things . . . *(Betty Jean burst out laughing at this, and Inez, in spite of better instincts, does too. Betty Jean goes back to look over Lena's shoulder.)*

PEARL: Well jist listen to you all! What is it? What are you savin' it up for, the Fourth of July? Tell me before you bust your seams!

LENA: Shoot! Now will you look at her? Miss Curiosity! Honey, you're too young. I don't want to dirty up those lily white ears! *(Betty Jean finds this incredibly funny; she shrieks with laughter.)*

PEARL: Go on! Is she . . . ornery?

LENA: Ornery? Well I don't know as I'd call it that . . . exactly. Besides it ain't really her . . . it's that bum she thinks is gonna marry her! *(Lena trumps the trick.)*

PEARL: What's wrong with him?

LENA: Everything! *(Lena stops game now to devote full attention to telling this.)* He has got himself a reputation all over this office I mean to tell you! He used to work here.

INEZ: Till he got himself fired! Lena had to let him go. *(Betty Jean crosses to her own desk to powder face.)*

PEARL: Oh . . . he was the one was . . . ornery then?

LENA: Shoot, he was way past ornery. Dirty! That's the word to describe that man. Filthy dirty man!

PEARL: No! Right here in this office?

LENA: Mmm. Why he was always takin' anybody he could git a hold of out behind the candy machine in the hall, and you better believe he wasn't shovin' nickels in a machine for no *Hershey* bars out there!

PEARL: No!

LENA: Shoot! Once I seen him back that Dago girl, Marie . . . you remember Marie, don't ya, Inez? Worked for Dooley?

INEZ: Married some Hunkie in Chicago?

LENA: Yeah, that's her. Anyhow I seen Wanda's intended back this Dago girl, Marie, up against a wall and about rip her blouse off her, out there by the candy machine. Right from my desk I had a complete view. Poor thing was so scared she didn't know which end was up!

PEARL: All right here in this office? Law!

LENA: Well don't drop your pants about it, Pearl honey. I'm tellin' you the man was trash!

PEARL (*pouting*):   Pshaw! We haven't go nobody like that up in Underwriting. All we got is Mr. Johnson? Lives with his mother in Clive!

INEZ: Well thank your stars, Pearl, honey, on that account. It was a terrible influence on us havin' him here. Why he never even went to church Easter morning!

PEARL: No!

LENA: And the stories he used to pass around! Why . . . he told Betty Jean here . . . and before she was even married, you understand . . . told her how he'd gone to this sideshow out by Hampton and seen some girl performer do something with a stud pony! Well! I don't mean to spell it out for ya, but Law, when Betty Jean here told her Earl Henry about it, didn't he about knock her cuckoo for knowing about such disgustin' things!

BETTY JEAN (*coming back from her desk*):   He was terrible mad!

PEARL: No! In Hampton they do that?

LENA: Crime 'n Itly! That's jist nothin' to how low he was! He came right over to Inez at her desk, right before Inez had her baby, James Orville, and he yells jist as loud as a fire truck: "Hey, Inez." He yells, "Why don't you send that husband of yours up to Merrimack and git that doctor up there to fix him for ya!"

PEARL: The nerve! They do that in Merrimack?

INEZ: Doesn't that beat all? Why the very idea! Could have spoiled the rest of my married life?

LENA: Oh, I don't know as *that's* true. Lola What's-Her-Name, used to work on the IBM Machine on two? She sent her husband up to that doctor in Merrimack.

PEARL (*trying to place Lola*):   Really?

INEZ: I didn't know that.

BETTY JEAN (*pressing in her back*):   Well, she already had five kids.

PEARL: Mmm. This Lola happen to say what happened after her husband got himself fixed?

LENA: Nothin' . . . so she says! Didn't do nothin' but make him worse than he already was! Wasn't anything could hold him down after the operation Lola said. Wasn't ten months later she had her a set a twins! Both boys! A course, all you girls'd know more about that sorta thing than me! (*Hand of cards is over. Lena crosses to water cooler to get drink.*)

INEZ: Pshaw! Lena . . . you gonna go through life like that? Fudge? I'd die of the curiosity! It's just a cryin' shame you can't hook somebody or the other! Law! *(Betty Jean sits. Inez deals the next hand.)*

LENA: Maybe I don't want to. Ever think of that? Maybe there ain't no dang man this side of the Mississippi I'd give the time of day to, let alone have livin' off my good salary the rest of my natural life! And cashin' in on all my insurance if I pass first!

BETTY JEAN *(soothingly)*:   Well, sure! Can't say as I blame you in the least, Lena, honey. What with the kinda money you make and all the insurance you musta piled up from here for your retirement. *(Lena comes back and sits. Pearl is watching Lena.)*

PEARL: You ever been in River Falls? Visitin' or anything? Or Mountain Point?

LENA: Nope. Why?

PEARL: You . . . you look like I know you from someplace. Only I can't locate where.

INEZ: Isn't she the limit? Shoot! Somebody's always lookin' like somebody else to old Pearl. Every Tom, Dick or Harry on Mulberry Street puts her in mind of someone else!

PEARL: No, but Lena *really* does! *(Inez finishes the deal. They sort their hands.)*

INEZ: Pass.

BETTY JEAN: One club.

PEARL: Pass.

LENA: Pass.

INEZ: You got it Betty Jean for one club.

BETTY JEAN: Hardly worth it. Mangy little ole bid. Well, Pearl, lead out. Law! I'm so hot I'm stickin' to this seat! *(Pearl leads.)*

PEARL: So, they met here . . .

INEZ: Who met here?

LENA: He was in the stockroom. Doesn't that take the cake? A forty-year-old man stackin' envelopes at 60¢ per?

PEARL: Tommy Paul gets one-fifty out to John Deere now.

BETTY JEAN: Earl Henry just got raised to two!

LENA: It was the only job I figured he could handle, don't ya know? I was the one hired him to start with and first few years he was okay.

PEARL: But you fired him?

LENA: Had to, finally. After Wanda Sue started workin' here he wasn't the same man. Couldn't even handle his stupid little job. And I had to tell him so in front a everyone and yell at him and everything cause he was makin' such a mess of that room!

BETTY JEAN: It was an awful scene the day she let him go. Upset me to me stomach the whole afternoon. And Wanda Sue! Law, she threw up!

PEARL: What she look like? She pretty?

INEZ: Not bad. Big blue eyes. A natural blond. *(Inez glances at Betty Jean.)*

LENA: Ain't her looks that's gittin' us down about her. It's that she's turnin' out to be so blame stupid and ignorant.

BETTY JEAN: Yeah. It's all jist comin' out now. Why, Pearl, it takes her a solid morning to type a row of figures down a page!

LENA: She come in here after her junior year of high school. Doesn't have no diploma a course. So she don't make the same as the rest of my Research girls!

INEZ: Not by half! *(Pearl has spilled jelly from doughnut on dress. Goes to water cooler to clean it off.)*

BETTY JEAN: She is so dumb! Can you believe she's *makin'* her own wedding dress? And after I told her ninety-eleven times about them gorgeous little numbers over at "Three Sisters" where I bought mine. Jist gobs and gobs of lace and tulle for $29.98. She didn't listen. She jist keeps bringin' in her silly old veil to work and sewin' on it at her lunch. Isn't that dumb? She got the mayonnaise on it jist last week! *(The other girls all laugh.)*

PEARL: Hey, she got her an engagement ring? *(Pause. The others look at each other, begin to smirk and wink.)*

INEZ: Uh . . . what'd you say, honey? Has she got her an engagement ring? That's the question you have asked?

PEARL *(Bewildered. Turns at cooler to look at them.)*: Yes.

INEZ *(winking)*: That's what the girl asked, Betty Jean. What do you say to that? Has Wanda Sue got her an engagement ring?

BETTY JEAN: An engagement ring, huh? Well, I don't know . . . Lena, what'd you say? Does Wanda Sue got her an engagement ring?

LENA: Has she got a ring? Well . . . I would say . . . she has got her the most unusual ring this side of the Pennsylvania mines! That's what I would say! *(Betty Jean and Inez and Lena all burst out laughing very loudly, splattering their cards on the table and floor, totally disrupting the game.)*

PEARL: Hey, you all! What's goin' on? What is this?

LENA: Honey, she's engaged all right! And she's got a ring! A *coal diamond!* All of her very own! *(Girls laugh more at this.)*

PEARL: A *what?*

LENA *(magnanimously)*: Oh, let's let Inez tell it. She saw the thing first!

INEZ *(For the occasion she lights up a Camel, takes a drag, sticks her gum under the desk, tilts back in her chair and clears her throat)*: Well! Wanda Sue Turner used to sit next to me. Right side, against the back wall.

LENA *(can't keep out of it)*:   Left side. Against the front wall.

INEZ *(giving Lena a look)*:   As I was sayin'! This Wanda Sue's a close mouth. Never tell ya anythin' you want to know. But, anyhow. In she pops this one morning and announces right outa the blue she's gittin' engaged the very next day and is gittin' a half-carat ring!

PEARL *(stunned)*:   Half-carat? You kiddin' me?

LENA: That's what we all said. We couldn't hardly wait till the next day in fact to git a look.

INEZ: Next day, 8:30 on the nose, in she pops. And sure enough there she is wavin' her hand around with this great big ring. And . . .

LENA *(can't keep out of it)*:   And, it was a half-carat all right. But, honey . . . it had a black spot in the center big as a dime. A chunk a coal nobody could polish into diamond and so they left it stickin' in there, black as the ace of spades!

PEARL: What?

LENA: And she went around like she didn't even see that big black blob in the center. She was jist flashin' the thing around!

INEZ: And we didn't want to say nothin' on accounta its bein' the first day she'd got herself engaged. We never did say nothin'.

LENA: Only it is the sorriest lookin' ring you'll ever see in this world. *(A pause.)*

PEARL: Seems like I seen her in that ring. In the washroom I bet.

LENA: Mmm. Probably. She's still wearin' it. Won't take it off for love nor money. She thinks he's comin' back to her.

PEARL: He left? What's he doin'?

LENA: Sittin' on his dinghy somewhere! *(Girls laugh at this.)*

INEZ: Crime 'n Itly, Lena, don't tease Pearl so much! He joined the Navy this week . . . took Wanda out to dance to Pee Wee Hunt's band at the Bel-Air. . . .

PEARL: Law! I can't abide Pee Wee Hunt!

INEZ: Well, he sprung it on her out there about how he couldn't git another job in town because Lena kept disrecommendin' him every place called her up. So Red joined the Navy and is gonna save up and sail home to her in two years with a genuine kimono from Tokyo, Japan! He says!

BETTY JEAN: And she believes it! The rest a these are mine . . . *(Betty Jean shows her cards, others concede the game, laying down their cards.)* Sits here all week typin' him mushy letters on company time! Sewin' away on that sorry lookin' veil, draggin' around with that coal diamond on her hand! And doin' her reports wrong so Lena has to make her do 'em again.

LENA: Law, I jist don't know how long I can put up with it all before I have to let ole Wanda Sue go too! 'Cause I think she's gonna be actin' like that till Judgement Day!

INEZ: Same day you git you a man, huh?

LENA: Inez, you ever let up on that? Here . . . I got to go to the john. Deal out, Betty Jean, and I'll be right back . . . we haven't got much time left. *(She gets up, starts out.)* Don't none of ya cheat on me, hear? *(She exits.)*

PEARL *(the minute Lena's gone, rising, very conspiratorially)*: Hey! What was that guy's name?

BETTY JEAN: Huh? Who? What guy?

PEARL: *That* guy . . . that guy you was all jist talkin' about.

INEZ: Who?

PEARL: The guy with Wanda Sue!

INEZ: Oh, Red.

BETTY JEAN: Red.

INEZ: Red Haner.

PEARL: Red?

INEZ: Mm. Had this big bushy mess a red hair and freckles. Why? What's eatin' you?

PEARL *(triumphant)*: That's jist what I thought!

INEZ: What do you mean that's jist what you thought?

PEARL: Boy, have I got a story for you all! Thank the Lord Lena left!

BETTY JEAN: Why?

PEARL: You know how I said Lena looked familiar to me?

INEZ: Oh, everybody looks familiar to you. What's that got to do with the price of eggs?

PEARL: I kept thinkin' all hour I knew Lena from before only I couldn't locate where. Then jist a few minutes ago right outa the blue, I commenced to think on my Aunt Fannie! Used to run this boarding house in Clearview. And I used to go visit summers when I was a little kid. Nineteen, twenty years ago.

INEZ: Well who cares what you did twenty years ago?

PEARL *(getting very excited)*: But that's when I seen Lena. The summer I graduated grade school and went to visit Aunt Fannie. Lena was rentin' a room off her and had a job in some dinky little hicktown office in Clearview. And Lena was young then, ole Lena was—real young—

BETTY JEAN: Yeah?

PEARL: Mmm. But jist as sorry lookin' then as she is now. An Old Maid in her Youth!

BETTY JEAN: Well—feature that!

PEARL: Never did have any boyfriends like the rest of the girls in the roomin' house, you know? Jist her job. That's all Lena ever did talk about was that dumb ole hicktown office job a hers!

INEZ: Oh, Law!

PEARL: Other girls kept on goin' out on their Saturday night dates while Lena jist sat there with me and Aunt Fannie on the front porch. All the nights of August she jist sat. Until this one night we seen her comin' down Willow Street, runnin', shoutin' at us and wavin' her left hand! And then she come up on the porch and sticks it in our faces and shows us this big ole half-carat engagement ring!

BETTY JEAN: What?

PEARL: And tells us she has met someone on the job and has got engaged and is gonna git married!

BETTY JEAN: Oh, Land!

PEARL: Only thing of it was that ring had a chunk of coal in the middle of it big as a dime!

INEZ: What do you mean?

PEARL (*exultant*):   That Lena was engaged to Red too! And wore that coal diamond jist like Wanda Sue! I knew I seen that ring before! (*A long pause. The revelation has stunned Inez and Betty Jean.*)

BETTY JEAN: Crim 'n Itly girl, you mean it?

PEARL: Mmm. And to beat all she pretended there wasn't no coal in the middle of it either! That it was the most perfect ring ever existed in the world of God! (*Betty Jean and Inez are very excited now, laughing and giggling.*)

INEZ: I can hardly believe it at all.

PEARL: Well, it's the Lord's truth. Didn't last more 'n two, three months. After I left, Aunt Fannie said Lena used to sneak him up to her room, and then he started eatin' in the roomin' house and she footed his bill! But by the time I went back to Clearview for Christmas vacation, it was over. Lena said he had to "support his mother" so had to "postpone the wedding" and take back the ring because he loved Lena "so dearly" and didn't want to spoil Lena's chances with all the other men! 'Course we knew Red jist give Lena that ring to git himself that job!

BETTY JEAN: And then Lena got her *this* job here in Valley Center and moved here and hired him again? Thinkin' she'd git him in the end I bet!

PEARL: Mmm. And then along comes Wanda Sue! Well! How's that for a story, girls? Guess that takes the cake about that swell boss you all keep braggin' on! (*In triumph Pearl chuckles, takes a big bite out of her apple, tilts back in her chair.*)

BETTY JEAN: My Land! How many years was it he was—*(Lena enters.)*

LENA: Well, now, nobody cheated on me did they? *(Girls laugh, thinly.)*

INEZ: Cheated? Shoot, Lena, not on you!

BETTY JEAN: We were jist killin' time . . .

INEZ *(busying herself with cards)*: Tryin' to keep cool . . .

BETTY JEAN: Shootin' the breeze . . .

INEZ: Jist waitin' on ya, Lena . . . to come back . . .

LENA *(putting her purse away)*: Well, I bumped into old Mavis Jones in the washroom. From Claims on Four? And you know how that girl goes on!

BETTY JEAN *(busying herself too)*: Oh, Law!

LENA: Mmm. She told me they're hirin' two more Claims Investigators over there at Boone Ridge.

BETTY JEAN: Two more?

LENA: Pshaw! They could use eight more over there! And that's a fact! *(Pause. Lena sits down again to continue game. Girls are trying to suppress giggles. There is much tension—then Inez blurts out mischievously:)*

INEZ: Mmm. We got ole Pearl here talkin' . . . about her past . . .

BETTY JEAN *(laughing lightly)*: Which she kin hardly remember . . .

INEZ: 'Cause she got a memory like a frog . . . although she did remember as how she'd visited in Clearview . . . when she was a kid? Came to visit her Aunt Fannie. Ran a roomin' house in town . . . for girls . . . isn't that what you said, Pearl, honey? *(A long pause. Pearl looks at Inez, terrified. Lena looks at Pearl. Finally:)*

LENA: That a fact, Pearl?

PEARL: Oh, but it was so long ago I disremember everything about it. I can't remember a thing! Not a thing! *(She smiles weakly.)*

INEZ: That's ole Pearl for you! Always did have a memory like a sieve! *(Pause. Lena is shaken. Arranges her hand, regaining her composure. Finally:)*

LENA: Well, now, let's see can we finish the rubber off. Betty Jean? Your bid!

BETTY JEAN *(looking at Inez, then Lena)*: I pass . . .

LENA: Pearl?

PEARL: Pass.

LENA: One spade. Inez?

INEZ: Pass.

BETTY JEAN: Two spades.

PEARL: Pass.

LENA: Pass.

INEZ: Pass.

PEARL: You got it, Lena. For two spades.

LENA: Well. Then it's ours Betty Jean. Inez, lead out! *(Inez leads. Lena becomes very dictatorial now, ordering everyone.)* Betty Jean, lay down your hand! *(Betty Jean does.)* Uh-huh. Put the eight on the three! Pearl, what you gonna do?

PEARL: The King . . . I got no choice . . .

LENA: That's a shame! Here comes the Ace! Put down that King! *(Lena takes the trick.)*

BETTY JEAN: Oh my! Lena's that's good! *(She crosses and stands looking over Lena's shoulder.)*

LENA: Okay, here we go! There's mine! Inez put down yours! *(She leads, Inez plays.)* So, Pearl, you're in Underwriting, huh?

PEARL: Yes . . . yes, ma'am, I am . . . I . . .

LENA: Me and Jessie a course are such good old girlfriends . . . we go back must be fifteen years . . .

PEARL: Oh, Jessie's just a wonderful boss to work for, I can tell you that.

LENA: Thought you said she was mean?

PEARL: Jessie? Oh no I didn't . . .

LENA: Oh well . . . it don't matter . . .

PEARL: Leastways I . . . I disremember . . .

LENA: *Memory* matters though. Memory's just a terrible important asset for the insurance business. A person would have trouble doin' a good job on their work without a good memory. Don't you think so girls? *(A short pause.)*

INEZ: Why I think memory's the most important thing to have of all!

LENA: Betty Jean?

BETTY JEAN: Oh, definitely the most important thing of all. Why everytime I have to type a report I have to remember all them things in my head . . .

LENA: Mmm. In my experience you can't hardly handle the work without it. Most of the girls who stay on and advance theirselves have superior memories. Without that a girl could be a downright detriment to the firm. I think all the Bosses of the Sections feel exactly the same way . . . in point a fact I'm sure they do . . . at least the ones I know . . . *(Lena has been taking trick after trick.)* 'Course, I'm a little more lenient than some. I say, sometimes people *do* forget some things that aren't important to them at all . . . *(Lena looks at Betty Jean and Inez.)*

INEZ: Shoot, I'm like that!

BETTY JEAN: Me too.

LENA: Other people have a more general problem . . . *(Bell rings.)* That's it! End a lunch!

BETTY JEAN: And we didn't even finish the rubber off! Fudge!

PEARL *(jumping up)*:   I . . . I got to go. I got to finish my report . . . I . . . I'll see you all . . . I . . . *(She is terrified. She starts hurrying out.)*

LENA: Pearl?! *(Pearl stops.)* You come on back next Friday, hear? We'll make it permanent on Fridays. At least for a while . . . see how everything goes . . . 'Cause you're jist like us Pearl honey, you hear? You play one mean hand of bridge! *(A pause. Pearl exits quickly as Inez and Betty Jean begin to set up office desks for the afternoon work. As they move around her, Lena sits staring after Pearl. Lights dim to black.)*

AMERICANSAINT

ADAM LeFEVRE

First production May 26, 1987, at Actor's Theatre of Louisville, with Bob Krakower as director; sets by Paul Owen; lighting by Cliff Berek; costumes by Kevin McLeod, with the following cast:

BROTHER VINCENT	David Garcia
BETTINA SMOOCHES	Jenny Robertson
CAPTAIN MIKE*	Nick Phelps
ARLO PENNYPACKER*	Kevin Fabian

Setting
Various, at sea and in Vermont

Time
1903

■   ■

Scene 1: Burial at Sea

CAPTAIN MIKE: Et cetera, et cetera, and so we commit his soul to the deep. (*He lifts the board and a body slips from under a shroud and falls down into the sea.*) Ung-ah!

BROTHER VINCENT: Wait!

CAPTAIN MIKE: Kerplunk. What is it, Padre? Did you want to say a few words? Oops. Looks like I jumped the gun. Oh, my backbone! He was a big one.

BROTHER VINCENT: Now he's light. God will lift him.

CAPTAIN MIKE: Worse case of *mal de mer* I ever seen. Well, go ahead and say your piece. Don't mind there's no body. It's the thought that counts. I got to get back to the poop, though. The mate can't chart a course for beans. Got us turned toward Terra Horribilis.

BROTHER VINCENT: Bless you, Captain.

CAPTAIN MIKE: And vicey versa to you, Padre. Elmo! Steady as she goes, I says! You got bilgewater for brains, boy!

BROTHER VINCENT (*kneels*): Dear Lord, grant me the strength to finish alone the work you set before Father Dominick and myself,

* May be played by the same actor.

his humble novice, whom no one could blame if I just turned around and went right back to the Vatican because my stated duties were strictly secretarial and the unlettered world abashes me, but now, should I pluck this flower it is solely to *my* credit, and then, who knows what elevation? so I will forge on to find this child of God and confirm her saintly deeds so that we might greater glorify your name here on earth, and, who knows? though I desire no honor other than to better serve you, I would certainly be somebody in Rome. Arrivederci, Padre. In Jesus' name we pray. Amen.

CAPTAIN MIKE *(off)*:   Land ho!

Scene 2: On the Road

Brother Vincent, exhausted and dusty, plops down his duffle near a signpost of three arrows. One says "Brattleboro." One says "Rutland." One says "Peru."

BROTHER VINCENT: Lord! The roads of America are long.

(Bettina Smooches, a girl of 13, comes skipping down the lane, stopping periodically to scratch the dust with her stick. She sings a little ditty.)

BETTINA: I love
                                            Eddie Stalinky.
                                            I wear
                                            his face on my pinky.

BROTHER VINCENT: Hello, little girl. What are you doing with that stick?

BETTINA: Looking for something I want. *(She sings.)* I love Eddie Stalinky . . .
Can you touch your tongue and your butt? I can. *(She touches her tongue with the finger of one hand, and her behind with the finger of her other.)* Ha! This is Vermont, you know.

BROTHER VINCENT: How far to town?

BETTINA: Over the bridge and round the bend. Hey! "Railroad crossing. Look out for the cars. How do you spell it without any *Rs?*" I-T. Ha! Get it? My brother taught me that one. He's home in bed, dying from diarrhea. I found a snake with two heads. Wanna see?

BROTHER VINCENT: That's terrible.

BETTINA: It's dead, don't worry.

BROTHER VINCENT: I mean your poor brother.

BETTINA: He'll be dead too, before sunset. So will you—someday.
Me too. I can see the future sometimes. Plain as my hand.

BROTHER VINCENT: What is your name, child?

BETTINA: Bettina. Bettina Smooches. But someday it will be Stalinky. I just know it.

BROTHER VINCENT: Are you the one they call the Virgin of the
Valley?

BETTINA: Are you kiddin'? I'd smack 'em. If you give me a nickel,
I'll show you my bellybutton. There's somebody's face in there.
Guess who? Oops, I got to go. My brother just died. Here's my
stick. It's magic, so don't point it nowhere lest you mean it. Just
a loaner, you understand, case you need some magic. 'Bye, now.

Scene 3: The Telegraph Office

Vincent enters with duffle and stick. He rings bell for service.

BROTHER VINCENT: Hello? Anybody there? Hello? Somebody?

ARLO: Right you are. I was readin' out back. *Plutarch's Lives*. Gonna
be President someday, or bust tryin'.

BROTHER VINCENT: I'd like to send a telegraph.

ARLO: I'll show these pumpkin heads a thing or two. Be statue of
me right next to Ethan Allen in the square. All right, stranger,
let 'er rip.

BROTHER VINCENT: Arrived in America and Peru . . .

ARLO: Peru, Vermont. A nice place to live if you got no ambition.
Me, I got bigger fish to fry. Go ahead.

BROTHER VINCENT: May have located the Virgin of the Valley.
Stop.

ARLO: Stop?

BROTHER VINCENT: There's more.

ARLO: Let's hope so.

BROTHER VINCENT: How must phenomena be confirmed? Please
advise. Stop. Sad . . .

ARLO: Wait. Lucky for you I got a little Greek. All right, go on.

BROTHER VINCENT: Sad to inform Father Dominick died at sea.
Sign it "Brother Vincent," and send it off to the Vatican.

ARLO: Rome?

BROTHER VINCENT: Correct.

ARLO: I ain't punched nothin' through the cable since McKinley
got shot. Jeezum Crow, what a treat!

BETTINA (*enters*):   Mister? I need my stick.

ARLO: Get out of here, Goo-goo Eyes! You already been told.

BETTINA: I need my stick. Daddy wants me to fetch Silas back.
Says he didn't finish his chores. How I feel about it don't matter.
Daddy is Daddy, simple as that.

BROTHER VINCENT: Here, child.

BETTINA: Holy smokes, be careful! I figured a man wearin' a dress ought to know which is the business end of a stick. Guess I pulled a boner. Well, no harm done.

ARLO: Has I got to call the constable, Goo-goo Eyes?

BETTINA: Name's not Goo-goo Eyes, you crook. Oops. A duck just ate a June bug gonna make him choke. 'Bye, now. (*Exits.*)

BROTHER VINCENT: Is she the one they call the Virgin of the Valley?

ARLO: She's been called just about everything. Kinda famous around here.

BROTHER VINCENT: Is it true that in her presence statues have wept tears of blood, and the crippled have jumped up and danced?

ARLO: Well, she's a caution, I'll tell you that.

BROTHER VINCENT: Did not a local haunt of Sodomites, an avowed parlor of harlotry, recently, spontaneously burst into flames when the girl walked by?

ARLO: That'd be Ethel Mae Houligan's. They couldn't for sure pin that on Goo-goo Eyes, but, tell you this—I wouldn't leave that child and her curiosity alone in the same county with a box of matches.

BROTHER VINCENT: Where does she live?

ARLO: Down the road, same as everybody.

Scene 4: In the Air

BETTINA: You can't see me. You don't even know I'm here, and that's just the way I like it. Shh. (*She makes radio noise—squeaks, hums, static.*) Come in. Come on in out of the in-between. Shh. It's a long ways off, but, if you listen, you can hear time begin. It sounds like . . . Shh. Come in now. Come on in. (*She makes radio noise.*)

Scene 5: Goin' Fishin'

Lem Smooches enters with a fishing pole.

BROTHER VINCENT: Mr. Smooches?

LEM: Maybe. Fishin' helps me think.

BROTHER VINCENT: I'm Brother Vincent, agent of the Holy See in Rome.

LEM: "And Jesus said unto him, 'I will make you a fisher of men.'" Well, he weren't talkin' to me. I'm a fisher of fishes. A nuts and bolts believer, honest enough to call a misery a misery. Born up on that there mountain. Or that one. Hard to tell. Cloudy.

BROTHER VINCENT: Bettina is your daughter?

LEM: Some years ago my wife took off with an auctioneer, so I'm somethin' of a doubtin' Thomas.

BROTHER VINCENT: She's a remarkable girl.

LEM: You know Doris?

BROTHER VINCENT: Doris?

LEM: Doris. What? She changed her name?

BROTHER VINCENT: I'm referring to Bettina.

LEM: Oh, Goo-goo Eyes. She's remarkable, all right. Been that way ever since her brother near drowned her in the duck pond.

BROTHER VINCENT: I've been sent by the church to confirm the wonderments of which we have heard.

LEM: Come again?

BROTHER VINCENT: Is it true she has caused the crippled to jump up and dance?

LEM: Well, her own brother she did once, when she laid that stick into him. See, Silas was kicked in the . . . how can I put it? . . . gonadals by a milkcow when he was three year old. Upshot of it was his left arm and leg quit growin'. He got on okay 'cause as the rest of him growed, we tied a milkin' stool to his bum side to even him out. He's down to the duck pond one day, chuckin' rocks at the frogs and turtles like a boy'll do, and Bettina, she got Christian names for all them critters, so she took her stick to 'im. He danced all right. That's when he decided to drown her.

BROTHER VINCENT: There are reports of statues she touches weeping blood.

LEM: Well, I wouldn't doubt it.

BROTHER VINCENT: Did you yourself ever see such a wonder?

LEM: A statue, you say? Not actually. I did see her make a tomcat *piss* blood, though. Her and that stick.

BROTHER VINCENT: Is it true her mere gaze caused a brothel to burn?

LEM: If you're speakin' of Ethel Mae's, that's the first I heard that particular theory. If'n it's true I'll take a strap to that girl. Every man needs his horns scraped somehow, and, whatever else Ethel Mae may have been, and that, I repeat, is her own damn business, she was always a clean woman, rest her soul. Smelled like strawberries she did.

BETTINA (*enter with stick*):   Hard as I smack him, Silas jest won't get up.

LEM: Course not. The boy is dead. He's crossed over. He's gone.

BETTINA: Where's he gone to, then?

LEM: A better place than this, bet your face on it. Where his limbs is all one size and he don't need no milkin' stool to stand straight.

BETTINA: Hey, Mister. Wanna try? *(She extends the stick to him.)*

LEM: Put that stick down, girl, and tell me true. Did you set Ethel Mae's on fire?

BETTINA: I never done nothin' but walk on by.

LEM: Did you gaze at it?

BETTINA: I did. One time. Yes, I did.

LEM: And what did you see?

BETTINA: Flames. Flames of many colors, like the tongues of angels. And they was prettier than the privy lilies and Black-eyed Susans.

BROTHER VINCENT: Praise God. They'll make me a bishop.

LEM: If I thought it'd make one lick o' difference I'd whup you senseless. 'Scuse me, Roman, I'm off to wet a line. Leave the boy alone, girl. He's dead. *(Exits.)*

BROTHER VINCENT: How blessed I am to have found you. Dear child, do you know? God is in you.

BETTINA: Whereabouts? *(She looks for him.)*

BROTHER VINCENT: You have great and wonderful power.

BETTINA: Truth is my stick ain't workin' like it should. Silas won't budge.

BROTHER VINCENT: You shall be known around the world as Saint Bettina, Virgin of the Valley.

BETTINA: No sir, I shall not. I shall be known as Mrs. Eddie Stalinky. We will be married between the wars in a cathedral made entirely of music. And I will wear his name proudly as my own skin right to the stone on top of my grave. The rest is all turtle talk. Hey! Can you touch your tongue and your butt? *(He does.)* You're learnin', mister.

Scene 6: Back in the Telegraph Office

Brother Vincent sits eating an apple. Arlo enters, loaded with books.

ARLO: This country needs a man in the White House who knows his hydraulics as well as his history. Not to mention poetry. Been readin' poetry to sharpen my tenderness. *Poetry is the alibi of the soul.* I thought that up myself, and you may quote me.

BROTHER VINCENT: It's odd, but, you know, I've begun to feel at home here. I'm beginning to understand how peace passeth all understanding. Perhaps, when I'm a cardinal, I'll return to supervise the building of a shrine. That little girl is going to be a saint, you know. The rest is just formalities.

ARLO: Too bad you never met Ethel Mae. Now there was a saint. Trust ya till payday. Oh, by the by, somethin' come in for you last night on Elroy's shift. Asked me to get it to you. *(Arlo hands him a telegraph message.)* What's the matter? Is the spellin' off? Elroy is a chowderhead at spellin'. Here. Bet I can translate for ya. *(Takes message and reads.)* "You are lost. Stop. Virgin of Valley proved hoax by parish priest two months ago in Peru, South America. Stop. You are lost. Stop. Find your way home." Signed, Cardinal Quisadicci. Peru, *South* America. Oops. Looks like you pulled a boner. The 3:15 out of Brattleboro will get you to Boston by morning. Here, read some hydraulics along the way. Put some color back in them cheeks. I'll look you up on my European tour.

Scene 7: On the Road and in the Air

Brother Vincent trudges by with duffle.

BETTINA: Hey, Mister. I know where you're goin'. I kin see the future sometimes, clear as this day. Ever since Silas drowned me in the duck pond. He pushed my face right down there in the turtles and the lilytails, and held me there till a bubble burst in my head. You're goin' home. And you'll live there a long time— longer than you want. And, on a snowy morn there in the Eternal City, you'll die in your bed wonderin' if the things I said is true. They're true. You ain't never gonna be Pope, nor cardinal, nor titmouse, but that's all right. 'Cause it was meant that way. They will be wars and wars and wars, and children will have children, and children will have beasts, and beasts will take numbers for names. And somewhere between the wars, on a day not unlike this one, I will marry Eddie Stalinky, clown prince of radio. And our children will make music at the wedding out of tubes and bones. And they will decide in the middle of the music not to be born, for the sake of his career, for they will understand, as only the unborn can, how important it is. And then at the darkest hour of midnight, when the whole world thinks the sky is comin' down, he will make the people laugh. And the laugh will be deep and round, and for a moment the world will be like one person. And when he dies folks will say, "All of us have died a bit today." It was meant. I was born to be his bride. Ladies and gentlemen, Mr. Eddie Stalinky, Clown Prince of Radio. This is what he told me on our wedding day. "Someday, my little airwave, you will understand everything. Clear as the hand on your face."

(She puts her hand on his face and that is the end of the play.)

THROWING YOUR VOICE

CRAIG LUCAS

THROWING YOUR VOICE was written for Naked Angels and produced by them as part of their evening of one-acts, collectively titled *Naked Rights,* which ran from December 6* through December 21, 1991. The production was directed by Jace Alexander. The designers were: George Xenos (set), Brian MacDevitt (lighting), Aural Fixation/Guy Sherman (sound) and Rosi Zangales (costumes); the production stage manager was Jenny Peek, with the following cast:

DOUG	David Marshall Grant
LUCY	Jenifer Estess
RICHARD	Tim Ransom
SARAH	Lisa Beth Miller

■ ■

After dinner. Lucy, Doug, and Richard have coffee; Sarah has herbal tea. She is hugely pregnant. Gentle music plays on the sound system; it will end at some point and no one will rise to put on another CD.

RICHARD: But to have them killed? Or maimed?

LUCY *(to Sarah)*:   Some honey? *(Sarah shakes her head.)*

RICHARD: To *pay* somebody to do that for you? I mean, I understand killing somebody in the heat of passion. Or if they had something you really really wanted.

LUCY: They did.

DOUG: But they did.

RICHARD: I guess. I mean . . . 'cause, but I actually have no trouble imagining killing somebody when they walk in the middle of the subway stairs in front of you really slowly—

LUCY: Yes.

RICHARD: —and are just incredibly, *incredibly* fat—

SARAH: Watch it.

RICHARD: No, you know, you try to go this way, they move—

---

* The opening night was a benefit for Amnesty International U.S.A.

DOUG: Right.

SARAH: They're doing it on purpose, just to incense you. *(Pause. The music plays.)*

DOUG: . . . Or those jerks who block the aisles at Food Emporium, staring at some foodstuff—

RICHARD: Those are the ones.

DOUG: —as if they'd just woken up from a fifty-year sleep and are trying to pick the really right . . .

LUCY: They're having a stroke, probably.

DOUG *(overlapping slightly)*:   . . . brie. . . . No, they're not having a stroke. Why would you take their side? I hate those people.

LUCY *(smiles)*:   You're right. They should die.

RICHARD: I just . . . I don't know . . . to *pay* somebody . . . to kill the mother of you daughter's main competition for the cheerleaders so she'll be too distraught to audition. . . . It worries me.

DOUG: Well, it's passive aggressive.

LUCY: It is.

RICHARD *(to Sarah)*:   Are we going to be like that in sixteen years?

SARAH *(nodding)*:   Mm-hm.

RICHARD: Plotting . . . living our entire lives through little Grendel? Having no life of our own?

LUCY *(to Doug, overlapping from "Having—")*:   She should've killed the daughter's friend directly.

DOUG: That would've—

LUCY: That would've been healthier.

DOUG: Don't you think? *(Doug hears Richard's words late as he replays them in his head.)* Little Grendel? Is that what you call it?

RICHARD: Mm-hm.

LUCY: But . . . you know . . . if I think about it . . . I would probably . . . if I thought I could get away with it?

DOUG: Mm-hm.

LUCY: I would do the exact same thing to Orrin Hatch and Arlan Specter.

SARAH: Yes.

LUCY: Wouldn't you?

SARAH: No question.

LUCY: Kill their mothers so they're too distraught to go to the Senate.

SARAH: Yes. Or . . . actually I've thought about this . . . a little bit . . . and I would make them . . . take old rusty fishing knives used for cleaning, you know . . . squid . . .

LUCY: Mm-hm.

SARAH: And I would make them cut each other's tongues out and eat them live on television while Anita Hill stands over them and . . .

LUCY: Screams.

SARAH: No . . . Actually, I would have her *shit* in their bloody mouths. Is my image. *(Tiny beat before:)*

RICHARD: Dinner was delicious, thanks . . . Being pregnant has brought out such a warmth of fellow feeling in Sarah.

SARAH: No, come on.

RICHARD *(overlapping, continuous)*: It's very moving.

SARAH: They're horrible people.

RICHARD: Yes. *(Beat. To Doug and Sarah, referring to the music.)* What is this?

LUCY: It's . . . *(Looks at Doug.)*

SARAH: It's beautiful.

DOUG: Schubert?

LUCY: Schumann?

RICHARD: One of the Shoe People. No, don't get up.

LUCY *(moves toward the sound system)*: No, I wanted to get some water. Anybody else?

RICHARD: No, thank you.

SARAH: No. Thanks.

LUCY *(overlapping "thanks," looking at the CD case)*: Schumann.

RICHARD: Schumann?

DOUG: But . . .

LUCY: Doug?

DOUG: No. Thanks. But . . . if you think about it?

RICHARD: Uh-huh?

DOUG: This whole . . . thing about not wanting to get caught? *(Pause.)* To *get* the other person but not to be held responsible?

SARAH: Uh-huh?

DOUG: Like the woman in Texas?

SARAH: She wanted what she wanted but she didn't want to—

DOUG: Right . . . right.

RICHARD: Exactly.

DOUG: It's like . . . I don't particularly . . .

LUCY *(returning with water)*: What is this?

DOUG: I was saying . . .

SARAH: The woman in Texas.

DOUG: I don't particularly want, say, to go to Iraq and kill a hundred thousand Iraqis even if I do think their President is . . .

RICHARD: A putz.

DOUG: Well, a little Hitler and dangerous.

RICHARD: Right.

DOUG: I don't want to see the faces of the people we kill.

RICHARD: Right.

DOUG: So I pay taxes to a government which pays an entire underclass to go—

RICHARD: Right.

SARAH (same time):   Yes.

DOUG: —and do it for me, so I can still have my air conditioning in the summer.

LUCY: Which, of course, we don't have.

DOUG: I mean, it's sort of the same. It's still murder.

LUCY: I think that's ridiculous.

DOUG: I know you do.

LUCY (overlapping):   I'm sorry. I think if we hadn't done it he would have eventually blown us all to smithereens or we would have all—history would have been set back centuries by this medieval crazy man and the Iraqi people are—Wait—responsible for their actions and their own nation and I'm sorry they're all dead. That's all. (Pause.)

DOUG: My point . . . was only that . . . we often . . . people often pay other people to do their dirty work so they don't have to look at the consequences—

LUCY: Yes.

DOUG: —of their actions.

LUCY: I don't think it was dirty work. I think it was . . .

DOUG: God's work?

LUCY: We don't agree on this subject. (Pause.)

RICHARD: But . . . you know? One way, too, of looking at it is that people . . . if everyone was actually responsible for their own actions and nothing else. If the woman in Texas were not held responsible, even though she paid this guy—

DOUG: Legally?

RICHARD: Legally, morally, any way. If . . . see, I didn't go to Iraq.

DOUG: But you paid taxes.

RICHARD: Right.

DOUG: And you pay taxes—

LUCY: Let him finish.

DOUG: Wait, you pay taxes to support a government that practices murder in this state. Capital punishment.

LUCY: There's no—

RICHARD: Not in New York.

DOUG: No?

LUCY: There's no capital punishment in New York State.

DOUG: Are you sure? That's right.

LUCY: Not for twenty years.

DOUG: Well, there goes my argument. But . . . I mean—*(To Sarah.)* Would you buy fur?

SARAH: With what?

DOUG *(overlapping)*: If you could? . . .

SARAH: If I could? No. Probably not. I can't even . . . imagine.

DOUG *(overlapping slightly)*: Would you buy . . . ?

LUCY: I would. And I would wear it in grandeur.

DOUG: We know you would. But you're poor and you'll always be poor . . . W—?

LUCY *(overlapping, sung)*: "Marat, you're poor,
"And the poor stay poor."

DOUG: That's right.

SARAH *(overlapping)*: Right! *(Joins Lucy and they sing together:)*

LUCY & SARAH: "Marat, don't let us wait anymore!
We want our rights!"

DOUG: Thank you.

LUCY *(overlapping)*: "And we don't—*(Sarah has momentarily forgotten the words; she rejoins Lucy on:)*

LUCY & SARAH *(overlapping)*: "—care how!
We want our revolution
Now!" *(They crack up.)*

DOUG: Yes, me too. All right . . .

LUCY: I can't believe it!

DOUG: Just tell me: would you buy—

LUCY: I still know those words.

SARAH: I know!

DOUG *(overlapping, continuous)*: Would you buy coffee from Colombia if you knew—*(To Lucy.)* Where is this coffee from?

LUCY: D'Agostino's.

DOUG: If you knew people had died . . . culling it.

LUCY: Harvesting.

SARAH: No, I suppose . . .

RICHARD: But wait.

LUCY: Culling?

RICHARD *(overlapping, continuous)*: Wait, wait.

LUCY: Dougie, you always do this. It was so peaceful here.

DOUG: We're not having a bad time. Are we?

SARAH: No.

RICHARD: No.

LUCY: But you're gonna make all the people feel bad. They're gonna go home—

DOUG: No, they're not.

LUCY: —feeling guilty and defiled, sorry that they're Americans.

RICHARD: But. I just . . . Here's my point.

LUCY: Okay.

DOUG: Okay.

RICHARD: If people were responsible for their own actions alone . . .

DOUG *(to Lucy)*: No one's unhappy.

RICHARD: If the soldiers who went to Iraq—

DOUG: I understand.

RICHARD: —were wholly responsible for their going there and I didn't feel any responsibility whatsoever.

DOUG: But you're saying that you do.

RICHARD: Yes, I do. But I'm als—I'm saying that's stupid. Even if I agreed that it was entirely wrong for them to go there which . . . I don't know about—

DOUG: You don't.

RICHARD: No. But let's say . . . I voted for George Bush and I supported the war . . . totally . . .

DOUG: Okay.

RICHARD: I still . . . in an existential way . . . don't think I should be responsible for someone else's actions. *(Pause.)*

DOUG: Would you invest in South Africa?

RICHARD: I already have.

DOUG: What do you mean?

RICHARD: That's probably where . . . I mean, I don't know, that's probably where Sarah's ring is from. I didn't ask when I bought it, I was all of twenty-two.

DOUG: Uh-huh.

RICHARD: But . . . I've read that most diamonds, new diamonds come from there. *(Pause.)*

DOUG: Well, okay.

LUCY: It is okay, don't say it like that.

RICHARD: I also read that . . . people are killed in the diamond mines. Children, for all I know. It's horrible. And I didn't know. What are we supposed to do.

DOUG: Would you buy ivory?

RICHARD: No. But I also wouldn't throw away *old ivory*, if I had it.

DOUG: You wouldn't?

RICHARD: No.

DOUG: Why?

RICHARD: Because I think the damage is already done.

DOUG: But then you're saying there is damage.

RICHARD: No—

DOUG *(overlapping)*: I caught you! You admit—

RICHARD *(overlapping)*: No, I'm saying, *if* there's damage, if you're right, which I don't agree with—

DOUG: You do and you don't, you mean.

LUCY (*to Sarah, quietly, indicating Doug with her head*):   Arlan Specter here.

RICHARD: The damage, you've already paid for the ivory or the diamond or—

DOUG: But if you keep it and treat it as if it's precious, somebody else could sell it someday, thus contributing to the ivory market, thus contributing rather directly to the slaughter of elephants.

RICHARD: Well, I think that's kind of . . . a long chain of command.

DOUG: But it is that. You're still in command. You sell that diamond someday, if it's from South Africa—

RICHARD: Oh, come on, look—

LUCY: Doug. (*Pause.*)

DOUG: What? (*Pause.*)

RICHARD: I think . . . when you boycott a nation, the entire economy suffers. Including the poor people. (*Silence. The music has ended.*) And I don't think . . . because I buy a diamond . . .

LUCY (*to Doug, very quiet*):   You did this.

RICHARD: I mean, first of all it's the only thing I've ever bought that's worth anything.

DOUG: Fine.

SARAH (*overlapping*):   Don't get defensive.

RICHARD: I'm not. Have you ever even taken it off, though? In eight years?

SARAH: No.

LUCY: That's very romantic.

SARAH: I'm not sure I could get it off now that I'm all swollen.

RICHARD: Well, you may have to when the baby comes, because we're gonna probably need the money.

LUCY: Ohhhh.

RICHARD: I mean . . . Is that what we should do?

DOUG: No, Richard.

RICHARD: If . . . here. If I knew for certain . . . people had died in the mining of this diamond. A little thirteen-year-old black girl . . . who had to work in the kitchen of one of the mines . . . and she stole a sliver of diamond to pay for her . . . sick . . . parents . . . and was beaten for it . . . beaten to death. (*Pause.*) Should I get rid of the diamond? Not sell it because that would contribute to the diamond mine?

DOUG: I—

RICHARD: Should we just . . . throw it in the gutter? (*Pause.*)

LUCY: I wish I didn't have to get up so ear—

DOUG (*overlapping*):   I wouldn't presume to tell you—

RICHARD: Where are your *shoes* from, Doug? Where was this wonderful meal grown? Do you know? Do you check all the labels?

DOUG: No. (*Pause. No one moves. Sarah's head makes a sudden, sharp little turn.*)

LUCY: What? Are you okay? (*Sarah nods.*)

RICHARD: That's all. I'm just . . .

DOUG: I understand.

RICHARD: I mean— . . . I'm sorry. I guess you hit a nerve. (*Pause.*) My father left me exactly twenty-five thousand dollars in his will and I went out and bought the diamond for Sarah. (*He looks at her.*) That was all the money I've ever had at one time and probably ever will. (*Pause.*)

SARAH: Does anyone hear that? . . . I'm sorry.

RICHARD: What?

SARAH: Like . . . a *voice*?

RICHARD: A voice?

SARAH: Is someone throwing their voice?

RICHARD: Why . . . (*He gives a little nervous laugh.*)

SARAH: Don't . . . Please don't everyone look at me like I'm Joan of Arc. Ever since I gave up caffeine and alcohol, I have this buzzing. *That.*

RICHARD: I don't . . .

DOUG: I know what it is. (*He stands.*) I hear it too.

SARAH: You do?

DOUG: Yes. It's the stereo.

LUCY: That's right.

DOUG: It picks up police signals.

SARAH: Oh, thank god. (*Laughs with great relief.*)

RICHARD: What did you think the voice was saying to you?

SARAH: It was screaming, actually.

RICHARD: It was?

SARAH: Yes.

RICHARD: Oh, my little mystic. (*He takes her hand in his.*) That was probably Joan of Arc's problem, she was picking up police signals.

LUCY: It drives me crazy. We hear it at all hours. It doesn't even have to be on.

DOUG: Yes, it does. (*Sits back down.*)

RICHARD: Okay? (*She smiles, weakly. Her expression changes.*) What? . . . You still . . . ?

SARAH: There. (*She looks down at her hand in Richard's hand; she pulls it free and sees the ring. She lifts it to her ear. She gasps.*) I'm sorry.

RICHARD: Oh very funny. Fine, get rid of the ring, I don't care.

SARAH (*overlapping*): "Don't hit me!" It's saying . . .

RICHARD: Yes, I'm sure.

SARAH: I'm sorry, Richard, I hear something, I can't help it.

RICHARD: No, it's fine.

LUCY: I hear it, too.

RICHARD: Oh good. *(He stands up.)* You all have your little joke. *(Doug is now staring down at the ring.)*

SARAH: No.

RICHARD: It's been a lovely evening. *(He puts on his jacket. Very quietly at first, from the direction of Sarah's ring, we hear a tiny voice screaming:)*

VOICE: Don't hit me! Please don't hit me.

RICHARD: Do you want to come with me now or do you want to . . . ? *(The tiny voice screams a blood-curdling scream and Richard stops, also staring down at ring.)*

VOICE: Please! Please god! Don't hit me! *(Sarah tears at her finger, removing the ring and dropping it. From the floor, it continues to call:)* Please! Please don't hit me! Help! Help me, god! Please god. *(The lights begin to fade as all four of them stare at the floor and the tiny voice continues screaming.)*

ANDRE'S MOTHER

TERRENCE McNALLY

ANDRE'S MOTHER was originally part of an evening of vignettes and songs entitled *Urban Blight*, first seen at Manhattan Theatre Club on May 18, 1988. *Urban Blight* was directed by John Tillinger and Richard Maltby, Jr.; sets by Heidi Landesman; costumes by C. L. Hundley; lighting by Natasha Katz; Ed Fitzgerald was production stage manager; the cast was as follows:

CAL	John Rubinstein
PENNY	Faith Prince
ARTHUR	Rex Robbins
ANDRE'S MOTHER	E. Katherine Kerr

Terrence McNally subsequently expanded ANDRE'S MOTHER into a tele-play for American Playhouse, first aired in March 1990.

Characters
CAL, a young man
ARTHUR, his father
PENNY, his sister
ANDRE'S MOTHER

Time
Now

Place
New York City, Central Park

■ ■

Four people—Cal, Arthur, Penny, and Andre's Mother—enter. They are nicely dressed and carry white helium-filled balloons on a string.

CAL: You know what's really terrible? I can't think of anything terrific to say. Goodbye. I love you. I'll miss you. And I'm supposed to be so great with words!

PENNY: What's that over there?

ARTHUR: Ask your brother.

CAL: It's a theatre. An outdoor theatre. They do plays there in the summer. Shakespeare's plays. *(To Andre's Mother.)* God, how much he wanted to play Hamlet again. He would have gone to

Timbuktu to have another go at that part. The summer he did it
in Boston, he was so happy!

PENNY: Cal, I don't think she . . . ! It's not the time. Later.

ARTHUR: Your son was a . . . the Jews have a word for it . . .

PENNY (*quietly appalled*): Oh my God!

ARTHUR: Mensch, I believe it is, and I think I'm using it right. It
means warm, solid, the real thing. Correct me if I'm wrong.

PENNY: Fine, Dad, fine. Just quit while you're ahead.

ARTHUR: I won't say he was like a son to me. Even my son isn't
always like a son to me. I mean . . . ! In my clumsy way, I'm trying
to say how much I liked Andre. And how much he helped me to
know my own boy. Cal was always two handsful but Andre and
I could talk about anything under the sun. My wife was very fond
of him, too.

PENNY: Cal, I don't understand about the balloons.

CAL: They represent the soul. When you let go, it means you're
letting his soul ascend to Heaven. That you're willing to let go.
Breaking the last earthly ties.

PENNY: Does the Pope know about this?

ARTHUR: Penny!

PENNY: Andre loved my sense of humor. Listen, you can hear him
laughing. (*She lets go of her white balloon.*) So long, you glorious,
wonderful, I-know-what-Cal-means-about-words . . . *man!* God
forgive me for wishing you were straight every time I laid eyes
on you. But if any man was going to have you, I'm glad it was my
brother! Look how fast it went up. I bet that means something.
Something terrific.

ARTHUR (*lets his balloon go*): Goodbye. God speed.

PENNY: Cal?

CAL: I'm not ready yet.

PENNY: Okay. We'll be over there. Come on, Pop, you can buy
your little girl a Good Humor.

ARTHUR: They still make Good Humor?

PENNY: Only now they're called Dove Bars and they cost twelve
dollars.

(*Penny takes Arthur off. Cal and Andre's Mother stand with their
balloons.*)

CAL: I wish I knew what you were thinking. I think it would help
me. You know almost nothing about me and I only know what
Andre told me about you. I'd always had it in my mind that one
day we would be friends, you and me. But if you didn't know
about Andre and me . . . If this hadn't happened, I wonder if he
would have ever told you. When he was sick, if I asked him once

I asked him a thousand times, tell her. She's your mother. She won't mind. But he was so afraid of hurting you and of your disapproval. I don't know which was worse. *(No response. He sighs.)* God, how many of us live in this city because we don't want to hurt our mothers and live in mortal terror of their disapproval. We lose ourselves here. Our lives aren't furtive, just our feelings toward people like you are! A city of fugitives from our parents' scorn or heartbreak. Sometimes he'd seem a little down and I'd say, "What's the matter, babe?" and this funny sweet, sad smile would cross his face and he'd say, "Just a little homesick, Cal, just a little bit." I always accused him of being a country boy just playing at being a hotshot, sophisticated New Yorker. *(He sighs.)*

It's bullshit. It's all bullshit. *(Still no response.)*

Do you remember the comic strip *Little Lulu*? Her mother had no name, she was so remote, so formidable to all the children. She was just Lulu's mother. "Hello, Lulu's Mother," Lulu's friends would say. She was almost anonymous in her remoteness. You remind me of her. Andre's mother. Let me answer the questions you can't ask and then I'll leave you alone and you won't ever have to see me again. Andre died of AIDS. I don't know how he got it. I tested negative. He died bravely. You would have been proud of him. The only thing that frightened him was you. I'll have everything that was his sent to you. I'll pay for it. There isn't much. You should have come up the summer he played Hamlet. He was magnificent. Yes, I'm bitter. I'm bitter I've lost him. I'm bitter what's happening. I'm bitter even now, after all this, I can't reach you. I'm beginning to feel your disapproval and it's making me ill. *(He looks at his balloon.)* Sorry, old friend. I blew it. *(He lets go of the balloon.)*

Good night, sweet prince, and flights of angels sing thee to thy rest! *(Beat.)*

Goodbye, Andre's mother.

(He goes. Andre's Mother stands alone holding her white balloon. Her lips tremble. She looks on the verge of breaking down. She is about to let go of the balloon when she pulls it down to her. She looks at it awhile before she gently kisses it. She lets go of the balloon. She follows it with her eyes as it rises and rises. The lights are beginning to fade. Andre's Mother's eyes are still on the balloon. The lights fade.)

I CAN'T REMEMBER ANYTHING

ARTHUR MILLER

I CAN'T REMEMBER ANYTHING and "Clara," two one-act plays, were
presented under the title *DANGER: MEMORY!* by Lincoln Center Theater
(Gregory Mosher, Director; Bernard Gersten, Executive Producer) at the
Mitzi E. Newhouse Theatre in New York City on February 8, 1987. It was
directed by Gregory Mosher; the sets were by Michael Merritt; the costumes
were by Nan Cibula; the lighting was by Kevin Rigdon; the production
manager was Jeff Hamlin; the general manager was Steven C. Callahan; the
general press representative was Merle Debuskey; the production stage
manager was George Darveris; and the assistant stage manager was Neel
Keller. The cast of I CAN'T REMEMBER ANYTHING, in order of speaking, was as follows:

> LEONORA   Geraldine Fitzgerald
> LEO   Mason Adams
> Understudies:
> For LEONORA, Kathleen Claypool;
> for LEO, Vince O'Brien

■ ■

The time is now.

*Leo's living room—kitchen in a nondescript little wooden house on a
country backroad. A woodburning stove near a handmade plywood dining
and drawing table; some canvas folding chairs, one of them repaired with
needle and thread; a wicker chair; a couple of short benches; a well-worn
modern chair and a lumpy couch—in short, a bachelor's heaven. A couple
of fine, dusty landscapes on one wall as well as tacked-up photos and a
few drunken line drawings of dead friends.*

*At the big table Leo is carefully lettering with a marker pen on a piece
of cardboard, a newspaper open at his elbow. There are a few patches on
his denim shirt and his pants are almost nothing but patches. They are
his resistance to commercialism in the last quarter of the twentieth century.
He has a stubborn little face.*

Leonora enters through the front door; she is a large woman who opens her long, many-colored woolen shawl and shakes it out as she sits in a chair not far from him, giving a little cough and swallowing a few times and catching her breath. Now she turns to him. Her speech is New England with a European aristocratic coloration of which, however, she is not aware.

LEONORA: Well. You might at least look up.

LEO: I saw you.

LEONORA: That's a greeting, isn't it. "I saw you."

LEO: I've got chicken again.

LEONORA: I don't care, everything tastes the same to me anyway. May I have my colored water?

LEO: It's over there.

LEONORA: Thank you. *(She goes, pours some bourbon, holds up the glass, adds a bit more.)*

LEO: You always have to pour it twice.

LEONORA: Because I have to see whether it's enough or too much.

LEO: But it's never too much, it's always too little.

LEONORA *(taking a pitcher and holding it in her hand)*:   May I have some water?

LEO: There's some in there.

LEONORA: I see that. May I have it?

LEO: You certainly may. *(Finishes his drawing, inspects it, sets it aside. Takes a pencil and starts on a crossword puzzle.)* I see you bashed in your new car.

LEONORA: It's what I said the last time; they are placing these light poles too close to the road.

LEO: The light poles are the same distance they have always been.

LEONORA: Well, they're not, but there's no use arguing about it.

LEO: Maybe you ought to forget about driving under certain conditions.

LEONORA *(sits some distance from him, facing front)*:   There's simply no use talking to you.

LEO: Not about the distance of light poles to the road there isn't.

LEONORA *(takes a thin package out of her enormous bag)*:   I got this in the mail this morning; it's from Lawrence.

LEO: It might be one thing if you could be sure to kill yourself. But you're liable to end up crippled or blind or killing somebody else, then what?

LEONORA: Oh, what's the use? *(Sips; a deep relaxing sigh, then:)*

LEO: Where is Lawrence?

LEONORA *(glancing at the package)*:   In Sri Lanka, apparently.

LEO: Is he still in that monastery or whatever the hell it is?

LEONORA: It's not a monastery, it's one of those retreats, I think. —But I can never finish reading one of his letters. He just goes on and on and on until I fall asleep. Do you have a knife?

LEO: On the table. *(She gets up, goes to table, picks up knife, starts cutting package open, indicates whiskey bottle.)*

LEONORA: You know you're almost out.

LEO: I know, but I couldn't get to town today. Isn't there enough for you?

LEONORA: What about you?

LEO: I haven't touched whiskey in at least a year, since I got my arthritis. Haven't you noticed?

LEONORA: I was just trying to be polite.

LEO: That bottle was full day before yesterday . . . just to remind you.

LEONORA: You've had guests?

LEO *(pointedly)*:   No, just you.

LEONORA: Well, what's the difference?

LEO: By the way, if you come in here one night and I'm dead, I want you to call Yale–New Haven Hospital and not this . . . whatever you call him . . . mortician what's-his-name in town.

LEONORA: What good is a hospital if you're dead, for God's sake?

LEO: I just finished making arrangements for them to take my organs.

LEONORA: Really!

LEO: For research. So call Yale–New Haven. This mortician here used to have a Nixon bumper sticker.

LEONORA: What do they expect to find from *your* organs?

LEO: Why?—My organs aren't good enough?

LEONORA: But I should imagine they would want people with some interesting disease. All you've got is arthritis. Aside from that, you'll probably die in perfect health.

LEO: Well, I might get something.

LEONORA: Where, for heaven's sake? You never go anywhere but the post office or the grocery store.

LEO: I go to the gas station.

LEONORA: The gas station! What do you expect to pick up at the gas station?

LEO: I don't know. Gas disease.

LEONORA *(laughing)*:   Gas disease!

LEO: This is another one of those conversations.

LEONORA: Well, I certainly didn't start it.

LEO *(showing her his newly drawn sign in block letters)*:   This is Yale–New Haven, see? I'm going to tack this number over the phone.

LEONORA: But I'll certainly be dead before you.

LEO: In case you're not dead and you walk in and there I am with my eyes crossed and my tongue hanging out.

LEONORA (*grimacing*):   Oh, stop that, for God's sake.

LEO: Well, that's how you look when you have a stroke. (*Returns to his newspaper. Pause.*)

LEONORA: There's nothing in the paper, is there?

LEO: Yes, a few things.

LEONORA: Well, don't tell it to me, it's all too horrible.

LEO: I wasn't going to tell it to you. (*Pause.*) You want rice?

LEONORA: I hate rice. (*He returns to his paper.*) Why are you being so difficult, Leo?

LEO: Me? I'm the one who invited you to have rice, for Christ's sake.

LEONORA: I can't for the life of me figure out why I haven't died.

LEO: Well, maybe it'll come to you.

LEONORA: I used to believe, as a girl—I mean, we were taught to believe—that everything has its purpose. You know what I'm referring to.

LEO: My mother was the only atheist in Youngstown, Ohio; she never talked about things having purposes.

LEONORA: Well, in New England you tended to believe those things!—But what purpose have I got? I am totally useless, to myself, my children, my grandchildren, and the one or two people I suppose I can call my friends who aren't dead. . . .

LEO: Then why don't you stop being useless?

LEONORA: How can I stop being useless, for God's sake? If a person is useless, she is *useless*.

LEO: Then do something.—Why don't you take up the piano again?

LEONORA: The piano!

LEO: Oh, come on now, for Christ's sake, you used to play Mozart and Chopin and all that stuff. You can't tell me you don't remember playing the piano, Leonora.

LEONORA (*without admission or denial*):   I don't know where I'd ever begin a thing like that.

LEO: Well, the accordion, then.

LEONORA: *What?* I certainly never in my life played the *accordion*.

LEO: Except with thirty or forty people dancing on the grass, and everybody pissed to the gills, and Frederick banging on a soup pot, and a big salami tied between his legs.

LEONORA: Really? (*A sudden laugh.*) A salami?

LEO: Sure, and a pair of oranges. Waving it around at the women.

LEONORA (*stares*):   Sometimes . . . I *think* I remember something, but then I wonder if I just imagined it. My whole life often seems imaginary. It's very strange.

LEO: I know something you could kill time with.

LEONORA: There is nothing. I don't even have the concentration to read anymore. Sometimes I wonder if *I'm* imaginary.

LEO: Why don't you try to get people to donate their organs to Yale–New Haven? You could just sit at home with the phone book and make calls.

LEONORA: You mean I'm to telephone perfect strangers and ask them for their organs?

LEO: Well, it's important; they really need organs.

LEONORA: Where do you *get* these ideas?

LEO: I tell you, I just wish I had your health.

LEONORA: Something's burning.

LEO: Christ, it's the rice! *(Struggles to get up.)*

LEONORA: May I . . . ?

LEO *(waving at her)*:   Yes! Take it off the stove! *(She hurries to a point, returns with a pot into which she is looking.)*

LEONORA: It looks terrible. You can't eat this.

LEO: Well, I was just using it up. I have salad, it'll be enough.

LEONORA: You only have one plate out.

LEO: Oh? I must have got distracted. I think somebody phoned when I was setting the table.—Who the hell was that, now . . . ?

LEONORA: Perhaps you don't want me to dinner.

LEO: Oh, get a plate, will you? They're right up there in the cabinet.

LEONORA: Good heavens, after all these years I know where the plates are. *(She goes, brings down a plate, knife and fork, and napkin.)*

LEO: I'm having some bread; *you* don't want any, though.

LEONORA: Bread! I haven't eaten bread in a decade.

LEO: You ate some last week . . . that that girl brought me from the nature store.

LEONORA *(stops moving)*:   I can't remember anything.

LEO: Well, you did. You ate three slices.

LEONORA: I can't have eaten three slices of *bread*.

LEO: You did, though.

LEONORA: I simply cannot remember anything at all. *(They are seated at their plates facing each other, and he has served the chicken and they eat. He picks up his pencil and enters a word in the puzzle as he eats.)* Oh! Do you mean that young girl with the braids?

LEO *(preoccupied)*:   Uh-huh.

LEONORA: The one with the lisp.—She's quite pretty.

LEO: Oh, she's some doll.

LEONORA: "Doll!"—I will never understand your attraction for these women when you really don't like women at all.

LEO: I like women. I just don't like dumb women.

LEONORA: Oh, is she clever?

LEO: She's writing a master's thesis on Recurrence. That's a mathematical principle.

LEONORA (*doesn't know what to say*):   Well!

LEO: Yes. But you couldn't understand anything like that.—You can talk to that girl about something.

LEONORA: I don't recall you being so intellectually particular in the old days.

LEO: I used to drink more in the old days.

LEONORA: Oh, I see; and now that you can't drink you discuss mathematics.

LEO: Who was the President of France when the War started?

LEONORA: Good God, how should I know?

LEO: Well, you were living there then, weren't you?

LEONORA: Yes, but nobody *ever* knows who the President of France is.

LEO: Well, you wouldn't have known anyway.

LEONORA (*slamming her fork down*):   I would certainly have known if it was of any importance.

LEO: No you wouldn't.

LEONORA (*Throws her napkin straight at him, speechless with anger. Pause. He goes on with the crossword.*):   May I have my napkin?

LEO (*returning the napkin to her*):   I think it begins with a P.

LEONORA: I hate crossword puzzles. They do nothing but add triviality to the boredom of existence.—"President of France"! Before the War no one *cared* who the President was. It's not like being the President of the United States.

LEO: Everybody knows that, for Christ's sake.

LEONORA: You don't. You don't know anything about France.

LEO: Could it be Poincaire?

LEONORA: "Pwancare"! It's Poincaré.

LEO: Well, Pwancaray.

LEONORA: I believe Poincaré was Prime Minister at some point, but not President. Why do you ask me questions like that? I can't remember anything political. Will they take out your brain too?

LEO: I guess so. For sweetbreads.

LEONORA (*screwing up her face*):   Why do you *say* things like that!

LEO: And my liver with onions. (*She laughs painfully, and then they both eat in silence.*)

LEONORA: This is really quite good. Is that thyme?

LEO: Rosemary.

LEONORA: I mean rosemary. God, I simply can't keep anything straight.

LEO: You used to use a lot of rosemary.

LEONORA: Did I?

LEO: On gigot. You had a wonderful touch with any kind of lamb, you always had it nice and pink, with just enough well-done at the ends; and the best bread I think I ever ate.

LEONORA: Really!

LEO: You don't remember Frederick holding the bread to his chest, and that way he had of pulling the knife across it, and handing it out piece by piece to people at the table? *(Slight pause.)*

LEONORA: Well, what difference does it make?

LEO: I don't know, it's just a damn shame to forget all that. Your lamb always had absolutely clear pink juice, like rosé wine. And the way you did the string beans, just exactly medium hard. Those were some great dinners.

LEONORA: Were they?

LEO: Yes.

LEONORA: Well, I'm glad you enjoyed them. To me—when I do think of anything like that—it's like some page in a book I once read. Don't you often forget what you've read in a book? What earthly difference does it make?

LEO: But it's not a book, it's your life, kiddo.

LEONORA: Yes, well . . . so what? Look at these millions of people starving to death all over the place, does anyone remember them? Why should I remember myself any more than I remember them?

LEO: Well, it's not the same.

LEONORA: Naturally. That's because you come from central Ohio.

LEO: What the hell's that got to do with it?

LEONORA: In central Ohio everything always turns out for the best.

LEO: Youngstown doesn't, for your information, happen to be in central Ohio.

LEONORA: Well, it might as well be.

LEO: Well, I have work to do tonight.

LEONORA: I won't stay, I'll just sit here for a bit and look out the window. Is that all right?

LEO: Sure. *(Gets with difficulty to his feet, picks up plates . . .)*

LEONORA: Here, let me . . .

LEO *(a command)*: I'll do it! *(He shuffles to the sink as she sits staring front.)* What'd Lawrence send?

LEONORA: Oh! *(She had forgotten and reaches to the table and the package, from which she takes a record.)*

LEO: Another record? Oh, Christ.

LEONORA *(uncertain)*: He never sent me a record before.

LEO: Sure he did, about three years ago, that goddamn Indian music, it was horrible.

LEONORA: Yes, I remember now. . . . It was wonderful for a certain mood.

LEO: Sounded like a bunch of cats locked in a toilet.

LEONORA: What do you know about music, for heaven's sake? *(She finds a note with the record.)* I don't have my glasses. *(Hands him the note.)*

LEO *(reads)*:   "Dear Mother. This one is quite different. Let me know how you like it. My group has been invited to play in New Delhi, isn't that terrific? Love, Lawrence."

LEONORA: Well!—That's short and sweet, isn't it? After three years, did you say?

LEO: Wait, there's a P.S. "P.S. Moira and I have decided to separate, you'll be glad to hear."

LEONORA: Moira? Who is Moira? *(She stares ahead tensely, struggling to remember.)*

LEO: Sounds like somebody he married. *(He hands back the note. Her eyes moisten with tears which she blinks away, looking at the record.)* I hope you're not going to play that here.

LEONORA *(an outcry)*:   I have no intention of playing it here . . . or anywhere, since my machine has been broken for at least five or six years!—When did it all begin getting so vile, do you know? *(He sits at table again and picks up a pencil, poring over some diagrams.)* Are you working at something?

LEO: I promised my friend Bokum I would check out some of his calculations that he made for the new bridge in town.

LEONORA: I didn't even know there was an *old* bridge.

LEO: Across the river; you drive over it half a dozen times a week.

LEONORA: Oh, that one!—Strange, I never think of that as a bridge.

LEO: What do you think of it as?

LEONORA: I don't know . . . just the road. Are you going to rebuild it?

LEO: I'm not doing anything, just checking out Bokum's numbers. *(Opening a file folder.)* But everything keeps slipping out of my head. I could do this stuff in twenty minutes and now I can't calculate worth a damn.

LEONORA: Well, now you know what I mean . . .

LEO: That was one thing I admired about Frederick, he never once slowed down mentally.

LEONORA: Didn't he?

LEO: For Christ's sake, you remember whether he slowed down mentally, don't you?

LEONORA: Well, I'm sorry if it irritates you!

LEO: It doesn't "irritate" me, I just don't think you ought to be forgetting that, that's all.—The man was sharp as a tack to his last minute!

LEONORA: You know, I could criticize you too, if I wished to.

LEO: Well, go ahead!

LEONORA: I wouldn't bother. (*Pause.*) By the way, I am never going back to your dentist.

LEO: Neither am I. I'm sorry I recommended him.

LEONORA: What gets into you? You are forever sending me to doctors and dentists who are completely incompetent. That man nearly killed me with his drill. Why do you do that?

LEO: I don't know, he seemed okay for a while there.

LEONORA: It was the same thing with that awful plumber. And that idiotic man who fixed the roof and left me in a downpour. I think there's something the matter with you; you get these infatuations with an individual and just when you've got everybody going to them you stop going.

LEO: He just seemed like a nice guy; I don't know.

LEONORA: He seriously wanted to pull out all my teeth.

LEO: Did he? Son of a bitch.

LEONORA: Well, he actually pulled all yours, didn't he? (*She silently swallows a drink.*)

LEO: Well . . . not *all*.

LEONORA: But all the front ones.

LEO: He didn't like my gums.

LEONORA: And you allowed him to pull out all your front teeth?

LEO (*defensively angry*):   Well, he seemed okay! I liked him!

LEONORA: Yes, you certainly did. (*She looks at her glass.*) May I have another? (*He nods, studying his puzzle. She goes and pours.*) All it is is a little color for conviviality. (*She returns to her chair, sits.*) I saw the most beautiful young deer today. Near the waterfall, so she couldn't hear me until my car was right next to her. She turned to me and there was such a look of surprise! I felt ashamed. Imagine how frightening we must be to them! And how we must stink, when they feed on nothing but grass and green things. And we full of dead chickens and rotting cow meat . . . (*She drinks. He does his puzzle.*)

LEO: You know it's Frederick's birthday tomorrow.

LEONORA (*with a faint guilt in her eye*):   Tomorrow? (*He gives her an impatient, nearly angry look.*) Why do you look at me like that? I simply didn't think of it. (*With defiance.*) I never think of anything. I just drive around the countryside and look at the trees, I don't see what's wrong with that. I love the trees; they are strong and proud and they live a long time, and I love them very much.

(She is filling up, takes a breath to suppress her feelings.) Everything is so awful, Leo; really and truly this is not the same country.

LEO: You don't have to convince me. I've been a Communist all my life and I still am, I don't care what they say.

LEONORA: I believe you really are, aren't you?—And why not?— You've always given everything you have away. It's your finest trait. But I think . . . were we in Russia once . . . ?

LEO: Sure you were, about twenty years ago . . .

LEONORA: All I remember is that it was all perfectly dreadful.

LEO: Well, you were rich.

LEONORA: Oh, by the way . . . *(Digging into her large bag, brings out a large handful of unopened envelopes and lays them on the table before him.)* The lawyers say I ought to give away a lot more, would you look at these? I've been meaning to bring them all week.

LEO: Jesus!—They've really got your name down. But I don't know anything about these organizations. Christ, here's the Baptist Mission to Pakistan.

LEONORA: Good God!—There's something there for African Relief, isn't there?

LEO: You sent them something last time, didn't you?

LEONORA: But there are so many of those children. Would five thousand seem too much? I'd like it to matter.

LEO: If that's what you want, go ahead.

LEONORA: Except that I read that some of the money never gets there; it's stolen, they say.

LEO: I don't know what to tell you.

LEONORA: How terrible it is. . . . In the old days I never once thought of someone stealing money we donated to . . . like the Spanish Republicans, for instance. Did you?

LEO: Well, people believed in something those days.

LEONORA: But what do they have to *believe*?—It's just common decency. Or is that a stupid thing to say? Tell me honestly—wasn't there something more precious about human life before . . . let's say . . . before the War?

LEO: Maybe. Although not in Ohio. I mean my father died drunk in the entrance of a coal mine—the other guys just forgot he was in there and they came back next morning and he'd froze to death, just croaked.

LEONORA: Why do you use that *language*?

LEO: It'll be dark in a few minutes, you're going to have to drive that car.

LEONORA: I'm perfectly fine. May I have what's left?

LEO: Well . . . if that's what you want, sure. *(He watches her, not approvingly, as she pours the whiskey and water.)*

LEONORA (*sitting*):   Have you ever seen that raccoon again?

LEO: Which raccoon?

LEONORA: The one who stole your hamburgers off the outdoor griddle.

LEO (*laughs*):   Oh, him! Yeah, he comes by occasionally.—Although not for a couple of weeks now.

LEONORA: I will never forget your description of how he tossed the hot hamburger from one paw to another to cool it off.

LEO (*chuckling*):   Oh, yeah . . . (*Mimes tossing a hot hamburger from hand to hand. She guffaws.*)

LEONORA (*through her laughter*):   And how did you describe him? —Like a chef in a fur coat?

LEO: Well, he looked . . . kind of annoyed, y'know? Like a French chef. Haven't seen him around for quite a while, though. Probably got shot by now. (*Pause. She sips, staring out the window.*)

LEONORA: Why don't they leave those poor animals alone?

LEO: Well, for one thing, the deer are ruining the apple trees.

LEONORA: Well, maybe that is what they're supposed to be doing. Would you like to be shot because you ate something? (*He works his crossword puzzle. She sips, stares out the window.*)

LEO: It's your birthday too, of course. (*She glances at him. He returns to his puzzle.*) Happy birthday. (*She stares front, a certain distress in her eyes.*) I guess there's no reason not to tell you . . . I still miss him. He was the greatest man I ever met in my life.

LEONORA: Was he?

LEO: Yes, he was. It's over ten years and I don't think a day goes by that I don't hear his laugh or that nasal voice. God, he had common sense.

LEONORA (*after a long sip, and an inhale*):   He shouldn't have died first, Leo.

LEO: I know. (*Pause.*) Listen: just in case you come in here some night and find me dead, I think he'd have wanted you to . . . live. I'm sure of that, kiddo. (*Pause.*)

LEONORA: We were married just a month over forty-five years; that's a very long time, Leo.

LEO: But even so . . .

LEONORA: One can't just skip off and start over again.

LEO: You're twelve years older than me and you've got more life in you than I have. Chrissake, you hardly look sixty-five, if that; you might have ten years to go yet . . .

LEONORA: Oh, God help me.

LEO: How about taking a trip somewhere, maybe find somebody to go along with you?

LEONORA: Everybody is dead, don't you realize that? Everybody except you.

LEO: It doesn't seem possible. . . . All those hundreds of people that used to be at your parties . . . Three days later there'd still be people sleeping it off in the flower beds or out in the cars.

LEONORA: All dead.

LEO: Well, they can't *all* be . . .

LEONORA: . . . For God's sake, Leo, the last party must have been at least fifteen years ago! There's something the matter with you. You are not growing old, or something.

LEO: How about Asia? You've never been to Asia.

LEONORA: You're getting worse than I am. When Frederick did that Ganges bridge, and we were six months with the Maharajah . . . ?

LEO: Maybe you could visit him?

LEONORA: Good heavens, he was nearly seventy twenty years ago . . . Anyway, I hated it there; all that bowing and scraping, and those poor elephants. And everyone telling you nothing but lies.—And besides, those people were Frederick's friends, not mine. All our friends were.

LEO: Even so, Frederick was absolutely nuts about you, Leonora, you can't ever forget that.

LEONORA: Of course. I'm not talking about *that*. (Pause. A smile grows on her face.) The very first time we met . . .

LEO: . . . On a train, wasn't it?

LEONORA: Of course . . . to California for one of his bridges there. And he found my mother alone in the dining car and said, "Your daughter has the finest backside I have ever seen."

LEO: Ha! She wasn't scandalized?

LEONORA: Why? It's a complimentary thing to say, isn't it? Besides, she was still headmistress of the Boston College for Women.

LEO: So?

LEONORA: Well, she had plenty of means of comparison. (Laughs her high, hawking laugh.)

LEO: See now?—You remembered all that.

LEONORA (a tension rises in her, which she suppresses): Well, that was so long ago it hardly matters. (Nearly blushing.) I want to ask you something personal, may I? (He turns to her, waiting.) Well, may I?

LEO: What?

LEONORA: Why do you pretend that you aren't discouraged?

LEO (surprised by this): Well, I'm not as down on everything as *you* are, but . . .

LEONORA (*her anxiety intensifying*):   But why can't you just admit that it's all nothing? You *know* it's nothing, Leo.

LEO (*stalling*):   What's nothing?

LEONORA: Why, our lives, the whole damned thing.—That's what is so irritating, you simply refuse to . . . to . . . (*A new idea.*) I mean you go on and on reading that stupid newspaper with the same vileness every day, the same brutality, the same lies . . .

LEO: Well, I like to know what's happening.

LEONORA: But nothing is "happening"! Excepting that it keeps getting worse and more brutal and more vile . . .

LEO: What the hell are you getting so angry about if I read a newspaper?

LEONORA: Because after thirty or forty or whatever goddamned awful number of years it is, you are still a sort of *strangeness* to me. I ought to know you by now, oughtn't I? Well, I don't. I don't know you, Leo! (*He is mystified but impressed with the depth of her feeling, and wondering what she is trying to say to him. He watches her profile.*)

LEO: Well, what would you like to know?

LEONORA: Every evening I feel this same condescension from you, when you know perfectly well that it is all continually getting worse.

LEO: Listen, I'm depressed too . . .

LEONORA: No, you are not depressed, you just try to *sound* depressed. But in the back of your mind you are still secretly expecting heaven-knows-what incredible improvement just over the horizon.

LEO: I still don't understand what you're trying to . . .

LEONORA: This country is being ruined by greed and mendacity and narrow-minded ignorance, and you go right on thinking there is hope somewhere. And yet you really don't, do you?—but you refuse to admit that you have lost your hope. That's exactly right, yes—it's this goddamned hopefulness when there is no hope— that is why you are so frustrating to sit with!

LEO (*lets her steam for a minute*):   The trouble is you don't understand science.

LEONORA: Science! I am asking you for your truthful opinion about your *life*! What has that to do with science, for God's sake?

LEO: Well, I don't think I'm as important as *you* think *you* are.

LEONORA (*caught by a suggestion now*):   Ah. That's interesting.

LEO: I never accomplished anything much except . . .

LEONORA: Why?—You helped Frederick immensely for . . . more than twenty years, wasn't it? And before that you taught so many students . . .

LEO: Well, the thing is, I figure I've done what I could do, more or less, and now I'm going back to being a chemical; all we are is a lot of talking nitrogen, you know . . .

LEONORA (*outraged, and laughing*):   Talking nitrogen!

LEO: And phosphorus and some other elements . . . about two dollars' worth if you discount inflation. So if you're wondering why you're alive . . . maybe it's because you *are*, that's all, and that's the whole goddamn reason. Maybe you're so nervous because you keep looking for some other reason and there isn't any. (*Pause.*)

LEONORA: It's not that, Leo.

LEO: I know.

LEONORA: What do you know?

LEO: Frederick was your life, and now there's nothing.

LEONORA (*with a wild, furious grin*):   So if I told you how unimportant I think I am, I might disappear in thin air, like a speck of dust on the nose of a mouse.

LEO: Okay, well . . . I've got to work.

LEONORA: I don't even remember why we started talking about this.

LEO: That's better than me—I don't even remember what we were talking about.

LEONORA (*laughs, throwing her head back, deep prolonged laughter filled with pain*):   . . . Oh, dear, dear . . . (*A pause. Leo arranges papers before him with over-elaborate care.*)

LEO: I finally went to the doctor's on Monday.

LEONORA: Really. What for?

LEO: What for! Chrissake, you know I've been feeling terrible!

LEONORA: Well, you're always so healthy, I forgot.

LEO: I haven't been healthy at all, I haven't been sleeping and I'm nerved up all the time.

LEONORA: Oh?

LEO: Yes. (*Uneasily shifts his papers, then takes the plunge.*) He looked me over thoroughly, and then he sat me down and gave me a long talk. He really goes into things, I never knew he was practically a psychiatrist.

LEONORA: Oh, is he?

LEO (*takes a breath, then . . .*):   He says I'm under tension. High tension. The medicine isn't bringing my pressure down anymore. So he asks if there's anything making me tense.

LEONORA: Oh?

LEO: And I said yes, there was. And that's what I have to talk to you about, Leonora.

LEONORA: Talk to *me*?

LEO: I'd be more relaxed if you didn't . . . you know . . . come over quite so often. That's what I've been wanting to tell you. *(Pause. She simply sits blinking, motionless.)* Not that you're not welcome, but you come for breakfast and don't leave till nearly ten or so, and then for dinner again which . . . well, it used to be half past five but now its three-thirty and sometimes two in the afternoon. And it makes me nervous, every single day like this. I've been trying to hint around about it but it's my health now and I just have to ask you not to come over more than maybe once or twice a week or so. Okay? *(She remains motionless, blinking. He waits expectantly, flushed, tense . . .)* I'm an old man now; I mean I just am; I can't start up a whole new life around another person in this house all the time. *(She still doesn't react.)* I mean after Frederick died it was a question of easing you out of the shock for a few months, which I was more than happy to do. But the years are going by and you . . .

LEONORA: My friends all died.

LEO: I know that, but I am an old man, Leonora. I'm very old! And you upset me being here practically all day long! So I'm having to . . . just tell you. Okay? I'm very serious about this. *(His hands are shaking; furious at her obdurate silence.)*

LEONORA *(draws the record out of its envelope)*: Could I play just one minute of it? My machine is really broken.

LEO: Okay, a minute, but that's all.

LEONORA *(puts record on the turntable)*: Am I wrong? Didn't you and I dance once?

LEO: Once?

LEONORA: More?

LEO *(shaking his head as though all they did was dance)*: Phew!— Okay, forget it.

LEONORA: Oh, of course!

LEO: Christ, there must have been a couple hundred nights when I'd come over and just the three of us would play records, and Frederick and I would take turns dancing with you 'cause you'd never get tired . . . and drink a dozen bottles of wine . . . and he had that fantastic French corkscrew . . .

LEONORA *(as she lowers the tone arm on the record . . .)*: I think I still have that corkscrew . . . *(Music: A samba beat, but with wild, lacy arpeggios and a driving underbeat.)*

LEO *(They both listen for a moment. He is pleasantly surprised.)*: Chrissake, that's nothing but a samba. *(She listens.)* Isn't it? *(He moves his shoulders to the beat.)* Sure, it's just a plain old-fashion' samba. *(She begins to move to it. She is remarkably nimble, taking little expert steps . . . and her sensuality provokes and embarrasses him, making him laugh tightly . . .*) You dancing, for Christ's sake? (*She lets herself into the dance fully now, and he lets his laughter flower, and, laughing, he struggles to his feet and, unable to move more than an inch at a time, he swings his shoulders instead, clapping his gnarled hands. And she faces him tauntingly, reddening with shyness and her flaunting emotions; one moment bent over and backing nearly into him, the next, thumbing her nose at him, and as the music explodes to its crescendo she falls into a chair, breathless, and he collapses into another and they both sit there laughing, trying to breathe. The music ends.*) Well, that's sure as hell not Indian music. Maybe he decided to stop wasting his time and start playing human music.

LEONORA: He does what is in him to do. Just like you. And everyone else. Until it all comes to an end. . . . Well, thank you for dinner. (*She stands a bit unsteadily, he turns back to his calculating.*) Shall I come by for breakfast? (*He stares down at his papers.*) Is something wrong?

LEO: Now you do remember what I was just saying to you. Don't tell me you don't remember that.

LEONORA: What do you mean?—Oh! *that.* (*She peers into the air at some incredible thing.*) You mean I am never to come back?

LEO: I didn't say never! I said once or twice a week.

LEONORA: Well isn't that wonderful of you! I will never set foot in this house again! (*She almost staggers as she starts for the door.*)

LEO: Wait! You can't drive like this.

LEONORA: I certainly can! It's only a few hundred yards. Why are you so stupid! (*She tries another stride to the door and presses on a chair to steady herself.*)

LEO: Maybe stay tonight. It's awful dark out, I don't even think there's a moon.

LEONORA: Are you blind, too? (*Points.*) The moon happens to be right there.

LEO: That's my outside lamp, for Christ's sake! Will you stay the night or not!

LEONORA: I certainly will not.

LEO: Then go, will you? Goodnight! (*With an iron effort she makes it to the door.*) . . . Maybe you ought to call me when you get home.

LEONORA (*outraged and agonized and enunciating*):   Call you! Why, for God's sake? It'd only be a relief to you and everyone else, wouldn't it? It would certainly be to me! My God, imagine not having to wake up tomorrow! What a dear, dear blessing! (*Straightening, or trying to.*) Well, Leo, I hope you recover soon, but wouldn't it be funny if I turned out not to be the cause of your tension after all? If it's simply that you are a stupid, stupid old man? (*She exits, with a burst of angry weeping. Shaken, he goes to a window and looks out. Her motor is heard starting, and the car roaring away. He shakes his head, thinks for a moment, then lowers his suspenders and takes off his shirt and shuffles toward his bedroom door. From a hook he takes down a nightgown, slips it over his head, and seated on a chair slips his pants off. Conflicted, he looks down at the phone now. After a moment . . .)*

LEO: Good, Good! At goddamn last! *(His conflict behind him he goes to table, takes the cardboard sign and with a couple of pushpins fastens it to the wall over the phone. It reads, "Yale–New Haven 771-8515." He starts toward his bedroom, then comes to a halt, turns back to the silence of the phone.)* Calling *me* stupid! You idiot, don't you know there's nothing between us?—I did it for him, that's all! Because of his greatness, because he was my friend and made me feel like somebody! Which any woman would know if she wasn't so dense! You've got no demands on me! You're nothing to me, nothing, and thank God it's over now. *(Triumphantly, arms raised to heaven.)* Frederick! It's over!! *(The phone rings. He is startled. Refuses to pick it up. It rings again. Picks it up, and without giving her a moment to speak . . .)* Okay, goodnight, goodnight.—What's that! Oh now Leonora, Leonora, you certainly do remember what I said tonight. But you do, dear, you remember every goddamned thing you ever heard since the year one! All right, then listen. . . . Listen . . . will you listen to me, Leonora! The doctor said to me today . . . *(Lights begins fading . . .)* he said that I am very tense . . . and he asked me if I had any idea why, if there was some anxiety happening in my life, and I said yes there was . . . I said there was this woman who meant absolutely nothing to me, but who kept coming . . . what? *(He contains himself.)* The doctor said to me today that I am very tense, and whether I had any idea . . .

(The light is out.)

FLYER

(*FROM* ROOTS IN WATER)

RICHARD NELSON

FLYER is from *Roots in Water* (early version), which was first performed in 1988, River Arts Repertory, Woodstock, New York, with Lawrence Sacharow as director; Loy Arcenas, set designer; Marianne Powell-Parker, costume designer; Arden Fingerhut, lighting designer; Peter Gordon, composer; Renée Lutz, stage manager.

BUSTER   Daniel Jenkins

Roots in Water is composed of eleven thematically related scenes between 1976 and 1988. No single character appears in more than one of them. Each scene has a date and a title. These should be projected through the given scene.

FLYER, which takes place in 1976, is the first.

Projection
1976
FLYER

■ ■

Buster, twenties, sits on a small wooden stool, dressed only in his underwear, and a baseball cap. He talks toward the audience, to a woman who is not seen.

Buster

Now this, what I'm doin', this ain't Nam. I ain't sayin' it is. That was that. And this is this. Now I ain't sayin' that was bad, though course I weren't in favor of Nam. Nobody is no more. I'm just sayin' that was tanks and stuff and this, well it's food and shit. And the only gun I transport now is the one I keep on my hip and that's more a souvenir or something like to do with my hands. So this is real different okay?

(Beat.)

You ever been up in one of them big boys? It's like flying a fuckin' boat, really. Or a whale. Or a tuna. Yeh, it's like sittin' in the eye of some big fat tuna. Like I got these big ol' ropes around the head of this tuna and I'm tellin' it where the fuck to go. I'm flying it, see. I'm the flyer. Fourteen trips so far and I don't think I've slept more than a wink or two in all that time. 'Bout three weeks, I guess. But that's okay, 'cause I know what I'm doing, my mission, see, it's gotta be done. The food, you understand. I bring the food.

(Beat.)

God, it's pretty up there. With the tuna. Passing through black clouds. That's clouds that the smoke has reached and that's like death. Like you was moving through closets. And then through the white clouds and that's Heaven, really. Heaven in the sky. And leaning to get a good look at the green hills down there, the thickness that's sort of gone wild, sort of like it's calling up to me, "Buster, that a-boy, Buster, you bring us some of that rice 'cause we ain't growing shit but green down here." Shit.

(Beat.)

Sometimes I just let Billy, he's my co., let him take the reins, let him turn that tuna for a while and I go back into the belly—the part that's pressurized—and I see those crates. Eight ton of crates and I dig my fingers into one and feel the grain like it was gold or something and I'm the king who's got all the gold and that's nice. I like that.

(Beat.)

So's then as we're coming into the strip, and I see the lights and they hear me coming and sees my eyes lit up, if it's night and not raining or what, and down there I'm watching all them groups of folks and I know as soon as my rubber feet hit that earth they are gonna be off and running after me, and they are gonna be being kicked back like they was asses or something, starving asses, like they've been lost in the desert for a year, 'cause they're so thin, see, and there's so many of them. But I don't look no more, that's at their faces, I mean. I don't look. I mean what's the point in looking, I've looked at too many faces already looking for her.

(Beat.)

When I was still looking for her. Which I guess I still am.

(Beat.)

But anyway, you can't let yourself be touched, can you. Gotta be like thin steel if you're bringing home the bacon like I am doing. So's I don't look, just taxi that big mother tuna to where the guys with the white sticks can keep the ones who don't got no faces away. Gotta be steel. Or you are gonna die, I says.

(*Beat.*)

My sister, she thinks I'm some throwback ape 'cause I think like this. Well if I'm a macho bastard, so what? She's got a briefcase, but she ain't never been faceless. So what the fuck does she know, I says. Fuck her, I says. Fuck.

(*Beat.*)

You sort of look like her.

(*Beat.*)

Not like my sister, I mean. I mean her. Like my wife.

(*Beat.*)

I'd ask you if you know her, but I asked that everywhere already and if I ask it one more time I think I won't be steel no more. Okay?

(*Beat.*)

How'd a gal like you, you know. This business ain't for a pretty gal like you. But gotta eat, right? That's it, right? But shit, I don't like it. Especially 'cause you sort of look like her. Liu Sung. I wish I knew where she was.

(*Beat.*)

But shit, you know. Shit.

(*Beat.*)

Eight tons, sometimes ten tons in a tuna that ain't supposed to carry six tons, but I'm flying it, see. So that's my worry. So's I'm in a hurry, you know I gotta feed 'em. That's what I say to mister clip-board. He says—six-ton limit, Buster, and I say, sure; the rest, I tell him, the other four tons, well that's my carry-on-luggage. So fuck off. I gotta feed a nation, 'cause she's my wife and if I can't find her in this mess then damn it I'll feed a whole god-forsaken country 'cause if I've fed that country then I know I've fed her and that's my job, ain't it, 'cause she's my wife, damn it. She's gonna eat my rice, that I bring. So go to hell.

(Beat.)

It's my only way to be a husband. Hell.

(Beat.)

So's Buster is steel. And I'm gonna cut through the night like I was a knife, you know, cut through the night with my eyes, my tuna eyes ablaze and bring home the bacon. It's something.

(Beat.)

I'm gonna feed a whole son-of-a-bitch continent.

(Beat.)

It's something.

(Beat.)

It's something.

(Pause.)

You gonna suck me off now?

(Blackout.)

MOUNTAIN LANGUAGE

HAROLD PINTER

MOUNTAIN LANGUAGE was first performed at the National Theatre, in London, on October 20, 1988. It was directed by Harold Pinter; the set design was by Michael Taylor. The cast was as follows:

ELDERLY WOMAN	Eileen Atkins
YOUNG WOMAN	Miranda Richardson
SERGEANT	Michael Gambon
OFFICER	Julian Wadham
GUARD	George Harris
PRISONER	Tony Haygarth
HOODED MAN	Alex Hardy
SECOND GUARD	Douglas McFerran
WITH	Jennifer Hill, Irene MacDougall, Kika Mirylees, Charlotte Seago

MOUNTAIN LANGUAGE received its United States premiere at the Classic Stage Company (Carey Perloff, Artistic Director; Ellen Novack, Managing Director), in New York City on October 31, 1989. It was directed by Carey Perloff; the scene design was by Loy Arcenas; the costume design was by Gabriel Berry; the lighting design was by Beverly Emmons; the sound design was by Daniel Moses Schreier; and the music was by Wayne Horvitz. The cast was as follows:

ELDERLY WOMAN	Jean Stapleton
YOUNG WOMAN	Wendy Makkena
SERGEANT	Richard Riehle
OFFICER	David Strathairn
PRISONER	Peter Riegert
GUARD	Miguel Perez
HOODED MAN	David Strathairn
SECOND GUARD	Thomas Delling
WOMEN IN LINE	Katie Cohen, Ellie Hannibal, Mary Beth Kilkelly, Gwynne Rivers

1
A Prison Wall

A line of women. An Elderly Woman, cradling her hand. A basket at her feet. A Young Woman with her arm around the Woman's shoulders.

A Sergeant enters, followed by an Officer. The Sergeant points to the Young Woman.

SERGEANT: Name?

YOUNG WOMAN: We've given our names.

SERGEANT: Name?

YOUNG WOMAN: We've given our names.

SERGEANT: Name?

OFFICER *(to Sergeant)*: Stop this shit. *(To Young Woman.)* Any complaints?

YOUNG WOMAN: She's been bitten.

OFFICER: Who? *(Pause.)* Who? Who's been bitten?

YOUNG WOMAN: She has. She has a torn hand. Look. Her hand has been bitten. This is blood.

SERGEANT *(to Young Woman)*: What is your name?

OFFICER: Shut up. *(He walks over to Elderly Woman.)* What's happened to your hand? Has someone bitten your hand? *(The Woman slowly lifts her hand. He peers at it.)* Who did this? Who bit you?

YOUNG WOMAN: A Doberman pinscher.

OFFICER: Which one? *(Pause.)* Which one? *(Pause.)* Sergeant! *(Sergeant steps forward.)*

SERGEANT: Sir!

OFFICER: Look at this woman's hand. I think the thumb is going to come off. *(To Elderly Woman.)* Who did this? *(She stares at him.)* Who did this?

YOUNG WOMAN: A big dog.

OFFICER: What was his name? *(Pause.)* What was his *name*? *(Pause.)* Every dog has a *name*! They answer to their name. They are given a name by their parents and that is their name, that is their *name*! Before they bite, they *state* their name. It's a formal procedure. They state their name and then they bite. What was his name? If you tell me one of our dogs bit this woman without giving his name I will have that dog shot! *(Silence.)* Now—attention! Silence and attention! Sergeant!

SERGEANT: Sir?

OFFICER: Take any complaints.

SERGEANT: Any complaints? Has anyone got any complaints?

YOUNG WOMAN: We were told to be here at nine o'clock this morning.

SERGEANT: Right. Quite right. Nine o'clock this morning. Absolutely right. What's your complaint?

YOUNG WOMAN: We were here at nine o'clock this morning. It's now five o'clock. We have been standing here for eight hours. In the snow. Your men let Doberman pinschers frighten us. One bit this woman's hand.

OFFICER: What was the name of this dog? *(She looks at him.)*

YOUNG WOMAN: I don't know his name.

SERGEANT: With permission sir?

OFFICER: Go ahead.

SERGEANT: Your husbands, your sons, your fathers, these men you have been waiting to see, are shithouses. They are enemies of the State. They are shithouses. *(The Officer steps toward the women.)*

OFFICER: Now hear this. You are mountain people. You hear me? Your language is dead. It is forbidden. It is not permitted to speak your mountain language in this place. You cannot speak your language to your men. It is not permitted. Do you understand? You may not speak it. It is outlawed. You may only speak the language of the capital. That is the only language permitted in this place. You will be badly punished if you attempt to speak your mountain language in this place. This is a military decree. It is the law. Your language is forbidden. It is dead. No one is allowed to speak your language. Your language no longer exists. Any questions?

YOUNG WOMAN: I do not speak the mountain language. *(Silence. The Officer and Sergeant slowly circle her. The Sergeant puts his hand on her bottom.)*

SERGEANT: What language do you speak? What language do you speak with your arse?

OFFICER: These women, Sergeant, have as yet committed no crime. Remember that.

SERGEANT: Sir! But you're not saying they're without sin?

OFFICER: Oh, no. Oh, no, I'm not saying that.

SERGEANT: This one's full of it. She bounces with it.

OFFICER: She doesn't speak the mountain language. *(The Woman moves away from the Sergeant's hand and turns to face the two men.)*

YOUNG WOMAN: My name is Sara Johnson. I have come to see my husband. It is my right. Where is he?

OFFICER: Show me your papers. *(She gives him a piece of paper. He examines it, turns to Sergeant.)* He doesn't come from the mountains. He's in the wrong batch.

SERGEANT: So is she. She looks like a fucking intellectual to me.

OFFICER: But you said her arse wobbled.

SERGEANT: Intellectual arses wobble the best.

(Blackout.)

2
Visitors Room

A Prisoner sitting. The Elderly Woman sitting, with basket. A Guard standing behind her. The Prisoner and the Woman speak in a strong rural accent. Silence.

ELDERLY WOMAN: I have bread—*(The Guard jabs her with a stick.)*

GUARD: Forbidden. Language forbidden. *(She looks at him. He jabs her.)* It's forbidden. *(To Prisoner.)* Tell her to speak the language of the capital.

PRISONER: She can't speak it. *(Silence.)* She doesn't speak it. *(Silence.)*

ELDERLY WOMAN: I have apples—*(The Guard jabs her and shouts.)*

GUARD: Forbidden! Forbidden forbidden forbidden! Jesus Christ! *(To Prisoner.)* Does she understand what I'm saying?

PRISONER: No.

GUARD: Doesn't she? *(He bends over her.)* Don't you? *(She stares up at him.)*

PRISONER: She's old. She doesn't understand.

GUARD: Whose fault is that? *(He laughs.)* Not mine, I can tell you. And I'll tell you another thing. I've got a wife and three kids. And you're all a pile of shit. *(Silence.)*

PRISONER: I've got a wife and three kids.

GUARD: You've what? *(Silence.)* You've got what? *(Silence.)* What did you say to me? You've got what? *(Silence.)* You've got *what*? *(He picks up the telephone and dials one digit.)* Sergeant? I'm in the Blue Room . . . yes . . . I thought I should report, Sergeant . . . I think I've got a joker in here. *(Lights to half. The figures are still. Voices over.)*

ELDERLY WOMAN'S VOICE: The baby is waiting for you.

PRISONER'S VOICE: Your hand has been bitten.

ELDERLY WOMAN'S VOICE: They are all waiting for you.

PRISONER'S VOICE: They have bitten my mother's hand.

ELDERLY WOMAN'S VOICE: When you come home there will be such a welcome for you. Everyone is waiting for you. They're all waiting for you. They're all waiting to see you. *(Lights up. The Sergeant comes in.)*

SERGEANT: What joker?

(Blackout.)

3
Voice in the Darkness

SERGEANT'S VOICE: Who's that fucking woman? What's that fucking woman doing here? Who let that fucking woman through that
fucking door?

SECOND GUARD'S VOICE: She's his wife. (*Lights up. A corridor. A
Hooded Man held up by the Guard and the Sergeant. The Young
Woman at a distance from them, staring at them.*)

SERGEANT: What is this, a reception for Lady Duck Muck? Where's
the bloody Babycham? Who's got the bloody Babycham for Lady
Duck Muck? (*He goes to the Young Woman.*) Hello, Miss. Sorry.
A bit of a breakdown in administration, I'm afraid. They've sent
you through the wrong door. Unbelievable. Someone'll be done
for this. Anyway, in the meantime, what can I do for you, dear
lady, as they used to say in the movies? (*Lights to half. The figures
are still. Voices over.*)

MAN'S VOICE: I watch you sleep. And then your eyes open. You
look up at me above you and smile.

YOUNG WOMAN'S VOICE: You smile. When my eyes open I see
you above me and smile.

MAN'S VOICE: We are out on a lake.

YOUNG WOMAN'S VOICE: It is spring.

MAN'S VOICE: I hold you. I warm you.

YOUNG WOMAN'S VOICE: When my eyes open I see you above me
and smile. (*Lights up. The Hooded Man collapses. The Young Woman
screams.*)

YOUNG WOMAN: Charley! (*The Sergeant clicks his fingers. The Guard
drags the Man off.*)

SERGEANT: Yes, you've come in the wrong door. It must be the
computer. The computer's got a double hernia. But I'll tell you
what—if you want any information on any aspect of life in this
place we've got a bloke comes into the office every Tuesday week,
except when it rains. He's right on top of his chosen subject. Give
him a tinkle one of these days and he'll see you all right. His name
is Dokes. Joseph Dokes.

YOUNG WOMAN: Can I fuck him? If I fuck him, will everything be
all right?

SERGEANT: Sure. No problem.

YOUNG WOMAN: Thank you.

(*Blackout.*)

4
Visitors Room

Guard. Elderly Woman. Prisoner. Silence. The Prisoner has blood on his face. He sits trembling. The Woman is still. The Guard is looking out of a window. He turns to look at them both.

GUARD: Oh, I forgot to tell you. They've changed the rules. She can speak. She can speak in her own language. Until further notice.

PRISONER: She can speak?

GUARD: Yes. Until further notice. New rules. *(Pause.)*

PRISONER: Mother, you can speak. *(Pause.)* Mother, I'm speaking to you. You see? We can speak. You can speak to me in our own language. *(She is still.)* You can speak. *(Pause.)* Mother. Can you hear me? I am speaking to you in your own language. *(Pause.)* It's our language. *(Pause.)* Can't you hear me? Do you hear me? *(She does not respond.)* Mother?

GUARD: Tell her she can speak in her own language. New rules. Until further notice.

PRISONER: Mother? *(She does not respond. She sits still. The Prisoner's trembling grows. He falls from the chair on to his knees, begins to gasp and shake violently. The Sergeant walks into the room and studies the Prisoner shaking on the floor.)*

SERGEANT *(to Guard)*:   Look at this. You go out of your way to give them a helping hand and they fuck it up.

(Blackout.)

THROWING SMOKE

KEITH REDDIN

For Peter

THROWING SMOKE was presented at the West Bank Theatre, October 1984. Lewis Black and Randy Forestter, Artistic Directors; the play was designed and directed by Mark Linn-Baker. The cast was as follows:

EARL	Budge Therkald
BUZZ	Keith Reddin
SPARKY	Reg E. Cathey
ROACH	John Gould Rubin
ERNIE	Peter Crombie
FRANK	Dan Deraey
DAVID	Rusty MacGee

An earlier version was presented by the Alliance Theatre, Atlanta.

Characters
EARL, the coach
BUZZ, third base
SPARKY, short stop
ROACH, left field
ERNIE, catcher
FRANK, the umpire
DAVID SAVILLE, a fan

Setting
A dugout.
An August afternoon.

"Don't forget to swing hard, in case you hit the ball."   —*Woodie Held*

■ ■

A dugout. Roach and Ernie sitting on the bench inside. Ernie is reading a comic book, while Roach is watching a small portable TV. Sparky is swinging two bats outside the dugout in the on-deck circle. The Coach is standing inside the dugout, chewing tobacco. He spits out a wad occasionally as he speaks.

COACH: I first saw Jesus down in the Canal Zone around April of '45. It was in this little dinky bar called the China Clipper, run by this Chink called Roberto. That's why he called it the China Clipper, cause he was a Chinaman, see. What he was doing down in Panama during the war, you got me. Have I told you this one before, Sparky?

SPARKY: Yeah, but go ahead, coach.

COACH: So I'm sitting in this bar see, like usual. It was pretty classy then, had this propeller fan on the ceiling, stuff like that. I'm in the Navy, I'm putting together busted-up P-36s from the carriers that go into dry dock down at the yard. And every night a bunch of us guys go down there, right? We go down to this piss poor bar to get really fucked up, you know what I'm saying? You listening to me, Sparky?

SPARKY: I'm listening coach, but jeez it's almost time for me to go out there.

COACH: Yeah, yeah. Nobody's listening to the coach anymore. He's burnt out now, they say, nothing but some old fart in a uniform. Don't think I don't know what they're saying behind my back, Sparky. The coach knows. He can't coach no more, that's what they say. They say I'm fat and I smell like old cheese, can't do nothing but sell Yoo-Hoo, but I know better.

SPARKY: Finish the story coach.

COACH: Yeah, so anyway, Sparky, I'm in the China Clipper, really putting it away with these other guys when in walks this guy. About 7 foot tall, has real long hair, this big beard. When He walks in, the whole place stops. I mean dead, nobody talking, nobody drinking. Jesus doesn't order anything. He just come in, and He kinda squints, like this, like I'm doing now, He squints and He's looking everybody over. Then, get this, then He walks straight over to me. People are moving out of His way. I mean He ain't looking at anybody but me, but everybody's moving out of His way, they're moving tables and chairs out of His path, He's walking in some kind of trance almost, you know. You know what I mean, Sparky?

SPARKY: Yeah.

COACH: So then He comes up to me. He puts these big hands, these huge hands on my shoulders and He says Earl (how He knew my name I'll never figure out) Earl, He says, after this thing is over (meaning the war) you are gonna go into professional baseball. You are gonna be one of the greatest baseball players on the face of the earth, in all history. Me, I look at Him right? I hate baseball, to me baseball is one of the most boring games in the world. But I tell ya, Sparky, when this guy looks at me and tells me I'm gonna play ball, you can be sure then and there that the rest of my life is devoted to baseball. *(Loud "boos" heard.)*

SPARKY: See ya, coach. *(He exits, Buzz enters, dragging his bat.)*

BUZZ: Boy, I tell ya, Lopez is really throwing smoke today.

COACH: You struck out again shithead.

BUZZ: I'm sorry coach. I really tried this time. But nobody can get anything off of Lopez today. The guy is pitching great.

COACH: Right.

BUZZ: Why does he have to be on the other side? Why don't we got Lopez?

COACH: That is twice you have struck out. Two strike outs in a row.

BUZZ: Coach, I know you're disappointed.

COACH: Just sit down and keep quiet. I don't want to talk to you.

BUZZ: Sorry.

COACH: Enough with the sorry. Sorry doesn't get us on base, now does it?

BUZZ: No, coach.

COACH: Roach, get on deck, you asleep or something?

ROACH: Huh? Oh yeah. Hey look, coach, Sparky's gonna strike out, we're gonna be on the field in two minutes.

COACH: Roach, I told you to get on deck.

ROACH: Come on, coach, nobody's hitting anything off Lopez.

BUZZ: Right coach, he's really throwing smoke out there.

COACH: I don't wanna hear nothing from you. You, you're lucky you're playing at all.

BUZZ: I'm sorry.

COACH: What would happen to the team if everybody acted like you Roach, huh? What would happen if everybody gave up and went home before the game is over?

ROACH: But just about everybody has left.

COACH: What? Hey, where the fuck is everybody? Where'd the fucking team go?

BUZZ: Guess they all went home coach.

COACH: But the game isn't over yet.

BUZZ: Yeah, but Lopez is . . .

COACH: I don't care about Lopez, where's my team? I don't have a team here.

ROACH: We're here. Me and Buzz and Ernie are here. *(Ernie raises his hand.)*

ERNIE: Ja.

BUZZ: And Sparky's striking out.

COACH: Where'd my team go?

BUZZ: They were here a minute ago.

COACH: I know that, but where'd they go? *(A loud booing.)*

ROACH: Sparky just struck out, coach. *(Points to TV.)*

COACH: He what? Sparky's out!

ROACH: That's three outs. We gotta take the field.

COACH: Yeah, we gotta . . . wait a minute. We only got five guys here. Where's Harrington?

BUZZ: I don't know.

COACH: Any you guys see Harrington?

OTHERS: No. Nope didn't see him. No Harrington's not around.

COACH: Where's our pitcher? *(Sparky enters.)*

SPARKY: Lopez is hot. I gotta hand it to him, he's got a no-hitter going and he's hot.

COACH: This is terrible.

SPARKY: It's not every day you're part of a no-hitter.

COACH: But we're the guys that are doing the non-hitting here.

SPARKY: But I tell ya coach, Lopez is hot.

BUZZ: Nobody can touch him.

SPARKY: Hey, are we missing a few guys?

COACH: Sparky, you seen the rest of the team?

BUZZ: We're missing a couple of guys.

COACH: We don't have a goddamn team and we gotta take the field.

ROACH: So let's go.

COACH: We can't take the field with four guys.

BUZZ: We can move around a lot. Make it look like there's more of us.

COACH: Buzz, you are really a jerk you know that.

BUZZ: Yeah, I'm sorry, coach.

COACH: Don't keep saying you're sorry.

ROACH: Hey, coach, the umpires are looking over here.

SPARKY: I think he wants us to take the field.

COACH: I know that. What the hell are we supposed to do?

BUZZ: I'll go look in the locker room. *(He exits.)*

SPARKY: Coach, you better stall 'em. Go out there and tell 'em we're bringing in a new pitcher.

COACH: Good idea. Sparky, see who we got in the bull pen warming up.

SPARKY: The thing is, coach, we don't got anybody in the bull pen.

COACH: Okay, who here can pitch? *(Silence. Buzz runs on.)*

BUZZ: Nobody's in the locker room, coach.

COACH: Okay, Buzz, here's your big break, are you ready?

BUZZ: Sure, coach.

COACH: I want you to go out there and pitch an inning.

BUZZ: What?

COACH: I said I want you to pitch this inning, till we find one of our pitchers.

BUZZ: But I'm a third baseman. I don't know how to pitch.

COACH: Anybody can pitch, get a glove, here's a ball. Throw a few to Ernie.

BUZZ: But I'm telling you I can't pitch, coach.

COACH: Okay, okay. It was just a wild card.

BUZZ: Sorry coach.

COACH: That's okay. You had your one shot at greatness and you blew it. It's okay though.

ROACH: The ump's coming over here.

COACH: Shit. Shit shit shit. What are we gonna do guys.

SPARKY: I don't know.

COACH: I'm hanging by my fingernails here, and you tell me you don't know? What kind of team is this?

ERNIE: Was ist los? Kannst du mir helfen?

COACH: Shut up Ernie.

SPARKY: I say we just forfeit the game. Lopez has got a no-hitter going anyway, let's give it to him.

COACH: Sparky, are you out of your mind?

ROACH: We're in last place anyway, coach. We lose every game, what difference does it make?

COACH: We can't give up, it's un-American. *(Umpire enters.)*

UMP: So, what's the story here, Earl?

COACH: We're bringing in a new pitcher.

UMP: So where is he?

COACH: He's in the bull pen. Buzz, go get, uh, whatshisface from the bull pen.

BUZZ: But coach . . .

COACH: Just tell him to get his ass on the mound, now move it. You retarded or something, move!

BUZZ: Okay. *(He runs off.)*

UMP: So let's play ball, okay, Earl?

COACH: No problem. He'll be here in a minute.

UMP: The crowd is getting antsy, Earl. We got a perfect game here, and the crowd wants to know what's going on.

COACH: I gotcha.

UMP: The crowd gets restless, then they start getting angry. They get angry on a hot day they start throwing stuff. Popcorn, beer bottles. They get into fights, start cursing, going wild. When they go wild the first they attack is the ump. I don't need that stuff this afternoon, Earl.

COACH: No problem, we're ready to go.

UMP: I'm wearing a face mask and chest protector but that don't stop an angry mob, you know what I mean?

COACH: No sweat.

UMP: Okay, as long as you're ready to go. I don't want to fine nobody. *(Buzz runs on.)*

COACH: Okay, so where is he?

BUZZ: Who?

COACH: Who? The pitcher, the new pitcher, where is he?

BUZZ: Ah . . . like, um, he's taking a shower.

UMP: What's going on here?

COACH: We got everything under control here.

UMP: I want somebody on that field in two minutes, that's all I got to say.

COACH: Right. *(Ump exits.)* We're screwed. We are up shit creek without a paddle.

BUZZ: Nobody's in the shower, coach. I just made that up.

COACH: I figured, Buzz.

SPARKY: So, what's the plan?

COACH: The plan is we need four guys, and most of all, now this is essential, we need a new pitcher.

SPARKY: Maybe Ernie could pitch. I mean he catches all the time, he handles the ball as much as any of the pitchers.

COACH: I hate talking to Ernie.

ROACH: We only got a minute, coach, we got to try something.

COACH: Okay. Hey, Ernie, Ernie boy, how you doing?

ERNIE: Ja?

COACH: Wie gehts heute, Ernie?

ERNIE: Es geht mir gut, und Sie?

COACH: I'm not doing too well right now. Look, Ernie, the thing is, in case you haven't noticed, we're missing a few players here.

ERNIE: Was ist los, Coach?

COACH: Ernie, listen. I want you to listen a second.

ERNIE: Ja?

COACH: Ernie, I want you to pitch an inning.

ERNIE: Was?

COACH: I want you to throw the ball, spielen Ernie, we got to finish the game.

ERNIE: Ich kann nich verstan.

COACH: Why can't the guy talk English. I don't know what the hell he's saying. Why can't he talk Spanish. Shit, I know Spanish. I learned it in Panama.

ERNIE: Der illustrate fertig. Ich bin schon mit.

COACH: I mean we got a lot of Puerto Ricans in the pro's, why do we get traded an East German.

BUZZ: Lopez speaks Spanish.

COACH: I don't want to hear anything about Lopez.

BUZZ: Sorry, coach.

SPARKY: Just put him on the mound and give him the ball, he'll know what to do.

COACH: The man does not know anything we are saying.

ERNIE: Ich kann nicht . . .

COACH: Okay, just get him out there. Let's move. *(Roach and Sparky exit with Ernie.)* Now, Buzz I want you to search this place out.

BUZZ: Sure.

COACH: I want you to check every locker, every shower, every stall for somebody from our team. Then I want you to check the parking lot. Then you look around the concession stands. You can't find anybody from our team, pick up somebody.

BUZZ: But coach . . .

COACH: Buzz, we're falling apart here and we need somebody out on the field. Now, I don't care how you do it, but I need at least five guys, now move out.

BUZZ: Hey wait a minute . . . you could play, couldn't you, coach?

COACH *(pause)*:   Naw. I can't play. Get out of here, Buzz. *(Buzz runs off.)* I couldn't play . . . *(Buzz runs on.)*

BUZZ: You want anything coach?

COACH: What?

BUZZ: Since I'm out there, I was wondering if you wanted something to eat. You want a beer or something? *(Coach stares at Buzz.)* You all right, coach?

COACH: Buzz, I thought I told you to find our team.

BUZZ: Yeah, I'm going. *(Buzz runs off. Roach enters.)*

COACH: Okay, what's the story, Roach?

ROACH: We got ol' Ernie on the mound, but he looks confused.

COACH: I figured.

ROACH: He just keeps looking up at the stands and waving.

COACH: Great.

ROACH: Well, he's never been on the mound alone, in front of everybody, maybe he's scared.

COACH: He better be scared, he's got to pitch. *(Loud crowd noise.)*

ROACH: Oh-oh, something's going on.

COACH *(looking up)*:   Please don't let the crowd hurt one of the players, please . . . we need every one.

ROACH: Something's happening out there.

COACH: Roach, find out what the hell Ernie's doing . . . and Roach—

ROACH: Yeah?

COACH: Don't let me down, okay?

ROACH: Right, coach. (*Roach runs off. Ballpark music heard—Buzz runs on.*)

BUZZ: I got somebody coach.

COACH: What is that?

BUZZ: Where?

COACH: In your hand, what is that?

BUZZ: It's a hot dog.

COACH: What the hell are you doing with a hot dog now, Buzz?

BUZZ: Well, gee, I'm hungry, coach.

COACH: We've got a goddamn game here with no team and you are out getting food?

BUZZ: Well, I was out there and I figured . . .

COACH: Never mind. Now, where are these guys you found?

BUZZ: Guy. I could only get one guy.

COACH: I sent you out to find me a team, and Jesus Christ, Buzz, you got mustard all over your uniform.

BUZZ: Aw, sorry, coach.

COACH: Okay, where is this guy?

BUZZ: He's in the locker room, suiting up. I gave him Adler's stuff.

COACH: Okay, now what can he play?

BUZZ: Huh?

COACH: What position can he do, Buzz?

BUZZ: I'm not really sure what he can do, I'm not sure he's into baseball. Like, he told me he plays cricket.

COACH: Cricket?

BUZZ: That's almost the same thing, isn't it? Like, they use a bat and a ball and run around like we do.

COACH: Buzz, cricket and baseball are not the same thing I . . . (*Roach and Sparky drag Ernie on.*)

ROACH: You're not gonna believe this, coach.

COACH: What? What happened?

ROACH: We're out there with Ernie on the mound, right?

SPARKY: We . . . well . . . we try to move around, look like we're ready to play and . . .

ROACH: Ernie starts going crazy.

BUZZ: I'm gonna get the guy now. (*He goes off.*)

COACH: What?

ROACH: Ernie, coach.

SPARKY: He sees the cameras and the crowd . . .

ROACH: He starts yelling at the top of his lungs.

SPARKY: He keeps yelling this stuff.

(Buzz enters with Saville.)

BUZZ: Here he is.

SAV: Super of you to let me play. I've watched all the time. Never thought I'd get to play. Kind of like a dream come true you might say.

BUZZ: I told coach here you play cricket, not baseball, but it's the same thing, right?

SAV: Well you might say that. Not that I don't know how to play some baseball. Watched ever so much on the telly.

BUZZ: You hear that, coach, he says he can play baseball too. What position you want play?

SAV: I thought, if you don't mind, I'd like to pitch.

BUZZ: That's fantastic, you can pitch, can you. That's great.

COACH: What did Ernie do now?

SPARKY: He kept saying this one thing over and over.

ROACH: Something to do with some wall.

COACH: What?

SPARKY: He was yelling "Eine mauer trennt das deutsche volk."

COACH: What the hell does that mean?

ROACH: What?

COACH: What does that crap mean?

SPARKY: Well, I looked it up in the phrase book, coach.

COACH: And?

SPARKY: Roughly it means One Wall separates the German People.

COACH: Great. Ernie, why do you do these things to me? Ernie, you listening to me?

ERNIE *(in German)*: Do you see me, I was great. They had the cameras on me and everything.

COACH: What? Slow down, Ernie.

SPARKY: He's pretty excited.

COACH: What do you want?

BUZZ: Here's the guy, coach. He says he can pitch.

COACH: Hi. (Now I thought you said he played cricket.)

BUZZ: He plays, played baseball . . . before, in high school, is that right?

SAV: That's correct.

COACH: Where did you find this guy?

BUZZ: Out by the souvenir stand, he was buying one of our caps.

SAV: My son, David junior, is a regular fan of yours.

COACH: Great.

BUZZ: He says he'd like to pitch.

ERNIE *(in German)*: I really told them. The crowd went crazy.

COACH: Ernie, be quiet a minute, willya.

ERNIE *(in German)*: I have told them the truth. I have spoken the true feelings of the German people.

COACH: Ernie . . .

ERNIE *(in German)*: We must reunite the separate states. That is what I told them.

SPARKY: Ernie, I can't find all this stuff. *(Flipping through the phrase book.)*

ERNIE *(in German)*: Only in America can I speak the truth. That is why I made my escape.

SPARKY: He keeps saying something about . . .

ERNIE *(in German)*: That and to play American baseball. I love baseball.

SPARKY: He said something about baseball.

SAV: So, when do we start?

ERNIE *(in German)*: I love the uniforms.

COACH: Buzz, does this man know anything about baseball?

BUZZ: He told me he used to play.

COACH: The man is wearing a leisure suit and sandals, Buzz.

BUZZ: I gave him a uniform.

ERNIE *(in German)*: It's interesting that they serve frankfurters, beer, pretzels, all German food here.

SAV: So, I don't mind pitching for you.

COACH: Thanks but no thanks. I'm gonna kill you, Buzz.

BUZZ: What can I do coach?

COACH: I ask for one simple thing . . .

ERNIE *(in German)*: Say where is the rest of the team? We are missing some people.

SPARKY: Coach, the ump is coming back here.

COACH: Now look what you've done.

BUZZ: I'm sorry, coach.

ROACH: He looks plenty pissed off.

COACH: I'm ruined. This is the end of my career. *(Ump enters.)*

UMP: I'm feeling like death taking a shit so it better be good, Earl.

COACH: Frank, it's like this, we don't have a team right now.

UMP: What?

COACH: Seems most of the team has disappeared.

BUZZ: They were kidnapped by a terrorist group.

COACH: Shut up, Buzz. See, the team left. We've been losing a lot of games lately and nobody was getting a hit off of Lopez . . .

BUZZ: Yeah, he was really throwing smoke today.

COACH: It's been bad couple of weeks, Frank.

UMP: So you want me to call off the game?

COACH: No, don't do that.

UMP: You don't have a team, we can't have a game.

COACH: Have pity Frank . . .

UMP: How many guys you got?

COACH: Four.

BUZZ: Five.

COACH: We got four guys, and some guy from the parking lot.

UMP: I don't see how we can finish. And Lopez had a perfect game.

COACH: Frank, you can't do this to me.

UMP: You only got four guys.

COACH: I'll play. Me and the guy in the slacks make six, that's pretty close.

BUZZ: Coach, you're gonna play!

UMP: 'Fraid not, Earl. Sorry.

COACH: You can't do this, I'll be ruined. They'll laugh me out of the league. I'll be the biggest joke in baseball.

UMP: I'd like to help, but the crowd's getting ugly.

COACH: Frank, do me a favor, please.

UMP: Ugly crowds go for the ump. I've learned this through the years.

COACH: I'm asking nicely, I'm saying please, Frank.

UMP: The whole team up and left, huh? *(Starts laughing.)*

COACH: They just left. We only had another inning.

UMP: A forfeit's not so bad, Earl, it's not the end of the world.

COACH: It's the end for me. I won't be able to go anywhere without everybody shitting on me.

UMP: See you tomorrow, boys. *(He exits.)*

COACH: I feel like killing myself.

BUZZ: Don't worry about it, coach.

SPARKY: We would of lost anyway.

ROACH: I mean we lose every game. We're the worst team in the league.

SPARKY: We just play a little harder next time. We just dig in and play a little better ball, right coach?

COACH: Everybody get out of here.

ROACH: We'll do okay tomorrow, coach.

COACH: Everybody hit the showers, go home.

BUZZ: You wanna go out later, coach. You want to get a couple of beers or something?

COACH: Leave me alone, all right.

SPARKY: Sure. *(Loud boos heard, crowd noise.)*

ROACH: See ye, let's go Ernie. Game's over. *(Ernie, Sparky and Roach exit.)*

SAV: Better go get my kid. Thanks again. *(Exits.)*

BUZZ: I'll put this stuff away.

COACH: Throw it away, I don't care, I'm finished anyway. It doesn't matter.

BUZZ: Aw, gee, coach, you shouldn't say that. That's not a very positive attitude.

COACH: Buzz, you irritate me a lot, you know that.

BUZZ: Yeah, I guess so.

COACH: Get out of here. I want to cry.

BUZZ: You don't want to really, coach. So, I mean we lost a game so what? We lose games, we win games, that's baseball. That's life, right? Whoa, that was a very heavy thing I just said there. Did you hear that? Did you hear that last thing I just said, coach?

COACH: Yeah.

BUZZ: That part about life being like a baseball game. Sometimes you tie, sometimes you get rained out. There's a lot of truth to that. *(Pause.)*

COACH: Is it hot today, Buzz, or is it just me?

BUZZ: No, I think it's pretty hot today.

COACH: And I haven't sweat at all. Usually on a day like this, I'm wet, you know I sweat like a pig.

BUZZ: Yeah. Everybody's going home now. They announced the game is over and so everybody's leaving.

COACH: Yup, all over.

BUZZ: Everybody going out to the parking lot, out to their cars. Heading on the highway back to their houses. Watch another game on TV tonight. Watch a night game, maybe Boston–New York, maybe Chicago–Pittsburgh, could be any game.

COACH: I hate it when this place empties out, everybody leaving garbage all over the park.

BUZZ: Yeah, wrappers and stuff all over the place. Beer bottles.

COACH: You know whenever it's real hot like this, always reminds me of ol' Panama. I was in Panama in the war, Buzz.

BUZZ: Yeah.

COACH: It gets very hot in Panama. Hot, a lot of humidity. Certain times of the year it rains a lot there. Most of that place is jungle there. They cleared up the Canal Zone, though.

BUZZ: I guess.

COACH: Hey, Buzz, I ever tell you my story about Panama. The one while I was down there during the war.

BUZZ: Yeah, coach. *(He starts picking up equipment.)*

COACH: Oh. Okay.

BUZZ: You can tell me again if you want to.

COACH: I was telling Sparky, before, but I don't think he was listening, you know.

BUZZ: Sure, coach.

COACH: See, Buzz, I was down in Panama, like I said, down at the Canal Zone, this was in '45.

BUZZ: Is this the one where you saw Jesus in the bar, and He told you you was gonna be a baseball star?

COACH: That's it. Fuck it. I been telling that dumb story, nobody pays attention anymore.

BUZZ: Listen, coach . . . so you tell me the story, I'm listening.

COACH: So Jesus, He walked up to me in this bar and He told me . . . baseball. Baseball and nothing but baseball. And, Buzz, for close to thirty-seven years I been traveling in buses, eating crappy food outta cardboard containers, wearing smelly uniforms. I had a good career, but I wasn't any star. In 1954 I won a car, was voted MVP by the sports writers, that was pretty good. *(Pause.)* So ol' Jesus picked me out. But somebody, some jerk in the bar, starts yelling at Him, at Jesus. You got to remember that Jesus had real long hair, and He spoke very quietly, in 1945 He was real funny looking, you know? So this guy starts making some crack like Jesus is a queer cause He has this long hair. Then pretty soon everybody in the bar is laughing at Him, pushing Him around. Jesus don't say nothing. Then a bunch of guys trying to prove how tough they are, they start punching Him out. Really hurting Him, He just sat there, letting 'em. Then they dragged Him outside, down to the docks, by the canal and . . . I couldn't watch no more. I went home and I . . . see I knew it was Jesus. He never said this, I don't have no proof, but somehow . . . somehow Buzz I knew it was Jesus come to Earth to talk to me. I'm this fucking nobody and He came to tell me about baseball. About my fate. And Buzz I didn't do anything to stop those guys. And then you guys . . . today you guys walk out of here before the goddamn game is over and I feel really terrible. We would of lost sure, but it still broke my heart.

BUZZ: Don't get mad at me coach, but I'm sorry. I know it don't mean much, me always saying I'm sorry, but I'm sorry anyway. I wish I didn't strike out so much, wish I could hit a lot of home runs but I guess all I'm good at is hanging around third base and trying to improve my lifetime RBI average. I never done commercials and they got this goofy picture of me on my trading card, but coach I love playing baseball. You putting me on this team was the best thing ever happened to me. I guess that's all I gotta say, coach.

COACH: Listen, would you call me Earl, okay?

BUZZ: Okay, Earl. You can call me Buzz. *(Pause.)* I think there's a breeze now. Maybe it'll cool off.

COACH: Buzz, you know, I'm gonna have me a cigar. You want one?

BUZZ: Fine by me, Earl. *(They both light up their cigars, and smoke in silence. Buzz coughs a couple of times.)* These are good.

COACH: I don't smoke cigars often, but somebody gave me these. I just felt like smoking a cigar now. *(Pause.)*

BUZZ: You know we got a double header scheduled tomorrow.

COACH: Yeah, a double header. *(They smoke, as a few crumpled papers and wrappers blow across the stage.)*

(Slow fade to blackout.)

SLAUGHTER IN THE LAKE

JOSÉ RIVERA

SLAUGHTER IN THE LAKE was first produced at the Ensemble Studio Theatre's One-Act Play Marathon on July 6, 1988, Curt Dempster, Artistic Director; Laura Barnett, Producer. Directed by Joan Vail Thorne; scenic design by Anne Sheffield; costume design by Abigail Murray; sound design by Bruce Ellman; lighting design by Greg MacPherson; stage manager was Dean Gray.

BILL TYSON	Dan Desmond
STEVE BROWNING	James Rebhorn

Marathon '88 was presented as part of the First New York International Festival of the Arts.

Characters
BILL TYSON, a businessman in his forties
STEVE BROWNING, a businessman in his late forties

Time
The present. Late summer.

Place
A man-made lake in Central Park, New York

■ ■

Central Park. A small, man-made lake. Late Summer. Bill Tyson and Steve Browning, businessmen in their forties, are throwing rocks into the lake. They are on their lunch hour. Tyson is taller, more forceful; he's hiding his nervousness. Browning is stockier, darker, not as successful; he can barely hide his enthusiasm for being there.

TYSON: Yeah, you can sit here, hours will go by, you'd never know you were surrounded by the city, would you?
BROWNING: It's beautiful here. You picked a great spot.
TYSON: Uh-huh, it's peaceful. I'm glad you like it, Steve.
BROWNING: Another great job, Mr. Tyson. Another coup.

TYSON: Yeah. You can spend hours here and not see a single jogger, or hear a single radio. . . .

BROWNING: It's hard to believe we're both here. That's what I—

TYSON (*not listening*):   It's very close to Columbus Circle—what, Steve?

BROWNING: I didn't mean to interrupt your train of thought. You were saying.

TYSON: Just . . . that it's hard to believe that millions of people surround us . . . like huge, choking hands. . . .

BROWNING: Interesting way to put it, but true.

TYSON: I've brought my son here. Paul used to love coming into the city with me and going to Central Park.

BROWNING: I don't mind telling you, it's great to see you again. Thanks for calling me.

TYSON: I'm glad you were free. I . . . uh, planned to call you many times before yesterday, believe me.

BROWNING: Oh, I know. At least once a week, the phone would be in my hand and my book open to "T"—Tyson. Bill Tyson.

TYSON: Same here.

BROWNING: But I always put it down, closed the book, bagged the whole idea.

TYSON: Same here.

BROWNING: Great minds think alike.

(*They laugh quietly.*)

TYSON: I discovered this little oasis when it was frozen. In January . . . after having "one of those days" at S and S. I mean . . . of course, things have gotten somewhat better since then . . . but *that* day, I don't mind telling you, I was ready to kill. Against my advice, they signed up the absolute worst high school biology text . . .

BROWNING: Bet I know who did that.

TYSON: Who else? So I grabbed my coat and marched up to the park . . . and spent my lunch hour throwing rocks through the ice.

BROWNING: Look at the ducks. Reminds me of Stony Brook.

TYSON: Oh, there are flocks of ducks here.

BROWNING: I'm actually surprised you didn't pick Clancy's Bar for this meeting.

TYSON: No. If I'm in a bar, I'll drink, and I don't need to drink during the day too.

BROWNING: I didn't know you were drinking at night.

TYSON (*testily*):   Well . . . you're *not*?

BROWNING: Sorry. I just thought a duck pond didn't seem like your style.

TYSON: Styles change, Steve. You know. A man gets bored. *(Beat.)*

BROWNING: You should have seen Janet's face when you called! Oh Jesus, you'd have thought the President of the United States had called me.

TYSON: She's a sweetheart. Louise and I have really missed her.

BROWNING: She misses you two. *(Beat.)* It's been nine months, almost to the day, you realize that? Nine months since Bloody Thursday.

TYSON: Bloody Thursday? Is that what historians are calling it?

BROWNING: Nine months since you fired me. And nine months since we've had a friendly face-to-face conversation. That's quite a record for friends that go back to double dates and first cigarettes.

TYSON: Steve . . . if there's any way I can say I'm sorry—

BROWNING: Oh fuck it. I made no secret how pissed off I was . . . I'm tired of that shit now. The thing is, we're finally back together. How's Louise?

TYSON: Well . . . we have our moments.

BROWNING: You know, Jan really thought it was over between the two of us.

TYSON: Well. It nearly was. *(Beat.)* You know, I took Paul here to fly a little Japanese kite once. Louise won't come in because Manhattan scares her. This lake has become what I rely on during the day . . . as a place to think, to file things away . . . a place where I can go and think of Paul. . . .

BROWNING: I missed Louise's birthday this year, didn't I?

TYSON *(sadly)*: Yeah. It was last week.

BROWNING: First time I've done that since you two got married. Please wish her a happy one for me.

TYSON: She was very upset, actually, because Paul . . . who's really getting big . . . Paul forgot to get her a birthday present.

BROWNING: Sounds like something Danny would do.

TYSON: Paul claimed to have forgotten, then he changed his story to say that he was *broke,* which is untrue, I know he has money. I give him a good allowance. *(Beat.)* Paul's been acting very strange lately; I'm frankly a little worried about him. Does Danny ever talk to you about Paul?

BROWNING: I think Danny would rather stick his hand in a blender than volunteer a conversation with Dad. The boys are at that goddam age, you know? What? Fifteen now? Oh, you'll never guess what I did.

TYSON: What?

BROWNING: I took the rest of the day off from work.

TYSON: Why? For me?

BROWNING: Come *on,* don't be so dense. I thought maybe you'd take the rest of the day off too, and we could spend the day drifting around the city. . . .

TYSON: Well . . .

BROWNING: . . . or go back to the Island, rent a little boat in Port Jeff—

TYSON: . . . no, I have to get back. I'm meeting an author, a series editor, and I can't just disappear on everyone—

BROWNING: What are you afraid of? That you'll have to fire yourself? *(Pause.)*

TYSON: Actually, I *do* see people here sometimes. Once, I watched a school of these ducks being attacked by a man who had a radio controlled boat in the water. I'll never forget that halfwit trying to kill these ducks with his radio-operated remote control boat.

BROWNING *(a smile)*:   Seriously?

TYSON: He was trying to kill them! A dozen little baby ducks, Steve, paddling behind their mother, and the remote control boat is going right for them. . . .

BROWNING *(big smile)*:   Really? To kill them?

TYSON: The mother tried to decoy for her children, swimming off to attract the boat . . .

BROWNING *(laughing)*:   A toy boat? And the ducks? That's pretty funny.

TYSON: What's wrong with you, Steve? They were innocent living things about to be slaughtered in the lake by some *sadist.* . . .

BROWNING *(subsiding)*:   I'm sorry, Bill, I really am.

TYSON: You don't understand, do you? It was a typically selfish New Yorker taking out his aggressions . . .

BROWNING: Yes, yes, he was. I'm sorry.

TYSON: Disrespect for life, Steve.

BROWNING: What did you do? Throw a depth charge?

TYSON: Not hardly. I did pick up a stone. I had it in my hand, hidden, watching the boat getting closer, the mother flapping crazily in the water . . . *(Chuckles nervously.)* . . . I guess it could seem funny, to an outsider.

BROWNING: Did you throw the stone?

TYSON: No. I think one of them was killed. A little slick of blood appeared on the water . . . little feathers here and there. . . .

(Tyson looks away. Browning studies his friend for a while, not saying a word.)

BROWNING: Did something happen? Is there something you want to tell me? (*No answer.*) It's why you called me, isn't it? Something's wrong with Louise?

TYSON: Louise is fine.

BROWNING: Okay, it's Paul. (*No answer.*) Is there some trouble with Paul?

TYSON: I called you because I wanted to see you again.

BROWNING: Awwww! Now it all comes back to me! The trials of being Bill Tyson's friend! The agonies! The torture!

TYSON: Jesus.

BROWNING: Quiet, brooding Mr. Tyson . . . seething in his little corner, like a gargoyle, eaten to death and spitting up blood . . . but ever the stoic, uncomplaining, tight-lipped Protestant.

TYSON: Steve, as Paul is fond of saying to his father, "Fuck you, okay?" (*Beat.*) Thank you. (*Pause.*) How's Macmillan treating you?

BROWNING: You don't want to know. I'm having a bad time.

TYSON: Really?

BROWNING: Yeah. It's . . . you know, the same old Steve Browning story.

TYSON: You hate your job. You hate your books. You hate your authors.

BROWNING: Give that man the door prize! I'm sick of these writers' attitudes . . . of the hand-holding I have to do . . . the pissy amounts of money we have to work with. And you'd think a house like Macmillan would be run like a *business*! They're killing me!

TYSON: I had no idea.

BROWNING: No one does, not even Janet. It's the industry in general . . . the compromises in quality . . . I go in, open a few veins, perform auto-lobotomy . . . for what? A text that'll cost students fifty dollars and be obsolete in a semester?

TYSON: What are you going to do?

BROWNING: Maybe start my own small press. Be my own boss. Maybe put out low-priced books I can care about.

TYSON: You'll make it.

BROWNING: Convince me. (*Beat.*) You're looking pretty good, old man.

TYSON: I've been to the gym a lot, pumping iron, swimming . . .

BROWNING: Another big change in your life.

TYSON: Well, it makes good sense. We are, after all . . . uh, instruments, to a degree. I know that sounds flakey, but it's true.

BROWNING: Yeah yeah yeah. I bet you've taken up photography too.

TYSON: I have not.

BROWNING: Hang gliding.

TYSON: No.

BROWNING: Gourmet cooking.

TYSON: No.

BROWNING: Sculpting in clay.

TYSON: Well. Okay. Now don't make fun of me!

BROWNING: Would I do that to you—?

TYSON: In the past nine months, our paths have gone in different directions—and I hope you don't sneer at some of the choices I've made.

BROWNING: Sneer? At the thought of you making cute little nudes in clay?

TYSON: They haven't been easy choices for me to make! I won't have you criticizing me!

BROWNING: Come on, lighten up!

TYSON: I won't lighten up! *Dammit,* Steve! It's not a very easy thing for me to talk about—

BROWNING: Okay, okay . . . I'm sorry; forgive me. (*Beat.*)

TYSON: I'm sorry.

BROWNING: What the hell is eating you today?

TYSON: I uh . . . feel all opened up . . . like my skin's been pulled off me? Paul's inherited my temper: that short fuse I more or less conquered. He destroyed half his wardrobe the other day. Took a pair of scissors and slashed his shirts and jeans because I wouldn't let him wear some T-shirt his pals were wearing. Uh, some *group* . . . Iron Fist or something. Iron Toilet. It had some guy in chains and a straightjacket being tortured.

BROWNING: Danny's got one like that.

TYSON: Then Paul must've seen Danny's. At any rate, I wouldn't let him wear it to school, he got mad at me and tore his clothes to shreds.

BROWNING: We should form a club. "Men with Teenage Sons." Long Island chapter. I'll publish the newsletter and provide my readers with recipes for raising intelligent, independent young men.

TYSON: I don't need anyone to tell me how to raise a boy of fifteen. (*Pause.*) You started me on cigarettes, do you remember that? That was you who started me smoking. (*Beat.*)

BROWNING: What?

TYSON: I had a big fight with Louise about it. The other night. She said my brother started me, but I was sure, positive, it wasn't: it was you. (*Beat.*) After school, at your house. You had a pack of Camels . . .

BROWNING: What are you talking about?

TYSON: Oh, it's stupid—a coincidence! You started me smoking cigarettes and I'm trying to make connections.

BROWNING: To what?

TYSON: To my *son*! Paul, like me, has always excelled. But Danny, like you, has always been the adventurous one, the groundbreaker. I mean, Danny started Paul playing the trumpet. Danny started Paul running track, liking girls—

BROWNING: You're losing me completely.

TYSON: Jesus, Steve, it's my obsession with Paul. No my obsession with *us*—with Paul and me—with father and son relationships in general. *(Beat.)* I read a story in the papers recently about a father-son relationship. The father and son were beggars, working street corners and subways as a team. Well, for whatever reason, business was drying up, people were simply not giving. *(Beat.)*

The two of them were on the verge of starving, when the father realized what the problem was. He realized it was because his son was no longer the pathetic little boy people were used to—enjoyed—giving to. The kid was bigger and stronger. So he took his son home and broke the kid's arm with a crowbar . . . just battered his son's arm until the bones gave in. He made his son pathetic again . . . a more effective beggar. Now the dimes and dollars are just falling in their laps.

(A long silence.)

I didn't *want* to come across that story in the paper. Didn't want to know what the other animals were doing. I'd rather watch the kids flying Japanese kites in the park . . . but those stories manage to find me . . . even at home, Steve. *(Tyson throws a rock in the water.)*

I wanted to look the other way when I suspected Paul's problem. I thought I was being paranoid, just *reading* into his behavior. But his grades began to fall. His teachers complained about absences. There was household money suddenly missing. He became sullen, willful, disrespectful. I didn't want to think it, but the evidence was clear . . . and Louise's tears convinced me. *(Beat.)* All I know is this didn't start by itself. *(Beat.)* Danny is the leader in my son's life as you were the leader in mine. And lately I've watched my son going slowly to hell because of your son's influence. *(Beat.)*

BROWNING: What exactly . . . now wait . . . what exactly are you saying?

TYSON: Oh, Steve, for crying out loud . . . I never should have called you. *(Tyson turns from Browning and starts to exit.)*

BROWNING: Get back here! You can't just run off like that! You're accusing my son of . . .

TYSON: Be up front with me! You know what your son's been doing! For goodness sakes, your son's been known to sell drugs in school, he's been—

BROWNING: Known? *Known??* Was it printed in *Newsday?*

TYSON: Paul has bragged about Danny selling pills, and what have you, in school . . .

BROWNING: Mary, Mother of God.

TYSON: . . . Danny and Paul share everything, they've been inseparable since kindergarten, so what the hell do you expect me to believe?

BROWNING: This is incredible.

TYSON: My son has been taking pills, smoking pot, taking God-knows-what for God-knows-how-long *and he's only fifteen years old,* Steve! I blame Danny for starting him on it. Let me say that flat out.

BROWNING: My son is not a drug pusher—

TYSON: Then tell me what's happening to Paul!

BROWNING: He's rebelling against you!

TYSON: Rebelling—?

BROWNING: Christ, offer a man his first cigarette and look what he does to you! UP YOURS, BILL!

TYSON: WHAT THE HELL AM I SUPPOSED TO THINK?

(Tyson grabs Browning by the lapel and shakes him. Browning pulls away. Tyson, shaking from head to foot, moves away. A long silence. Browning fumbles for a cigarette. Neither man can quite look at the other.)

BROWNING: Cigarette?

TYSON: Absolutely.

BROWNING *(handing Tyson a cigarette)*:   Camels.

TYSON *(Takes the cigarette.)*:   Very funny.

BROWNING: Sure it won't kill you? *(Lights Tyson's cigarette. They smoke.)* Whew. I feel better already. Hmmmm, the narcotic effects are taking hold, yeah, I'm seeing God. . . .

TYSON: I'm sorry, Steve. My son's in trouble.

BROWNING: So's your sense of humor.

TYSON: What do you expect me—?

BROWNING: I'm sorry. All right? Calm down. You've already ripped my new jacket, which I'll have to replace. So let's keep our cool. *(Beat.)* You really believe my son got your son started on drugs.

TYSON: Yes I do.

BROWNING: Do you hear what you're saying? Do you know what that does to the pit of my stomach?

TYSON: Steve, I've seen Danny *working* on Paul, manipulate Paul. Paul was a sweet, mild-mannered, easygoing little kid and Danny's got him wrapped around his finger.

BROWNING: And from that and nothing else, you actually concluded—

TYSON: Well, I haven't specifically *seen* them do this. They don't exactly do it out in the living room.

BROWNING: You can't *prove* it, can you?

TYSON: No. But it's something I know, an overwhelming feeling I have about your son.

BROWNING: Has Paul actually *told* you? Has he complained to you—?

TYSON: No. *(Beat.)* I haven't asked him.

BROWNING: You haven't talked to him about it.

TYSON: No. By the time I get home most nights, he's exiled himself into his room . . . then each weekend, he's at your house.

BROWNING: You haven't actually spoken, sat down, and in a face-to-face manner, discussed any of this with your son.

TYSON: No Steve, I haven't.

BROWNING: It's just a feeling.

TYSON: Louise shares it. *(Beat.)*

BROWNING: Look, why don't we . . . we get out of this stupid park, go to Clancy's and talk about this there? I mean, there's nothing we can't solve if we put our heads together, right? We'll get a private little booth, a few sobering drinks, and we'll attack this like one of those Byzantine manuscripts we used to work on together.

TYSON: I know the solution to this problem, Steve, we don't need to *work* on this. I want you to keep your son away from Paul. I want Danny to cease being a factor in Paul's life. I mean, it won't be easy with school starting soon, but if you talk to some of Danny's teachers; I'll talk to Paul's teachers—

BROWNING: No. *(Beat.)* No, Bill. *(Beat.)* Danny's not Paul's problem. *You're* Paul's problem. You are. *(No answer.)* It's rebellion. It's *that*; I know; I've been there. *(Beat.)* Danny gets further and further from me. More secret. More remote. I quickly learn his new languages and he quickly changes them . . . until no translation is possible for us. Until there's no crossing from my country to his because he's burnt his bridges, the river, the whole damn countryside. *(Beat.)* The peanut-brain got caught, you're absolutely right, with pot in school. But he's not a *dealer* for Petesakes

. . . you have to trust I know him better than you do. And he's certainly never fooled around with anything harder than grass. If he had, you would have been the first person I would have called for help—

TYSON: I never should have come here.

BROWNING: But you did. You reached out to your oldest friend —and I'm not going to let you down. So I'll give you the truth as I see it. Danny did not drag Paul into this. Paul started down this road because he wants to tell you something about the life you represent.

TYSON: The life I represent is a good life.

BROWNING: I agree, Louise agrees, Jan agrees, but you have a son who violently, insanely disagrees.

TYSON: You make it sound like he woke up one fine day and said, "I don't like Dad's politics, I think I'll take a little angel dust and teach him a lesson!"

BROWNING: In essence, yes.

TYSON: Bullshit! A child's an empty vessel, filled every day by TV, music, movies, peers, teachers, his best friend!

BROWNING: And his father! His father, who's feeling a little old, a little mortal, so he pumps iron . . . who is almost certainly unchallenged by his job in publishing . . . who probably will continue to experiment with hobbies, to fill the time, until he dies. (*Beat.*) Your life is changing. That's okay. It's just a thing some men of our age go through. (*Beat. Tyson turns his back on Browning.*) So why don't we go to Clancy's . . . find a booth with a nice-looking waitress, a real ten . . . and let's talk about our kids and your fucked-up midlife crisis . . . (*Big smile.*) . . . okay, big guy?

TYSON: What makes you think I want to go to a bar with you? If it hadn't been for this crisis—do you think I would have called you? (*Beat.*)

BROWNING: That's what I'm hoping.

TYSON: Well, don't. I've told you, specifically, what I need from you and if you can't give me that, then . . . well, I have to go back to the office. (*Beat.*) We've both changed a lot in a year's time. I'm getting, uh . . . I'm *fighting* more . . . *I'm fighting with both of my fists!* So much of what I love is being polluted by others, including Paul, and I'm fighting to stop that, whether it occurs at the office, or at home, on Long Island, wherever. There are simply too many threats. (*Beat.*) And I can't feel sympathy for you any-more. The old Steve Browning story is boring me. I'm tired of watching you blow great opportunities in the field in the name of independence, whatever *that* means. No . . . the life I allegedly represent is a good one . . . and Paul knows that. I just wish Paul's friends did.

BROWNING (*Takes a long look at Tyson, shakes his head—then sadly smiles*):   Please come to Clancy's with me? (*Beat.*)

TYSON: I have to go back to the office. I have an author. (*Starts to walk out.*)

BROWNING: I did my best for you. All those years we worked together . . . building a reputation, discovering writers . . . and in all that time, I did my best for you.

TYSON: I have to go right now—

BROWNING: And! And the last nine months have been pure hell for me. I wasn't even able to tell Janet, for *two months,* that you had fired me from S and S. I pretended I had a job to go to for two months. Do you know what it was like waiting for you to ask me back?

TYSON: My hour's over—

BROWNING: Billy. (*Beat.*) Uhm, okay. Okay. I'll do it. I'll do what I can to keep Danny away from Paul. (*Beat.*) So now, why don't you call in and let's get on the railroad and hit beautiful downtown Port Jefferson together?

TYSON: I really should go back. (*Beat.*) I wish you luck, in going into business for yourself. I hope you make a killing. (*Pause.*) Will you walk me to Columbus Circle?

(*Beat. Browning stays in place, thinking, as Tyson walks to the edge of the stage. The two men look at each other. Tyson walks off, leaving Browning alone. Fade out slowly.*)

I'M NOT STUPID

DAVID E. RODRIGUEZ

I'M NOT STUPID was first presented at Playwrights Horizons as part of the Dramatists Guild Foundation's 1991 Young Playwrights Festival. The play was directed by Seret Scott; set design by Allen Moyer; costumes by Elsa Ward; lighting by Pat Dignan; sound by Janet Kalas; stage manager was Liz Small; dramaturg was Paul Selig. The cast was as follows:

ROGER	Curtis McClarin
DR. GREEN	Peter Francis James
MARGRET FLETCHER	S. Epatha Merkerson

■ ■

Scene 1

Scene begins with spotlight on Roger. He is sitting in a chair, rocking back and forth.

ROGER: I was watching the Little Rascals on TV, they had a clubhouse . . . and I wanted a big clubhouse like the Little Rascals . . . I'm not stupid! You need WOOD to build a clubhouse, and there is a lot of wood in the junkyard. I could get wood from the junkyard to make me a little house like the Little Rascals. I was going to sleep in it, and Pa, too. We were going to sleep in the clubhouse like the Little Rascals. I went to the junkyard and got a lot of wood . . . I'm not stupid! You need nails, I had a lot of nails . . . and you need a box, you build it like a big box, but it's turned upside down . . . I'm not stupid! I could make a clubhouse, you need a hammer for the nails. Pa had a hammer, he had a big hammer. Like this big. It was in the house . . . and I went into the house to get the big hammer. I asked Ma for Pa's hammer. She started to cry. She told me Pa wasn't coming back. . . . *(Pause, Roger begins to cry.)* . . . I'm not stupid! I know Pa was dead. Sleep killed him. Sleep! . . . I was a bad boy.

(Lights come up revealing a doctor's office. Dr. Green is sitting behind a desk.)

DR. GREEN: How were you a bad boy?

ROGER: I was bad. I was a bad boy.

DR. GREEN: How were you bad, Roger . . . Roger?

ROGER: Yeah?

DR. GREEN: Tell me, it's okay. How were you a bad boy?

ROGER: All I wanted to do was build a clubhouse . . . *(Pause.)* . . . like the Little Rascals.

DR. GREEN: Roger? . . .

ROGER: Yeah? . . .

DR. GREEN: It's okay. . . . Okay?

ROGER: Okay!

DR. GREEN: Is it bad to build a clubhouse, Roger?

ROGER: Yeah!

DR. GREEN: Why? . . . Why? . . . *(Pause.)*

ROGER: I wasn't thinkin' about Pa. I wasn't thinkin' about Pa.

DR. GREEN: Roger? . . .

ROGER: Yeah. You keep sayin' my name.

DR. GREEN: Was that bad?

ROGER: Yeah!

DR. GREEN: Why? Tell me. Why was that bad?

ROGER: I was supposed to be thinkin' about Pa. I didn't want to hear . . . hear that Pa was dead. All I wanted to do was build my clubhouse. I was suppose to be thinkin' about Pa. . . . That's bad. Why? Why she don't tell me after I make my clubhouse? I never finish the Little Rascals clubhouse. I wanted Pa's hammer. I wanted Pa's hammer. Ma never gave me Pa's hammer, she never gave it to me!

DR. GREEN: Roger? . . .

ROGER: Stop sayin' my name. . . .

DR. GREEN: Do you want to talk more?

ROGER: No.

DR. GREEN: Do you want to be alone?

ROGER: I want to be alone.

DR. GREEN: Okay.

ROGER: Okay!

(Roger exits. Ma enters opposite of Roger's exit.)

MA *(sitting)*:   So, what did he tell you?

DR. GREEN: The usual.

MA: Bad things about me again?

DR. GREEN: Well, not exactly . . . bad.

MA: Oh . . .

DR. GREEN: Although, there were some things said that . . . concern me.

MA: Like bad things right? That boy has always got something bad to say about me. . . .

DR. GREEN: Now, Mrs. Fletcher . . .

MA: It's true. What did he say about me last week?

DR. GREEN: Well, the same thing he said for several weeks, the same thing he said today. . . .

MA: I'm not giving him the hammer. *(Pause.)*

DR. GREEN: Why don't you give him what he wants?

MA: Isn't it enough that he got all the money?

DR. GREEN: Not all of it Mrs. Fletcher.

MA: Oh, you're talking about my share. The third I get to take care of Roger with, and the rent, and the bills. . . .

DR. GREEN: You got what you were entitled to by law.

MA: What I'm entitled to, and what I deserve are two different things.

DR. GREEN: We're here to talk about Roger.

MA: Why don't you buy him a hammer? You take care of his money.

DR. GREEN: It's not that simple. He doesn't want another hammer.

MA: I won't give it to him. He's taken far too much from me already.

DR. GREEN: Okay . . . Mrs. Fletcher, I know your late husband's will didn't come out exactly as you had hoped. . . .

MA: It's not only the money . . .

ROGER *(enters)*:   Hi, Ma. I didn't say nothin' bad about you this time, Ma, I swear.

MA *(to Roger)*:   Why don't you shut up.

DR. GREEN: Mrs. Fletcher!

ROGER: That's okay.

DR. GREEN: Roger?

ROGER: Yeah?

DR. GREEN: Would you mind waiting outside?

ROGER: Yeah.

DR. GREEN: Please?

ROGER: Okay. I'll be right outside, Ma. Waiting right there. Ma . . . Ma . . . 'bye Dr. Green.

DR. GREEN: Good-bye, Roger. *(Exit Roger.)* What was that?

MA: What was what? I don't know what you're talking about.

DR. GREEN: He's your son.

MA: No, he is not. He's no son of mine.

DR. GREEN: No? What is he to you, then?

MA: He's just this stupid, good-for-nothing that took everything I ever lived for!

DR. GREEN: That is not true!

MA: It's true! Since the day he was born I no longer had a husband. Now he's dead because of him.

DR. GREEN: It was a heart attack. Blaming Roger—

MA: Henry was strong! He worked day in and day out to pay doctor bills . . . *Doctor!* He'd come home tired every night. . . . So tired and pale, Dr. Green. How long do you think a man could last doing that without one day his body giving in? I saw it. I told him to stop. I told him to send Roger away so he wouldn't have to work so hard. But no, he loved Roger. That man gave more love to that idiot than he gave me in seventeen years!

DR. GREEN: I see. So what are you going to do now? Make him suffer? Treat him as if he were some kind of animal? What do you want?

MA: I want what I deserve!

DR. GREEN: And what is that? Money?

MA: I said, it isn't about the damn money!

DR. GREEN: Okay . . . What then? . . . What? *(Pause.)*

MA: If you don't like the way I treat him, why don't you have him sent away? *(Pause.)*

DR. GREEN: This is all about the money. . . .

MA: You're wrong. . . .

DR. GREEN: We both know that if Roger is sent away, you'll be awarded his trust money. . . .

MA: I want to go on with my life. . . .

DR. GREEN: . . . I won't be able to provide services for him, thus, I will no longer oversee the account . . .

MA: . . . I deserve some peace. . . .

DR. GREEN: . . . making you the beneficiary of your husband's will, isn't that right? What else could it be?

MA: You don't know everything, you have no idea!

DR. GREEN: Come now, Mrs. Fletcher, you said it yourself, he's not your son. All Roger is, is one big dollar sign. . . .

MA: He's an idiot.

DR. GREEN: Roger is very high functioning, he does not present a danger to himself or to others. He has proven able to cope with the everyday challenges, you are physically fit to care for him, and it goes on and on. Mrs. Fletcher, all that I can suggest to you is what I have requested in the past.

MA: No, I don't need a shrink.

DR. GREEN: You need to learn how to deal with Roger. I'm not going to diagnose you, or put you on any medication. We'll just sit down and talk, talk about your husband's death, most of all, talk about Roger, so you can get a better understanding—

MA: No thanks.

DR. GREEN: I can help you—

MA: You know how you can help me!

DR. GREEN: Give it a chance. What do you have to lose? If you have one bit of love left in you for that boy, do it for him?

MA: No!

DR. GREEN: Do it for yourself, then?

MA: You think you know everything! You're so smart! You think you got everything all figured out!

DR. GREEN: I think you need more help than Roger. And I don't think I know everything. I don't know how a woman like yourself could be so full of hate . . . but if you continue on this path, one day it may very well lead you to break, and I don't think that's something for Roger to experience.

MA (exiting): I've heard enough of your know-it-all talk. Good-bye, Dr. Green.

DR. GREEN: For your sake, listen to me!

MA: Whatever you say, Doc. . . . 'Bye. . . .

DR. GREEN: Before you go, just answer this, did you ever love him?

MA: Bye-bye. . . . (Exit. The lights fade to black.)

ROGER (as if holding a hammer): Heavy . . . Roger, hit the nail on top . . . if you don't, the nail will bend. . . . Look Roger . . . BOOM! BOOM! BOOM! . . . I hit it on top. BOOM! No Roger . . . BOOM! You're bending the nail! BOOM! Hit it on top! On top . . . Boom! . . . On top! . . . Boom! Stop . . . it's bending, Roger! Try it . . . BOOM! . . . I can't, Pa . . . BOOM! . . . It's heavy . . . BOOM! . . . Try it . . . BOOM! . . . I can't, Pa. . . . BOOM! . . . Hit it! . . . BOOM! . . . I can't. . . . Hit it, Roger! . . . I can't. . . . Hit it, Roger! . . . I can't. . . . On top! . . . BOOM! Again! . . . BOOM! (Pause.)

Good boy Roger, good boy. Good boy Roger, good boy.

Scene 2

In the Fletcher household, living room. We see Ma sitting in a chair watching television. There is a knock at the door. It is Dr. Green.

MA (drunk but not noticeably): Dr. Green?

DR. GREEN: Good afternoon, Mrs. Fletcher. Please, pardon this intrusion. I tried calling, but your phone is out of order. Roger didn't keep his appointment. Do you know where he is or if he left?

MA: He's at the junkyard.

DR. GREEN: This is most peculiar. All the years I have known him, he has never missed an appointment.

MA: Wait for him here. He'll be right back, and I do have to talk to you.

DR. GREEN: I see. Then I'll wait. *(Settled.)* So, what is on your mind?

MA: I was thinking about that question you asked me, if I loved Roger. And I've been thinking; I love Roger. It's the kind of love you have for a pet . . . a dog, maybe. You give it a bath, feed it, clean up after it. Don't get me wrong, Dr. Green, did you expect me to love him as a son? How can I? He can't do anything, except eat and sleep, like a dog. I'm not mean. That does not make me mean. Did you ever wonder if a dog loves? I say that people say that dogs love, but that is just because you take care of it. They'll go back to sleep until they're hungry again, and then come back for more. They don't know where the food comes from, as long as it tastes good. They'll eat it, then they'll go back to sleep. . . . Roger sleeps a lot. In a way, Roger isn't a person. He's a dog. You give him what he wants, and he stays happy, right? That's right! It's true! So why should I love him as a son, when he's a dog. Don't look at me like that Dr. Green, you know what I'm saying is true. Why don't you just put away all that mumbo jumbo about a person is a person, and wake up and see that Roger is really a dog, that talks. A talking, walking, big ol' dumb dog, and maybe you could understand what I'm saying. So you can stop looking at me like that! I'm not stupid, I'm smart. Do you think I'm smart? I think I'm smart, this is my opinion. It is my opinion that Roger is a dog. So what? What's so wrong with that? Kill me, for cryin' out loud, but at least I loved him. I kept him happy. No, I mean, I love him and I keep him happy. Sometimes I mix words around, but I'm still smart, and he's still happy. So you see, there's nothing wrong. Roger would even tell you himself, and he will when he comes back, you'll see.

DR. GREEN: I can't believe you just said that.

MA: Why not? He's never going to get married and have kids. He's never going to have a job, much less take care of me when I get old. I'm lonely, even if Roger is around. Maybe . . . maybe I should get a real dog or something, what do you think? I'll bathe it, take it for walks, clean up after it. I have had years of experience. . . .

DR. GREEN: You're drunk.

MA: So I'm drunk, what does that have to do with it? I'll still feel the same when I'm sober. I'll still want a dog. . . .

DR. GREEN: Mrs. Fletcher, I think we ought to talk about this again, when you sober up. Obviously you're not yourself. Until then, I will look for Roger. If you will excuse me—

MA: No, stay here. Roger will come back. He's probably on his way, and it's so cold outside.

DR. GREEN: I appreciate your concern, but I think I really ought to—

MA: I gave him the hammer.

DR. GREEN: What?

MA: I did. After that, he went rushing out the door to the junk-yard.

DR. GREEN: Well, that explains it. It was good of you, you know. You did something.

MA: I know I've been really hard on him for some time. You see, I'm not mean. I think I'm turning over a new leaf. I was just angry over Henry's death, that's all. Now, I'm over it.

DR. GREEN: Really?

MA: You say that as if you don't believe me. I may be drunk now, but this is the last time. I'm going to be a new woman, you'll see.

DR. GREEN: I see. A moment ago, Roger was a dog.

MA: Oh that. Really bad example, wasn't it?

DR. GREEN: I would say so, but—

MA: You know, I never knew what the "K" stands for in Dr. K. Green.

DR. GREEN: Karl.

MA: Karl, that's a nice name. Do you mind if I call you Karl?

DR. GREEN: If you prefer.

MA: I would. I don't know, Dr. Green sounds so formal. Don't you agree? So distant, and I would like us to be closer, Karl. After all, you'll be treating me.

DR. GREEN: Treating you?

MA: Yes, didn't I tell you? No, I didn't, did I?

DR. GREEN: I don't believe so.

MA: Well, now you know. I've decided to take you up on your offer. I figured some treatment will do me some good.

DR. GREEN: I see.

MA: What's wrong, you don't want to treat me? I know, I'm blowing your mind, right? Oh, don't be surprised, Karl. I was on my bad side for a while like I said before, I'm over that now.

DR. GREEN: Well, then I think that Dr. Green would be more appropriate.

MA: Why?

DR. GREEN: I think it would make our relationship more profes-sional. Now that you are under my care—

MA: Oh, don't be such a stiffy! Wanna drink, while you wait? Oh, I forgot, doctors don't drink, right?

DR. GREEN: I don't know about other doctors. I don't.

MA: That's good. I wouldn't want you to either, Karl. Oops, I forgot! I'm sorry.

DR. GREEN: That's all right.

MA: Since you're here, maybe we can have my first session right now.

DR. GREEN: You've been drinking.

MA: Never mind, I'm sobering up already.

DR. GREEN: Really, Mrs. Fletcher.

MA: Call me Margret, or is that not professional enough?

DR. GREEN: That's quite all right, if you prefer, but as I was saying before—

MA: Yes, as you were saying, Dr. Green.

DR. GREEN: —I think it would be more appropriate, if I asked my secretary to make an appointment.

MA: There you go again, Mr. Stiffy. Do you always have to do things by the book? There's no bending you, is there?

DR. GREEN: I don't know. What do you mean?

MA: You know what I mean. Didn't you do anything wild and crazy when you were young?

DR. GREEN: Like what?

MA: You know, like play a practical joke on your friends, or steal the neighbor's dog? Play a big trick?

DR. GREEN: I have. Not that in particular, but yes, when I was young.

MA: That's what I mean. Come on, loosen up. Let's get a session going here.

DR. GREEN: All right, if you insist.

MA: Great. So what do I do now, lie down?

DR. GREEN: Whatever makes you feel comfortable.

MA: I'm comfortable. What do I do now?

DR. GREEN: Tell me what's on your mind?

MA: Where do I start?

DR. GREEN: Anywhere.

MA: I don't know, I feel funny. Give me a suggestion.

DR. GREEN: All right, why the sudden change in you?

MA: I told you, I'm letting go of the past.

DR. GREEN: Why?

MA: Why not? I can't stay bitter for the rest of my life. Now that Henry is gone, I'm over it. Why don't I start a new life with Roger? Have a chance to be a mother to him? After all, he is my son, isn't he? Forget all that nonsense about him being a dog. I do love him. I guess I've been denying it for so long. . . . Well?

DR. GREEN: Well, what?

MA: Aren't you going to say something?

DR. GREEN: Like?

MA: Well, like, I think that you're making a change for the better.

DR. GREEN: I think you're making a change for the better.

MA: You really mean that?

DR. GREEN: Honestly?

MA: Yes.

DR. GREEN: No, I don't believe one word you've said.

MA: What? I can't believe it!

DR. GREEN: I'm a psychiatrist, Mrs. Fletcher. I don't believe in miracles.

MA: But I'm telling the truth! I swear, I gave him the hammer, and he's at the junkyard! Who the hell do you think you are calling me a liar?!

DR. GREEN: When did you give him the hammer?

MA: Today! I gave it to him today!

DR. GREEN: What did you make him promise? What did he have to do?

MA: Nothing. Why are you doing this to me?! I just wanted him to be happy.

DR. GREEN: How do you know he is at the junkyard?

MA: I took him there myself.

DR. GREEN: Really? Why?

MA: He wanted me to see him build his goddamn clubhouse!

DR. GREEN: Then why isn't he here now? Tell me! Why?

MA: What? What are you accusing me of? Do you think I'd go that far?

DR. GREEN: Go as far as what? GO AS FAR AS WHAT?!!! WHAT DID YOU DO TO HIM?

MA: I'm changing, don't you see? I'm not lying! I swear!

DR. GREEN: I'm going to the junkyard.

MA: No!

DR. GREEN: Why not? I'm going, Mrs. Fletcher.

MA *(clings fiercely to him)*:   Don't go please, please don't go! He's there! Believe what I'm saying! He's there!

DR. GREEN: Let go of me! Let go of me!

MA: Alright, alright, go then! Go! *(Doctor exits.)* You think you know everything! Go! *(Breaks down in tears on the floor. Lights fade to black.)*

Scene 3

In the Fletcher household. The lights are dim, one lamp is on. Green bursts in with the hammer in his hand.

MA: I told you he was at the junkyard, but you didn't believe me. *(No response.)* Now do you believe me? You thought you knew everything. I'm a new woman, now. I've changed for the better. I gave him the hammer.

(Green drops the hammer.)

I did it to make him happy. Why are you looking at me like that? He built the clubhouse, didn't he? You should've seen the look on his face. First time I've seen him smile since Pa died. I haven't seen a more satisfied look. I wasn't satisfied though. No . . . Sure, Roger got something else he wanted. He always gets what he wants, he's always satisfied! It was special this time. I've seen that look before. It was the time I took him to the city. Roger wanted to get Pa a birthday present. So did I. We were at the hardware store, and when Roger saw the hammer—there were hundreds of hammers—Roger wanted this one. I told him that Pa already had one, but Roger didn't listen. He went on and on about the stupid goddamn hammer! So, I smacked him real good, and he went running out in the store. I figured he'd come back, but after a long while, he didn't. Good! So I just took the bus back alone. I wanted him to stay in the city. I swear, I never wanted him to come back. I didn't see him for two days. Henry didn't notice. He would work day and night. I began to think what happened to that dummy. I thought he'd come home. And I realized that I can't do such a thing. I may never see him again! Oh my god! What if he's starving, or cold? It wasn't my fault he left. That night I found myself in the city. "Excuse me, did you see my son? My son? My little boy? Did you see him? Are you blind? Are you stupid? How can you not see him?" And all around, I saw people walking, laughing, eating dinner, wearing warm coats. How can they have fun? Don't they realize what happened? I lost my son, don't they care? How can I have been so stupid? I said, "God, please god, if I find him I swear . . . I swear I won't ever touch him again. I'll give him anything he wants." And what was I going to tell Henry? And at that moment, I loved Roger more than anything in the whole world. "Just let me find him." I wasn't going back home without Roger. I'd been walking for five hours, and every alley I passed, I prayed and prayed that I wouldn't find him there, face down in the gutter. It's funny, how everybody started to look like him. Thre blocks away I saw someone with the same stupid walk. I started to first walk faster and faster, then jog, then run faster and faster. "Roger! Roger! Roger!" I went up to him and it was a bum. It was Roger. Roger is a bum. Roger was, still is, and always will be a bum. AND THIS BUM HAD

THE GODDAMN HAMMER IN HIS HAND! And the first thing he says is, "LOOK, I GOT THE HAMMER!" So what? And then the same look of satisfaction was there! And I wasn't satisfied. The same day, I beat the living daylights out of that boy, and I still wasn't satisfied. But I am satisfied for the first time in my life, right now. I'm satisfied. I don't care what happens now. He was like a pet. All I have to do now is get a dog, a big dog, then I'll be satisfied.

DR. GREEN (*advances violently*): HOW! HOW CAN YOU BE SO EVIL!, He was doing so well. He had a chance!

MA: He wasn't a person, he was a dog! You saw him yourself, didn't you, in a dog house?

DR. GREEN: I saw your son—your son—with a hammer in his head!

MA: He was your patient. That's all he was to you! That's all he was to you! You don't know what it was like!

DR. GREEN: I loved Roger as a son!

MA: A son? He didn't even know your first name, Karl. If he was my son, if he was a human being, I wouldn't have done it!

DR. GREEN: You actually believe it. You're not just calling him a dog. You actually believe it. I will have you committed for life! You will pay for this! You will rot in a cage where you belong!

MA: So you can get the money.

DR. GREEN: What?!

MA: You brought the hammer. People saw you coming out of the junkyard. And you came here to attack me.

DR. GREEN: What are you talking about?

MA: Yes Karl, because the neighbors heard you when you left, and when you came back. Now we are arguing because you killed Roger!

DR. GREEN: What?

MA: It's a lot of money, isn't it? Enough for a shrink to kill for!

DR. GREEN: You're insane!

MA: And now you want to blame it on me, and send me away, and call me crazy so you can get the money! You knew Roger for many years. He would go anywhere with you!

DR. GREEN: Stop it!

MA: And I'm saying this loud enough so all the neighbors can hear! No, don't hurt me! Doctor Karl Green, please don't hurt me, I'll give you the money! I'll give you what you want, don't kill me, too!

DR. GREEN (*tries to shut her up*): I said stop it! Shut up!

MA: Help! Help! He's killing me! Let me go!

DR. GREEN (*withdraws*): All right! All right! I'm not touching you! Don't do this . . .

MA *(lower)*:   You think you know everything, Mr. Know-it-all. I'm not stupid Karl. A nice long trip to Mexico will do me some good. After all, I am a new woman. Don't look at me like that, Karl. I'm not a mean person. That doesn't make me mean. I just want to be satisfied.

DR. GREEN: You'll never get away with this!

MA: Like I said, Mexico. I'll leave after I get the money.

DR. GREEN: You'll never . . . How could you have done this?

MA: I'm not stupid. A poodle sounds real good right now.

VITO ON THE BEACH

SAMUEL SCHWARTZ

VITO ON THE BEACH is dedicated to Greg, Doug, and Robert.

The play was first performed by Love Creek Productions at the Westbeth Theatre Center, New York City, on April 30, 1991, directed by Sharon Fallon, with the following cast:

VITO	Dustye Winniford
CHASE	Kendel D. Smith

Characters
VITO, midthirties, an ex-boxer, heavyweight.
    Looks younger than he is, extremely handsome, ragged around the edges.
CHASE, late twenties, slight, thinning blond hair.
    Affected at times, moves like a dancer.

Place
A deserted residential area in the Ocean View section of Norfolk, Virginia. It is late August, very hot. Chase has a beach chair, an easel, a sketchpad and charcoal pencil. Vito has a simple bar he holds over his head to simulate pull-ups.

Time
August 1990

■ ■

Lights up on Vito in swimming trunks and tank top. He simulates pull-ups by lowering a steel pipe under his chin and then raising it above his head again. He counts as he lifts.

VITO: . . . four, five, six, seven . . .

(Chase sits at his easel, drawing with charcoal. He has a Walkman. He hums to himself as he draws and Vito continues to do his pull-ups.)

    . . . fourteen, fifteen, sixteen, seventeen . . .

(Chase's movements become more erratic, more undisciplined. He now sings to himself as counterpoint to Vito's counting.)

CHASE *(singing to himself):* Shoobe do wop . . . *(Hums a bit.)* Shoo shoo sha do wa . . . Wa, wa, wa, wa

VITO: . . . eighteen, nineteen, twenty, twenty-one, twenty-two, twenty-three . . .

(Vito stops his pull-ups. Chase has become louder and Vito extends the bar above his head and just keeps it there as if he's hanging from the bar. Chase is in his own world now—singing as his piece of charcoal sweeps around the pad. Vito drops from his bar. He walks over to Chase.)

VITO: Hey. *(Chase continues to sing.)* Hey. You. *(No response.)* Chase. *(Chase does not respond. Vito finally takes off Chase's earphones.)* What you doing?

CHASE *(tongue in cheek):* Dancing.

VITO: You're supposed to be drawing my picture—

CHASE: I am.

VITO: For money you already seen—

CHASE: I know.

VITO *(suddenly puts his hand over his face.):* Mother fucker—

(Chase immediately takes a lace handkerchief from his bag and puts it up to Vito's nose. When he takes the handkerchief away, it's red with blood.)

CHASE *(concerned):* Does it hurt?

VITO: No.

CHASE: Nosebleeds are common in summer—*(Vito takes the handkerchief.)* I'll wash it. *(Chase takes it back.)*

VITO: The fucker's got blood on it.

CHASE: Some bleach . . .

(Vito suddenly puts his hand on his nose again, pretending there's blood. Chase surrenders the handkerchief.)

CHASE: Here.

VITO: Fooled you. I'll give you money for it.

CHASE: Keep the handkerchief.

VITO *(looks at it, surprised):* It's lace.

CHASE: I like lace.

(Vito shakes his head. He balls up the handkerchief and places it in the band of his swimsuit.)

VITO *(sitting):* Was a time I could take fifty of them mothers—

CHASE *(incredulous):* Nosebleeds?

VITO: Pull-ups.

CHASE: Oh. *(Beat.)* I can't do one.

VITO: Bullshit. Little guy like you.

CHASE: That's the problem.

VITO: You got less meat to haul up. *(Gets the bar.)*

CHASE *(tries to change the direction of the conversation)*:   What do you call these things by the way?

VITO: What?

CHASE: I always thought they were called chin-ups. But you just said pull-up.

(Vito hands him the bar and forces him to hang on it. Chase suspends it above his head and stays there.)

VITO: Stop thinking about it and fucking do it. *(Chase halfheartedly tries a few times and then gives up.)* You're not going to the bar. The bar's coming to you. *(Vito stands behind Chase and helps him struggle to do one. Chase falls to the ground, breathless. Vito applauds.)* See. There. You done it.

CHASE: No. You did it.

VITO: What you talking? My English bad or something?

CHASE: No. You did it. You did all the work.

VITO: Then why am I standing pretty here and you're panting like a dog in heat?

CHASE: Good point.

VITO: You gotta take a shit. I tell you where the bathroom is. You still gotta do the rest.

CHASE: O.K. O.K. So I did one.

VITO: Yeah. So good. So fuckin' A.

CHASE: Now I have to do two.

VITO *(shakes his head)*:   You're a trip, man. And not one I want to be on. *(Chase gets up and goes back to the easel.)* Now what you want me to do?

CHASE: Why don't you just sit still for a second. I need to fill in some detail on the head. It's interesting. For a neck as wide as yours, you have small cheekbones. *(Vito nods and sits down. Chase begins working on the portrait.)* Why are you having this done, Vito?

VITO: You sent in the best sample drawing.

CHASE: No, I mean, why are you having a portrait done when there must be thousands of pictures of you?

VITO: 'Cause that's why.

CHASE: What?

VITO: They're pictures. Photographs. Snapshots. Ring shots.

CHASE: So?

VITO: Round ten rip-offs.

CHASE: I don't understand.

VITO: Don't you got it yet? They're me. *(Holding his face.)* They're this. They smack a punch better than Cortez. They're real, man.

They don't smooch up and kiss your ass like a portrait. They shine a light on the gashes and salve. They're old news dusted off, blown up and pasted on page one. They're me.

CHASE: This is you, too.

VITO: No. I told you—I want all the shit taken out. I want it clean and smooth and soft—like it were back fifteen years ago. Like it were back on Coney Island—before the Navy. Tender and not knowing so much as it does now.

(Chase goes on painting. Vito fidgets a bit. He picks up a bell weight and starts doing some curls.)

CHASE: Vito—

VITO: Yeah.

CHASE: So you really are gay?

VITO *(guffaws)*: Christ—I'd pay you just to make me laugh.

CHASE: But you really are?

VITO: Is the Pope Polish?

CHASE: What about all those articles about Carol LaMer and the paternity suit?

VITO: All made up.

CHASE: Planted—

VITO: Yeah—fucking planted. Carol needed the money. She was good at acting. She was pregnant. Nice gal, Carol. She did do a good acting job. Don't matter now I'm retired.

CHASE: Vito—

VITO: You're full of fuckin' questions.

CHASE: You complained when I talked. So I put the earphones on. Then you complained when I didn't talk.

VITO: You ask too many fuckin' questions. *(Gentler.)* That's all. *(Beat.)*

CHASE: You use that word quite a bit.

VITO: What word?

CHASE *(embarrassed)*: The "F" word.

VITO: So?

CHASE: It doesn't upset me. I like that word. Have you ever thought about it?

VITO: I don't gotta think about it. Only people who don't do it gotta think about it.

CHASE: It's just—listen to it—It starts with a whisper. Fffffffffffff. Seductive. Very soft. Like a real, gentle, soft breeze. And then bang—*(Claps his hands together.)* That "K." Ka. Ka. Ka. Whisper. Bang. Starts with a whisper. Ends with a bang. Promises something so soft. And then ends so hard.

VITO: Get on with the fuckin' picture. *(Chase goes back to his canvas.)* What you want me to do now?

CHASE: Why don't you strike a—pose.

VITO: What've I been doing here for the last hour?

CHASE: I mean a real pose. *(Gets up and strikes a pugilistic pose.)*

VITO: Oh—you mean like I was boxing still.

CHASE: Yes.

VITO *(rather proudly strikes a pose on the beach)*:   This?

CHASE: Yes. Very good. *(Continues to draw. Vito begins hitting out—punching at an imaginary opponent. Vito's back in the ring now.)* What are you doing, Vito?

VITO: Dancin' to music you can't hear.

CHASE: Who you dancing with?

VITO: Cortez.

CHASE: The main event.

VITO: Top card.

CHASE: Standing room.

VITO: A roar, you know. Like one of them waves coming in.

CHASE: Seven thousand with matches in the air.

VITO: Even the bell was heavy that night.

CHASE: Up against the turnbuckle.

VITO: Ba Bam, Ba Bam, Ba Bam, Boom.

CHASE: Never drew your blood.

VITO: I gaffed him, though. Sewed and gobbed after number three.

CHASE: That was ten straight for you.

VITO: Sweet, sweet number ten. After that, they named me—

CHASE: The Shadow.

VITO: Yeah. Hey—how'd you know all this?

CHASE: I was there.

VITO: You—

CHASE: Fourth row.

VITO: Really. You was there?

CHASE: Yes.

VITO: My right went through his skull. *(Chase mimes the punch.)* It did. You seen it, right?

CHASE: You almost killed him.

VITO: The Shadow knows.

CHASE: Yes.

VITO: Busted his brain.

CHASE: You did. He looked like Oedipus Rex when you finished with him.

VITO: Who the fuck is Oedipus Rex?

CHASE: Greek fighter—before your time.

VITO: Not many before my time. *(Strikes his pose.)*

CHASE (*starts looking through his bag*):   You know—I have a clipping from that fight.

VITO: Cortez?

CHASE: Yeah. Here it is. (*Takes out a clipping from his bag.*) I'm sorry it's a little faded. It's kind of old.

(*Vito goes to his gym bag and takes out a pair of glasses and puts them on.*)

VITO (*belligerent*):   Not that fucking old. (*Looks at the clipping, obviously thrilled.*) So why you have this?

CHASE (*sinks to one knee and spreads his arms in a dramatic gesture*):   I'm a fan.

VITO (*wipes his forehead*):   A fan. Yeah? (*Gives him the clipping.*)

CHASE (*puts the clipping away*):   That's why it was such a surprise. . . . Seeing that advertisement in a gay paper. Vito Carbone—as close as a whisper to the heavyweight champion, a real main-event fighter—wants someone to paint his picture. I thought—my God—those rumors about him—they were all true—

VITO: The rumors was true, the facts was as straight as I am.

CHASE: Whatever happened to Cortez?

VITO: He done O.K. after that. Threw a fight, but done O.K. You know Cortez—he read Shakespeare, took this seaweed shit and loved fancy dishes—and you know the funny thing—

CHASE: He was straight.

VITO (*laughing*):   Yeah. The fucker was straight.

(*Chase begins laughing, too. They both are laughing.*)

VITO (*sobering*):   Manny, my trainer, always wanting to teach me things. Make me talk different. I always thought that was bullshit, because it would make me sound like a queer—

CHASE (*not knowing what to say*):   It turned out O.K., though.

VITO: Yeah—so now I'm a stupid queer.

(*Silence. And then both start to laugh, again.*)

CHASE (*goes back to his easel*):   Do you have a lover?

VITO: Me?

CHASE: Yes.

VITO (*suppressed grin*):   I'm a fighter—not a lover.

CHASE: There must be someone.

VITO: Some one, some two, some hundred or so. Ten, twenty, thirty in a month. A few guys stuck around awhile. I had to be careful—not be too obvious—and the same guy sticks around awhile—a thorn in the ass, you know?—now I'm retired, don't matter much.

CHASE: You've had hundreds?

VITO: Yeah. *(Pugilistic punches.)* Bang. Bang. Killed every one of 'em.

CHASE: Lovers.

VITO: No, man. Fucks.

CHASE: There must have been someone—special—different—someone—

VITO: Manny bought me boys. Back door stuff. Buying me steaks to keep me outta the pasture. It's so dumb, though, when you think about it. All that money. All that time. Trying so hard to make the world think the Shadow was straight. But then you look at what I did out there. In front of millions of people. Me standing in a ring in my underwear, kissing a cheek with my palm, slapping a hand here and here, and that dance, you know, that dance, with your arms around the guy—even then, I'd be moving, the—the Shadow and his partner, greased down one side, up another, arms locked, smoke and that roar, that light, eyes tight shut, a kiss. . . .

CHASE: Life isn't fair, is it?

VITO: What?

CHASE: Just stating the case. Life isn't fair.

VITO: You ever had to piss with a hard-on?

CHASE: No.

VITO: Try it sometime. That's fucking unfair.

CHASE: O.K.

VITO: I mean—I've hit myself in the face before. Trying to piss with a hard-on.

CHASE: Why don't you just wait?

VITO: Wait?

CHASE: Wait till it goes down.

VITO: Mine don't go down that quick.

CHASE: Think.

VITO: Think?

CHASE: Yes.

VITO: Think about what?

CHASE: Your parents—naked.

VITO *(laughing)*: It'll work, huh?

CHASE: For me it does.

VITO: You're smarter than you look. You know that?

CHASE: Sometimes.

VITO *(serious)*: You ever think maybe it's punishment like some people says?

CHASE: Intelligence?

VITO: No.

CHASE: What?

VITO (*uncomfortable*):   AIDS.

CHASE (*unclear about this*):   Punishment?

VITO: For—for fucking—too much.

CHASE: No. I don't think so.

VITO: Really, though. You never thought it maybe—

CHASE: Sometimes, but—

VITO: See, I know I was born Catholic and stuff—and Catholics— I mean we trip and say a Hail Mary—but, you know, ever since—ever since I found out—about this thing—this sickness thing—

CHASE: You mean AIDS?

VITO: Yeah—at night—before I go to bed—I do the whole confession—Hail Mary, full of Grace—all that—but I just do it there in the dark and try to remember all the bad things I done that day and I tell the shadows each one—said twenty-three fucks, fifteen shits, two damns and one buttfuck—and—when I finish I kiss my hand—

CHASE: Why?

VITO: I don't know—I do—I kiss my hand. Like I forgive myself, or something.

CHASE: Like going to confession?

VITO: Yeah. It's like going to confession. And the Priest forgives you. (*Wipes himself with the handkerchief.*) Can I see?

CHASE (*surprised*):   See what?

VITO: The picture?

CHASE: Oh. Not till it's done.

VITO: So you finished soon?

CHASE: Almost. I want this one to be right.

VITO: This one?

CHASE: This picture.

VITO: You make money doing this shit?

CHASE: No.

VITO: No?

CHASE: No. I never did.

VITO: Your samples were fucking great. You never sold anything.

CHASE: I don't.

VITO: You try?

CHASE: Once.

VITO: Once?

CHASE: Yeah.

VITO: What happened.

CHASE: The dealer said, "You're very talented."

VITO: That's good.

CHASE: No. It's not.

VITO: When someone tells me that, it makes me feel good.

CHASE: He said—"you're very talented" because he wasn't interested in my picture. It translates as—"yes, you can draw, but you haven't drawn anything that I'm interested in."

VITO: When was this?

CHASE: About five years ago.

VITO: Five years ago? What the fuck? You keep drawing till someone says yes.

CHASE: I'm almost thirty.

VITO: So? You keep doing it long enough—someone's gotta say yes, right?

CHASE: I suppose.

VITO: I said yes.

CHASE: You're the first—

VITO: It's the odds, man. Of five-card draw. You stay in the game long enough—you gotta come up with a winning hand.

CHASE: So why aren't you still in the ring?

VITO: 'Cause I'm too old.

CHASE: There you go.

VITO: It ain't the same. Hah. I bet if I made pictures, I'd sell 'em.

CHASE: You probably would.

VITO: So whataya do, then?

CHASE: What do I do?

VITO: To eat?

CHASE: Oh. I teach.

VITO: Like in school?

CHASE: Yes. I'm an art teacher.

VITO: An art teacher. You say it like you're apologizing.

CHASE: It's O.K. Sometimes it's good.

VITO: Tell me about when it's good.

CHASE: I had this class—and I put a vase on a table—plain, white vase on this simple, wooden table—I had about fifteen students sitting around the table and I said to them—"draw what you see." That's all. Just "draw what you see." So I go away and I come back in an hour. Fourteen kids drew a plain, white vase on a simple, wooden table. But there's this one kid, a sixteen-year-old girl and she's drawn a picture of an acorn in a spider web. Perfect detail—an acorn in a spider web. I asked her about it and she said, "You told us to draw what we see." And I nodded. Then she pointed across the room and there below the plain, white vase on the simple, wooden table was a spider web with an acorn in it.

VITO: Yeah?

CHASE: I'm boring you.

VITO: Where you from? I know you live in New York, but where you from?

CHASE: Coney Island.

VITO: Coney Island?

CHASE: Yes.

VITO: I'm from Coney Island.

CHASE: I know.

VITO: Fuckin' A.

CHASE: Coney Island.

VITO: Coney Island?

CHASE: Yes.

VITO: You're shitting me?

CHASE: No.

VITO (*suspicious*):   So why you don't talk like me?

CHASE: We moved when I was twelve.

VITO: So you talked like me until you was twelve?

CHASE (*bemused*):   I didn't talk much.

VITO: Was you on the Brighton side of Coney?

CHASE: Yes—a little north. I could see the water from my parents' bedroom.

VITO: You spend a lot of time at the park?

CHASE: Mostly the beach.

VITO: We could hear the shooting gallery from our porch. You?

CHASE: When the wind was right.

VITO: I want to place you there, but I can't?

CHASE: We met once.

VITO: At the park?

CHASE: The beach.

VITO: Yeah?

CHASE: I was on the beach. I was building a sandcastle.

VITO: A sandcastle?

CHASE: Yes. (*Takes some wet sand and demonstrates.*)

VITO: I know what a sandcastle is.

CHASE: So I was making this sandcastle and you walked by. You had a bathing suit on.

VITO: When was it?

CHASE: I was eleven, so I guess you were twenty—

VITO: Nineteen, twenty—

CHASE: Nineteen, twenty, and you came by and you looked down at me and asked me what I was doing. I was scared—

VITO: Scared?

CHASE: Well—you were in the Navy then—had a reputation—I thought you were going to beat me up.

VITO: Did I?

CHASE: No. I said I was building a castle. You said it didn't look like a castle. And you smiled—

VITO: Smiled?

CHASE: Yes. Smiled. You didn't show teeth or anything—grinned—maybe, that's right, it was more like a grin—you have this way, Vito, of moving your teeth, but your mouth stays still—

VITO: What the fuck are you talking about?

CHASE: No—it was like your teeth smiled, but your lips didn't move.

VITO: And then?

CHASE: Then—you walked away.

VITO: That's it? I walked away?

CHASE: That's it.

VITO: You remember all that? The teeth moving and shit—

CHASE: It was a long time ago—

VITO *(absentmindedly)*: Not that long—

CHASE: But, yes. I remember.

VITO *(slowly, puzzled)*: I walked by—you was building a castle—I asked what it was—you said it was a castle—I smiled—I walked away—nineteen—Navy—yeah—nineteen—woulda been my first year—but don't remember—

CHASE: Like I said. It was a long time ago.

VITO: Guess it was.

CHASE: So how'd you end up in Virginia?

VITO: Here in seventy-five.

CHASE: Naval base?

VITO: Yeah.

CHASE: Why didn't you go back?

VITO: It's quiet here. It's also the only other place besides Coney Island where you can do a sand sauna.

CHASE: What?

VITO: Sand sauna. You being from Coney Island, Brooklyn, the State of New York and you never heard of a sand sauna?

CHASE: No. What is it?

VITO: I'll show you later. But the thing is, see, Coney Island and Virginia Beach are the only two beaches have gold in the sand. *(Come closer as he talks, trying to sneak a peak.)*

CHASE: What are you doing?

VITO: I want to see.

CHASE *(angry)*: No.

VITO: O.K., O.K. Fuckin' sensitive. *(Goes back to his shadow boxing while Chase draws.)*

VITO: I gotta take a piss.

(Chase continues to draw. Vito goes over to the other side of the stage and mimes unzipping his pants.)

CHASE *(concerned)*:   You going to do it here?

VITO: Yeah. Where you want me to do it? In the water?

CHASE: Well—yes.

VITO *(laughing)*:   It's a secret all of a sudden. *(Takes a piss while Chase looks on.)* So what you staring at? *(Annoyed.)*

CHASE: It's like television. As long as it's on—

(Vito finishes up—shakes himself and zips up. Chase starts to laugh.)

VITO: So now what's so fuckin' funny?

CHASE: The way you shake it.

VITO: What's so funny about the way I shake it? *(Chase mimes exaggeratedly what Vito has just done.)* So you gotta lover? *(Smirks.)*

CHASE: Me?

VITO: Who else?

CHASE: No.

VITO: You seem like the type.

CHASE: Why?

VITO: Guys who keep handkerchiefs handy. They always got lovers. People like me who lose 'em. We don't.

CHASE: I just have lots of handkerchiefs. *(Beat.)*

VITO: No. Come on. I confessed to you. You gotta do the same. *(Gets out his rope and begins to jump rope.)*

CHASE: Well. Once.

VITO: You mean you're almost fuckin' thirty years old and that's it. *(Chase doesn't say anything.)* What is it with you man? Is this a religious thing or something?

CHASE: It just takes me awhile.

VITO *(looks toward the painting)*:   Yeah. I noticed. *(Beat.)* Come on, man. You gotta give me a story.

CHASE *(resigned)*:   I put an ad in the paper. Just like you. I advertised for a model.

VITO: Yeah. So?

CHASE: It was a painting I was working on. A very special painting. I needed a model with a physique—a special physique—a physique like yours.

VITO: When was this?

CHASE: I was right out of school. Five, six years ago.

VITO: And a guy answered the ad.

CHASE: First one. Looked a lot like you.

VITO *(cocky, funny)*:   Knockout, huh?

CHASE (*getting the joke*): Yes. A knockout. First one who showed up. He was just right. And that was it.

VITO: You fucked?

CHASE: That's one way to put it.

VITO: Must have been some fuck. I mean if you ain't done it since.

CHASE: Yeah. I guess so. (*Vito takes the chin-up bar and pretends like he's putting Chase on it.*) What do you want me to do?

VITO: A chin-up. (*Crosses his arms.*)

CHASE: Why?

VITO: 'Cause I want you to do something in your life more than once. See how it feels.

CHASE: I can't.

VITO: Do it, goddammit. (*Chase struggles with the bar and then finally does a chin-up.*) O.K. Now. How's that?

CHASE (*resentful*): Great. I've done it twice.

VITO: You know—I lost my first fight.

CHASE: I didn't—

VITO: Didn't you know that—?

CHASE: —know that. No. I didn't.

VITO: Lyman Sullivan. Sixteen pounds lighter than me. Third round KO. (*Chase sits and looks at what he's done. A moment of silence.*) What you staring at? You done?

CHASE: No.

VITO: I'm getting tired here—(*Chase folds over the sketchbook.*) Hey, wait. I'm paying good money—

CHASE: It's just not turning out right.

VITO: You gotta at least let me look at it.

CHASE: No.

VITO: For chrissakes.

CHASE: I gotta go.

VITO: Go? Hey—

CHASE: What?

VITO: I'm serious here. I need a picture of myself.

CHASE: For what?

VITO: I told you—

CHASE: I still don't understand. You have pictures of yourself when you were young.

VITO: But I want one special—

CHASE: For what?

VITO: I was gonna put it in the paper when I die. (*Chase begins to laugh.*) You have some sick sense of humor if you find that bone-crunching funny.

CHASE: You're going to live forever, Vito. Look at you. You could

go ten rounds with Cortez and still come out on a split decision.
VITO: I got AIDS.

(Chase is silent.)

CHASE: But you look—
VITO: I don't actually got AIDS. I'm HIV asymptomatic. I got a T-cell count of four-seventeen. I'm on acyclovir and small doses of AZT. Ain't that a trip. I didn't even finish high school and the doctor's got me talking like I got a fucking Ph.D.
CHASE: So you're not dating—
VITO: I don't date no more. I don't box no more.
CHASE: I don't completely understand about the—
VITO: Picture? I go to this doctor, see—he's the only one in Norfolk who treats folks—even sailors come to him—anyway—I'm in his waiting room one day and this woman comes out of his office all pale and looking like she was sixty. She sits down and just stares at the floor for a while.

I offers her a gummy bear and she kind of smiled and said no. Then she starts sobbing. I mean buckets. And first I think maybe it's the gummy bear thing—maybe she don't like 'em.

But it turns out she's got AIDS see. Her husband's a fuckin' shooter, man—shared needles and all that shit—and she does it, too—so they're fuckin' their brains out and she has a kid. She's just found out the kid's got it too, right?

Well I ask her if there's anything she might be needing. She dries her eyes and smiles this little smile and tells me she don't have a camera.
CHASE: Camera?
VITO: Yeah. She tells me about the kid. Then says she don't have any pictures of him.
CHASE: So what'd you do, Vito?
VITO: First thing, I takes out a couple hundred dollars and give it to her and tell her to buy a camera. She don't wanna take it, see, 'cause she's the proud type. So I tell her she can have it, but she's gotta do one thing for me.
CHASE: What's that?
VITO: Send me a picture of her little kid.
CHASE: That was nice.
VITO: Yeah. But then I did somethin' kind of surprised me—
CHASE: What's that?
VITO: I put my arms around her and I just . . . held her. . . . *(Stops and looks out in space.)*
CHASE: Did she send you a picture?

VITO (*takes out his wallet and shows Chase a picture*): He's so cute.

CHASE: He has that same smile you do.

VITO: Yeah. Anyway, it's when the idea come into my head about the portrait. I wanted a picture of me, too.

CHASE (*looks scared all of a sudden and begins to pack up*): Hire someone else, Vito. I'm sure you received lots of samples.

VITO: Yeah. But yours was the best.

CHASE: I've got to go.

VITO: You can't go.

CHASE: Why not?

VITO: You hadn't done a sand sauna yet.

CHASE: Right.

VITO: Yeah. Sand sauna. That's why people come to Norfolk. That's why people go to Coney Island, Brooklyn, the State of New York.

CHASE: And I never heard of it.

VITO: Can't believe that.

CHASE: Well—

VITO: I don't care about the picture. But you can't leave and not do a sand sauna.

CHASE (*puts his things down*): O.K., Vito. I'll do a sand sauna. What about you?

VITO: The doctor says I can't get wet. But I'll walk you through it.

CHASE: O.K. First?

VITO: First—take off your shirt.

CHASE: O.K. (*Takes off his shirt.*)

VITO: Now—you gotta go out and get wet.

CHASE: O.K. (*Goes into the water area and stands.*)

VITO: Watch out for nettles. You gotta fuckin' get wet. Whataya doing—taking a piss? (*Chase looks up with a guilty expression.*) Oh. I forgot. You gotta fill up the bathtub and put on a bathing suit just to take a piss.

(*Chase makes a few divelike motions. Vito, meanwhile, begins digging a trench in the sand.*)

CHASE: Can I come out now?

VITO: One second. (*Continues digging, then gets up.*)

CHASE: O.K.?

VITO: O.K.

CHASE (*comes out of the water*): Now?

VITO: Now—get in this here hole here. (*Chase sits down. Vito covers him with sand until it's up to his neck.*) See—there are little bits of gold in the sand—and now we get it here up to your neck— and you're wet, see—already, you're wet, but there's some water in the sand, 'cause we're below sea level—and what happens is you start to sweat.

CHASE: Oh. (*Looks up with his head out of the sand. A beat while Vito smiles down at Chase.*) So how long do I stay here?

VITO: Long enough for me to look at my fucking picture. (*Goes over to the canvas and picks up what Chase has been working on.*)

CHASE (*loud, painful*): NO. (*Struggles, but he can't get out.*)

VITO: Hey, what the fuck is—

CHASE: That wasn't fair.

VITO: What's fair—you making me sit out here and there's nothing to show for it. (*Reveals that the canvas is nothing more than squiggles.*) Is this fucking fair?

CHASE: I'm sorry.

VITO: Yeah. You're sorry. I'm pissed.

CHASE: If you let me out, I'll tell you—why.

(*Vito begins digging Chase out, little by little, as if enticing the story out of him.*)

CHASE: That day I saw you on the beach at Coney. I was eleven. You were nineteen, twenty. I'd never seen shadows like that before. Not in a boy's body. Above the shoulders, the neck, ridges beneath your chest, the back of your legs.

VITO: I must have been twenty.

CHASE: I was in love with you. Back then. I started drawing you right after meeting you on the beach. I filled sketchbooks as fast as my mother could buy them. Then one day she found one under the bed while I was at school. She locked me in the closet when I got home. She kept me there all day.

VITO: They was pictures of me?

CHASE: Yes. I had done some nudes. She blamed the pictures. She didn't recognize you, though. She thought if I stopped drawing the pictures, I would be all right. But in the closet, I kept my eyes closed and I traced the lines over and over again.

VITO: You didn't know I was a faggot?

CHASE: No. But I kept drawing you. I abstracted you. I would draw a line on paper and know that was your arm, or a triangle and know it was your chest, or a series of spirals for your legs. I reduced you to dots and shadings and great bold strokes of black ink. I knew who you were.

VITO: But your mother didn't.

CHASE: Then when you started to fight and your picture was in the paper. That's all I needed. Mom was happy, because I'd always ask to see the sports section. And I'd go through it and find an article, or a description of you during a fight. Magazines, too.

Feature articles. Color photos. And then I'd make collages and fill up whole walls with pictures of you.

VITO: Fuckin' A.

CHASE: When I went to art school, I started drawing you with a vengeance. Different clothes. Different ages. As you might have looked as a baby. As you might look when you grow old. Different colors, different positions.

VITO: From the paper you did this?

CHASE: Oh yes. I'd go to fights. I wanted you to be more real. I magnified the pictures. I did hundreds of pictures of a strand of hair, a hand, a finger, a fingernail. Then I got tired with that—so I did miniatures. Then I got tired with that so I blew them up. I made you larger than life. More real than you are now.

VITO: What about the model?

CHASE: I got to the point, right after art school. I wanted flesh and blood. I was tired of the photographs and the descriptions and that memory of you on the beach. All of them kept getting smaller and smaller. But I wanted something larger. So I put an ad in the paper. I described you—

VITO: By name?

CHASE: No. Described someone that looks like you. And the model that showed up looked just like you.

VITO: So why'd you come here to do a picture of me? Don't sound like you needed me?

CHASE: I saw your ad in the paper—and I knew—you had to let me come down—you had to let me—

VITO: But you didn't come down here to draw a picture of me?

CHASE: No.

VITO: So why'd you come down?

CHASE: I never thought there was a chance before—but now—you know—all that time—I thought, maybe—

VITO: You mean you wanted to fuck?

CHASE (*turns away*):   I just wanted to meet you.

VITO: Well, I've got news for you fuckforbrains. I'm HIV infected—

CHASE: So am I.

VITO (*stops, he's quiet*):   But you said one time.

CHASE (*tries to struggle out of the hole, but Vito stops him*):   It was.

VITO: That was some fuck.

CHASE: Why do you care?

VITO: I told you. I thought it was punishment. I thought I was being punished all this time. But you didn't do anything wrong. You said the guy came over and—

CHASE: He raped me.

(Chase is in a pretty bad state at this point. Vito lifts him from the sand. He takes out the handkerchief he had and touches it to Chase's cheeks.)

CHASE: There was nothing I could do. He had a knife.

VITO: He hurt you?

CHASE *(calm, resigned)*:   Yes. He hurt me.

VITO: If I ever get my hands on that creep, I'd bury his head in his ass.

CHASE: He's already dead.

VITO: One fucker I ain't gonna miss.

CHASE: You still think it's punishment?

VITO: I mean, with me, I was sure that God was punishing me. Now I ain't so sure.

CHASE: Look at it this way, Vito. If it is a punishment, which I don't believe, but say, for the sake of argument, that it is a punishment.

VITO: O.K.

CHASE: The Bible says God punishes us. But it also says He forgives us, right?

VITO: Yeah.

CHASE: Well, if, in this world, I got punished for something I did once, I'm certain you'll be forgiven for something you did all the time. *(Chase is laughing and crying at the same time. Vito puts his arm on Chase's shoulder.)* The funny thing is—right after it happened—that's pretty much when I stopped painting. Didn't go out or anything. Then I found out about my HIV status. Ever since then, it's been different.

    See—five, six years ago—I never would have come down here. But now—it's like—I told myself—I have a chance to meet Vito Carbone—and I'm going to do it. *(Pause.)* We've got to forgive ourselves. Because no one else is going to. You paint what you see. A vase on a table. An acorn in a spider web. I mean—I used to look in the mirror and say "What?" Now I look in the mirror and say, "What the—fuck?"

VITO *(laughing)*:   Yeah. What the fuck? *(Goes over to the radio.)* Does this thing work without the earphones?

CHASE: Yes.

(Chase takes the earphones out. Vito plays with it. A romantic slow-dance song comes on. Chase stands next to the radio.)

VITO *(comes over and nods at Chase)*:   Hi.

CHASE: Hi.

VITO: My name's Vito Carbone.

CHASE: The boxer?

VITO: Yeah. Heavyweight.

CHASE: I've been a fan of yours for years.

VITO: Really? You sound like you're from Brooklyn?

CHASE: Coney Island.

VITO: If that ain't some coincidence.

CHASE: Yeah.

VITO: I'm from Brooklyn, too.

CHASE: I guess we have something in common.

VITO: Hear this song? I like it.

CHASE: So do I. *(Beat.)*

VITO: Ask me to dance, fuckforbrains.

CHASE: Would you like to dance fuckforbrains?

VITO *(laughing)*: Yeah. *(Takes Chase and hugs him around the waist. They dance. Chase is rather stiff at first. Vito takes his head and pushes it toward his chest. Chase relaxes into the position.)* Yeah.

(This should somehow mirror the image of "the dance" as Vito described it earlier. The music ends. The voice of the radio announcer comes on. Vito stops. Chase looks up. Vito is crying. Chase goes and takes out another handkerchief. He wipes Vito's eyes. He opens his bag and takes out another picture. Chase walks over to Vito and gives it to him. Vito looks at the picture.)

VITO: What's this?

CHASE: A gift.

VITO *(wipes his face and puts on his glasses, looks satisfied, smiles)*: It's a picture of me on the beach.

CHASE: Yes.

VITO: This is really good.

CHASE: Thank you.

VITO: When'd you do this?

CHASE: Five, six years ago.

VITO: You mean—

CHASE: The last picture I ever painted. The guy there—that was the model who—ah—I told you about.

VITO: But it looks just like me.

CHASE: It does.

VITO: Even the beach—that house there—you got it all right—you been here?

CHASE: Never.

VITO: And this is the one—

CHASE: —that I did from the model. Yes. *(He is packing his things now, about to leave.)*

VITO: I gotta pay you—

CHASE: You don't owe me anything. Please.

VITO: You mind if—

CHASE: Use it for whatever you want—

VITO: My face—you know—it looks like when I was twenty—

CHASE: Or nineteen. Not that long ago.

VITO: A long time ago. *(Chase is just about to leave when Vito calls out one more time.)* You know—

CHASE: Yes.

VITO: You really are good at this. You should . . .

CHASE *(about to leave)*: I'm going to.

VITO *(calls after him)*: Wait—I was thinking—my house is just up there—

CHASE: What?

VITO: You have time for some coffee or something? I have video-tapes of the fights—

CHASE: You have Cortez on video?

VITO: Yeah.

CHASE *(excited)*: You have the big one—

VITO: Top card.

CHASE: The one that was—

VITO: Ten straight for me.

CHASE: You faked him out in round two.

VITO: Yeah.

CHASE: I'd love to see that fight again.

VITO: I got it on tape.

CHASE *(hesitates)*: There isn't a later flight.

VITO *(matter of fact)*: You can take the shuttle in the morning. *(Chase pauses.)* Listen, fuckforbrains. I like you, O.K. I'm trying to tell you that in not so undirect terms here. This is kind of like a date and I'd be so fucking happy if you'd say yes so we can get on with it.

CHASE: Yes.

VITO: Get your stuff, then. Here— *(Goes to help him.)* Here—let me give you a hand here.

(Chase takes Vito's hand and kisses it. Vito smiles and puts his arm around Chase. They walk off as lights fade to black.)

THE RED COAT

JOHN PATRICK SHANLEY

THE RED COAT is part of an evening of six short plays by John Patrick Shanley titled *Welcome to the Moon*, which was first presented by the Ensemble Studio Theatre, in New York City, in the fall of 1982. It was directed by Douglas Aibel; scene design by Evelyn Sakash; costumes by Michele Reisch; lighting by Mal Sturchio; sound by Bruce Ellman; Barry Koron was music director; and Teresa Elwert was production stage manager. The Company was as follows:

Robert Joy, Anne O'Sullivan, John Henry Kurtz, James Ryan, Michael Albert Mantel, June Stein.

Characters
JOHN, seventeen-year-old boy
MARY, sixteen-year-old girl

Setting
A side street, nighttime

■ ■

Nighttime on a side street. A street light shines down on some steps through a green tree. Moonlight mixes in the shadows. A seventeen-year-old boy sits on the steps in a white shirt with a loosened skinny tie, black dress pants, and black shoes. He is staring off. His eyes are shining. A sixteen-year-old girl enters, in neighborhood party clothes: short skirt, blouse, penny loafers.

JOHN: Hi, Mary.
MARY: Oh! I didn't see you there. You're hiding.
JOHN: Not from you, Mary.
MARY: Who from?
JOHN: Oh, nobody. I was up at Susan's party.
MARY: That's where I'm going.
JOHN: Oh.
MARY: Why did you leave?
JOHN: No reason.
MARY: You just gonna sit here?
JOHN: For a while.
MARY: Well, I'm going in.

JOHN: Oh. Okay . . . Oh! I'm not going in . . . I mean came out because . . . Oh, go in!

MARY: What's wrong with you, John?

JOHN: I left the party because you weren't there. That's why I left the party.

MARY: Why'd ya leave the party 'cause I wasn't there?

JOHN: I dunno.

MARY: I'm going in.

JOHN: I left the party 'cause I felt like everything I wanted was outside the party . . . out here. There's a breeze out here, and the moon . . . look at the way the moon is . . . and I knew you were outside somewhere, too! So I came out and sat on the steps here and I thought that maybe you'd come and I would be here . . . outside the party, on the steps, in the moonlight . . . and those other people . . . the ones at the party . . . wouldn't be here . . . but the night would be here . . . and you and me would be talking on the steps in the night in the moonlight and I could tell you . . .

MARY: Tell me what?

JOHN: How I feel!

MARY: How you feel about what?

JOHN: I don't know. I was looking out the window at the party . . . and I drank some wine . . . and I was looking out the window at the moon and I thought of you . . . and I could feel my heart . . . breaking.

MARY: Joh . . .

JOHN: I felt that wine and the moon and your face all pushing in my heart and I left the party and I came out here.

MARY: Your eyes are all shiny.

JOHN: I know. And I came out here looking for the moon and I saw that street light shining down through the leaves of that tree.

MARY: Hey yeah! It does look pretty.

JOHN: It's beautiful. I didn't know a street light could be beautiful. I've always thought of them as being cold and blue, you know? But this one's yellow . . . and it comes down through the leaves and the leaves are so green! Mary, I love you!

MARY: Oh!

JOHN: I shouldn't've said it. I shouldn't've said it.

MARY: No, no. That's all right.

JOHN: My heart's breaking. You must think I'm so stupid . . . but I can feel it breaking. I wish I could stop talking. I can't. I can't.

MARY: I never heard you talking like this before.

JOHN: That's 'cause this is outside the party and it's night and there's a moon up there . . . and a street light that's more beautiful than the sun! My God, the sidewalk's beautiful. Those bits of shiny stuff in the concrete . . . look how they're sparkling up the light!

MARY: You're crying! You're crying over the sidewalk!

JOHN: I love you, Mary!

MARY: That's all right. But don't cry over the sidewalk. You're usually so quiet.

JOHN: Okay. Okay. (*A pause. Then John grabs Mary and kisses her.*)

MARY: Oh . . . you used your tongue. (*He kisses her again.*) You . . . should we go into the party?

JOHN: No.

MARY: I got all dressed . . . I tasted the wine on your . . . mouth. You were waiting for me out here? I wasn't even going to come. I don't like Susan so much. I was going to stay home and watch a movie. What would you have done?

JOHN: I don't know. (*Kisses her again. She kisses him back.*)

MARY: You go to St. Nicholas of Tolentine, don't you?

JOHN: Yeah.

MARY: I see you on the platform on a Hundred and Forty-ninth Street sometimes.

JOHN: I see you, too! Sometimes I just let the trains go by until the last minute, hoping to see you.

MARY: Really?

JOHN: Yeah.

MARY: I take a look around for you but I always get on my train. What would you have done if I hadn't come?

JOHN: I don't know. Walked around. I walk around a lot.

MARY: Walk around where?

JOHN: I walk around your block a lot. Sometimes I run into you.

MARY: You mean that was *planned*? Wow! I always thought you were coming from somewhere.

JOHN: I love you, Mary. I can't believe I'm saying it . . . to you . . . out loud. I love you.

MARY: Kiss me again. (*They kiss.*)

JOHN: I've loved you for a long time.

MARY: How long?

JOHN: Months. Remember that big snowball fight?

MARY: In the park?

JOHN: Yeah. That's when it was. That's when I fell in love with you. You were wearing a red coat.

MARY: Oh, that coat! I've had that for ages and ages. I've had it since the sixth grade.

JOHN: Really?

MARY: I have really special feelings for that coat. I feel like it's part
of me . . . like it stands for something . . . my childhood . . .
something like that.

JOHN: You look nice in that coat. I think I sensed something about
it . . . the coat . . . it's special to me, too. It's so good to be able
to talk to you like this.

MARY: Yeah, this is nice. That's funny how you felt that about my
coat. The red one. No one knows how I feel about that coat.

JOHN: I think I do, Mary.

MARY: Do you? If you understood about my red coat . . . that red
coat is like all the good things about when I was a kid . . . it's like
I still have all the good kid things when I'm in that red coat . . .
it's like being grown up and having your childhood, too. You
know what it's like? It's like being in one of those movies where
you're safe, even when you're in an adventure. Do you know what
I mean? Sometimes, in a movie the hero's doin' all this stuff that's
dangerous, but you know, becausa the kind of movie it is, that
he's not gonna get hurt. Bein' in that red coat is like that . . . like
bein' safe in an adventure.

JOHN: And that's the way you were in that snowball fight! It was
like you knew that nothing could go wrong!

MARY: That's right! That's right! That's the way it feels! Oh, you
do understand! It seems silly but I've always wanted someone to
understand some things and that was one of them . . . the red
coat.

JOHN: I do understand! I do!

MARY: I don't know. I don't know. I don't know about tomorrow,
but . . . right this minute I . . . love you!

JOHN: Oh, Mary!

MARY: Oh, kiss me, John. Please!

JOHN: You're crying!

MARY: I didn't know. I didn't know two people could understand
some things . . . share some things. (They kiss.)

JOHN: It must be terrible not to.

MARY: What?

JOHN: Be able to share things.

MARY: It is! It is! But don't you remember? Only a few minutes
ago we were alone. I feel like I could tell you anything. Isn't that
crazy?

JOHN: Do you want to go for a walk?

MARY: No, no. Let's stay right here. Between the street light and
the moon. Under the tree. Tell me that you love me.

JOHN: I love you.

MARY: I love you, too. You're good-looking, did you know that?
Does your mother tell you that?
JOHN: Yeah, she does.
MARY: Your eyes are shining.
JOHN: I know. I can feel them shining.

(The lights go down slowly.)

FINGER FOOD

NINA SHENGOLD

FINGER FOOD was commissioned by the Actors Theatre of Louisville and first produced by the Ark Theatre in New York City, 1984; it was directed by Chris McHale. The cast was as follows:

DENNY	Jeff Garrett
MONA	Mary Portser

Characters
DENNY, a food photographer
MONA, a hand model

Setting
A commercial photographer's studio, minimally indicated by a standing floodlamp focused on one end of a long table. The lit end is elegantly set with a lace tablecloth, cut crystal wineglass and bottle of wine. The rest of the table is tacky and bare. There's a canvas director's chair and an empty carton, a telephone, Denny's camera equipment.

■ ■

Lights up on Denny, staring intently at the wine-bottle set-up. He starts making adjustments, moving the glass, turning the bottle: an artist at work.
Perfection. He glares at the door, annoyed. Strides to the phone and dials.

DENNY: Mitchell? Denny. My talent is late again. . . . Runs in her *what*? I'm not shooting her panty hose. . . . Studio *Six,* Mitchell . . . No, not deodorant, Beaujolais! . . . Yeah, well she just better shake it, there's Reddi-wip coming at quarter past four!

(He hangs up and returns to his set-up. Turns on the floodlamp. Smiles. Holds one hand next to the wineglass and looks through his camera, rehearsing the shot.)

Oh, baby.

(He steps back for more distance and tries it again.)

Gorgeous.

(He steps back again and finds that he's too far away now to reach the glass. He tries anyway, stretching one arm toward the glass, leaning back with his camera. It looks ridiculous and it doesn't work.)

Damn.

(Sudden brainstorm. He rips off one shoe and sticks his bare foot on the table, gripping the glass with his toes. He picks up the camera and says to his foot:)

Love ya. You're beautiful.

(Mona rushes in, breathless. She is simply but prettily dressed and wears orange rubber dishwashing gloves. She carries a model's looseleaf book. Denny jumps up and runs to her.)

Carla!

MONA: Darling!

DENNY *(embraces her, kisses both cheeks, then draws back)*: You're not Carla.

MONA: No, I'm—

DENNY: I asked them for Carla. The hand model.

MONA: Then . . . you don't *know?*

DENNY: I have to have Carla.

MONA: Oh heaven. I thought they had told you. The agency.

DENNY: What happened?

MONA *(crosses herself with rubber gloves)*: She was in . . . She had— Carla—a terrible accident. An elevator door.

DENNY: No!

MONA: Yes.

DENNY: Carla?

MONA: Yes!

DENNY: Is she all right?

MONA: She was maimed! She broke *two* of her nails! The thumb and the index! Oh god. I have nightmares. *(She covers her face with her gloves.)*

DENNY: So the agency sent you instead?

MONA *(Lowers her hands. He's so insensitive. Glacial)*: I'm her understudy.

DENNY: I'm not sure I can do it with somebody else.

MONA: Try me.

DENNY: You've done this before?

MONA: Hundreds of times.

DENNY: A hand job.

MONA: I live for it.

DENNY: I've never seen you.

MONA: My face, perhaps. No. *(Touches a glove.)* May I hang up my things?

(Denny grabs the carton from under the table and drops it contemptuously in front of her. Mona looks at it. Looks at him. Then she pulls off one rubber glove, finger by finger, like a stripper. He watches, transfixed. Underneath she is wearing a lacy black fingerless glove and crimson nail polish. Denny moans. Mona smiles. She drops the glove into the box and takes off the second, finger by finger.)

MONA: My name—*(Drops the second glove.)*—is Mona.

DENNY: Um . . . Uhhhh . . . huh. Ah. Denny.

MONA: Denny. *(She touches his face. His eyes follow her fingers.)*

DENNY: I love what you're wearing.

MONA: Thank you.

DENNY: You, ah, only do hands?

MONA: I went to the elbows once. Laundry soap. It was awful. I felt like a slut.

DENNY *(rhapsodic)*:   Just hands.

MONA: I've brought my portfolio. Will there be makeup?

DENNY: I . . . I have to see. . . .

MONA: Pictures first. *(She indicates with a graceful, game-show assistant gesture that Denny should sit.)*

DENNY: Pictures. Yes.

(He sits. Mona stands over his shoulder and guides him through the book. We do not see the pictures described.)

MONA: Most of these are production stills from my video spots. Cold cream. Grape jelly. Men's shirts.

DENNY: Collar-smoothing. Oh Christ. Very nice.

MONA *(turning the page)*:   Dishwashing liquid. Which is the coed and which is the 62-year-old grandmother? Neither! They're me! They're both me!!!

DENNY: No!

MONA *(nods proudly)*:   I love doing character work. I *studied* that grandmother. I'm very Method. *(Turns another page. Breathless.)* Oh. This was my favorite job ever. Chocolate creme devil's food—*(She breaks off, staring.)* Denny. Your toes are nude.

DENNY *(Looks. They are.)*:   Yes, well, I—

MONA: Denny, they're stunning!!! *(She crouches and pets his toes.)* Oh, Denny. *(Grabs his right hand.)* God. You have wonderful digits.

DENNY: I do?

MONA: Have you ever modeled? You could, you know. You have incredible cuticles.

DENNY: Thank you.

MONA: Your palms . . . Your knuckle hair . . .

DENNY (*impassioned*):   Mona . . .

(*Their hands twine. They look at each other meltingly. Mona drops his hand suddenly, embarrassed. All business. Back to the model book.*)

MONA: Nail polish. Not my best finger.

DENNY (*turns the next page, reacts with surprise*):   Who's *that*?

MONA: My teacher. Giancarlo. He taught me to grasp. To find the caress in it. (*In a sensuous Italian accent.*) "You must never just reach for a thing. You must *yearn* for it. *Grasp*, never grab." (*Wistful.*) Giancarlo had knuckles like Brussel sprouts. Those who can't do. . . . He ran off with a thigh model.

DENNY: You were in love with him.

MONA: He was a genius. He taught Carol Merrill on *Let's Make a Deal*. (*She does a game-show display gesture.*) Door Number One . . .

DENNY (*grabs her hand*):   You're unbelievable!

MONA: Where can I change?

DENNY (*stalking her*):   Mona, I'm a professional.

MONA: *I'm* a professional.

DENNY: Trust me.

MONA: I trust you.

DENNY: This is not smut. This is advertising.

MONA: Stop *clutching*!

DENNY (*drops her hand, pulls himself together*):   And if you'll excuse me, I need to set up.

MONA: I need to warm up. Excuse *me*.

(*Denny makes an elaborate show of busying himself with wine props and light meter. Mona turns her back to him, peels off her lace gloves, and stretches her fingers. She takes a brown paper bag from her purse, unfolds it, and puts it over her head. Denny stares as she runs through a series of silly-looking finger exercises, the last few suggesting a cat. Petting, smoothing. Maybe a couple stray mews. Then she applauds herself.*)

MONA (*murmurs in Giancarlo's accent*):   Brava. Brava, mia Mona! (*She takes off the bag very matter-of-factly, stops when she sees Denny's stare.*) It helps my concentration. (*Referring to bag.*)

DENNY: Ah.

MONA (*stands, very composed and serene*):   Where's the cat?

DENNY: Cat?

MONA: Will you want petting or filling the kitty dish?

DENNY: Mona, we're doing a wine ad.

MONA: What? They told me tunafish Friskies.

DENNY: Beaujolais.

MONA: But the agency *told* me—

DENNY: They're wrong.

MONA *(starting to panic)*:   Oh my god. Wine? I have to rethink this. My whole preparation was tuna. Oh, Denny. Oh! This is so sudden!

DENNY: What's wrong?

MONA: Tension. Look at this tension. *(She holds up her clawlike hands.)*

DENNY: Here, let me rub them.

MONA: NO! Wine. Think of wine. *(Drumming her fingers.)* You asked them for Carla. I should have realized. Carla would never do cat food. She doesn't *have* to do cat food. Cheap trash like me does the cat food while *Carla* does Beaujolais! *(She bites on her thumbnail.)*

DENNY: Mona! Don't do it!!!

MONA *(realizing, in horror)*:   Oh god! I knew it! I knew this would happen. That's why I'll never be one of the greats. I'm such a neurotic!

DENNY: You're not.

MONA: You don't know. Denny, I was a nailbiter! Mom used to soak them in Lysol. I'd bite them and vomit. And that's not the worst of it! I sucked my thumb!

DENNY: Lots of kids do that.

MONA: Until I was twenty! I sleep in a straitjacket. I just can't trust myself. *(About to bite her nails again, she lets out a cry of despair. Runs to the chair and sits on her hands, rocking back and forth.)* Giancarlo, he warned me. He told me, "Carissima, you got the hands, but you don't got the temperament. I could make you a star, but you wacko!" Oh, Denny! *(She breaks down in tears. Denny reaches to comfort her.)* DON'T lay a finger! Hands OFF!

DENNY: You misunderstand, Mona. I'm a professional.

MONA: *I'm* a professional.

DENNY: Steel. Like a doctor. I promise you, flesh leaves me cold. Flawless skin and warm naked tapering fingers are nothing. Color and form. Raw material. Meaningless.

MONA: Meaningless??

DENNY: I didn't mean *mean*ingless.

MONA *(incensed)*:   Meaningless? Look at this, buster! *(She thrusts out a hand.)* This is the species, right here. Evolution! Opposable thumb! Scratch that and it's monkeyville!

DENNY: I didn't—

MONA: Where would we be without hands? No *applause*, Denny!

No backrubs! No volleyball! Think of great art. The Creation.
E.T.! *(She demonstrates Michelangelo's pose.)*

DENNY: Mona, please . . .

MONA: You think this just *happened?* I worked for this, buddy! I
started out slapping men's faces on soap opera! Packets I ripped!
I ripped packets! I modeled for aerosol roach sprays you see on
the subway! In Spanish! And *after* all that I went home and did
dishes!

DENNY: Hey, I've been there, too, lady. I didn't start out shooting
Beaujolais, nosirreebob. They used to give me the ugly foods.
Liverwurst. Cheez Whiz. Gefilte fish. I've had to shoot foods that
make pigs anorexic!

MONA: You only shoot food?

DENNY: We've got our specialties too, you know. Some guys shoot
black and white blue jeans. Some guys do nothing but lingerie.
Hey, I'm not knocking it. Half-naked girls wearing satin and lace
turns them on, that's *their* business. *(Looks at her.)* Me, I do food.
I do food like I'll have you in tears from how good it looks. Bulging
ripe melons with dew on their skins like a tropical rainforest. Corn
on the cob dripping butter. Napoleons oozing cream. Hot . . .
apple . . . PIE. A la mode and the ice cream's just trickling down
off the crust through those thick, juicy . . .

MONA: Chocolate creme devil's food . . . ?

DENNY: Pudding. Cannolis.

MONA *(rhapsodic)*:   Just food.

DENNY: If it goes in your mouth, I'm your man.

MONA: You inspire me.

DENNY: Your hands and my lens, kiddo. We could make beautiful
ad graphics.

MONA: Get your camera.

DENNY: I'm wearing it.

MONA: Shoot. *(With a dancerly flourish, she cups her hand under the
bowl of the wineglass.)*

DENNY *(comes in very close and circles seductively, firing off shot after
shot)*: Beautiful. Baby. Great palm. Stroke the bowl. Can you give
me more knuckle? Perfecto. That's super. A little more flex in
the wrist. Honey. Angel. Oh yes.

MONA *(breathing heavily)*:   Yes! You're wonderful!

DENNY: Fingers! More fingers! Oh, angel! *Oh!!!* *(He stops very
suddenly.)*

MONA: Keep shooting! Don't stop, Denny! Shoot me!

DENNY: I'm all out of film.

MONA: Hold my hand! Hold me! *(He clasps her hand ardently.)* God yes. You're ruthless. The sweat of your palms. *(She lies on the table.)* Take me!

DENNY *(on fire)*:   Mona! *(He yanks off his camera and moves in to kiss her. She thrusts her hands in front of his face, palms forward. Denny kisses them feverishly, licks her fingers.)*

MONA *(suddenly pulls one of his hands away)*:   Your ring! Take your ring off!

DENNY: I can't.

MONA: Take it off, Denny! Do it!

DENNY: It's stuck!

(Mona slaps him. Shocked silence. She clutches her hand.)

MONA: Oh god. Oh my god. *(Picks up the wineglass and gulps.)*

DENNY: You can't drink that! It's product!

MONA: Tough shit.

DENNY: Good point. *(Drinks from the bottle. Pause.)*

MONA: I feel so cheap. Put your shoe on.

DENNY *(Sits in the chair, puts his shoe back on. Looks at her.)*:   I'm sorry, Mona. I thought you had seen.

MONA: It's a wedding ring?

DENNY: Yes.

MONA: Married. My god. Every man on this planet is married! Well, tell me this: who are you married to??? *Women* I meet aren't married! You marry each other? *(She drinks. Calmer.)* Sorry. I live in New York.

DENNY: It's all right.

MONA: Is she a model? Your wife?

DENNY: A photographer.

MONA: What does she shoot?

DENNY *(Beat. Shamefaced.)*:   Laundry soap. *(Mona recoils. Impassioned.)* She's nothing like you! She's got dishpan hands!

MONA *(gathers up her portfolio, gloves)*:   Goodbye, Denny.

DENNY: Don't go.

MONA: I have to.

DENNY: Please!

MONA *(turns back)*:   The Italians wave . . . so. *(She does the traditional "ciao.")* As if they were holding a bird. Giancarlo. He taught me.

(She blows Denny a kiss on her fingertips, then goes. Denny stands for a moment. He does a small, wistful "ciao.")

DENNY: One hand clapping. *(He turns off the floodlamp and sits, heartbroken. Then he picks up the phone and dials.)* Mitchell? Yeah, Denny. Look, Mitch, I'm not feeling so hot. You think you could cancel the whipped cream?

(The door opens. It's Mona.)

MONA *(eyes shining, breathless)*: Did you just say . . . *whipped cream??*
DENNY *(a killer smile)*: Send it right up, Mitch.

(He hangs up and opens his arms toward Mona. Beaming, she tosses both pairs of gloves in the air. Bang in loud upbeat music and blackout.)

WOMEN AND WALLACE

JONATHAN MARC SHERMAN

The great question that has never been answered, and which I have not been able to answer, despite my thirty years of research into the feminine soul, is: What does a woman want?
—*Sigmund Freud*

WOMEN AND WALLACE was first produced at Playwrights Horizons in the fall of 1988 as part of the Foundation of the Dramatists Guild's Seventh Annual Playwrights Festival (producing director, Nancy Quinn.) It was directed by Don Scardino, with sets by Allen Moyer, costumes by Jess Goldstein, and lighting by Nancy Schertler. The production stage manager was Roy Harris and the playwright advisor was Albert Innaurato. Music was composed and performed by John Miller. The cast, in order of appearance, was as follows:

WALLACE KIRKMAN	Josh Hamilton
NINA	Joanna Going
MOTHER	Mary Joy
GRANDMOTHER	Joan Copeland
VICTORIA	Dana Behr
PSYCHIATRIST	Debra Monk
SARAH	Bellina Logan
LILI	Jill Tasker
WENDY	Erica Gimpel

Time
1975 to 1987

Note
All sets and props should be simple and spare. The lighting should be very suggestive. Scenes should flow quickly from one to the next. The actor playing Wallace should be about eighteen years old. The women's parts can be played in one of three ways.
1. One virtuoso actress can play them all, which is the idea I had in mind when I started but which scares the hell out of me now.
2. Three or four actresses can be used, each one playing more than one part. I would be careful about giving the actresses playing both Nina and Mother more than one part, for various reasons.

3. Eight actresses can be used, with one part per actress. This is, I think, the most desirable solution, but may be tough to achieve.

The four times that Wallace reads his writing directly to the audience can be handled simply by having him speak right to the audience, without a piece of paper before him or anything. The title is, so far, the only title I can stand, as well as being the first thing I called the play. Be Wonderful.

Order of Scenes

■ ■

Prologue

Wallace is standing to the left with a tomato in his hand and a crate of tomatoes at his feet. Nina is standing to the right, wearing a white dress. Pause. Wallace lobs the tomato. It splatters on Nina's dress. Pause.

WALLACE: I love you. *(Pause.)*

Scene One

WALLACE: "Mommy." By Wallace Kirkman. Age six. I love Mommy because she makes me peanut butter and banana sandwiches on Wonder bread and it tastes better than when I order it at a restaurant. And Mommy never looks at me funny like the waiters in restaurants do. And Mommy crushes aspirins and mixes them into jelly when I get sick. Because I can't swallow aspirins. They just sit on my tongue and wait for me to finish the whole glass of water. And then I spit them out. But when they're mixed into jelly, I hardly have any problem at all. I just eat the jelly and feel better. And Mommy washes my clothes, so I don't have to. And she does it so they smell nice when they come out. They come out smelling clean. And they even smell a little like Mommy, because she folds them for me, and her smell rubs off onto my shirts. She smells like perfume. Not really sweet, like Billy Corkscraw's mother. Mommy smells like she's getting ready to go out to dinner. And Mommy's read every book in the library downstairs. I couldn't do that. She can read three books in a week with no trouble at all. Real books, not *The Hardy Boys*. Mommy's really smart. She can read and take care of me. Both. That's why I love Mommy.

Scene Two

The kitchen. Mother is fixing a peanut butter and banana sandwich with a large knife. She puts it into a lunchbox on the table. Wallace runs in.

WALLACE: I'm going to miss the bus! Is my lunch ready?

MOTHER: All set. *(Wallace grabs the lunchbox and kisses Mother on the cheek.)*

WALLACE: Bye, Mommy.

MOTHER: Bye, Wallace.

WALLACE *(to the audience)*:   I love the second grade!

MOTHER: Don't shout, Wallace. *(Wallace runs out. Mother watches after him. She writes a note on a slip of paper and puts it on the table. She takes off her turtleneck shirt, so she is in her brassiere. She slits her throat with the large knife. She falls to the floor. Pause. Wallace runs in.)*

WALLACE: Mommy, I'm home! *(Wallace sees Mother on the floor. He picks up the note. Reading the note.)* "Cremate the parasite."

Scene Three

Wallace's bedroom. Wallace is lying on his bed. Grandmother walks in, holding a gift and a photograph.

GRANDMOTHER: Here you are. Your teacher gave me this gift for you.

WALLACE: It's not my birthday.

GRANDMOTHER: Well, something bad happened to you. When something bad happens, you get gifts to make you feel better.

WALLACE: Why do I get gifts on my birthday?

GRANDMOTHER: Well, because you're a year older.

WALLACE: Being a year older isn't bad.

GRANDMOTHER: It adds up. Open your gift. *(Wallace opens his gift.)*

WALLACE: Peanut brittle.

GRANDMOTHER: Isn't that *lovely*—

WALLACE: I *hate* peanut brittle.

GRANDMOTHER: So do I. Don't forget to send your teacher a thank-you note.

WALLACE: Why should I *send* her something? I see her every day.

GRANDMOTHER: So *give* her a thank-you note.

WALLACE: But I *hate* peanut brittle.

GRANDMOTHER: So throw the peanut brittle at her during the pledge of allegiance. Just give her *something* in return for her gift. It's good manners.

WALLACE: Okay.

GRANDMOTHER: She's a very pretty woman.

WALLACE: I guess so.

GRANDMOTHER: Why aren't you downstairs?

WALLACE: Too many people. Why'd they all come back home with us?

GRANDMOTHER: I don't know. They didn't get enough grief out, maybe.

WALLACE: I think they just like free food.

GRANDMOTHER: You're probably right. They're all bunched together like a big black cloud of perfume and cologne munching on little corned beef sandwiches. *Horrible.*

WALLACE: What's that?

GRANDMOTHER: What? *This?*

WALLACE: Yeah.

GRANDMOTHER: Oh, it's a photograph of your mother. The last one, as far as I know. Your father took it six days ago. I wanted to have it.

WALLACE: I wish Mommy would come back.

GRANDMOTHER: I know, Wallace, but for whatever reasons, she wanted to go—

WALLACE: She didn't want to.

GRANDMOTHER: What? Wallace—

WALLACE: I know she didn't want to, Grandma, I know. A pirate came in while I was at school and tore her open. He took everything inside of her and put it in his sack and escaped through the kitchen door. She didn't want to go, Grandma. And if I was here—if I pretended I was sick and stayed home—I could have saved her—

GRANDMOTHER: No. You couldn't have. Don't think you could have saved her, because I'm telling you, you couldn't have. Nobody could have. It was time for her to go. It'll be time for me to go soon, too. And someday, it'll be your time to go—

WALLACE: Not me. I'm going to live forever.

GRANDMOTHER: I wish you luck. You'd be the first person to do it.

WALLACE: I'm going to.

GRANDMOTHER: If anybody can, Wallace, I'm sure it'll be you.

WALLACE: And I'm going to find the pirate who did this. You wait and see.

GRANDMOTHER: I will, Wallace. I certainly will. *(Pause.)* You look very handsome in your suit.

WALLACE: Thank you.

Scene Four

The schoolyard. Wallace is sitting on a bench, eating a sandwich. Victoria walks in.

VICTORIA: Hi, Wallace.

WALLACE: Hi, Victoria.

VICTORIA: Can I sit down?

WALLACE: Free country. *(Victoria sits down next to Wallace.)*

VICTORIA: What you got for lunch?

WALLACE: Peanut butter and banana.

VICTORIA: Want to trade?

WALLACE: What do you have?

VICTORIA: Tuna.

WALLACE: No, thanks. Besides, I already ate some of mine.

VICTORIA: Peanut butter and banana's my favorite. Bet it's good.

WALLACE: It kind of sucks. My Dad made it. Dads can't make lunch. You can barely *taste* the banana.

VICTORIA *(pause)*:   I'm sorry about your mother.

WALLACE: Yeah. Me, too.

VICTORIA: She killed herself?

WALLACE: Who told you that?

VICTORIA: I don't know. Somebody.

WALLACE: She didn't kill herself. A pirate slit her throat, I think. I haven't finished checking things out yet.

VICTORIA: Uh-uh. That's not what they said. They said "suicide."

WALLACE: Who cares?

VICTORIA: I don't know. *(Pause.)* You want a hug?

WALLACE *(quiet)*:   Yeah. *(Victoria hugs Wallace for a few moments. He pushes her away suddenly and she falls.)* Get away from me! *(Pause.)* I gotta go. *(Wallace runs out. Pause. Victoria walks over to Wallace's sandwich and looks at it. She picks it up and takes a bite.)*

Scene Five

WALLACE: "Broken Glass." By Wallace Kirkman. Age thirteen. It's past four in the morning and I can't sleep. I go downstairs to get something to drink and maybe see what's on television. I open the refrigerator and take out the orange juice. I drink orange juice because I'm susceptible to colds. And because I heard that Coke rots your teeth. Whether it does or not makes no difference, because after you hear something like that, it stays in your brain. So I pour some orange juice into a glass and put the carton back in the fridge. And I drink. It goes down smooth and cold, and I just swallow it all without stopping. When I'm done, I look at the empty glass in my hand. My parents got a truckload of glassware for their wedding, and the glass in my hand is one of the set. It's older than me. Respect your elders, I think, but then I see her. She's laughing at me. She's inside the glass, laughing at me. I throw the glass against the refrigerator and hear it crash. I look at the shards on the floor. Like an invitation. I know that glass is made of sand, and I like walking on the beach, and I almost step towards the glass, but I don't. I think of blood. My blood. And I just kneel down and stare at the broken glass on the floor, watching for any reflection of the moonlight outside the kitchen window and waiting for my father to come downstairs, because he can't sleep through anything.

Scene Six

Psychiatrist's office. Psychiatrist is sitting in a chair, writing in a notebook. Wallace walks in.

PSYCHIATRIST: You must be *Wallace*.

WALLACE: Yeah, I'm him.

PSYCHIATRIST: Pleased to meet you. Would you like to have a seat?

WALLACE: Can I lie on the couch?

PSYCHIATRIST: If you'd like.

WALLACE: It seems like the proper thing to do.

PSYCHIATRIST: Go right ahead.

WALLACE: I should *warn* you that I've had my head measured by a close friend, and if you shrink it by so much as a *millimeter*, I'm taking you to *court*.

PSYCHIATRIST: I don't shrink heads.

WALLACE. If I say "*I do*," does that make me insane?

PSYCHIATRIST: It's not that simple. (*Wallace lies down on the couch.*)

WALLACE: Nice couch. Where'd you get it?

PSYCHIATRIST: Bloomingdale's.

WALLACE: Really? I would have thought there'd be some store that would sell special couches for psychiatrists. It doesn't feel as good when you know that anybody with a few bucks can get one.

PSYCHIATRIST: Tell me why you're here, Wallace.

WALLACE: It was either this or a straitjacket, I suppose.

PSYCHIATRIST: Why's that?

WALLACE: Come on, didn't my father tell you all this?

PSYCHIATRIST: I'd like to hear what you have to say.

WALLACE: Can't argue with that. You see, I've been breaking glasses. In the kitchen.

PSYCHIATRIST: Any particular reason.

WALLACE: I like to live dangerously. You know, in perpetual fear of slicing the soles of my feet open. I don't know what it is, but ever since they cut the umbilical cord, I've been obsessed with *sharp* things. Especially knives. I'm attracted to knives. I'm *incredibly* attracted to *doctors* with knives. Do *you* have a knife, Doctor?

PSYCHIATRIST: No—

WALLACE: Do you want to *buy* one?

PSYCHIATRIST: No.

WALLACE: Oh. (*Long pause.*)

PSYCHIATRIST: Tell me about your mother, Wallace.

WALLACE: She was like Sylvia Plath without the publishing contract.

PSYCHIATRIST: Do you remember much about her?

WALLACE: *Nothing.*

PSYCHIATRIST: Nothing at all?

WALLACE: Nope.

PSYCHIATRIST: Are you sure?

WALLACE: Why are you asking me this? Tell me, would you ask me this if my father weren't paying you?

PSYCHIATRIST: You're upset because your father made you come here.

WALLACE: No, I'm upset because he didn't pick a prettier psychiatrist.

PSYCHIATRIST: Was your *mother* pretty, Wallace?

WALLACE (*pause*):   Yeah, she was pretty. *Pretty* pretty. Pretty *suicidal*. And now she's pretty *dead*.

PSYCHIATRIST: You know, Wallace, you don't have to say anything you don't *want* to say.

WALLACE: Okay. (*Long silence.*)

PSYCHIATRIST: What are you thinking about, Wallace? (*Pause.*) Wallace? (*Pause.*) Wallace?

Scene Seven

The park. Wallace and Victoria walk in. Wallace is eating a Mallo Cup and drinking something pink out of a bottle. Victoria is eating Jujyfruits.

VICTORIA: Good movie.

WALLACE: Yeah.

VICTORIA: I like the kissing stuff.

WALLACE: I like when the girl died.

VICTORIA: You want to sit down here?

WALLACE: Here?

VICTORIA: Yeah. Sure.

WALLACE: Yeah. Sure. *(Wallace and Victoria sit down on a bench.)*

VICTORIA: You want a Jujyfruit?

WALLACE: No, they stick to your teeth. You want a Mallo Cup?

VICTORIA: Chocolate makes you break out.

WALLACE: Oh. *(Wallace takes a bite out of a Mallo Cup and drinks from his bottle.)*

VICTORIA: What is that?

WALLACE: What is *what*?

VICTORIA: *That*. In the bottle. The pink stuff.

WALLACE: Oh. You don't want to know.

VICTORIA: Sure I do. Wouldn't ask if I didn't want to know.

WALLACE: Uh, well, it's Pepto-Bismol mixed with seltzer.

VICTORIA: *What?*

WALLACE: I've got this perpetually upset stomach, and drinking this helps. It isn't all that bad, actually. Want some?

VICTORIA: No, thanks. I'll pass. *(Pause.)* It's such a nice day.

WALLACE: Yeah, it's not bad.

VICTORIA: I don't want to go back to school. Do you?

WALLACE: Oh, I'm just *dying* to sharpen my pencils and do tons of homework every night.

VICTORIA: Do you think eighth grade is going to be any different than seventh grade?

WALLACE: No chance in hell. It's all the same. I don't think it matters. They just keep us in school until we're safely through our growth spurts and all of the puberty confusion, then send us out to make the best of the rest of our lives. And we get so terrified of the real world that we pay some university to keep us for four more years or eight more years or whatever. It all depends on how terrified you are. My grandmother's brother is sixty-two, he's *still* taking classes up in Chicago. If they keep you long enough to get comfortable when you're young, they've got you for *life*.

VICTORIA: Not me, that's for sure. Once I'm out, I'm *out*. I'm not going to college, no *way*.

WALLACE: What are you going to do?

VICTORIA: Who knows? Sit on the beach and get a really solid tan. Watch a lot of movies. Dance.

WALLACE: Sounds pretty stimulating, Victoria.

VICTORIA: Don't tease me.

WALLACE: I wasn't.

VICTORIA: Yes, you were.

WALLACE: I swear, I was not teasing you. Why would I tease you?

VICTORIA: I don't know. *(Pause.)* You didn't like the kissing stuff?

WALLACE: Huh?

VICTORIA: You know, in the movie.

WALLACE: Oh, I don't know.

VICTORIA: Sure you do.

WALLACE: I was getting candy. I missed it. Leave me alone.

VICTORIA: You want to try?

WALLACE: Try what?

VICTORIA: *That.*

WALLACE: What's *that?*

VICTORIA: Kissing.

WALLACE: You mean, with *you?*

VICTORIA: Yeah.

WALLACE: You mean, *now?*

VICTORIA: Yeah.

WALLACE: Umm—

VICTORIA: Scared?

WALLACE: Yeah, *right.* Go ahead. Kiss me.

VICTORIA: You sure?

WALLACE: As Shore as Dinah.

VICTORIA: *Dinah?*

WALLACE: Forget it. Will you kiss me already?

VICTORIA: Okay. *(Victoria takes out the Jujyfruit she was eating and throws it away. They kiss.)*

WALLACE: You didn't fade out.

VICTORIA: Nope.

WALLACE: I think I love you, Victoria.

VICTORIA: Really? *(Wallace grabs Victoria and starts kissing her with great passion, holding her in his arms. After a few moments, she breaks away.)*

WALLACE: What's wrong?

VICTORIA: What's *wrong?* You're too *fast* for me, Wallace, *that's* what's wrong. *(Victoria walks out.)*

WALLACE: Too *fast?* *(Pause.)* I mistook love for a girl who ate Jujyfruits. *(Wallace drinks from his bottle.)*

Scene Eight

Grandmother's kitchen. Wallace is sitting at the table. Grandmother walks in with a glass of milk and a plate of cookies.

GRANDMOTHER: Tollhouse cookies, baked this morning especially for *you*.

WALLACE: Thanks.

GRANDMOTHER: You look wonderful. Such a *handsome* thing.

WALLACE: This is delicious.

GRANDMOTHER: Of *course* it is. Would I serve you anything *but?* The first batch went to Grandpa, so *terrible*. *(Pause.)* I'm so *happy* you came to visit.

WALLACE: I love to visit you guys.

GRANDMOTHER: That's like sugar on my heart. It makes me feel so good. *(Wallace points to a photograph in a frame on the table.)*

WALLACE: Who's this?

GRANDMOTHER: That's Grandpa's second cousin, Jerry. He just died. That's the last picture of him, taken *two minutes* before he went. He was at a wedding there, sitting at his table, in between two pretty young girls—you see? The photographer snapped this picture, Jerry was joking and flirting with these young girls—he was like that, Jerry, so *bad*—two minutes later, he just *shut his eyes* *(Pause.)* *Gone*. But still smiling.

WALLACE *(pause)*:   Nice picture. *(Pause.)* Grandma, can I ask you something stupid?

GRANDMOTHER: If it makes you happy, I don't see why *not*.

WALLACE: What was your first kiss like?

GRANDMOTHER: My first *kiss?* You really have faith in my memory, don't you?

WALLACE: You don't have to tell me.

GRANDMOTHER: No, no, no. Let's see. It was with Grandpa, and we were—

WALLACE: Your first kiss was with *Grandpa?*

GRANDMOTHER: Sure. We were steadies in *high* school, you know.

WALLACE: I just never really thought about it. *(Pause.)* Was it nice?

GRANDMOTHER: I was petrified, but he made me feel comfortable. Still petrified, but in a comfortable way. Comfortably petrified. It was on a Saturday night, in nineteen-thirty-six, I think. We were in Wentworth Park, about four blocks from here.

WALLACE: Wow.

GRANDMOTHER: I remember thinking he kissed really wonderfully. I mean, we were just in high school, and kissing him made me feel like the movie stars must have felt. I almost fell *backwards*, I was so taken away. Then I got suspicious, asking myself where'd he *learn* to kiss like that. When I asked him—

WALLACE: You *asked* him?

GRANDMOTHER: I *asked* him, and he told me he had been practicing on his pillow for almost five years. That made me feel better.

Besides, with those eyes, I couldn't help but believe him. *(Pause.)* I was sixteen then. Generations are different.

WALLACE: Yeah.

GRANDMOTHER: Each generation changes. It either improves or declines.

WALLACE: Yeah, trouble is, you can't tell one from the other. I mean, what *your* generation calls decline, *mine* calls improvement. It's so confusing. Along with everything else.

GRANDMOTHER: Don't waste your time thinking of it. I will say one thing, though. Hair is important. Secondary, but important nonetheless. Find a girl with *hair*.

WALLACE: *Hair?*

GRANDMOTHER: Sure. I mean, I can't run my fingers through Grandpa's hair. All I can do is rub his scalp. *(Pause.)* Which some say brings good luck.

WALLACE: I think that's when you rub *Buddha's* scalp.

GRANDMOTHER: Well, Grandpa's certainly not *Buddha*. And I'm certainly not *lucky*.

WALLACE *(pause)*: Do you ever miss Mommy?

GRANDMOTHER: All the time.

WALLACE *(pause)*: Me, too. *(Pause.)* All the time.

GRANDMOTHER *(pause)*: Drink your milk. It's good for your teeth.

Scene Nine

WALLACE: "My Mother's Turtlenecks." By Wallace Kirkman. Age sixteen. My mother loved my father and hated her neck. She thought it was too fleshy or something. If I hated *my* neck, I'd have it removed, but my mother never trusted doctors, so she wore turtlenecks. All the time. In every picture we have of her, she's wearing a turtleneck. She had turtlenecks in every color of the rainbow, she had blacks, she had whites, she had grays, she had plaids, she had polka dots and hound's-tooth checks and stripes and Mickey Mouse and even a sort of *mesh* turtleneck. I can't picture her without a turtleneck on. Although, according to Freud, I *try* to, every moment of every day. We have a photograph of me when I was a baby wearing one of my mother's turtlenecks. *Swimming* in one of my mother's turtlenecks is more like it. Just a bald head and a big shirt. It's very erotic in an Oedipal shirtwear sort of way. It's a rare photograph, because I'm smiling. I didn't smile all that much during most of my childhood. I'm taking lessons now, trying to learn again, but it takes time. I stopped smiling when my mother stopped wearing turtlenecks. I came home from a typical day in the second grade to find her taking a bath in her own blood on the kitchen floor. Her turtleneck was on top of the kitchen table, so it wouldn't come between her neck and her knife. I understood then why she had worn turtlenecks all along. To stop the blood from flowing. To cover the wound that was there all along. They tried to cover the wound when they buried her with one of her favorite turtleneck dresses on, but it didn't matter. It was just an empty hole by then. My mother wasn't hiding inside. *(Pause.)* She wrote a note before she died, asking to be cremated, and I asked my father why she wasn't. He said my mother was two women, and the one he loved would have been scared of the flames. *(Pause.)* I look at that photograph of little me inside my mother's shirt all the time. It's the closest I can get to security. There are no pictures of me inside mother's womb, but her turtleneck is close enough.

Scene Ten

Wallace's bedroom. Wallace and Sarah are sitting on the bed. Sarah is reading something on a piece of paper.

SARAH: Oh, I *really* like it.

WALLACE: *Really?*

SARAH: *Really.* It's very good.

WALLACE: *Why?*

SARAH: Well, it's funny, but it's also *sad.* It's really *sad.* And it's so *true.* I mean, there's so much of *you* in there. I mean, if I didn't know you, I'd *know* you after I read this. You know what I mean? I think it's really talented work. What's it for?

WALLACE: *For?*

SARAH: I mean, is it for English class or something?

WALLACE: No. I just sort of *wrote* it. Not really *for* anything. For me, I guess.

SARAH: You should submit it to the school newspaper. I bet they'd publish it.

WALLACE: I don't think I want the whole school reading this.

SARAH: Why not? I mean, you shouldn't be *ashamed* or anything—

WALLACE: I'm not *ashamed.* It just seems a little *sensationalist,* you know?

SARAH: I don't know. I guess so.

WALLACE: *So. (Pause.)* What do you want to do?

SARAH: Oh, I don't know.

WALLACE: We could go see a movie.

SARAH: Sure.

WALLACE: Or we could stay here.

SARAH: Sure.

WALLACE: Well, which one?

SARAH: Whichever.

WALLACE: Come on, I'm horrible with decisions.

SARAH: So am I.

WALLACE: Sarah, you're the valedictorian of our *class*, for Chrissakes. If you can't make a decision, who can?

SARAH: Umm, do you want to . . . stay *here?*

WALLACE: Yes.

SARAH: Okay. Let's stay here, then.

WALLACE: Settled. Do you want something to drink?

SARAH: Umm, sure.

WALLACE: What do you want? Some wine? A screwdriver?

SARAH: Oh, you mean something to *drink*. I don't drink.

WALLACE: Oh. (*Pause.*) Do you mind if I drink something?

SARAH: Oh, no, don't let me stand in your way.

WALLACE: I'll be right back.

SARAH: Okay. (*Wallace walks out. Sarah looks around the room. She looks at a photograph in a frame by the bed. Wallace walks in, sipping a glass of wine.*)

WALLACE: *In vino veritas.*

SARAH: Who's this?

WALLACE: It's my mother.

SARAH: She was beautiful.

WALLACE: She was okay. I'm going to light a candle, okay?

SARAH: Sure. (*Wallace gets a candle. He takes a lighter from his pocket.*)

WALLACE: My great-grandfather was lighting a pipe with this lighter when he died. It's a Zippo. Pretty sharp, huh?

SARAH: It's very nice. (*Wallace tries to light the lighter. It won't light.*)

WALLACE: I think it has to warm up. (*Pause. Wallace tries to light the lighter a few more times. It won't light.*) Uhh, I guess my great-grandfather forgot to refill it before he died. It's just as well. I hate candles. They're so *cliched*. (*Pause.*) You want to listen to some music?

SARAH: Sure.

WALLACE: What do you like?

SARAH: Oh, *anything*.

WALLACE: You like James Taylor?

SARAH: Sure.

WALLACE: Let me just find the tape. (*Wallace looks for the tape.*) I don't know where I put it. Maybe it's out in the car. I can go check—

SARAH: That's okay. We don't *need* music. Do we?

WALLACE: Uhh, *no*, I guess *not*. (*Pause.*) Well.

SARAH: What was your mother like, Wallace?

WALLACE: What was she *like*?

SARAH: Yeah.

WALLACE: She was like Sylvia Plath without a Fulbright scholarship.

SARAH: What do you mean?

WALLACE: I mean—I don't know what I mean, I'm *sixteen*. (*Wallace drinks his glass of wine.*) Would you mind if I kissed you?

SARAH: The wine works fast.

WALLACE: No, *I* do. Can I?

SARAH: Umm, can't we *talk* for a while—

WALLACE: I don't *want* to talk, I want to *kiss*. Can I kiss you?

SARAH: I'd really feel better if we just—

WALLACE: Oh, come *on*—(*Wallace kisses Sarah, long and hard.*)

SARAH: Maybe I should go.

WALLACE: What? Oh, come on—

SARAH: No, I mean, maybe this wasn't such a good idea.

WALLACE: Don't you *like* me?

SARAH: Very much, Wallace. But I don't want this to be just—I don't know, a lot of *stupidity*. Just kissing and nothing else. I wanted to *talk* to you, you know?

WALLACE: Yeah, whatever.

SARAH: Oh, Wallace, don't do that—

WALLACE: Just go, please.

SARAH: What?

WALLACE: You said maybe you should leave, so leave. I don't want to—I just don't want to *deal* with this, okay?

SARAH: But—

WALLACE: But *nothing*. Just, please, go, okay?

SARAH: I—*fine*. Bye, Wallace.

WALLACE: Yeah, yeah, see you—

SARAH: I'm sorry this didn't work out. (*Pause.*) I'll see you in school on Monday. Okay? (*Pause.*) Okay, bye. (*Sarah walks out.*)

Scene Eleven

Wallace's bedroom. Wallace is sitting on his bed, talking on the phone.

WALLACE: Yeah, I wanted to see if I could make a song request and a dedication. . . . Umm, "Something in the Way She Moves." . . . By James Taylor. . . . You *don't*? I mean, it's on "Greatest Hits." You see, I'm trying to right a wrong, as they say. . . . I don't know, it's an expression. . . . Umm, do you have any, I don't know, like, Cat Stevens or something, somebody *close* to James Taylor? You know, one man and a guitar, that sort of thing. . . .

Only top forty? . . . Who's in the top forty? Anybody named James? . . . No, that's not really appropriate. . . . Umm, could I just make a dedication, then? . . . Well, I *know* it's supposed to be for a song, but you don't seem to have the song I *need*, so if I could just maybe make the dedication and then you could maybe not play anything for about three minutes in *place* of the song I need and that way—*hello*? (*Pause.*) Shit. (*Wallace hangs up the phone.*)

Scene Twelve

Sarah's front door. Sarah inside, Wallace outside.

SARAH: Wallace.

WALLACE: Sarah.

SARAH: What are you doing here?

WALLACE: I wanted—umm, I wanted to *apologize*.

SARAH: You don't *have* to—

WALLACE: Yeah, I do.

SARAH: Okay. (*Pause.*) So?

WALLACE: You know, I just—it's funny, you know, sometimes I just wish I were a little kid again, when "sorry" was okay, you know?

SARAH: Yeah, well, we're not little kids, Wallace.

WALLACE: We're *not*? Umm, no, no, we're *not*. We're *certainly* not. Umm—*okay*. Well. I was acting *really* stupid before, I mean, just very—*stupid*. It was—I was being, umm—

SARAH: Stupid.

WALLACE: *Yeah*. And it was *wrong*, and it was—you know, it made you—it was *unfair*. And I *apologize*.

SARAH: Okay—

WALLACE: And I thought maybe we could try *again*.

SARAH: Again?

WALLACE: Yeah, you know, maybe I could come *in*—

SARAH: My parents are sleeping.

WALLACE: Oh. (*Pause.*) I could try to be quiet.

SARAH: It's kind of *late*.

WALLACE: Umm, well, you know, maybe you could come back over to my house and we could start from the *beginning*.

SARAH: *Wallace*—

WALLACE: I mean, I know it *sounds* like a stupid idea, but trust me, I'll behave this time, I know what to do. We can *talk*. We can have a *conversation*. We don't even have to kiss, we'll just *talk* and then you can go. *(Pause.)* Or we can just sit in *silence* for a while. We don't *have* to talk.

SARAH: I don't think that's a very good *idea*, Wallace.

WALLACE: All I'm *asking* for is another chance, Sarah. Don't make me beg.

SARAH: There's no need to *beg*, Wallace, I just don't think—

WALLACE: Okay. I'll beg. *(Wallace drops to his knees.)* I'm *begging*, Sarah, give me another shot.

SARAH: Wallace—

WALLACE: I'll be *good*.

SARAH: *Wallace*—

WALLACE: Look at the moon, Sarah. It's *full*. It's *romantic*.

SARAH: Wallace, get off your knees.

WALLACE *(pause)*: That's okay. I kind of like it down here. *(Pause.)* I was going to bring a guitar and maybe *serenade* you, but I can't sing. And I don't play the guitar. I did have Romantic Thoughts, though.

SARAH: That's very sweet, Wallace. *(Pause.)* I really should go back *inside*—

WALLACE: Yeah, I understand. You know, I tried to dedicate a song to you on the radio, you know, something by James Taylor, and they didn't *have* any James Taylor. Can you *believe* that?

SARAH: That's pretty funny.

WALLACE: Yeah. Pretty Funny World.

SARAH: Sure is.

WALLACE: So, umm, you wouldn't want to maybe try again, say, *next* weekend? A movie or—

SARAH: *Wallace*.

WALLACE: No, I understand. Okay.

SARAH: I'm *sorry*, Wallace.

WALLACE: Yeah, no, *I'm* sorry.

SARAH *(pause)*: Are you going to *stay* down there?

WALLACE: For a little while, yeah. If you don't mind.

SARAH: No, I don't mind.

WALLACE: Thanks.

SARAH: Yeah, well, okay. Goodnight, Wallace.

WALLACE: 'Night.

SARAH: Bye.

WALLACE: Bye. *(Sarah walks out, closing the door behind her. Pause. Wallace looks up at the moon.)* Thanks a lot, Moon. You really came through for me.

Scene Thirteen

Psychiatrist's office. Psychiatrist is sitting in a chair, writing in a notebook. Wallace walks in.

PSYCHIATRIST: Hello, Wallace. It's been a long time since I've seen you.

WALLACE: About five years.

PSYCHIATRIST: Yes. Nice to see you again.

GRANDMOTHER: I'll bet.

PSYCHIATRIST: Would you like to have a seat?

WALLACE: No.

PSYCHIATRIST: Okay, then. What's on your mind?

WALLACE: Lots. *(Pause.)* I came here last time because my father made me, but now I'm here because I want to talk to you. You see, I'm confused. My mother makes me a sandwich for lunch. I take it. She, in turn, slits her throat. And after the funeral, when I go back to school for the first time, my *father* makes me a sandwich for lunch, or at least he *tries*, so as not to screw up my daily routine any more than it already has been. And I'm thinking, all day while I'm in school, that *he's* going to be lying on the kitchen floor when I get home. It's the same thing, you see, because I *took* the sandwich. If I didn't *take*, I think, they'll be okay. But I *take*, and that kills them. And when I came home from school and he *wasn't* on the floor of the kitchen, but instead sitting in his study, *alive*, I was disappointed. Let down. Because my system didn't work. It *failed* me. Everything was *failing* me. And when I *expected* my father to fail me, he failed me by *not* failing me. He was just sitting there in his study. Alone, deserted by the woman he loved and planned to—I don't know, move to Florida with, and he can manage to stay alive, to go on living. *How?* And, I mean, Victoria, this twelve-year-old *girl*, is *sitting* there, practically *begging* me to kiss her, I mean, she would have been on her *knees* in a second, in more ways than one, that's how it seemed, and when I finally let down and actually *do* what she's been *asking* me to do—I *kiss* her and *bang*—all of a sudden, *I'm* too goddamn *fast* for her. I told her I *loved* her, and she runs off, *skipping*, and the next week she's kissing somebody else, and I heard he got up her *shirt*, and *he's* not too fast, *I'm* the one who was too *fast*. So I get this reputation that scares the hell out of me, because, not only will no *decent* girls *look* at me, I can't even think about any of the *in*decent girls, because I'm scared to death of having to live up to my own reputation. And, now, I mean, when my big mistake has always been talking too much, so I try, finally, on this girl I *really* like, okay, I mean, *bright*, *pretty*, actually *nice*, *caring*, I try not to screw it up by talking too much, and I go *right* for the kiss and she won't ever see me again because I didn't talk too much. I mean, I can't *win*. They *desert*. Women *desert*. And I know it all stems back to my fucking *coward* mother, and if she hadn't *offed* herself, I'd have no problems, but what I'm trying to say is I don't know what the hell to *do* about all of this, Doctor, and it's my life, so can—you know, can you give me some *advice* or something, Doctor? *(Pause.)* Doctor? *(Pause.)* Doctor?

Scene Fourteen

Wallace and Psychiatrist.

WALLACE: "Tyrannosaurus Rex." By Wallace Kirkman. Age eighteen. *(Psychiatrist gets up and starts to walk out.)* Don't go. I need *help* with this one. Stay right there. Please. You'll like this. It's very *Freudian*. In fact, it's a *dream*. *(The lights change rather dramatically. Psychiatrist sits and Wallace walks out. He walks in a moment later with a crate of props.)* I need a *mother*. *(Pause.)* I need somebody who can *act* like a mother. *Please*. *(Victoria walks in.)* You'll do. I always wanted to be a dinosaur when I was young. Youn*ger*. I have a lot in common with Tyrannosaurus. We both walk on two legs, we both eat meat, and we both occasionally answer to the nickname "King of the Tyrant Lizards." Anyhow, the recipe for this dream is something like two parts *Oedipus Rex*, two parts Freud, and nineteen parts me. In the beginning, the eventual parents are both thirteen years old. *(Wallace pushes Psychiatrist and Victoria onto their knees.)* And Jewish. *(Wallace pulls two pairs of gag glasses out of the crate of props. He puts one—with a plastic nose—on Victoria and the other—with a plastic nose and a plastic moustache—on Psychiatrist.)* They get bar mitzvahed and bat mitzvahed on the same day and sleep with each other on the same night. Kids today. God bless 'em. On with the dream. The girl gets pregnant, as girls will do. *(Wallace pulls a baby doll out of the crate of props and hands it to Victoria.)* She wants to get an abortion so the baby won't get in the way of the seventh grade, but neither of the partners got any cash for their *mitzvahs*, only savings bonds. *Lots* of savings bonds. So, they pack several pairs of underwear and go to stay with the girl's grandmother, a mentally ill fortune teller from Boston. *(Grandmother walks in—a grand entrance—wearing a turban.)*

GRANDMOTHER: This baby is *trouble*. He's going to fight with you and *shtoop* you.

VICTORIA: *Shtoop?*

PSYCHIATRIST: How do you know the baby's going to be a "he"?

GRANDMOTHER: I'm a fortune teller. Give me a break.

WALLACE: When the baby is born, they immediately sell it on the black market. (*Victoria tosses the baby doll to Wallace. Wallace pulls a packet of play money out of the crate of props and hands it to Victoria.*) They use the money to pay a few months' worth of rent on a Beacon Street apartment. (*Wallace takes the packet of play money from Victoria and replaces it in the crate of props. He pulls a pair of boxing gloves out of the crate of props and hands them to Psychiatrist, who puts them on.*) The father starts to take boxing lessons. The mother spends her spare time in their spare apartment reading spare Japanese literature. (*Wallace pulls a Mishima paperback out of the crate of props and tosses it to Victoria.*) They earn rent money and grocery money and boxing lesson money and Japanese book money by becoming kiddie porn stars. (*Psychiatrist and Victoria look at one another in* horror.) *Cut.* And, at this point, the dream leaps ahead about seventeen years or so. The father is a very popular amateur boxer. (*Wallace pulls Psychiatrist up off her knees so she is standing. Wallace pulls Victoria up off her knees so she is also standing.*) The mother is about to commit ritual suicide. (*Wallace pulls the large knife Mother used to slit her throat out of the crate of props and hands it to Victoria.*)

VICTORIA: I've tried and tried and *tried.* And I'll just *never* be Japanese. (*Victoria plunges the large knife into her bowels and falls to the floor. Dead. Wallace stares at her for a moment, then tosses the baby doll into the crate of props and pulls out a pair of boxing gloves. He puts them on.*)

WALLACE: The son is a boxing necrophiliac who masturbates. A lot. (*Wallace approaches Grandmother.*) Hello.

GRANDMOTHER: *Shalom.*

WALLACE (*to the audience*): I *hate* when people say *"shalom."* I never know whether they're *coming* or *going* or just a *pacifist.*

GRANDMOTHER: How may I serve you?

WALLACE: I'd like to know my fortune.

GRANDMOTHER: Easy. You're going to fight with your Dad and *shtoop* your Mom. Ten bucks, please.

WALLACE: This is *horrible.* I don't want to fight with Dad. I *love* Dad.

GRANDMOTHER: Ten bucks, please.

WALLACE: And I don't want to *shtoop* Mom. Because Dad would get mad. And we'd fight.

GRANDMOTHER: Ten bucks, please.

WALLACE: And I don't want to fight with Dad. I *love* Dad. Boy, this makes me tense. I need some *release*.

GRANDMOTHER: Ten bucks, please. *(Wallace punches Grandmother and knocks her out.)*

WALLACE: I wonder if there's anything good over at the *morgue*. *(Wallace looks at Victoria.)* She's *beautiful*. She's *everything*. She's *dead*. And she's a nice Jewish girl. I wonder where her bowels are. *(Wallace leaps onto Victoria, kisses her madly for a few moments, then rolls off onto the floor.)* It's time to *box*. *(Wallace approaches Psychiatrist. A bell rings. Psychiatrist punches Wallace and knocks him out.)*

PSYCHIATRIST: 10, 9, 8, 7, 6, 5, 4, 3, 2, 1. *(Psychiatrist slaps Wallace's face and he comes to.)*

WALLACE: Did I win?

PSYCHIATRIST: Nope.

WALLACE: *Shit.*

PSYCHIATRIST: Come on, I'll buy you a beer.

WALLACE: I'm underage.

PSYCHIATRIST: You don't have a fake i.d.?

WALLACE: I was always too busy *masturbating* to buy one.

PSYCHIATRIST: Oh. *(Pause.)* Come on, I'll buy you a ginger ale.

WALLACE: Yeah, okay. You're on. *(Psychiatrist helps Wallace up and they walk a few steps.)*

PSYCHIATRIST: One beer and one ginger ale, barkeep.

WALLACE: Excuse me for a moment, I've got to go to the bathroom.

PSYCHIATRIST: But you haven't had anything to drink.

WALLACE *(pause)*: *Excuse me for a moment, I've got to go to the bathroom.*

PSYCHIATRIST: Oh. Sure, go right ahead.

WALLACE: Be right back. *(Wallace walks out. He runs in a few moments later, without the boxing gloves on, his hands covering his eyes. He is screaming. Grandmother, Psychiatrist, and Victoria clear the stage and walk out. The lights change back. Wallace takes his hands off his tightly closed eyes, opens them, sees nobody around, and stops screaming. He yawns, as if waking up.)* I've been having this dream every night for the past two months. It's always pretty much the same, although sometimes it's in color and sometimes it's in black-and-white, and once the black-and-white version was colorized, which pissed me off. I mean, it's more or less my life story, and who wants their life story *colorized*?

Scene Fifteen

Wallace's dormitory room. Wallace and Lili walk in.

WALLACE: This is my room.

LILI: Nice. How did you get a single room your first year?

WALLACE: I had a psychiatrist write the school a note saying essentially that if I had to live with another person I'd probably kill them.

LILI: Seriously?

WALLACE: Not really. But the school believed it. *(Pause.)* You must be tired.

LILI: Why?

WALLACE: Well, I mean, you were on the stage for practically the entire time.

LILI: It's an important part.

WALLACE: And you did it so well. *Really*. The whole thing was—*beautiful*.

LILI: The choreographer's pretty talented.

WALLACE: I mean, who the hell would ever think to do *Catcher in the Rye* as a *ballet*?

LILI: The *choreographer* would.

WALLACE: I—well, I mean, I *know*, but it's just—*wow*. You know, I never realized there was so much stuff about *lesbians* in *Catcher in the Rye*.

LILI: It's all in the *subtext*.

WALLACE: Yeah. But I think, you know, having *you*—you know, having a *woman* as Holden Caulfield really made everything *quite* clear.

LILI: I'm glad you liked it. *(Pause.)* You're very *cute*, Wallace.

WALLACE: *Me?*

LILI: Yes, you. I'm really *drawn* to you, you know?

WALLACE: Umm, *sure*.

LILI: What are you waiting for?

WALLACE: Huh?

LILI: *Kiss* me.

WALLACE: Umm, are you—umm, *sure*. *(Wallace kisses Lili.)* How was that?

LILI: That was nice. Do you want to sleep together?

WALLACE: *What?*

LILI: Do you want to *make love*?

WALLACE: Umm, with *you*?

LILI: *Yes*, with *me*.

WALLACE: Umm, sure, yes, yeah, *sure*. *(Pause.)* What do we do?

LILI: Are you a *virgin*?

WALLACE: Umm, *technically*, no.

LILI: What do you mean, "technically"?

WALLACE: Well, what is the definition of male virginity?

LILI: Is that a rhetorical question?

WALLACE: A male virgin is a male who has never had his thing inside a female's thing. Right?

LILI: Anybody still calling it a "thing" is probably a virgin, I know that much.

WALLACE: Well, when I was born, I had a thing. A very tiny, bald thing, but a thing nonetheless. And I entered this world through my mother's thing—the infamous "tunnel of love." Therefore, my thing has been inside of a female's thing, although it had to share the space with the rest of my body. In fact, pretty much all men are born nonvirgins. The only exceptions would be men born Caesarean style.

LILI: You're saying you lost your virginity—with your *mother*?

WALLACE: Yeah.

LILI: You're pretty weird, Wallace.

WALLACE: Thank you.

LILI: So, will this be your first time having sex with somebody outside your immediate family?

WALLACE: You've got me there. Yes.

LILI: I'm *honored*.

WALLACE: I'm *terrified*.

LILI: It's simple. Don't worry, you'll be fine. Before we get started, do you have any protection?

WALLACE: Umm, no.

LILI: Here, take this. *(Lili hands Wallace a condom.)*

WALLACE: You really come prepared.

LILI: I don't want to even joke *around* with AIDS, you know?

WALLACE: I know. Remember when AYDS was just a dietetic candy? There's a stock that must have done *real* well. Can you picture the president of the company right before the end? "Call the damn thing Dexatrim, it's a *superb* name for a disease!"

LILI: You don't have to make jokes, Wallace, everything's going to be fine. *Better* than fine.

WALLACE: How did you know I was nervous? I thought I was covering it pretty well.

LILI: A woman knows.

WALLACE: Hey, tell me something.

LILI: Yeah?

WALLACE: What can you possibly see in me?

LILI: What do you mean?

WALLACE: I mean, how did I end up here with *you*? You're a beautiful senior, I'm a nervous little freshman.

LILI: You've got great eyes.

WALLACE: I *do*?

LILI: Really intelligent eyes. Like they've seen a *lot*, that's what they look like.

WALLACE: You're here with me because of my *eyes*?

LILI: Yeah, sort of.

WALLACE: The brochures don't do college justice.

LILI: Let's get on the *bed*, Wallace.

WALLACE: Let me just hit the lights.

LILI: No, keep them *on*, I want to *see* you.

WALLACE: You keep the lights on with a guy named Biff who pumps iron and gasoline. With a Jew from Jersey, you do it in the dark. (*Wallace flips the light switch. Blackout.*)

LILI (*pause*): Why do you wear so many *layers*?

WALLACE: Wearing layers of clothing keeps you warmer than wearing one *thick* garment.

LILI: But it's not cold out.

WALLACE: All right, so I hate my body. I'm too skinny. Is that such a crime?

LILI: You've got a nice body.

WALLACE: In the *dark*, maybe. You're so *sweaty*—

LILI: I want to *see* you, Wallace, I want to see *all* of you. Can't you turn the lights on?

WALLACE: If the lights go on, I go in the closet.

LILI: Do you have a candle or something, at least?

WALLACE: I *hate* candles. (*Pause.*) Am I doing okay?

LILI: You're doing *fine*. Just *fine*.

WALLACE (*pause*): Why did the chicken cross the road?

LILI: This isn't the *time*, Wallace.

WALLACE: Sorry. (*Long pause. Wallace flips the light switch. The lights come up. They sit up in bed together.*) Wow. (*Pause.*) You know, I always wondered what this would be like, I always tried to imagine, and it's just—now it's *actual*. Now it's *real*. Now—I just slept with an older woman. An older woman who *dances*. Billy Corkscrew would never believe it.

LILI: *Who*?

WALLACE: This kid I was friends with growing up, Billy Corkscrew. He talked about sex all the time. He told me everything, little Mister Know-It-All. You know, told me that the only way to *really* satisfy a woman was to put Spanish fly in her drink, and if you were dating a girl who spoke French instead of Spanish, you had to get your Spanish fly "translated," which Billy said could only be done at the French embassy and it cost a hell of a lot of money, and he said we would probably just be better off paying professionals. *(Pause.)* He moved to Arizona when we were eleven. Last I heard about him, he couldn't find a date for his senior prom.

LILI *(Pause)*:   You have to meet my little *sister.*

Scene Sixteen

Wallace's dormitory room. Wallace and Nina are sitting on the bed. She is looking at a photograph in a frame by the bed.

NINA: Is this your mother?

WALLACE: Yeah. She's dead.

NINA: Oh. I'm sorry.

WALLACE: For what?

NINA: For asking.

WALLACE: I don't mind. I mean, I've lived without her for so long—it's not all that bad, really.

NINA: What was she like?

WALLACE: Like Sylvia Plath without talent.

NINA: She killed herself?

WALLACE: Yeah. When I was six.

NINA: That's too bad. How'd she kill herself?

WALLACE: You really want to know?

NINA: Yeah. If you don't want to talk about it, though—

WALLACE: No, I do. It's just that it freaks most people out. *(Pause.)* She slit her throat with a kitchen knife.

NINA: Oh, god. I never understand why people don't just take pills and die painlessly.

WALLACE: I guess if you hate yourself enough to want to die—it's just like if you wanted to kill someone else. If you hate something, you want it to die painfully. I mean, I guess that's what it is. I know that pain belongs in there somewhere.

NINA: How did you deal with all that? I mean, how'd you get through it?

WALLACE: I used to break glass.

NINA: Huh?

WALLACE: I used to break glasses on the kitchen floor. That helped a little. It was destructive, but it eased the pain.

NINA: How *sad*—

WALLACE: It's no big deal. I mean, I guess it made me who I am today, and who knows what I would have been if she was still alive. Maybe I'd be somebody I'd hate, you know. Sure, there are times I'd kill to have her back, just for a day. So I could show her something I've written, or talk to her about my thoughts, or just even to see her smile when I did something silly. *(Long pause.)*

NINA: What are you thinking about?

WALLACE: I don't know. About my mother, and about how you listen to me talk, and—and about how I'd love to kiss you right now.

NINA: So why *don't* you?

WALLACE: What? Well, umm, Nina, do you—did your sister tell you—

NINA: I know. You and my sister were—*together*.

WALLACE: And it doesn't *bother* you?

NINA: A little. Not much. I mean, you were drunk—

WALLACE: *What*?

NINA: And all you did was *kiss*, right?

WALLACE: Umm—umm, *yeah*. Just a few drunken kisses, that's all it was.

NINA: A *few*? She said *one*.

WALLACE: Well, I mean, there were a few *within* the one. But we never pulled our lips apart, so technically, I guess, yeah, just *one*.

NINA: Okay. *(Pause.)* Well?

WALLACE: Well what?

NINA: *Kiss* me.

WALLACE: Nina, I think I *love* you. I know it sounds stupid, but—it that okay?

NINA: Sure.

WALLACE: Okay. I'm going to kiss you now, okay?

NINA: Okay.

WALLACE: Okay. *(They kiss.)*

Scene Seventeen

Wallace's dormitory room. Wallace and Wendy are sitting on the bed, kissing.

WENDY: Are you sure we should be doing this?

WALLACE: Why not?

WENDY: Well, what about your girlfriend?

WALLACE: What *about* her?

WENDY: Well—

WALLACE: I'm drunk, you're drunk, we don't know what we're doing. Right?

WENDY: Umm, *right*.

WALLACE: *Right*. Give me a kiss. *(They kiss.)*

Scene Eighteen

Wallace in a spotlight.

WALLACE: I fucked up. Mommy. I fell in love—*really*—for the first time. I mean, it wasn't romance for the sake of romance. It was romance for the sake of—*somebody. Nina.* Nina listened. And I got scared. I ran away. To somebody else. What do I do? Mommy. It *hurts. (Pause.)* I want my—I *need* my mother. *(Pause.)* I'm not asking for much. I just—all I want is to take the knife away from her. To go back and take the knife away from her. All I want to do is change history. *(The lights come up on the kitchen. Mother is fixing a peanut butter and banana sandwich. She is peeling the banana. Wallace looks at her. He looks at the audience, then looks back at her. He walks past the table picking up the large knife as he goes by. He walks out. Mother finishes peeling the banana and fixes the sandwich, breaking the banana up with her hands and spreading the peanut butter with a spoon. She puts the sandwich into a lunchbox on the table. Wallace runs in.)* I'm going to miss the bus! Is my lunch ready?

MOTHER: All set. *(Wallace grabs the lunchbox and kisses Mother on the cheek.)*

WALLACE: Bye, Mommy.

MOTHER: Bye, Wallace.

WALLACE *(to the audience)*:   I love the second grade!

WALLACE: Don't shout, Wallace. *(Wallace runs out. Mother watches after him. She writes a note on a slip of paper. While she is writing the note, Wallace walks in and quietly watches her from the side. She puts the note on the table. She takes off her turtleneck shirt, so she is in her brassiere. She wraps the turtleneck around her neck and pulls it taut, attempting to strangle herself. The lights on the kitchen slowly fade, and Wallace is in the spotlight again.)*

WALLACE *(To the audience. Pause.)*:   In countless science fiction stories about time travel, the moral is quite clear. When you go back in time, if you so much as step on an ant, the course of history will change drastically. Don't try to change history. It's dangerous. *(Pause.)* In my experience, trying to change history isn't really dangerous. It's just a waste of time—a futile, frustrating exercise where you exert yourself and use up boundless energies and—and everything stays exactly the same. With small technical differences, perhaps. One more dead ant. If you take a razor away from a man who wants to kill himself, he'll *still* kill himself—he just won't be clean shaven. The will is all that matters. If the will is there—*(Pause.)* I should dwell on the future. Dwelling on the past is hopeless.

Scene Nineteen

Wallace's dormitory room. Wallace is standing. There is a knock on the door.

WALLACE: Yeah. *(Nina walks in.)*

NINA: Hey there.

WALLACE: Sit down.

NINA: What's wrong?

WALLACE: Sit down.

NINA: Okay. *(Nina sits on the bed.)* What's the matter?

WALLACE: You deserve better.

NINA: Huh?

WALLACE: I'm not good enough for you.

NINA: What are you talking about? You're the *best*.

WALLACE: I'm the *worst*. You should *hate* me.

NINA: Why?

WALLACE: You don't want to know.

NINA: *What* don't I want to know?

WALLACE: I've been with somebody else.

NINA *(pause)*:   What?

WALLACE: I was with somebody else.

NINA *(pause)*:   Who?

WALLACE: Wendy.

NINA: Wendy. *(Pause.)* I think I'm going to be sick. *(Nina runs out.)*

WALLACE: *Nina. (Pause.)* Women *desert. (Wallace picks up a glass. He holds it in his hand, looking at it. He starts to throw it so it will break against the wall. Nina walks in.)*

NINA: Don't you dare break that glass or I'll turn right around and I won't come back. *(Wallace stops. He puts the glass on the bed and looks at Nina.)*

WALLACE: You came back. *(Pause.)* You should hate me.

NINA: I do. But I also happen to love you, and I'm not going to lose you without a fight.

WALLACE: You came back.

NINA: Do you want to work through this? I'll tell you right now, it's not going to be easy.

WALLACE: I know.

NINA: You betrayed me.

WALLACE: I know.

NINA: I know you may have been scared or whatever, but I swear to God, if you ever do this again, both you and her—*whoever* she is—will be lying on the street, okay?

WALLACE: Okay. *(Pause.)* You came back.

NINA: You want to work through this?

WALLACE: Yes.

NINA: Okay. Then we will.

WALLACE: You came back. *(Wallace goes to hug Nina. They hug. After a few moments, she breaks from the hug and slaps him, hard, across the face.)*

NINA: Don't you *ever* do that to me again, understand?

WALLACE: You came back.

Scene Twenty

Grandmother's kitchen. Wallace and Grandmother are sitting at the table.

GRANDMOTHER: And you *really* love her?

WALLACE: I *swear*. At least, I think I do. I mean, I know I do. And I was running away from her. You know, I was so terrified that she'd leave me, I wanted to leave first so I wouldn't have to deal with the pain. You know, I *wanted* to get caught with this other girl, Grandma, I *had* to tell her about it right away. It all made sense when I told her. Too much sense. She said she was going to be sick and walked out of my room. And something in me clicked. Something in me had been expecting it. Had been expecting her to leave me. And it made sense. And it was complete. *(Pause.)* And then she came *back*. That's what threw me for a loop. And right then I said, there is no way I am going to lose her. I am going to do everything in my power to keep her. Because she came *back*. And it scares the hell out of me that I almost lost her because Mommy killed herself. I mean, my mother deserts me for whatever reasons, but she almost made me lose the one girl I've ever really *loved*.

GRANDMOTHER *(pause)*:   You can't *blame* her until you die, you know.

WALLACE: What?

GRANDMOTHER: Your mother. I mean, sure, you can invoke her name once in a while to clear up a messy situation, but you've got to be responsible for *something* eventually. A dead mother does not give you *carte blanche* for a lifetime of screwing up. You can *do* it—you can screw *up*, go right ahead, but don't keep blaming her, or you'll just go through life fooling yourself and you'll die a blind man. *(Pause.)* Understand?

WALLACE: I think so. I'm not sure.

GRANDMOTHER: It's okay. You're still young. *(Pause.)* Are they feeding you enough up at school? You look thin.

WALLACE: They're feeding me fine, Grandma. *(Pause. Wallace points to a photograph in a frame on the table.)* Who's this?

GRANDMOTHER: Oh, that's Gertrude Mawsbaum, we grew up together. She just passed on. This picture was taken three weeks before she died.

Epilogue

Wallace is standing to the left with a tomato in his hand and a crate of tomatoes at his feet. Nina is standing to the right, wearing a white dress. Pause.

NINA: Well?

WALLACE *(pause)*:   I don't want to ruin your dress. *(Pause.)* I don't want to ruin your beautiful dress. *(Pause. The lights slowly fade.)*

HAIKU

KATHERINE SNODGRASS

HAIKU was produced in workshop under the auspices of The Philadelphia Theatre Company's new play project STAGES (Lynn M. Thomson, Program Director, Artistic Associate) on the TUCC Stage III, Temple University City Center, 1619 Walnut Street, Philadelphia, Pennsylvania, on April 26, 28, and 29, 1989, with the following cast and crew:

NELL	Karen Higgins-Hurley
BILLIE	Maryann Plunkett
LOUISE	Alla Nedoresow
Director	Christopher Ashley
Set Designer	Dan Boyles
Lighting Designer	James Leitner
Music	John Gromoda
Stage Manager	Claudia Park

Notes on Production

The draft that follows is the one closest to my original conception of the play. In acting it, character intentions should always come before any considerations of poetry.

It is my feeling that the play is weakest when the production tries to "answer" the questions that the script raises. The last moment in the play is meant to be ambiguous.

Kate Snodgrass

Characters

NELL, fifties, mother of Louise and Billie
LOUISE, twenties–thirties, Nell's youngest daughter
BILLIE, twenties–thirties, Nell's eldest daughter

Time

Present

Setting

A living room

Note

The set is suggestive rather than realistic. The flashback sequences may be signaled by light changes or sounds or both. A bamboo flute or porcelain wind chime may be substituted for the autoharp and/or used to signal the flashbacks, but the sound should remain delicate, almost eerie.

■   ■

At rise: The stage is black. We hear an autoharp. It goes from the top of the scale to the bottom. As lights come up, Nell has an obvious bruise on her wrist, a pad of paper and black magic marker in her lap, and a magnifying glass on a chain around her neck. Louise has a bandage on her forehead and is wearing a football helmet. The lighting suggests a mystery.

NELL: You were born in early winter. John and I planned it that way. I couldn't imagine having a baby in the summertime. It gets so sticky in August, humid. A breach baby. You tried to back into the world. I remember, the doctor had to pull you out. It was night when they finally brought you to me.

LOUISE: November evening.
                   Blackbirds scull across the moon.
                   My breath warms my hands.

NELL (*writes haiku, then checks it with the magnifying glass*):   John said you were too beautiful to live. It was true. You and Bebe together, you were like china dolls. Delicate, perfect. And then . . . that day I saw you through the window. Billie was on the swing set, and you were there. Outside. She was in red, and you had on that blue jumpsuit, the corduroy one with the zipper. The ball lay beside you. And that momma doll that winked. You were so quiet. You'd stared before, of course, when something fascinated you, as all children do when they . . . as all children do. But this time, you were . . . different. I called for you to come inside. *Lulu, come inside and have some lunch!* But you didn't hear me. *Bebe, bring Lulu and come inside!* I went out then. I had to get down on my knees beside you. I touched your hair and then your face. I held up that momma doll, but you stared through it in a way that . . . Funny, I don't remember being afraid. I remember the look on your sister's face.

LOUISE: Cold, chain-metal swings
                   Clang in the empty school yard.
                   Silent summer rain.

NELL (*writes haiku, same process as before*):   Do you know, I used to cry when school ended? It's true! I used to cry on the last day of school every year. My mother thought I was crazy. I'd come dragging my book bag over the fields, my face all wet. And my momma!

LOUISE: And my momma!

NELL: Nellie, she'd say . . .

LOUISE: Nellie, she'd say . . . you're the strangest girl I ever did see!

NELL: Yes, that's . . . What did you say?

LOUISE: That you're the strangest girl?

NELL: No, no. Before that. Are you tired?

LOUISE: Before that?

NELL: You are tired, and Billie's late.

LOUISE: Tell me again about John. Please. You haven't talked about John in a long time.

NELL: John. All right then. John was tall and thin like Icabod Crane, only not so scared.

LOUISE: John wasn't scared of anything.

NELL: He wasn't scared of anything, not John. He had a big, strong jaw and a tuft of yellow hair that stood up on his head, as yellow . . .

LOUISE: . . . as Mr. Turner's daffodils.

NELL: At least. And he would take you on his knee. Do you remember the song he used to sing? (*Nell clears her throat and sings.*) *Here come a Lulu! Here come a Lulu to the Indian dance.* (*Louise joins in.*) *All of them Indians, all of them Indians dance around Lulu's tent.* (*Like a drum.*) *Here* come a Lulu! *Here* come Lulu! *Here* come a Lulu! (*They laugh, remembering.*)

LOUISE: Icy branches bend
And break over stones. I hear
My dead father . . . laugh.

(*Nell writes haiku, same process as before.*)

LOUISE: Wasn't there a story about a fox? Who had a bushy tail?

NELL: You remember that?

LOUISE: And John would rub Bebe's back until she went to sleep. He smelled of soap and something . . . sweet?

NELL (*dryly*): Sweet! Cigars from Havana.

LOUISE (*repeating with Nell's exact inflection*): Cigars from Havana.

NELL: We'll stop now. (*During this next exchange, Nell fishes in her pocket for a bottle of pills and takes a pill out.*)

LOUISE: No! No, I want to do more.

NELL: Louise—

LOUISE: I'm not ready to go back. Please, not now.

NELL: But Billie's not here yet. We've got to be careful.

LOUISE: But I can do it! I promise. Please, Momma, I hate to go back. It's like being smothered!

NELL: I know.

LOUISE: Everything is so dim, and I can't hear you properly. Or see you or touch you or . . . *(Seeing the bruise on Nell's wrist—)* Did I do that?

NELL: It's not bad.

LOUISE: That was before I knew what to do. Please. I can stop it now, I know I can. You said so yourself.

NELL: I know what I said.

LOUISE: If you don't let me try, I'll never learn what to do.

NELL: We can talk to Bebe tomorrow. Today, it would be better—

LOUISE: Today, it would be better—if I saw Bebe first. Then I can stand it.

(During this next exchange Nell tries to give Louise a pill. Louise refuses. Nell removes the helmet.)

NELL: No. Not today!

LOUISE: Not today!

NELL: You're too tired.

LOUISE: I can control it.

NELL: Louise. I don't want to wait too long. You'll hurt yourself.

LOUISE: You'll hurt yourself. I mean, no! I won't. You promised I could talk to Bebe. You said I *had* to talk to her.

NELL: Yes, yes, we will. Tomorrow. *(Nell holds out pill.)* I want you to take this now.

LOUISE *(stubborn)*: You promised I could wait for Bebe.

NELL: I want you to—

LOUISE: I need some water. *(Nell is silent.)* I do! I can't swallow.

NELL: Louise.

LOUISE: I can't swallow. My throat is dry.

NELL *(sighing)*: Yes, all right, just a minute. *(Nell exits.)*

LOUISE: Just a minute. Just a minute.

(A loud door slam startles Louise. Abruptly, lights come full up as Billie enters with a suitcase and packages. There is a moment of recognition between Louise and Billie. Louise might say Billie's name, but Nell enters with a glass of water. There is an awkwardness in this next exchange. Nell greets Billie and moves to Louise with the pill.)

BILLIE: Nell, how are you? You look exhausted. I thought I'd never make it. The traffic at the airport is worse than ever.

NELL: You're here.

BILLIE: Yes, I'm here.

NELL: You're late.

BILLIE: I'm sorry. Are you all right? You sounded strange on the telephone.

NELL: I? Yes. *(Pause. Louise refuses to take the pill.)*

BILLIE *(half-kidding)*:   Shall I leave again and come back?

NELL: No. No, of course not. We don't mind at all, do we, Lulu? *(Holding up pill, asking.)* Can you *tell* Bebe how we don't mind?

LOUISE *(to Billie)*:   We don't mind.

NELL *(putting pill away)*:   Michael's not with you?

BILLIE: No. No, he's not coming. *(Then quickly to . . .)* Look what I came across in a little shop in Boston. They had both of your books, is that unbelievable? And get this, they actually had them in the poetry section. I get so tired of searching through the books on Japanese culture. Do you need them, or can I keep them? You know, I really love the cover on this last one.

NELL: Oh, Billie, I wish you'd waited. I was going to send you a copy, but . . .

BILLIE: They're finally getting the hang of it at that place. Black and white photography is much closer to what you wanted all along, isn't it?

NELL: I've been so busy. I don't know how I could have forgotten to send you . . .

BILLIE: Of course, I had to see that lovely dedication. I'm such a push-over. It always gives me a little thrill to see my name in print even if it *is* after the fact.

NELL: Let me go upstairs and—

BILLIE: I was just so surprised to run across them, and I was really impressed with this new cover. Where did they find the photographer?

NELL: I'll give you your copy now.

BILLIE: No, mother, mother, really! This one's fine. Well, it's not as if I can't afford it. At least it's not one of those dry biographies you used to write, the lives of the saints or some such thing? Somehow with you I always feel like a groupie at the stage door. "Please, ma'am, it's a first edition and would you sign it, please?"

NELL: I've already signed your copy. But if you want me to sign this, too . . . Why don't I do it later, all right? Let me do it later when Lulu's asleep. That way, we—

BILLIE: Fine, sure. Later is fine, whatever. Oh, I brought something for Lulu, too. *(Billie brings out package from her large bag and holds it out to Nell. It is wrapped in very shiny wrapping paper with a bright ribbon.)*

NELL: You did? Why, that was thoughtful. What is it?

LOUISE: What is it?

BILLIE: Open it. Oh hell, it's another music box.

LOUISE: Oh hell.

NELL: It's wrapped so prettily, why don't you let Lulu open it?

BILLIE: Do we have time before Easter?

NELL: Billie.

BILLIE: I'm sorry. Really. But she won't care what's inside. She just likes the wrapping paper.

NELL: That's not true. Lulu loves music.

LOUISE: Lulu loves music.

BILLIE: Lulu loves wrapping paper.

NELL (*to Billie*):   Go on. You give it to her.

(Flashback sequence begins. They are children. Dolls are mimed.)

BILLIE: I have to give this to you. This is the baby doll, and this is the momma doll. Now you take the baby doll and rock her to sleep, like this. (*Singing.*) *Rock-a-bye baby in the treetop. When the wind blows* . . . That's right. You be the babysitter. And now the momma comes to play with the baby. Hello, baby.

LOUISE: Hello, baby.

BILLIE: My, you are sleeping so soundly I don't want to wake you up. How did my baby do today, Mrs. Lippoman? Was she a good baby?

LOUISE: Was she a good baby?

BILLIE: Let me see her. Isn't she the most beautiful baby in the whole—No, give it back. No you can't have the momma doll. You have the baby doll.

LOUISE: You have the baby doll.

BILLIE: No, let go.

LOUISE: No.

BILLIE: Give it back, you can't have both of them.

LOUISE: Both of them.

BILLIE (*new tactic*):   All right then, give me the baby doll.

LOUISE: Give me the baby doll.

BILLIE: Give it to me. It's my momma doll, and it's my baby doll. Let go, let go . . . !

LOUISE: Let go, let go! (*Baby doll breaks.*)

BILLIE: You broke it! That was my baby doll. It was mine, and I'm going to tell on you, you . . .

LOUISE: You . . .

BILLIE: I didn't want to play with you anyway. You're stupid, stupid!

LOUISE: Stupid!

BILLIE: I'm going to tell, and then I'll *never* have to play with you again. Not ever! (*Billie shoves Louise's forehead with the palm of her hand.*)

LOUISE: Not ever! *(Louise begins hitting herself in the forehead.)*
BILLIE: Stop hurting yourself!

(Flashback sequence ends.)

BILLIE: Is she hurting herself again? What's that bandage for?
NELL: No, no, of course not. We just had a little accident.
BILLIE: Isn't the medicine working?
NELL: Of course, yes.
BILLIE: Let's look at it.
NELL: No, it's perfectly fine now. Almost healed.
BILLIE: Did you get that bruise at the same time?
NELL: Oh, this? It's nothing. I don't even remember where I got it.
LOUISE *(holds up her hands for a hug)*:   Bebe.
BILLIE: Good lord. *(Louise and Billie hug.)*
NELL: That's new, isn't it?
BILLIE: What?
NELL: She's different than when you saw her last, isn't she?
BILLIE: Because she hugged me? We all know how much that means.
NELL: Billie, what will we do with you?
BILLIE: Well, they're supposed to get more affectionate as they get older. I might as well be a rag doll that she's fond of. But if that's what you mean, that she's more responsive, then yes, we can thank whatever gods there be that she's not gone the other way. At least the medicine is doing that for her.
NELL: The medicine.
BILLIE: Yes.
NELL: But don't you think she's getting better, though? Honestly, isn't she more alert?
BILLIE: Alert.
NELL: She knew you, Billie. She wanted to touch you.
BILLIE: Of course she knows me. I'm her sister. She's wanted to get her hands around my neck for years.
LOUISE: For years.
BILLIE *(laughing)*:   There, you see? All right, all right, let's try this. *(She takes wrapped present and holds it out to Louise.)* Ah, it's a lovely bow, isn't it? And look at that shiny wrapping paper. You love that, don't you? Look at her. I tell you, Nell, I wasted my money on the music box. This wrapping paper's going to be enough.
NELL: Let's just take this bow off. Here.
BILLIE: No fair, no fair helping.
NELL: Now this paper comes off.

(Louise tears the paper off the music box. She opens the box as it tinkles out a song. She is enthralled.)

NELL: There, now. There. Why, that's beautiful, isn't it, Lulu? That's beautiful. See, see how she loves the music?

BILLIE: Yes.

NELL: Look, look at her. And she unwrapped it herself.

BILLIE: Mother.

NELL: She knew exactly—

BILLIE: No.

NELL: —what to do. Don't you see a difference in her?

BILLIE *(During this speech, Billie takes the box, handing the shiny paper back to Louise)*:   You never change, do you? No, I don't see any difference. She's not more alert, and she's not getting any better. All right. All right, maybe she's a little more affectionate. Maybe. But that's natural. Most of them become more affectionate. They learn to feed themselves and to go to the bathroom and to hug their sisters when they come home to visit.

NELL *(taking shiny paper from Louise)*:   You don't understand. You can't possibly know, you don't see her every day.

BILLIE: Yes, and you do, and you take every gaze out the window and rationalize it into some sort of normal reaction.

NELL: I don't rationalize. I don't need to. I see real change for the better!

BILLIE: Better, momma?

(Second flashback sequence. Again, they are children.)

BILLIE: Better bring her inside, momma. She's staring at the sun again. Maa-maa! *(There is no answer, so Billie uses a shiny necklace or a prism from around her own neck and holds it up for Louise, who is captivated with the shine. Singing.)* Twinkle, twinkle, little star, how I wonder who you are. Oooo, pretty twinkle, pretty twinkle. Maa-maa! *(She sings a song to the tune of "Frère Jacques." Louise hums some notes.)*

> Where is Lulu? Where is Lulu?
> Here I am, here I am.
> How are you this morning?
> Very well, I thank you

(Billie pulls Louise to her feet.)

> Please stand up. Please sit down.

(Billie pulls Louise back down.)

> Where is Booboo? Where is Booboo?

(Pointedly.)

Here you are, here you are.
How are you this morning?
Very well, I thank you.

(Billie pulls Louise to her feet.)

Please stand up. Please sit down.

(Billie pulls Louise back down. She begins to substitute different sounds for Louise's name. Louise imitates, repeating only the last sounds.)

Where is Poopoo? Where is—
LOUISE: —Poopoo. *(Pause.)*
BILLIE: *Where is . . . Bongbong?*
LOUISE: Bongbong.

(Billie gives up on the song and does the sounds rhythmically and playfully as Louise follows, repeating each set of sounds. Billie begins enjoying Louise, who mirrors even facial expressions. {Different sounds may be repeated or substituted as the actors play.})

BILLIE *(and Louise after, grunting)*:   Ugghh-Ugghhh. *(Tongue out.)*
Blah-blah. Eeeek-eeek. *(Like a villain.)* Heh-heh-heh. *(Rolling the tongue.)* Thrrrrrthrrrr. *(Like a pig.)* Snort-snort. Snort-snort. Snort-snort. *(As the sounds become funny to her, Billie laughs. Louise laughs. Billie laughs again. Louise imitates. When she realizes that Louise is not playing with her but only repeating, Billie holds up the chain/prism again.)*

BILLIE: Pretty twinkle, pretty twinkle. I wish . . . *(End of flashback sequence.)* I wish I could understand you, Momma.
NELL: I know you've never been able to understand. You were too young, I suppose. It was asking too much of you.
BILLIE: Was it? Strange. I don't remember being asked. Is that why you don't dedicate your books to Lulu?
NELL: What?
BILLIE: Yes, is that your way of asking me to understand now?
NELL: No, Bebe, I never—
BILLIE: Why not to Lulu? Because she can't *ever* understand?
NELL: No, that's not it at all. We've been wanting to talk to you. That's why I telephoned.
BILLIE: Because of the dedication?
NELL: Yes, and . . . and—
BILLIE: I thought it was because of your eyes.
NELL: Well, yes. That too.
BILLIE: How much can you see, anyway?

NELL: I can make out your shape, but it's getting worse.

LOUISE: It's getting worse. *(Silence.)*

BILLIE: All right, then. Will Daddy's trust fund cover a nurse for Lulu?

NELL: Even if it would, I don't want some stranger in the house caring for Lulu. I'll do it myself.

BILLIE: Yourself? Mother, how?

NELL: I'll manage. I've done it up until now.

BILLIE: But what if she dirties her clothes? What if she has a reaction? What if you were to fall? Lulu couldn't help you. She wouldn't know what to do. Why, she wouldn't even understand that anything was wrong.

NELL: I do not have to have help.

BILLIE: Then why did you ask me—?

NELL: I've managed this long, and besides . . .

BILLIE: Yes?

NELL: Lulu understands more than you know.

LOUISE: More than you know.

BILLIE: Lulu understands what *you want* her to understand. Momma, you can't go on ignoring Lulu's illness.

NELL: I'm not ignoring—

BILLIE: Mother, listen to me. Put her in a hospital where she can be taken care of properly. No, wait, I can help you. Please. Michael and I have talked it over, and . . . Really. I'd be happy if you'd come live with us. I thought that's what you wanted. You can visit Lulu every day if you want to. You can sit with her. Please. It's not as if she's going to know where she is.

NELL: Of course she knows where she is! What are you talking about? You haven't heard what I've been trying to say.

BILLIE: What haven't I heard?

NELL: That she's different. She's changed.

BILLIE: Changed how? And if you say she's more affectionate—

NELL: It's not just that. It's more. Much more. I haven't told you before this because I knew you wouldn't believe me. But you don't live with her, Billie, you don't see. You asked why I dedicate the haiku to you and never to Louise. It's because . . . I don't write the haiku.

BILLIE: What?

NELL: It's Louise.

LOUISE: It's Louise. *(Silence.)*

BILLIE: No.

NELL: It's true.

BILLIE: That's impossible.

NELL: No, I swear it.

LOUISE: I swear it.

BILLIE: Momma.

NELL: It started three years ago after we changed to that new medication.

BILLIE: What started?

NELL: I was reading a book. Very absorbed. Lulu was sitting, as she always does, next to the window. Suddenly, I realized that I had forgotten to give her the afternoon pill. I glanced up, and she was sitting forward in her chair, leaning on the sill. *(Louise does this as Nell speaks.)* It was odd. I knew she wouldn't notice me, but I said her name, *Lulu?* And she turned to me and looked at me, *really looked at me,* for the first time. She asked me to forgive her. Hah! As if there was anything to forgive. She was so frightened, so frightened. Bebe, it's as if she's trapped, trapped in a maze, and everything's all white, like cotton, or clouds, and . . . and she can't get out. Everything moves so slowly. And when she trys, sounds come in to distract her. They pull her away, and she can't concentrate. She can't be herself. But she was there. She is. *Louise* is there.

LOUISE: Can't concentrate.

BILLIE: You mean she's . . . normal . . . without the medication, or—?

NELL: No, it's not that. She still—Well, she can't go on without the medicine. I have to give her the medicine. She needs it.

BILLIE: Then what—?

NELL: Because it was late! The medicine has to be late. I don't understand it. I don't pretend to.

BILLIE: Wait. Are you saying that now you deliberately hold back her medicine?

NELL: Yes, yes! She can't get out without my help!

BILLIE: Dear God.

NELL: I used to think I was making it up.

BILLIE: I can imagine.

NELL: But I'm not. I'm not. The haiku is real. Louise is real.

BILLIE: Why didn't you tell me this before?

NELL: I didn't dare believe it myself. Then when we started working, we decided it was better if no one knew for the time being.

BILLIE: Why?

NELL: It was so fragile, don't you see? So delicate. It doesn't happen all the time. Sometimes when her medicine is late. But even then, not every day. And she only stays for a little before we have to take the medicine.

BILLIE: I see. And she speaks . . . in poetry.

NELL: No, no. We were at the window. It was October and just about dusk. Mr. Turner was burning leaves in his incinerator out back. I said, "Look how beautiful the colors are. Late autumn." And she said, "Late autumn evening/Swallows circle overhead/Wood smoke curling up." By concentrating on what we could see through the window, we'd make a haiku together. After that, she began making them up on her own. I simply sit and talk, and . . . Billie, it's as if she sees my thoughts, my innermost feelings, and translates them into images.

BILLIE: Almost as if she were you.

NELL: Yes.

BILLIE: What do you talk about?

NELL: Nothing important. Memories. The past. But she'll take the most ordinary event and make it so personal somehow.

BILLIE: Yes. How long do you talk?

NELL: Not long.

BILLIE: *How* long?

NELL: Half an hour at the most. But she's trying very hard. She wants to practice. She wants to be . . .

BILLIE: You want her to be normal.

NELL: No. More than that. Extraordinary. And she is.

BILLIE: Mother, if this is true . . . I mean, *when* this happens . . . Why haven't you told the doctors?

NELL: No doctors and no more hospitals. They brought on this problem in the first place. If I hadn't rushed her to the doctors so quickly, maybe she would have come out of it. No! We don't know! If they didn't have her taking all these drugs . . . Nobody knows what might have happened!

LOUISE: Nobody knows.

BILLIE: All right, if you mean that, then take her off the drugs entirely.

NELL: We can't do that.

BILLIE: Why not?

NELL: She hurts herself. She could—!

BILLIE: Momma, if that's what you believe, take her off the drugs. We could put her in the hospital and have the drug levels monitored.

NELL: No. I told you no hospitals.

BILLIE: But they could even wean her off the drugs slowly, and then we could—

NELL: No!

BILLIE: *Why not?*

LOUISE: *Why not?*

NELL: She needs the drugs. She's not herself yet. She needs them to . . . to protect her until . . . It's a question of will power.

BILLIE: Whose, yours?

NELL: I knew you wouldn't understand. I warned her, but no! She said she wanted to let you in. She said we *had* to tell you.

BILLIE: *She* said that?

NELL: She loves you, Bebe. The way she hugged you today was only a tiny indication of that.

BILLIE: Why did you ask me here?

NELL: I can barely see to write the words anymore. Don't you understand?

BILLIE: I'm sorry.

NELL: I need your help, Bebe. We need you.

(Flashback sequence. Billie is teaching Louise about makeup. The lipstick, mirror, etc., is mimed. Billie pushes hair back from Louise's forehead).

BILLIE *(to Louise)*:   You need to keep your hair out of your face. Okay, now, you take the lipstick and you put it on like . . . that. See? Okay. Pucker up. *(Billie puckers, and Louise imitates her as Billie applies lipstick to Louise's mouth, then to her own.)* Mmmm, luscious pink!

LOUISE: Mmmm.

BILLIE: Now then, you take this pencil. And *don't* put it in your eye!

LOUISE: *Don't* put it in your eye!

BILLIE *(to mirror)*:   You draw around the eye . . . underneath . . . above . . . but not too much. There. See?

LOUISE: *Don't* put it in your eye!

BILLIE: Right. And now for the shadow. What color shall we use? Let's use turquoise or . . . What about this purple? Yeah, let's use the purple!

LOUISE: Yeah, let's use the purple!

(Billie puts it on for the mirror while Louise picks up the turquoise and draws big circles over her neck, her face, her cheeks, and forehead.)

BILLIE: And we put it above the crease of the eye, not just on the lid. Then we take this black pencil and we draw it out, just like Elizabeth Taylor did in *Cleopatra*. Now, then, what's next?

LOUISE: Now, then, what's next? *(Billie looks at Louise and reacts as Nell enters.)*

BILLIE: Oh . . . !

NELL: Billie, how could you!

LOUISE: How could you!

NELL *(begins wiping off the makeup)*:   I thought you knew better than this. What were you thinking of? Oh, Lulu, such a mess.

LOUISE: Mess!

NELL: Her face is as red as a fire engine. And this turquoise! It'll take days for these colors to wear off. Why on earth . . . ?

(Louise begins slapping her legs.)

NELL: Now you've done it! Here, hold her hands. This is not the first time this has happened, but by God it will be the last. For the final time, do not take it upon yourself to teach her. You leave that to me, or you can leave this house! Do you understand? *(Billie lets go of Louise's hands.)* Oh, now I've got it all over me. Lulu, *be still! (Surprisingly, Louise is still.)* Bebe. *(End of flashback sequence.)*

NELL: Bebe.

BILLIE: What do you want me to do?

NELL: I want for you, I *need* for you to listen to her and believe in her so that she can be who she is. If we believe, she can get well. We can help her, I know it. Let us show you. Louise? Louise, Billie's here.

BILLIE: She's not listening.

NELL: Billie's here, and you wanted to talk to her. Remember? *(Louise looks at Billie.)* You see? There. Now, Bebe, say something to her. Go on.

BILLIE: Mother, don't make me do this.

NELL: Lulu. It's Billie.

LOUISE: Bebe.

BILLIE: Lulu.

NELL: Ask her something.

BILLIE: Mother.

NELL: Ask her.

BILLIE: All right. Lulu. Is it really you?

LOUISE: Is it really you?

BILLIE: Yes, it's really me. Is it true?

LOUISE: True?

BILLIE *(looks back at Nell for encouragement; Nell is insistent)*:   It's been a long time since I've seen you, Lulu. It's been months and months, I think. How . . . how are you?

LOUISE: How are you?

BILLIE: I've been fine, but how are *you? (Pause.)*

LOUISE: I've been fine.

BILLIE: She's just repeating, Mother.

NELL: She's tired. We were writing just before you got here. It's hard, but she can do it. Concentrate, Lulu. This is important. It's Billie. *(To Billie.)* Ask her about the poems.

BILLIE: Yes, I've read the poems. They're lovely.

LOUISE: We were writing just before you got here.

NELL: You see?

BILLIE: Momma told me. I want so much to believe it's true.

LOUISE: Believe it's true.

BILLIE: No, no, say something else. Say anything else. Make up a poem. Can you do that for me? Make up a poem. Please do that.

LOUISE: Make up a poem?

BILLIE: Yes, yes, please.

NELL: Look out the window. Describe it to her.

BILLIE *(to Louise):* Look, look out there. Winter's nearly over. Mr. Turner's daffodils are in bloom. And the hydrangea bushes we planted that year daddy died. Remember? They're big now. Why, they cover the whole side of the porch. Momma's already put out that old bird feed—I can't do this.

NELL: Keep going, she's listening.

BILLIE: She's not. You are, momma.

NELL: Please.

BILLIE: Well then . . . *(To the window.)* It's almost sunset. The sky is . . . red.

NELL: Yes. Red sky at dusk.

LOUISE: Red sky at dusk.

BILLIE: One gray cloud . . . . lies just . . . over the trees. . . .

LOUISE: Over the trees . . . one gray cloud lies—

BILLIE: She's mimicking me.

LOUISE: —in my sister . . .

BILLIE *(comforting):* That's right, I am your sister, aren't I?

LOUISE *(grabbing Billie's hand):* —in my sister's . . . sister's—

NELL: In my—

LOUISE *(gesturing):* —sister's—

NELL *(prompting):* —sister's . . .

BILLIE: Mother.

NELL *(understanding):* . . . eyes!

LOUISE: —eyes!

NELL: There. *((Nell claps.)* Bravo, Lulu! Good girl!

BILLIE: Stop it!

NELL: What.

BILLIE: She's repeating.

NELL: No.

LOUISE: No.

BILLIE: She's repeating what I say and what you say.

NELL: No, no! Louise, help me now.

BILLIE: Don't put us through this.

NELL: Louise?

BILLIE: I can't bear it.

LOUISE: I can't bear it.

NELL: Try a little harder, baby.

BILLIE: Mother, listen to me!

NELL: Concentrate now.

BILLIE: Please, don't!

LOUISE: Listen to me!

BILLIE: Mother, you have got to—

NELL: Louise, look at me and—

BILLIE: *Mother, stop!*

(Louise is startled by the shout and begins screaming and banging her head. Both Nell and Billie shout over the screaming. Billie gets the football helmet but can't get it onto Louise.)

NELL: The helmet. Lulu, Lulu, there.

BILLIE: Where is her medicine?

NELL: Oh, my hand! Hold her arms!

(Instead, Billie gets the music box and opens it for Louise to see. Louise immediately calms and focuses on the music. Nell gives Louise the pill and some water. Billie and Nell recover.)

BILLIE: Will she be all right now?

NELL: Yes. If we can keep her quiet, the pill should take hold. We startled her.

BILLIE: How can you do this?

NELL: I hate to see her leave. I know what you're going to say. But every word I've told you is true. You didn't want to believe.

BILLIE: That's not true. I want to believe. Just don't ask me to see something that isn't there.

NELL: Then let us prove it to you. We'll try again tomorrow.

BILLIE: No, no. I don't want to try anymore. I've tried before. I can't keep trying and have it not be true.

NELL: It doesn't always happen, so I'm not promising anything.

BILLIE: No.

NELL: Bebe.

BILLIE: No, it hurts too much. You talk to her as if . . .

NELL: . . . as if she's real. As if she's there. And she is.

BILLIE: Yes. Yes.

NELL: She is. Let me try tomor—

BILLIE: No.

NELL: I'm not asking you to believe it.

BILLIE: Aren't you?

NELL: I'm only asking you to let me try. Wait and see.

BILLIE: Wait and see.

NELL: You'll do that, won't you? Just that? For me?

(Silence. Louise has closed the music box. Lights slowly begin fading back to the setting with which we began the play.)

BILLIE: For you? Yes.

NELL: You'll wait.

BILLIE: I think I can do that.

NELL: That's my Bebe. You can stay as long as you like, you know. As long as you need to. *(Silence.)*

BILLIE: It's spring.

NELL: Yes. Finally. Did I ever tell you—when I was a girl, we had a cherry tree in the backyard. It was just big enough for me to sit in. The thickest branch was my backrest. It was curved, like a hammock, and I could lean back into that tree and rest my legs on either side of the trunk. In the spring and summer, I took books out there and devoured them along with the cherries. The Brontës, Alexander Dumas. Jane Austen and I were surrounded by flowers. The perfume.

BILLIE: I was never very literary. I can't even make a good rhyme.

NELL: You're your father all over again.

BILLIE: He wasn't scared of anything, not John. But I am, momma.

NELL: No, John wasn't scared of anything.

BILLIE: I wish daddy could be here to . . . see his garden. *(Silence. Billie and Nell are together. They do not attend Louise, who is alone at the window, separate.)*

LOUISE: Walking in his garden,
                         Suddenly in the twilight—
                         White hydrangea.

(Fade to blackout).

FINAL PLACEMENT

ARA WATSON

To Mary Harden

FINAL PLACEMENT was commissioned and first produced by the Actors Theatre of Louisville in December 1980. It was directed by Amy Saltz. The sets were by Paul Owen; costumes by Kurt Wilhelm; lighting by Jeff Hill; sound design by John North. The cast was as follows:

MARY HANSON	Laura Hicks
LUELLEN JAMES	Kathy Bates

■ ■

Set: A large office containing a metal desk with a swivel chair behind it and a straight-backed chair beside it. The desk, as well as the straight chair, is piled with manuals, papers, books, etc. Prominent on the desk is a dictaphone. On top of the things on the chair are several individual boxes of baby clothes. There is a second straight chair with a few things on it including a thermos bottle.

At rise: The lights are brought up to a less than full level. There is a spotlight on the dictaphone. As the spot fades to full, the following dictation fades in:

MARY'S VOICE: . . . the worker will continue regular visits with this child. End of dictation. Next one. New case, so no CW number yet. Last name: James. First name: Jimmy. Age: four years. Date: October ten, eighty-one. On this date this office was contacted by Dr. Timothy Bowman of the Northside Medical Clinic concerning four-year-old Jimmy James. Dr. Bowman reported that he has treated Jimmy twice in the last six weeks—once for a cut over the eye and once for a broken wrist. The parents attributed both injuries to accidents. On each of the visits, Dr. Bowman noted the child had a number of bruises on his body which the mother explained resulted from Jimmy's—quote—"always falling down"—end quote. On the second of these visits with Jimmy, Dr. Bowman also noted burn marks on the child's buttocks which he believed were caused by a cigarette. He determined, at this point—(*The sound and spot begin to fade out and the lights begin to fade up to a full level.*)—to contact this office and request an investigation of the situation by the Department—(*Sound out—lights full.*)

MARY (*entering, overlapping the fading dictation—she calls over her shoulder as she hurries to her desk*):   No, you guys go on. I'll join you as soon as I see who—(*She picks up the phone and pushes a button.*) Mary Hanson. Hello.—Yes, Miz Price. How are you today?—Well, that seems to be the general consensus around here, too. I think it's the heat.—Nope, I haven't forgotten. I should be there about four.—O.K. Sure. Similac or Enfamil?—No, I won't forget.—I'll see you then. Bye. (*She hangs up and starts quickly away from her desk before she realizes she has left her billfold on the desk. She goes back and gets it, starts out again, but the phone buzzes, catching her. She answers.*) Yes?—Line two?—Thanks. (*Pushes button—brightly.*) Hi.—No, I was just about to sneak out with everybody else for a coffee break, is all.—Oh, you're a much better high than caffeine anytime. We're not all supposed to abandon our posts at the same time anyway . . . (*Smiles.*) . . . so I'll wait five minutes. Don't want to break any of those "state regulations." So. How's your day off been?—(*Mocking.*) Oh-h-h, you have to sit out by your big ol' pool all by yourself? Poor baby.—(*A laugh—then:*) So-so. (*She retrieves a carton of Similac from the floor behind her desk and sets it on the desk.*) Your usual quota of impregnated teenagers, paranoid foster parents, etc.—No. I just want you to feel sorry for me. (*Laughs—then:*) So, what's up for tonight? (*A laugh.*) Very funny. But please to remember this is a business phone.—Well. You have that shopping list for me?—(*Searching in the mess on her desk for a pencil.*) Jack and Laura coming?—Of course, I've got a pencil . . . (*Looking.*) . . . somewhere . . . (*A movement outside the door catches her eye, puzzles her, but she continues.*) No. I don't have one behind my ear, smarty. (*She checks anyway.*) I'm not that—(*The movement outside the door again and it stops her.*) Honey? Could you hold on just a sec?—Thanks. (*She puts the phone down and moves to the door. Just before she gets there, Luellen suddenly steps in. Mary, startled:*) What are—? (*A moment's hesitation.*) Hello. You . . . you startled me.

LUELLEN: There wasn't no one at the front desk.

MARY (*an almost indiscernible fear*):   Oh? Well, she . . . she must have stepped away a minute.

LUELLEN: I heard your voice, so I followed it, but I didn't want to disturb you while you was on the telephone.

MARY *(remembering)*:   Oh. Oh, yes . . . I . . . I need to just finish up with that and . . . Did you want to talk to me or . . . ? *(Luellen "kind of" nods.)* Well, let me . . .

LUELLEN: Oh, yeah. You go right on ahead. *(She stands there.)*

MARY: Would you like to have a chair out in the waiting room? I shouldn't be too long.

LUELLEN: No.

MARY: It's a private call.

LUELLEN: Oh. I'll . . . I'll stand out here in the hall till you're done.

MARY: It might take me a few minutes. . . .

LUELLEN: I'll . . . just stand out here.

MARY: All right. *(Luellen smiles and exits with Mary watching her. Mary then hurriedly returns to the phone.)* Hi. Sorry. Someone just . . . *(Her voice trails off as she stares toward the door preoccupied.)* What?—Oh. No. Just an old client.—No, no, it's all right. *(Searching again she finds a pencil—brighter.)* Go ahead and give me the list. *(Sits.)* I'll go by the liquor store, too, so . . . *(The lights begin to fade down and the sound of the dictation fades up under Mary.)* —I know. You're very lucky to have me.

MARY'S VOICE: . . . CW number is 240973. Last name: James. First name: Jimmy. Age: four. Date: October 14, '81. Following the report made by Dr. Bowman, the worker made a visit to the James apartment at 1804 N. Main. No response. New date. October 15. Worker again visited the James apartment and was met at the door by Ms. James who refused to let the worker in, stating that Mr. James was out looking for work and that he didn't want her to let anyone in when he wasn't there. The worker explained the reason for the visit and Ms. James became very upset, saying people were telling lies about her. Through the open door, the worker observed a sparsely furnished room with clothing, papers, and empty food containers strewn—that's S-T-R-E-W-N—about. There was also a strong odor of urine coming from—scratch that—a strong odor of urine *emitting* from the apartment. The worker informed Ms. James she would be returning the following morning and requested that Ms. James and her husband, as well as their son Jimmy, be present for this interview. As the worker was leaving the building, she was stopped by a neighbor of the James who stated she often— *(The sound begins to fade down, the lights up.)* —heard Jimmy crying loudly and said she and her . . . *(Out.)*

MARY *(overlapping)*:   A quart?—O.K. That it?—All right. I should get to your place about 5:30.—Well, because I'm gonna take off a little early, that's why.—Honey, I wish I could talk but— Right.—Me, too. See you later—Bye. *(She hangs up, looks toward the door a brief moment, collects herself, then moves a few steps toward the door as she calls—)* Ms. James? Luellen, you can— *(Luellen shyly enters.)* Hi. Hope I didn't keep you waiting too long.

LUELLEN: Boy, sure is quiet up here.

MARY: Yes. Yes, I guess it is.

LUELLEN: Where is ever'body anyway?

MARY *(tenses slightly)*: Oh-h—

LUELLEN: Looks like you're the only one in the whole place.

MARY *(quickly—lying)*: No. Everybody's here. They're all . . . just busy . . . keeping their heads down. But . . . they're all here.

LUELLEN: You got the air-conditionin' on? Nice and cool in here.

MARY *(slightly nervous but friendly)*: I know. Can you believe this? Air-conditioning at the end of September. I swear that when I was a little girl, September was a fall month. *(There is a slight awkward pause.)* Ninety-seven degrees they said today. The end of September and it's ninety-seven degrees. Ridiculous.

LUELLEN: I just got a big ol' fan at home. Keeps it cool, though. Keeps it pretty cool . . . 'cept it blows ever'thing around.

MARY: Maybe that's what I need in here. *(Indicating various piles of things.)* Help me get rid of some of this stuff. *(They smile at each other in a common understanding and some of the tension is eased.)* I like your hair like that.

LUELLEN: Needs cuttin'.

MARY: No, I like it longer. Makes you look . . . It's nice. *(Slight pause.)* How is—

LUELLEN: Do you reckon I could set down for a minute?

MARY: Of course. Here. Let me . . . *(And she removes the boxes of baby clothes from the chair to the corner of the desk.)* . . . move some of this stuff out of your way so you'll have a place . . . There. Afraid I'm not much of a housekeeper.

LUELLEN: Me neither.

MARY: Well . . . *(Indicating chair.)* . . . you can . . . *(Luellen walks gingerly toward the chair.)* Are you all right?

LUELLEN: I walked all the way here.

MARY: From your house?

LUELLEN: Must be ten miles, I bet. Don't you think it's about that? 'Bout ten miles?

MARY: Well . . .

LUELLEN: Pretty near ten miles.

MARY: It's certainly longer than I'd want to walk, anyway. Especially today. Did you . . . come just to see me or . . . ? *(Luellen nods, but avoids looking at Mary.)* Well, I'm glad to see you, Luellen, but, you know, it might have been better if you'd called me first . . . to make sure I was in, that I didn't have a client with me . . .

(Luellen still doesn't look at her.) You lucked out, I guess. Now, what can—

LUELLEN: That ol' Ray just took off in the car. He knowed, too. He don't care. Just took off. Don't say "boo, bless you" or nothin'. Didn't even leave me no money for the bus. So, I walked it. I can.

MARY: Yes, you did.

LUELLEN: I thought I was goin' to pass out of heat prostation.

MARY *(fighting a smile)*: Are you thirsty? *(Pointing toward door.)* There's a watercooler or I have—*(Indicating thermos.)*

LUELLEN *(continues as she carefully takes off one of her shoes)*: All them cars whoosin' by me and nobody even—*(Looking at her foot.)* Oh-h-h, I knowed it! I knowed it for the last three miles. I could feel it. Look. Look at that. I got a big ol' blister on my big toe.

MARY: Let me see. *(Goes to her.)* Uh-h-h. Does not look so great.

LUELLEN: Durn him.

MARY *(going to desk)*: I've got some Band-aids here. . . .

LUELLEN *(taking off other shoe)*: I bet I got one on . . . oh-h-h-h . . . it's ready to bust, too.

MARY *(looking)*: I know they're here somewhere. . . .

LUELLEN: Shoot! Double shoot!

MARY: Here, Band-aids. Where are—Ah-ha! *(She pulls out a can of Band-aids.)* I knew I had . . . *(Opens the can to find it empty—shakes her head.)* Mary, Mary. You've got to pull your act together.

LUELLEN: I can put some toilet paper—

MARY: No, no. I'm sure there's—*(Remembering.)* There's a first aid kit in the storage room. You just stay where you are. *(The sound and lights cross fade as she exits.)* We'll get you fixed up in no time. *(Luellen pulls one foot up on the chair with her and examines her foot during the major part of the following dictation.)*

MARY'S VOICE: . . . and the worker has visited twice weekly with Jimmy since his removal from the James home and his subsequent placement in foster care on October 19. During these three months in the Swinford foster home, Jimmy has become a most affectionate, outgoing child who is just a delight to be—scratch that—outgoing child period. His health is now quite good and is reflected in his physical appearance. He continues to express concern for his mother, but his nightmares have become much less frequent and the bedwetting has stopped altogether. New paragraph. Mr. and Ms. James have remained in group therapy and it is that group leader's judgement that both, but especially Ms. James, have made substantial progress. See attached report. As a result, the court has ordered that supervised trial visits between Jimmy and his natural parents begin immediately with the goal of eventual reintegration of the James family. The worker will begin preparing Jimmy for these visits at their next meeting. This worker cautions—Scratch that. This worker feels—Scratch that. *(Lights and sound cross fade.)* This worker recommends the close supervision of—(*Out. Just before the sound and lights begin to fade, Luellen gets up and moves cautiously to Mary's desk. She is examining things without touching anything when Mary enters. Luellen immediately pulls back from the desk.)*

MARY *(holding up kit)*:   Here we . . . *(Slightest pause on seeing Luellen.)* . . . go. Did you need something?

LUELLEN: I . . . I only . . . *(Indicating Similac.)* Jimmy drunk that stuff when he was a baby. Give him the colic.

MARY: Some of my foster mothers say the same thing.

LUELLEN: How come you reckon anybody'd want to do that, anyway? Take care of somebody else's kid for?

MARY: All sorts of reasons. Why don't you sit back down and we'll get those feet taken care of and, then, you can tell me why you wanted to see me today. All right? *(Luellen moves to her chair as Mary shakes the can of Band-aids she's taken from the kit.)* Looks like we hit pay dirt this time. Would you like for me to—

LUELLEN *(reaches out and takes can away from Mary)*:   I couldn't never do that—take care of somebody else's kid and then have to give it back.

MARY: Well . . . it can be very hard.

LUELLEN: You know what Jimmy told me? Jimmy told me that place . . . that Sween . . . Swen . . . What was their name now? *(Begins putting on Band-aids.)*

MARY: You know that's not information I can give you.

LUELLEN *(looks at her)*:   He already told me. I just forgot it right now. *(Continuing with her feet.)* I'll remember it, though. He said they never give him enough to eat. He was always hungry. That's what he told me.

MARY: Well . . . *(Indicating feet.)* You getting it?

LUELLEN: I reckon they do it for the money.

MARY: Awful lot of work and not much money.

LUELLEN: He said she whupped him, too. Hard. *(Before Mary can respond to this, Luellen stands up.)* There. Don't hurt none when I stand up. *(Walks.)* Or when I walk.

MARY: Good. But . . . no shoes.

LUELLEN *(not getting the point)*:   I like to go barefoot.

MARY: Tell you what. After we finish here, I'll give you a lift home. That way—

LUELLEN: Where do you live?

MARY: Southeast.

LUELLEN: Where southeast?

MARY: Won't be out of my way to drop you off. I have to go by—

LUELLEN: How come you can know where I live, but I can't know where you do?

MARY (*gently, but firmly*):   There's no reason for you to.

LUELLEN: You said you wanted to be my friend.

MARY: I did. I do. But . . .

LUELLEN: I ain't got no friend that I don't know where she lives.

MARY: Luellen, I meant "friend" in the sense of . . . of helping you . . . of not being against you, your enemy . . . A "professional friend." (*Realizes this doesn't sound right.*) A professional who is a friend. (*And she is sorry she's gotten into this.*)

LUELLEN: How long you been a "professional friend"?

MARY (*not going to get hooked again*):   I've been a social worker for . . . I don't know . . . couple of years . . . almost. Something like that. (*Determined to take control of the situation again.*) Luellen, I have an appointment in about . . . (*Looks at her watch.*)

LUELLEN (*moving around again—looking at her feet*):   It's 'cause they're new shoes is how come. I ought to have wore my tennis shoes, but I wanted to look good and tennis shoes don't look good with a dress, do they?

MARY: You look very nice.

LUELLEN: Jimmy surely does like you.

MARY: Luellen, I want you—

LUELLEN: When he come home after that time, you was all he could talk about. "Miz Hanson took me to the circus" and Miz Hanson bought me this and give me that and brung me there." You sure must of spent a lot of your time with him. One time, he said you even took him over to your house and he had supper in your big ol' dinin' room, then you took him to a movie. . . . He sure is a pretty little boy, ain't he?

MARY: Yes. He is.

LUELLEN: Got the longest eyelashes. Looks like my daddy. Ol' Ray thinks he looks like him, but he don't. Looks 'zactly like my daddy. My daddy surely was a looker, too. How come you to put him in a place where they never fed him and they whupped him all the time?

MARY: They didn't whip him. I wouldn't have let anyone—(*Stops herself.*) And he gained weight while he was there.

LUELLEN (*seeing the baby clothes on the desk*):   Oh-h-h. Oh, look at that. Ain't those cute? Can I take one out? (*Wiping her hands on her skirt.*) My hands is clean. (*Picks up a little yellow jumpsuit.*)

Ain't that the most precious . . . Look at how little! Oh-h-h, and look here. Look, it's got a little blue duckie on it. *(Laughs.)* A little blue duckie with a itty-bitty red eye. Did you see that part? *(Holds it out at arm's length.)* So little. You forget how little they was. Tiny arms . . . teeny little legs . . . so little . . . *(And suddenly she clutches the clothing to her, closes her eyes and bites her lip hard.)*

MARY *(after a brief pause, moves toward her comfortingly)*: Luellen—

LUELLEN *(moves away just before Mary touches her, clutching the jump-suit)*: You 'member that Miz Botts lives 'cross the hall from me? That one was so nosey and was always tellin' lies on me and Ray? She's in the hospital. They come and took her yesterday.

MARY: I'm . . . I'm sorry to hear—

LUELLEN: I ain't going to go visit her neither. She's probably got cancer. Gonna get all her insides eat up. That's what Ray says.

MARY: Luellen. When you quit going to group, did . . . did you ask about seeing someone privately over there? I could—

LUELLEN: And I don't care if she does either. Could I have some water now? I'm real, real thirsty. *(Luellen stands turned away from Mary who watches her for a moment. As Mary turns and starts to move, the lights fade down and the sound fades in. Mary has looked toward the door as though she might get the water outside, but decides it is better not to leave Luellen alone again and, so, she pours her a drink of whatever is in the thermos.)*

MARY'S VOICE: . . . brought Jimmy in for treatment of his burned hands and told the nurse he'd fallen against the stove. Mr. and Ms. James then left Jimmy in her care saying they would be right back, but did not return. On February 17, Jimmy was again placed in the Swinford foster home. Date: February 23. The worker was finally able to contact Mr. and Ms. James. After lengthy discussion in which they became alternately defensive and angrily aggressive—at times even threatening the worker—the worker succeeded in explaining that a petition would be filed—*(Out.)*

MARY *(over fading dictation)*: Here's your . . . *(Luellen turns, takes the cup and drinks.)* You walked a very long way on a very hot day to see me . . . Luellen? . . . *(Luellen looks at her quickly and then away.)* and I *would* like to know why—what I can do to help you—but you are going to have to tell me. *(No response.)* Will you? *(No response.)* Well. I'm sorry, I wish I had more time, but I do have this appointment, so, if you'll let me get my things together, I'll take you—

LUELLEN *(quickly and with a new energy)*: No, but, see, see, I got this real good idea. It's real good, too. See, I'm fixin' to move out on ol' Ray. He just don't know it yet, but I am. I'm goin' to get me a place to live and I'm goin' to get me a job maybe with the phone company maybe. My girlfriend works for the phone company. Or a waitress. I could do that.

MARY: Jobs are a little hard to find these days, but . . . but that sounds . . . I think you'd enjoy working—

LUELLEN (*big smile*):   I think I would, too. And my girlfriend lives in a duplex and her neighbors is goin' to move maybe and I could move in there if they did. It's got a fenced-in backyard and a big side yard and I wouldn't even let ol' Ray even come visit only if he got over doin' them things.

MARY (*realizing*):   Wait a minute—

LUELLEN (*going on*):   I know he don't mean to. He just loses his temper sometimes is all, but he's gettin' a whole lot better 'bout it since we went to that group. I sure to 'preciate you makin' us go to them meetin's. See, we had a lot of pressure on us and we was probably just takin' it out on—

MARY: Luellen. Wait a minute here.

LUELLEN: No, no. I still wouldn't let him come and stay. Not no matter how much he yelled at me or how much he begged me, he couldn't. A daddy don't need to be with his son like a mama does. (*Slightly choked, but going on.*) A mama needs to be with her child. You know that, don't you? I know you do and I'm goin' to get a place for me and Jimmy to live and you can—

MARY: You know that's—

LUELLEN (*going on*):   And you could come visit Jimmy ever'day. You could take him out in your car and you could buy him a Coke and ask him questions . . . I'd share him with you. We could share him. (*She looks pleadingly at Mary. Pause.*)

MARY: Luellen, please don't do this to yourself.

LUELLEN: I ain't—

MARY: You're hurting yourself with this. You're building up a fantasy that—

LUELLEN: It ain't a fantasy. I thought it all out.

MARY: Thinking it out doesn't mean it can happen that way.

MARY (*a protest*):   Yes!

MARY: No. I'm sorry.

LUELLEN (*looks at her a moment—quietly*):   You ain't sorry.

MARY: Yes, I am. I'm sorry for how you feel right now. I know how very—

LUELLEN: You know what? You know what it's like to have your kid stole by the Welfare? To sit in a room and remember that your little boy ain't bein' quiet 'cause he's sleepin' or into somethin', but that he's bein' quiet 'cause he ain't even there no more.

And you don't know where he is or when he's comin' back? You don't know.

MARY: No. I guess . . . no one can . . . really . . . but you have to . . .

LUELLEN (*watching her coldly*): What? I have to what? Forget about him? You ain't got no kids, do you?

MARY: No.

LUELLEN: No. You want one?

MARY: Someday.

LUELLEN: Like my Jimmy? (*Mary doesn't answer this.*) I know you like him a whole lot. You like him better than the other ones? He your favorite? You know what ol' Ray told me once after you'd come out to visit? He said, "You better watch out, Lu girl. That woman wants your baby for herself and she's a' gonna get him, too." That's what he said, but I didn't believe him. Sometimes, though, that Ray knows what he's talkin' 'bout. You got him?

MARY: What?

LUELLEN: You got him at your house, ain't you?

MARY: No. That's—

LUELLEN: You don't want me to know where you live 'cause—

MARY: This is a state agency. There are rules here, Luellen. Even if I wanted to do something like—

LUELLEN: Oh, you want to. You want to and you did. (*The two look at each other a long moment.*)

MARY (*reasonably*): No matter how much I care about Jimmy—and I do, I care about him—that simply isn't the reason he was taken out of your home. You know that. I did not "steal" him. He is not at my house. O.K.? Now. I want you to tell me precisely what it is you think I can do, so I can answer you in as clear a way as possible . . . so we understand each other.

LUELLEN (*trying to be "reasonable" in turn*): I want to see Jimmy.

MARY: I understand that, but what do you want *me* to do?

LUELLEN: I want you to go get him.

MARY: I can't do that. I don't have that authority. It's out of my hands.

LUELLEN: You go get him and bring him here.

MARY: I can't—

LUELLEN: Go get him.

MARY: You were in the courtroom. You heard what the judge said.

LUELLEN: Then call him.

MARY: Who?

LUELLEN: Call that judge. Right now. Tell him I can have my baby back.

MARY: I'm not going to argue with you—

LUELLEN: Call him.

MARY: This interview is ended.

LUELLEN: Call him. *(She moves in on Mary.)*

MARY: I can't call the judge!

LUELLEN: Yes, you can! *(Continuing to move in on Mary—cold and menacing.)* And you better.

MARY *(backing—fear showing)*:   Luellen.

LUELLEN: You better do it. *(She is almost in Mary's face.)*

MARY: Get out of my face.

LUELLEN *(fists clenched)*:   I mean it!

MARY: Now . . . stop this!

LUELLEN: If you don't, I'll do something. I'll hurt you. I can. I ain't kiddin' either. *(Luellen begins to raise her fists and as she does, Mary starts to turn to run from her, but instead knocks into the chair with everything still piled on it. The chair overturns making a loud crashing sound. The crash causes both women to stop. Mary is almost immediately shocked into fury and Luellen is cowed.)*

MARY: God-damn-it! God-damn-it! *(Turns on Luellen who steps back.)* Just who the hell do you think you are? What do you think you're doing here? You can't ever—not ever in this life—see that child again. Not ever.

LUELLEN *(more of a cry)*:   Yes, I can.

MARY: Do you think the state or the judge would put that little boy back after what you did?

LUELLEN: I didn't . . . I never done—Ray. Ray done it.

MARY: You! You! Face that reality at least. You. You admitted it to me, to the judge—

LUELLEN *(shaking her head)*:   Ray.

MARY: Ray may have done a lot of it, but not that last, Luellen.

LUELLEN *(childlike)*:   Well . . . he made me.

MARY: He made you hold that child's hands on a hot stove till he had first and second degree burns? I'll tell you one thing, Ray couldn't have made me do that!

LUELLEN *(meekly)*:   We was just teaching him—

MARY *(going on)*:   And, then, you ran off and left him, just left him—*and* in all the months we've had him in foster care, you haven't contacted me once, not one time, to find out how he was doing. So why today? Why do you people suddenly turn up out of the blue and think—Christ. *(Takes a breath to calm herself.)* We explained everything to you six months ago. *(Brief pause.)* You could hold a gun to my head or a knife to my throat and it still wouldn't get him back for you. *(Pause.)*

LUELLEN: What am I gonna do?

MARY: I don't know. *(Pause.)* See someone. Let me make an appoint—

LUELLEN: Talkin' to a stranger ain't goin' to help.

MARY: It can.

LUELLEN: I was right 'bout you wantin' Jimmy, wasn't I? *(No answer.)* I know I was. That's how come me to come to see you. It gets so quiet sometimes. I thought you'd understand about it. Ray told me. He said, "The Welfare don't understand nothin' 'bout people's feelin's. They ain't never goin' to help you." *(Brief pause.)* My girlfriend's fixin' to have a little baby. I been givin' her all Jimmy's baby things.

MARY: I'm sure that's very hard for you.

LUELLEN: I'm givin' her a baby shower at my house. *(Pointing to the clothes.)* Could I have one of those to give to her? *(Mary gives her two boxes.)*

MARY: I wish you'd let me get you in to see someone. *(Luellen goes over and puts her shoes on.)*

LUELLEN: Don't hurt none.

MARY: At least, let me take you—

LUELLEN: I don't want you to.

MARY *(taking change from her billfold)*: Let me give you bus fare, then. *(Mary hands her the money and Luellen takes it without saying anything.)* I'm . . . I'm sorry I lost my . . . I shouldn't have . . . *(Luellen, without ever looking at Mary, turns and walks out, leaving Mary standing there watching her. The lights and sound cross fade.)*

MARY'S VOICE: . . . and on the third visit the Jonsons presented Jimmy with a new tricycle which he loved. All in all, the worker felt that the three trial visits with the prospective adoptive parents were most successful. Jimmy was taken to the State Office for final adoptive placement with his new family on September 3, '82. This file is being transferred to the office in Sycamore County. *(A sigh.)* Right. Next case. *(Lights and sound start fading down.)* Last name: Albert. First name: Joan. CW number—*(Sound and lights.)*

FEEDING THE MOONFISH

BARBARA WIECHMANN

FEEDING THE MOONFISH was first performed at the Nat Horne Theatre, New York City, as part of the About Face Theatre Company's Julyfest, July 1988. Directed by Tony Kelly; set design by Diane Forbes; costume design by Tricia Sarnataro; light design by Dan Kelley; sound design by Tony Kelly; stage managed by Rona Bern; with the following cast:

EDEN	Mary B. Ward
MARTIN	Christopher Rath

Characters
MARTIN, midtwenties
EDEN, about sixteen
VOICES OF THE MOONFISH, to be played by two or more actresses of varying ages and vocal ranges

Setting
The play takes place on a dock on a saltwater lake in southern Florida.

■ ■

Darkness. In the darkness we hear two or three long whistles and then a series of overlapping voices.

VOICES:
Martin
Martin
Martin
What are you thinking about now Martin?
Did you have a long night at work?
Are you tired?
What are you thinking about now Martin?
We're so happy you're home.

MARTIN:
Can I see him?
I want to see him.

VOICES:
Talk to us first.
Close your eyes first.

MARTIN:
I'll close them for you.

VOICES:
Tell us we're beautiful.

MARTIN:
I want to see him first.

VOICES:
Talk to us first.
Tell us your dream.
Tell us we're beautiful.

MARTIN:
You're beautiful.
You're so beautiful.

VOICES:
He'll be here soon Martin.
He'll be here soon.

MARTIN:
I'm dreaming about flying.
In planes.
I want to fly so bad that as soon as I hit the mattress, whammo some
    stewardess is strapping me in.
Get it?
Soon as my head hits the pillow I'm taxiing down some runway,
I'm taking off—
Into the blue.
Sky so deep you could just tumble into it and
never fall.
Just float around.
I'm up there.
In blue heaven.
Movies, brunettes, cocktail almonds, the whole bit, the life.
One long cool glass of water.
Flying, zooming through all that space.
All that blue distance.
All that space.
All that distance.

I want to leave here.
I want to leave this place.

VOICES:
Where are you?

MARTIN:
Home.

VOICES:
What surrounds you?

MARTIN:
Trees.
The dark.

VOICES:
The air.

MARTIN:
The air.

VOICES:
What's it like?

MARTIN:
Hot.
Heavy.

VOICES:
Hard to breathe.

MARTIN:
Bring him to me.

VOICES:
Cool yourself.
Put your hand in the water.

MARTIN:
Cool myself.

VOICES:
Put your hand in the water.
Cover yourself.

MARTIN:
Cover myself.

VOICES:
Reach farther.
Put your face to the water.

MARTIN:
Bring him to me.

VOICES:
Face to the water.
We'll show him to you.

MARTIN:
If I put my face to the water,
I can see pieces of him
like white ivory
and pieces of him tangled in the coral
like gardens.
I can feel
back of my neck
currents
like wind.

VOICES & MARTIN:
Now it is night
We will walk to the end of the pier
and watch the moonfish feed.
Because it is night
and peering deep into wells of bottle blackness
we will see them.

(Eden enters from behind Martin on the dock.)

EDEN: Who are you talking to? *(Martin freezes.)* Who are you talking to?

MARTIN: How long have you been standing there?

EDEN: Not long.

MARTIN: You shouldn't spy on people.

EDEN: I wasn't spying. I just woke up and I heard you.

MARTIN: How long you been standing there?

EDEN: I told you.

MARTIN: Where'd you come from?

EDEN: Your car.

MARTIN: You were in my car?

EDEN: I stowed away. I been sleeping under that sleeping bag you got all balled up there in the back.

MARTIN: You were in my car.

EDEN: Ever since you left the restaurant.

MARTIN: All that time.

EDEN: Yep.

MARTIN: Under the sleeping bag.

EDEN: I told you. Jesus.

MARTIN: Why?

EDEN: I wanted to see where you go when you leave work. I mean you sweat to death side by side of someone in the kitchen of a Big Sizzler Restaurant, a hundred an eighty fuckin degrees in the middle of fuckin *Florida* for days on end, an they never speak a word to you, never pass the time of day, never basically even look at you, an you get curious—you know?

MARTIN: I talk to you.

EDEN: You know what I mean.

MARTIN: You want me to look at you. That's so pathetic. You waitresses are all alike.

EDEN: I'm not a waitress. I'm a sandwich maker.

MARTIN: Whatever. You just want to be told how beautiful you are over and over.

EDEN: That's not it.

MARTIN: So go home. *(She doesn't move.)* Go home.

EDEN: I can't now. This is practically wilderness to me. I don't know how you got here—I was asleep. Anyway I ain't walking in the middle of this swamp an I ain't hitchin neither. There are goddam maniacs in this state. I could get harassed or raped or chopped up or worse.

MARTIN: What's worse than getting chopped up?

EDEN: What's so bad about me staying here awhile. Don't you wanna talk?

MARTIN: I got nothing to say right now.

EDEN: Talk to me. Tell me who you were talking to.

MARTIN: Listen—I wasn't talking to nobody. It's not your place to ask. You know what I mean?

EDEN: It's goddamn creepy here you know? You like comin here and spookin yourself? I don't think it's safe. Whole place is just rotting away—dock's practically falling into the water. You're gonna fall in too if you keep leaning over that way. *(Pause.)* So what's so fascinatin down there anyway? What are you lookin at? Look at all them fish—they're so huge, god. What are they?

MARTIN: Moonfish.

EDEN: Bullshitter. They ain't called that.

MARTIN: They are.

EDEN: There ain't no kind of fish called moonfish.

MARTIN: Whatever.

EDEN: How do you know they're called that?

MARTIN: Dunno.

EDEN: Did you read it? Did you read it in an encyclopedia or somethin—did you look it up?

MARTIN: Jesus. Yeah, I guess. A long time ago.

EDEN: They're really called that. You ain't kiddin me?

MARTIN: No. *(Pause.)* It's no big deal what they're called.

EDEN: Oh. They look like big moons with lips. It's nice you got that spotlight shinin on em an all. What are they doing sucking off the dock like that?

MARTIN: Eating. They feed at night. They come out an feed off the dock when the moon shines.

EDEN: How can they fucking even see the moon through all that water?

MARTIN: Don't be stupid. They don't see it, they feel it.

EDEN: I ain't stupid.

MARTIN: Natural things are moved by forces see. Like the moon. The moon's got a force, an it pulls an pulls at the insides of these fish an locks em into a way of behaving—one single way of being. They got no minds of their own anymore. Once the moon's got em they're helpless beyond all control. All they got is moon minds. Stupid fish.

EDEN: Where are you going?

MARTIN: I'm just getting up off my stomach.

EDEN: Don't go. Don't leave me here.

MARTIN: What?

EDEN: Talk to me.

MARTIN: I been talking to you. Don't you have somewhere to go?

EDEN: What do you think moves people?

MARTIN: Don't you have somewhere to go—cause I'll take you there.

EDEN: You think human beings guts are pulled inside out all over the place by forces?

MARTIN: Come on—your mom's probably shitting tombstones somewhere worrying about you.

EDEN: My mom's up north.

MARTIN: Well your dad then.

EDEN: Don't have a dad. My mom killed him.

MARTIN: Right.

EDEN: That's why she's up north now. In Sing Sing.

MARTIN: Your mom's in prison?

EDEN: My mom's in Sing Sing. My grandma'd be there too 'cept she's too sick. They thought she'd croak or something so they got her under twenty-four-hour surveillance in a nursing home.

MARTIN: They wanted to put your grandma behind bars?

EDEN: Sure. She was an accomplice to my dad's murder. She helped my mom kill him.

MARTIN: She did.

EDEN: Yeah.

MARTIN: How?

EDEN: What?

MARTIN: How'd they do it?

EDEN: Frying pans. They beat him to death.

MARTIN: That's not funny. (*She just stares at him.*) Look, there must be some place you go home to—I'll take you home O.K.?

EDEN: I want to stay here with you.

MARTIN: You can't stay here.

EDEN: Why not?

MARTIN: It ain't safe.

EDEN: Why not?

MARTIN: You'd probably roll off the dock in your sleep and the barracuda'd get you.

EDEN: They got barracuda here too?

MARTIN: Sure.

EDEN: Fucking Florida—I hate this place.

MARTIN: It's all right, you can hate. It's just a place. It can't hate you back.

EDEN: You know all the fish by names. (*She moves closer to him.*) How come—how come you're smart like that?

MARTIN: Knowing names don't make you smart.

EDEN: You think there are forces between us?

MARTIN: No.

EDEN: What if there were. What if we was being zapped right now by outside forces. Iodes or microwaves or something.

MARTIN: We aren't.

EDEN: You don't think so?

MARTIN: No.

EDEN: Maybe I do. (*She attempts to kiss him.*)

MARTIN: Get off. You're just lonely. You're just fucking lonely. You're just fucking lonely.

EDEN: It ain't a crime being lonely you know. You treat it like it was a disease. I ain't a disease. You think I'm a disease.

MARTIN: I don't think you're anything.

EDEN: I bet you're lonely too. I bet you're lonely too, so you don't have to treat me like some piece of filth.

MARTIN: I ain't lonely.

EDEN: Like some greasy piece of booger you just picked outta your nose and can't flick off your finger. (*She gets up to go.*)

MARTIN: You don't have to go anywhere.

EDEN: I got my pride too you know. I'll just be on my way. I'll just go get swallowed up into the dark like some kind of free-floating disease.

MARTIN: You don't have to leave.

EDEN: I'll do what I want.

MARTIN: Don't leave.

EDEN: I'll do what I want.

MARTIN: Don't be stupid—you can't walk around out there alone.

EDEN: So I get killed. I know what I'm doing. *(She exits.)*

MARTIN: Hey. Hey. Hey! *(He looks after her.)*

Fuck.
I can't see anything.
I can't see you.

VOICES:
Imagine what it looks like.

MARTIN:
I can't.

VOICES:
Picture it and you will see it.
It's all pictures Martin.

MARTIN:
I can't see anything.

VOICES:
Picture the water.
Ink dark, green
bottle black.

MARTIN:
Something could happen to her.

VOICES:
Nothing can happen.

MARTIN:
She could get lost.

VOICES:
Nothing can happen you don't want to happen.
If you make the pictures.

MARTIN:
If I make the pictures.

VOICES:
Nothing can happen.

MARTIN:
I am just afraid.

VOICES:
We'll bring him to you.
Stay with us.
Don't go.
Don't leave me here.
We'll bring him to you.

MARTIN:
I will die without air.

VOICES:
You will never drown in water.

MARTIN:
I will never drown in water.

VOICES:
He'll tell you what it's like.
Underneath.
Watch us.

MARTIN:
I am just afraid.

VOICES:
Look for us.

MARTIN:
Can I see him then?
I want to see him.

VOICES:
Talk to us first.
Close your eyes first.

MARTIN:
I'll close them for you.

VOICES:
Put your face to the water.
What do you see?
Face to the water.
What do you hear?
His voice.

It says
Now it is night.
Look for his shadow.
See his shadow on the end of the pier.
See him Martin.
And watch the moonfish feed.
His shadow.

(*Eden enters with an old sleeping bag, which she dumps on the dock. Martin stares at her.*)

EDEN: You want a Bud?

MARTIN: Who gave you beer?

EDEN: I brought two Buds—one for you an one for me.

MARTIN: You shouldn't be stealing beer from the restaurant.

EDEN: God. It's just a coupla fucking beers.

MARTIN: Doesn't matter. You shouldn't swear neither.

EDEN: All right. All right. I ain't gonna swear but it's no big crime to drink a beer with me. I ain't no alchy or nothin so you don't have to worry I'm gonna throw up all over you or pass out or somethin. I just thought you might get hot out here that's all. (*She hands him the beer.*)

MARTIN: All right. Thank you. (*He starts to pull the beer tab.*)

EDEN: You might wanna be careful.

MARTIN: You shook this up? What are you giving me shook-up beer for?

EDEN: I didn't shake it up. I don't even know if it is shook up. I just was saying that it *could be. You* could have shooked it up when we was drivin—all that Evel Knievel stuff you was doing on them potholes. I was only doin you the courtesy of warnin you.

MARTIN: O.K. O.K.

(*They open the beers—which are not shook up—and sit drinking them a moment in silence.*)

EDEN: I like the nighttime. Sometimes did you ever notice at night the way you can open up to people. You can open right up the way you never could in the daytime?

MARTIN: I don't know.

EDEN: I think I come out at night—you know—like a creature— a sci-fi creature.

MARTIN: Yeah. You're a creature all right.

EDEN:
Sometimes I'll stay up all night just to talk to a stranger.
Just to meet a new person. (*Pause.*)

I wish I really lived in space.
In space you don't weigh nothing.
You could float around. Float all over the place.
You could do somersaults in the air even.
It'd be cool huh?

MARTIN: You used to be able to see all this crap floating by.
EDEN: What do you think?
MARTIN: Garbage an hubcaps. Bloated dead things.
EDEN: What kind of dead things?
MARTIN: Fish.
EDEN: Bloated dead fish.
MARTIN: Yeah.
EDEN: Oh.
MARTIN: The moonfish were dying. The living things were all dying.
EDEN: How come?
MARTIN: The living things were all dying. But not anymore. The moonfish are making a comeback.
EDEN: That's nice. *(Pause.)* You like them fish don't you?
MARTIN: This place used to be fantastic. There was a marina. Men would come here and fish.
EDEN: They fished for the moonfish? They ate the moonfish?
MARTIN: Sharks. They fished for sharks.
EDEN: Sharks.
MARTIN: They hunted em. Took their boats through the channel to the ocean and hunted em. They had contests. I watched them haul em in off their boats an dump em on the dock. Hammerheads, tigers, gray nurses. They slaughtered em.
EDEN: Yeah?
MARTIN: They dumped em in piles and left em. Bellies up, hooks in their mouths, piled to the sun.
EDEN: That's it? What else?
MARTIN: Nothing.
EDEN: That's it?
MARTIN: That's it. They slaughtered em.
EDEN: Well, they was killers.
MARTIN: It was cruel.
EDEN: I'm so sleepy.
MARTIN: What?
EDEN: I said I'm real sleepy.
MARTIN: So sleep. I don't care what you do.
EDEN: Aren't you sleepy too?
MARTIN: No.

EDEN (pause): What do you think people do in prison?

MARTIN: What?

EDEN: Do you think my mom's having an O.K. time behind bars? I brought her some stuff to make an afghan with but they took away the crochet needles. They said they was lethal weapons. I hope she ain't too bored. She don't know what to do without something in her hands.

MARTIN: Your mom's really in jail?

EDEN: I told you.

MARTIN: She beat your dad to death.

EDEN: She tried. My grandma's the one that killed him. That dealt the actual death blow.

MARTIN: Your grandma killed him?

EDEN: She sure did.

MARTIN: Why'd she do it?

EDEN: She couldn't stand him no more.

MARTIN: That's it?

EDEN: No. He used to beat my mom on a semi-regular basis, an this time she was fighting for her life—right? He was choking her. It wasn't even like she had time to think of possible consequences or nothing—she had no choice. She was makin the best of the situation. She found her only opportunity, grabbed the waffle iron with her one free hand, and beamed him with it. Then she called Gram to help her come finish.

MARTIN: He beat you too?

EDEN: Naah. He couldn't beat me—he weren't my blood dad. Just her he beat.

MARTIN: Don't it bother you?

EDEN: Well, what do you think, you must be a moron or something. I'm in homeroom talking to Tasha Paritees about how Kimmi Wiggins ripped off two full shopping bags a stuff at Sears and went right past the security guards without getting caught. Two bags. Tons of jewelry, these cool earrings. Just dropped the rack right in—four bikinis, a princess phone, two Cheryl Tiegs jogging outfits, and she's rich—she don't need the stuff—but you gotta admit it—that's what I was telling Tasha—you gotta admit it— she did something.

MARTIN: You don't steal anything whether you're rich or not.

EDEN: I didn't say it was me—God.

MARTIN: Do you steal?

EDEN: Don't interrupt if you wanna hear. So I'm in homeroom talking to Tasha about this big ripoff and this announcement comes over the P.A. "Eden Battaglione please report to the front office. Eden Battaglione please report to the front office. Eden Battag-

lione please report to the front office." Like that—so right away
the entire student body of my homeroom goes ape-shit cause they
think it's got to do with me taking these pills in the lav—only
they weren't pills they was only Tylenol—so I get to the office
and them ugly hairdos are looking at me kinda funny and then
they lay it on me—"Your dad's been bashed to death by a waffle
iron, Eden—Your ma's been hauled away to some mental prison,
and your grandma's nearly croaked herself in the process of the
beating. Now, here's a permission slip, go home honey."

Wouldn't it upset you? I gotta be questioned by the police for
days, I gotta miss astronomy club for three weeks, my friends
think I'm a psycho, and in the long run all I get is my ass hauled
down here to this swampland to live with my fat aunt Inez and
her Siamese cats and work in a steak house. Wouldn't it upset
you? I mean wouldn't it?

MARTIN: You're not a psycho.

EDEN: I know that. You got a joint?

MARTIN: You don't need a joint. You're a healthy girl, you don't
need that stuff.

EDEN: You don't know anything. You don't know me. You don't
know what I might need.

MARTIN: Jesus, calm down, you're all worked up.

EDEN: Of course I'm worked up. Why shouldn't I be? I bust my
ass to make one single friend and all I get is shutting doors. He
don't wanna talk, he don't wanna listen, he just wants to watch
these weird fish all night.

MARTIN: I been listening to you. I'm listening.

EDEN: No. Why should you listen to me. Why should you understand. There's no rational way to account for the disgusting things
I've seen in my life.

MARTIN: Yeah?

EDEN: What?

MARTIN: You can be a drag you know that? Maybe you're just
young but even if you ain't lying you ain't the only person's ever
seen disgusting things go on in this world, and if you are lying,
shit, I could make up stories same as you that'd make your heart
bleed into little pieces. So your mom's a little high-strung—I could
tell you that I didn't ever have a mom—

EDEN: And I could tell you I once worked bachelor parties in order
to put food on the table.

MARTIN: I could tell you a brick fell on her head and split her skull
wide open one day as she was breast-feeding me—

EDEN: I could tell you my grandma was a schizophrenic, I could
tell you my father was a junkie and made me his love slave—

MARTIN: I could tell you my father slit his throat—what do you want me to do? What's the matter?

EDEN: Nothing.

MARTIN: What?

EDEN: Nothing.

MARTIN: What is it?

EDEN: I miss everyone I've ever known.

MARTIN: Look, I'm sorry I ain't been nice to you. I guess I'm just not very nice, you know? You know, I can be an asshole.

EDEN: Bullshit. That's shit.

MARTIN: Don't swear. Come on. Come on. Come here. Aren't you sleepy? You wanna sleep here or something? *(She shakes her head.)* Here blow your nose. Don't get all snotty on me. You wanna eat something? I got a ham sandwich in the glove compartment.

EDEN: I already ate.

MARTIN: What?

EDEN: Burt's birthday cake.

MARTIN: What, back at the restaurant? You didn't eat any dinner. You didn't eat anything healthy. Don't give me that shit. That's disgusting.

EDEN: I'm not disgusting.

MARTIN: Grow up, I seen you. You let those guys up there—horny old pricks—you let them pinch your butt and feed you cake and beer.

EDEN: God, you're such a preacher.

MARTIN: Look, I'm sorry, you shouldn't wear those little cut-off shorts. Your butt hangs out, you know that? I mean don't take this wrong but it's just a plain come-on.

EDEN: Well, what do you want me to wear, overalls? It's hot in the kitchen.

MARTIN: I work there too.

EDEN: Look, you don't have to go playing saint on me or nothing. I ain't your kid or some ugly little sister of yours that can't get a date, and anyway you shouldn't talk. I heard about you too you know.

MARTIN: What about me?

EDEN: What you done to girls. What you done to that girl.

MARTIN: Which girl? What is it you hear? Who tells you?

EDEN: You're no saint. I hear things.

MARTIN: What are you doing here then? If that's what you hear?

EDEN: I ain't afraid of you.

MARTIN: What are you doing here. You come here and shove these goddamn lies at me.

EDEN: They ain't lies. Not one thing I told you is a lie.

MARTIN: What do you want from me?

EDEN: I ain't a slut, you know.

MARTIN: What does that have to do with anything?

EDEN: You're so fucking cool ain't you? And I'll swear if I want. I hear things. You thought she was some dumb slut so it didn't matter none. You thought she had no brains.

MARTIN: What are you even talking about?

EDEN: I hear. I hear. You come out here at night and some girl you think is scum gets drunk and you just let her wander around by herself cause she bugs you. You just let her wander around all miserable and throwing up—

MARTIN: People make up goddamn stories.

EDEN: All miserable and throwing up and you could care less she gets hurt out here on this rusty old piece of shit dock. You could give a shit she falls in, and can't see and can't swim and screams and screams and panics and you don't even come help her.

MARTIN: You don't know anything.

EDEN: You could care less. You never even bothered, you just let her drown.

MARTIN: Shut up. Shut up.

EDEN: You coulda saved her but you let her drown. You watched her drown I'll bet.

MARTIN: Shut up. (*He moves to strike Eden, but stops himself before his fist makes contact.*) I never touched you.

EDEN (*pause*):   I know. I know that. It's O.K. You think I'm a slut or something but you know something, it doesn't matter to me. You know that? I don't care you think that.

MARTIN: I don't think you're anything.

EDEN: That's O.K. too. You can say that. That's what he said about her. About my ma. That's what he told her. But it weren't true. She was real special to him. She could take him.

MARTIN: What are you talking about?

EDEN: He hit her. He could hit her again and again, and she'd be screaming and throwing furniture and heavy objects and shit, but she could take it. He could do anything and it was O.K. because she loved him so much and she knew how much he loved her cause she was the only one that could take him. You understand? She was special. He didn't do that stuff to no one else. He could fool around on the side but in the long run it was her. She weren't just nothing to him. She was it. She was his living end.

MARTIN: She killed him.

EDEN: Sure. Jealousy. She had to have him for herself completely.

MARTIN: I thought you said she was fighting for her life.

EDEN: Conveniently. She woulda killed him anyway sooner or later. Just to finally have him. She loved him so much. To this day his memory is sacred to her. She's got a framed eight-by-ten of him hanging on the wall of her cell in the slammer. See, their bodies was made to be with each other. That's what I think. Gravity was pulling em to each other. Forces was pulling em—just like them fish—only they could feel emotional pain in their minds too so it was worse. They was real helpless. They couldn't change nothing though. They couldn't *change* see. That's why it don't matter what you think of me—

MARTIN: I don't even know you.

EDEN: It don't matter. There ain't nothing you could say or do or think that would change anything so what's to be afraid of right? I'm not afraid of you. It don't matter what you done to some girl. You could burn people's furniture cause you didn't like the color, set fire to your neighbor's front lawn and watch the grass grizzle up and the flames reach the front door, you could kill someone —you could never speak another word to me in your life, and it wouldn't matter. I'd still care for you.

MARTIN: You know, I think you're a little sick.

EDEN: That's O.K. too, cause I'm like you. You could do anything in your life that you ever regretted but we'd still be here on this dock right now—and it's nice huh? That breeze blowing and all —it's getting cool. That nice breeze, huh? You got such a beautiful face. I like you so much.

MARTIN: You think it's beautiful here?

EDEN: Yeah, it's beautiful. Like a picture.

MARTIN: You like it here.

EDEN: I like it here with you. To be here with you.

MARTIN: I'm so tired.

EDEN: Close your eyes. You could just close your eyes, Martin.

MARTIN: Maybe. Maybe that'd be O.K. Tell me something.

EDEN: What?

MARTIN: What's it like where you're from?

EDEN: It's north. It's all right. It ain't so sticky. You ain't aware of your own body so much cause you ain't sweating all the time, right. It's nice.

MARTIN: I should go there. I never been out of this state. I should go places.

EDEN: Why don't you take me places then. Why don't you kidnap me?

MARTIN: You already kidnapped yourself. Sometimes I think I'll just go though—I'll get out of here. I'll just do it. But I never do. I can't. I come here. These pictures flash in my mind. I get these pictures. I see this place so beautiful. So perfect. I see it perfect. In my mind the air is cool. I can't feel the heat. I see the lake clear down to its floor, sand white on the bottom. All the fish and creatures huger, wilder than you see them now.

EDEN: It's all beautiful now.

MARTIN: No, it's not the same. *(Pause.)* My dad would take me here.

EDEN: When you were a little kid?

MARTIN: He'd take me here. He'd show me the fish, all the different kinds. The rays. The squirrel fish and the parrot fish. He'd show me how the parrot fish got teeth and eat the coral. This coral that will sting, will try to kill any other living thing that touches it, except the parrot fish. They alone can touch it because they are made to touch it. They got teeth.

EDEN: He knew a lot.

MARTIN: At night we'd walk out here. We'd look for the moonfish. They'd come. I couldn't take my eyes off them. All those many fish, swimming in and out of the light, doubling in and off of each other, changing in and out with themselves till they became one silver river wrapped around the dock. Just to get the food. They do that, they become so beautiful just for the food. Where you going?

EDEN: I'm just itching my bites. Too damn buggy out here.

MARTIN: You listening to me?

EDEN: I'm listening to you. I ain't going nowhere.

MARTIN: You wanna know something?

EDEN: What?

MARTIN: The fish talk.

EDEN: Huh?

MARTIN: The fish talk.

EDEN: The fish talk. The moonfish?

MARTIN: Yes.

EDEN: What do they say?

MARTIN: Different things. What's so funny?

EDEN: You think you're so mysterious. What kind of different things? Will they talk to me?

MARTIN: I don't know. I don't think so. *(Eden lies on her back staring up at the sky.)* What are you doing?

EDEN: I'm listening. I'm listening to what them fish are saying.

MARTIN: You can't hear them.

EDEN:
You wanna know what I hear, what they're telling me?
They're saying:

The man in the moon
Looked out of the moon
Looked out of the moon and said
It's time for all of God's children
To think about going to bed.

MARTIN: What's that?

EDEN: Shhh. Just be quiet, Martin. Aren't you sleepy now? We should sleep.

MARTIN: Maybe I am.

EDEN: We can sleep out here. We don't have to screw or nothing. I wanna be with you out here sleeping.

MARTIN: Maybe I am sleepy.

EDEN: That's good. We can just be here together. You wanna tell me something while I comb my hair? That's one thing, I comb my hair no matter what, every night one hundred strokes.

MARTIN: All right. Tell you something.

EDEN: You wanna tell me something. Tell me a story.

MARTIN: Don't know any stories to tell you.

EDEN: Tell me anything. Just make up some crazy thing.

MARTIN: There's nothing I could tell you that you'd think was crazy.

EDEN: Then just close your eyes and tell me what you see. Close your eyes.

MARTIN: I'll close them for you.

EDEN: That's good. What are you thinking about now Martin? What do you see?

MARTIN: I'm dreaming.

EDEN: What?

MARTIN: I'm waiting.

EDEN: What?

MARTIN: Him.

EDEN: Tell me.

MARTIN: I am waiting for my father. I sleep alone here. Each night I dream and in my dream I see him. Warmer, more real than in life. He watches me sleep and picks me up in his arms like I was a tiny boy and carries me out to the end of the dock. I am weightless. He points to the sky, there is no moon. The water. There is no tide. Only the world, our world in complete stillness. No flux, no pull, no gravity. Just me and him, me and him. We lie on our stomachs, stare down into the dock light, and he calls them. Waiting and waiting, I think "They won't come, they can't come, there's no moon. There's no moon." But they do come. And they take my breath away. Gigantic pale, and luminous silver, they're kissing the dock with their mouths, feeding on the life there, mingling with the dark water, and I watch till it's like I'm being hypnotized and then I feel him lift me up and up and his arms rock me and his voice in my ear, he tells me, he says to me:

MARTIN & VOICES:
Now it is night
we will walk to the end
of the pier and watch
the moonfish feed
because it is night
and peering deep into
wells of bottle blackness
we will see them
shafts of floodlight pouring like
false day over their pale bodies
the moonfish
will feed
sucking into the light
in secret they must think
but we will watch
their ghostly orbs
kiss the barnacled piles of the dock
because it is night
because that's what we do
because so much is moved
by the pull of the moon.

EDEN: You dad tells you this?
MARTIN: He lifts me up and up and his kiss goes warm on my cheek, and my forehead and I see the silver of the fish and silver of the razor in his hand, and starting at his ear he slices down, down around the throat, and the red pours onto the dock and through the planks and onto the moonfish—staining, covering, choking them. His hand goes limp, the razor falls, he crumbles to my feet and noiseless I push the body empty and light into the lake. Waves over him. Billows of blood and water. The downward spiral of flesh, of water. The sleep of water. Then it happens. They come for him. One by one gliding into his pool of blood, testing him with their mouths, each bite making him theirs, pulling him finally down with them into the darkness. They own him now.
EDEN: They own him now.
MARTIN: He was so lonely for her. After she left him. He was so lonely. He couldn't sleep in their bedroom anymore. I'd find him in the morning in a ball on the living room floor. That's where

he slept. A grown man. Cause he couldn't stand the loneliness.

EDEN: I wouldn't leave you.

MARTIN: He never hit her though. He never touched her, all them times they fought. He couldn't hurt anything. Not a bug, not a lousy fish. Only himself. He could do that.

EDEN: I would stay with you.

MARTIN: I guess it wasn't in him.

EDEN: Brush my hair for me.

MARTIN (*brushes her hair*): Sometimes I get this feeling, I'm walking down some road, this thing comes over me.

EDEN: You got such a nice face.

MARTIN: I don't know what it is. I'm just walking and I see someone—some guy, some woman—they've got nothing to do with my life, I see them and I think "I could take him."

EDEN: I like you so much.

MARTIN: I could kill that guy over there. I'd like to kill that asshole.

EDEN: You could do anything in your life that you ever regretted.

MARTIN: It's not a rational thing. I never killed anyone, but I think I could do it.

EDEN: Anything that you ever regretted.

MARTIN: I could do it. Maybe I'd like to.

EDEN: I'd still care for you.

MARTIN: You listen to me tell you this. You listen to me, and you just sit there like it was nothing. Like it was natural.

EDEN: Tell me I'm beautiful. (*She places his hand on her hair, he begins to stroke it.*)

MARTIN: You just don't understand anything.

EDEN: Tell me I'm beautiful. (*She takes his hand from her hair and places it on her breast.*)

MARTIN: Like it was natural.

EDEN: Tell me.

(*She takes his hand and places it on her throat—gently but in a choking hold—he holds it there for a moment, then finally begins to stroke her throat.*)

MARTIN: You're beautiful. You're so beautiful.

(*He continues to stroke her throat as the lights fade.*)

CONTRIBUTORS

MIGDALIA CRUZ was born and raised in the Bronx. Her plays include "Miriam's Flowers," "Lucy Loves Me," "Dreams of Home," "Occasional Grace," and "Not Time's Fool." Her play "The Have-little" was a runner-up for the 1991 Susan Smith Blackburn Prize. She is a 1990 NEA Playwriting Fellow and a member of New Dramatists.

CHRISTOPHER DURANG was born in Montclair, New Jersey. He is author of "A History of the American Film," "Sister Mary Ignatius Explains It All for You," "Beyond Therapy," "Baby with the Bathwater," "The Marriage of Bette and Boo," and "Laughing Wild." He is one-third of the cabaret act "Chris Durang and Dawn."

MARIA IRENE FORNES is author of more than two dozen works for the stage, including, "Promenade," "The Successful Life of 3," "Fefu and Her Friends," "Mud," "The Conduct of Life," "Abingdon Square," and "And What of the Night?" She is recipient of six Obie awards and teaches writing throughout the United States and abroad.

ATHOL FUGARD's plays include "Blood Knot," "Hello and Goodbye," "People are Living There," "Boesman and Lena," "Sizwe Bansi Is Dead," "A Lesson from Aloes," " 'Master Harold' . . . and the Boys," "The Road to Mecca," and "My Children! My Africa!" His works have been produced in South Africa, London, and throughout the United States.

PERCY GRANGER began his career as an actor at the Provincetown Playhouse, which also performed his earliest works. Plays include "Eminent Domain," "Leavin' Cheyenne," "Working Her Way Down," and "Coyote Hangin' on a Barbed Wire." He is a member of the Ensemble Studio Theatre.

RICHARD GREENBERG's works have been part of the Best Plays, and Best Short Plays series. Plays include "Eastern Standard," "The American Plan," "The Extra Man," and "Life Under Water." He is a member of the Ensemble Studio Theatre.

ZORA NEALE HURSTON (1901–1960), novelist, dramatist, and folklorist, was a close associate with the artists of the Harlem Renaissance. Major works include the novel *Their Eyes Were Watching God*, and an autobiography, *Dust Tracks on a Road*.

DAVID HENRY HWANG is the author of "FOB," "The Dance and the Railroad," and "Family Devotions." With composer Philip Glass, he has collaborated on two works, "1000 Airplanes on the Roof," and "The Voyage." For "M. Butterfly," Mr. Hwang was honored with the

1988 Tony, Drama Desk, Outer Critics Circle, and John Gassner awards.

DAVID IVES was born in Chicago, and educated at Northwestern University and the Yale Drama School. His one-act plays have been a staple at the annual comedy festival of Manhattan Punch Line for several years. He has also written for film, television, and opera.

HOWARD KORDER's play "Boys' Life," presented by Lincoln Center in 1988, was nominated for a Pulitzer Prize. Other plays include "Search and Destroy," "Nobody," "Night Maneuver," "Imagining 'America,'" and "Lip Service." For television, he was Story Editor of the CBS series *Kate and Allie*.

ERIC LANE's works have been performed at LaMama, Symphony Space, the Nat Horne Theatre, and others. His plays include "The Heart of a Child," "Glass Stirring," and "Blue Christmas." He is Artistic Director of Orange Thoughts Theater Company and is recipient of a Writer's Guild Award.

SHIRLEY LAURO is author of "Open Admissions," "The Contest," and "Nothing Immediate." Her work has been produced in New York at Ensemble Studio Theatre, Manhattan Theatre Club, and Circle Rep; nationally, at Long Wharf, Actor's Theatre of Louisville; and others throughout the United States, Canada, and Europe.

ADAM LEFEVRE's plays include "Yucca Flats," "Windowwashers," and "The Crashing of Moses Flying-By." A book of his poetry, *Everything All at Once*, is published by Wesleyan University Press. He has acted in films, television, and on Broadway in "Our Country's Good," and "The Devil's Disciple."

CRAIG LUCAS is a graduate of Boston University, where he studied with poets George Starbuck and Anne Sexton. He is the author of the plays "Reckless" and "Blue Window." Screenplays include "Longtime Companion" and the adaptation of his award-winning play "Prelude to a Kiss."

TERRENCE McNALLY's plays include "Lips Together, Teeth Apart," "The Libson Traviata," and "Frankie and Johnny in the Clair de Lune," which he later adapted for film. He has written books for the musicals *The Rink* and *Kiss of the Spider Woman*. He is Vice President of the Dramatists Guild.

ARTHUR MILLER has received the Pulitzer Prize, the Tony Award, and the Drama Critics' Circle Award. Plays include "Death of a Salesman," "The Crucible," "All My Sons," "A View from the Bridge," and "After the Fall." He has also written the screenplay *The Misfits*, the teleplay *Playing for Time*, and his autobiography, *Timebends*.

RICHARD NELSON's works have been produced in London, New York, and throughout the United States. Plays include "Two Shakespearean Actors," "Some Americans Abroad," "Principia Scriptoriae," and the book for the musical *Chess*. He has been nominated for the Tony Award and received an Obie.

HAROLD PINTER was born in 1930 in East London. His many plays include "The Birthday Party," "The Homecoming," "Old Times," "No

Man's Land," and "Betrayal." As well as adapting several of his plays for film, he has written the screenplays *The Servant*, *The Pumpkin Eater*, *The Go-Between*, and *The French Lieutenant's Woman*.

KEITH REDDIN's plays include "Life During Wartime," "Life and Limb," "Rum and Coke," and "Highest Standard of Living." He has received the MacArthur Playwriting Award, an NEA Fellowship, and the San Diego Drama Critics' Award for Best Play for "Nebraska."

JOSÉ RIVERA's plays have been produced at Ensemble Studio Theatre, Circle Rep, Berkeley Rep, and others. He is author of "The Promise," "Each Day Dies with Sleep," "Marisol," and "The House of Ramon Iglesia," which was also filmed for American Playhouse.

DAVID E. RODRIGUEZ has won several national play competitions and is currently studying at NYU. "As I progress in my writing, as I learn more about the world, I realize that I get closer and closer to my real voice. I am a student, and will remain that way for a very long time."

SAMUEL SCHWARTZ, a Virginia native, currently lives in the Washington, D.C., area. He earned an MFA in dramatic writing from NYU, where he won the 1986 graduate writing award. New York's Love Creek Productions presented "Your Uncle Arthur" and "Vito on the Beach" in their festival of one-act plays.

JOHN PATRICK SHANLEY is from the Bronx. His plays include "Savage in Limbo," "the dreamer examines his pillow," and "Italian American Reconciliation." Films include *Five Corners*, *Joe Versus the Volcano*, and *Moonstruck*, which won the Writer's Guild Award and Academy Award for Best Original Screenplay.

NINA SHENGOLD won the ABC Playwright Award and the L.A. Weekly Award for "Homesteaders," which was produced by Capital Rep, Long Wharf, and others. She adapted Jane Smiley's novella *Good Will* for American Playhouse and wrote the CBS movie *Blind Spot* for Joanne Woodward.

JONATHAN MARC SHERMAN's play "Women and Wallace" was produced by the Young Playwrights Festival and later filmed for American Playhouse. Young Playwrights also produced "Serendipity and Serenity," and the Los Angeles Theatre Center presented both "Veins and Thumbtacks" and "Sons and Fathers."

KATHERINE SNODGRASS's first play, "Haiku," won Actors' Theatre of Louisville's Heideman Award and was published in *Best Short Plays of 1989*. She lectures at Boston University and works with Circle Rep's Playwrights' Lab, where she is putting the finishing touches on "Observatory Conditions."

ARA WATSON has seen productions of her plays in New York and in regional theaters across the country. Her plays include "The Mesmerist," "A Different Moon," "Bite the Hand," "Scarecrows," and "Blue Light Dancing." She is recipient of a Humana Play Festival Award for Best Play, and a Writer's Guild Award.

BARBARA WIECHMANN has worked as a writer and performer with

The National Shakespeare Company, NADA, Ensemble Studio Theatre, HOME, and many others. She was raised in Middle Haddam, Connecticut, attended Hamilton College, and now lives in Brooklyn with her husband, playwright Michael J. Carley.

GEORGE C. WOLFE is author of "The Colored Museum," and the book for the Broadway musical *Jelly's Last Jam*, which he also directed. He is on the Executive Council of the Dramatists Guild and is an Artistic Associate of the New York Shakespeare Festival.

INDEX